Get the eBook FREE!

(PDF, ePub, Kindle, and liveBook all included)

We believe that once you buy a book from us, you should be
able to read it in any format we have available. To get electronic
versions of this book at no additional cost to you, purchase and
then register this book at the Manning website.

Go to https://www.manning.com/freebook and follow the
instructions to complete your pBook registration.

That's it!
Thanks from Manning!

Get Programming with Scala

Get Programming with

Scala

Daniela Sfregola

MANNING
Shelter Island

For online information and ordering of this and other Manning books, please visit www.manning.com. The publisher offers discounts on this book when ordered in quantity. For more information, please contact

Special Sales Department
Manning Publications Co.
20 Baldwin Road
PO Box 761
Shelter Island, NY 11964
Email: orders@manning.com

Development editor: Kathy Olstein
Technical development editor: Arthur Zubarev
Review editor: Mihaela Batinic
Production editor: Lori Weidert
Copyeditor: Michele Mitchell
Proofreader: Keri Hales
Technical proofreader: Jean-François Morin
Typesetter: Dennis Dalinnik
Cover designer: Monica Kamsvaag

Manning Publications Co.
20 Baldwin Road
PO Box 761
Shelter Island, NY 11964

ISBN 9781617295270
Printed in the United States of America

To Marco, the best lockdown buddy I could ever ask for.

Contents

Unit 3

HTTP SERVER   113

Unit 4

IMMUTABLE DATA AND STRUCTURES   155

Unit 5

LIST 225

Unit 6

OTHER COLLECTIONS AND ERROR HANDLING   291

Unit 8

JSON (DE)SERIALIZATION   451

Preface

When I first heard of Scala almost 10 years ago, I was immediately intrigued: a language that combines object-oriented programming (OOP) with functional programming (FP) sounded very interesting! And of course, at the time, I had no idea of what FP really meant or why I should care about it. When I decided to give this new language a try, I was lucky enough to work with great mentors who guided me in the learning process.

As I was learning new features of the language, I decided to start writing down my discoveries to further cement my understanding of them. After one or two months, I started writing my blog. My original motivation was to force myself to keep studying and improving my skills, but I soon realized that other people were finding my blog posts useful. In particular, readers of my blog enjoyed my writings because they were tackling practical problems that were explained with simple terms and that avoided unnecessary complexity.

Around the same time, I also started engaging with the Scala community by attending conferences and local meetups. By talking to fellow developers, I have recognized a similar pattern: folks were really intrigued by the language but surprised by a steep learning curve that was daunting for many newcomers due to the amount of complex and technical concepts that were assumed as common knowledge. Within six months, somebody nudged me into giving a presentation about a Scala library called Akka. When delivering the presentation, I decided that the best course of action was to offer my insights in a beginner-friendly fashion—helping several developers learn Scala one-on-one and sharing my knowledge of the Scala language and ecosystem in talks and workshops for beginners.

This book distills what I have learned about Scala and FP over the years and applies the lessons learned while teaching it to newcomers, trying to present the topic in a simple and accessible way so that you can learn the basics in a quick and pragmatic manner.

Learning new technologies can be overwhelming and intimidating, but it doesn't have to be. I hope this book will make you fall in love with Scala, a powerful yet approachable language that can be fun and increase your productivity at the same time.

Acknowledgments

This book has been the most exciting and ambitious challenge of my career so far, and it would have not been possible without the constant help and support of many people.

I'd like to show my gratitude to the reviewers and the MEAP readers: your invaluable feedback has made this book much better.

Thanks to the Manning team, for their guidance and mentoring, particularly to Rebecca Rinehart, Michael Stephens, and Bert Bates for their precious advice during development of this book. Special thanks also go to my development editor, Katherine Olstein, for helping me continue focusing on its progress and get to the finishing line. I'd also like to thank my technical development editor, Arthur Zubarev, for his enthusiastic encouragement and my technical proofreader, Jean-François Morin, for his invaluable and detailed feedback.

To all the reviewers: Andrew Jennings, Anto Aravinth, Bonnie Malec, Chad Davis, Damian Esteban, Dan Sheikh, David Clements, Dr. Davide Cadamuro, Edward G. Prentice, Emanuele Origgi, Evyatar Kafkafi, George Onofrei, George Thomas, Igor Karp, Jeff Smith, Jens Christian, B. Madsen, Jon Guenther, Kai Gellien, Kelvin Johnson, Kevin Orr, Michelle Williamson, Mike Jensen, Rambabu Posa, Ronald Tischliar, Sam Zaydel, Sanket Naik, Scott Dierbeck, William Wheeler, and Yvan Phelizot, your suggestions helped make this a better book.

I'd like to show my gratitude to my mentors and colleagues, particularly to Bruno Filippone for introducing me to Scala, and ScalaItaly for inviting me to speak at a conference for the first time. Thanks to the Scala Community for your engagement and appreciation of this project and the Scala Center, particularly to Darja Jovanovic for her enthusiasm and support. Thanks to Professor Martin Odersky for creating such a beautiful language and for his invaluable feedback.

Last but surely not least, thanks to my life partner, Marco, for his unconditional support during every stage of this book and for encouraging me during the countless nights and weekends spent writing this book.

About this book

Object-oriented programming (OOP) has been the mainstream programming paradigm for the past couple of decades. More recently, the growing need for handling concurrency and multi-core processing has encouraged developers to explore functional programming (FP) thanks to its concepts of immutability and purity, which allow you to safely share data and design applications that are composable and easy to test. We are currently in a transition period where developers are familiar with the OOP paradigm but would like to learn more about FP.

Scala is a beautiful and powerful language that combines the OOP and FP coding styles to offer the best of both worlds and hence appeal to a broad set of developers.

Get Programming with Scala gives you an overview of its core features and guides you through several exercises to consolidate your understanding. It also teaches you how to develop more and more complex real-life Scala applications. It aims to make you productive in Scala as quickly and easily as possible, making it an ideal book when diving in for the first time.

Who should read this book

This book is for anyone with some programming experience using any OOP language, who is looking for a practical introduction to the Scala language and FP. You do not need any experience developing on the Java Virtual Machine (although it will certainly not hurt you) or any prior FP knowledge; you'll learn about these subjects in this book.

How this book is organized: A roadmap

The structure of *Get Programming with Scala* is different from most of the programming books you may have read before. The book is divided into units, each containing bite-sized, easy-to-understand lessons. Each lesson has several quick check questions to help you verify your understanding (all of the answers are at the end of each lesson) and a final "Try This" exercise to help you consolidate the topic (solutions can be found on the book's GitHub repository). At the end of each unit, its capstone project shows you how to apply what you have learned so far in a real-life application. The units cover the following content:

- Unit 0 discusses why Scala is a great language to learn and the tools you need to install on your machine to start coding. You'll learn about the Scala REPL, which helps you discover the language by evaluating Scala expressions, and sbt, the Scala Build Tool you'll use for your Scala applications.
- Unit 1 introduces you to the fundamental code components of the language. In particular, you'll learn to define values and variables, conditional statements, functions, and classes.
- Unit 2 shows you how to code in Scala using classic OOP concepts you have used in other languages. You'll see how to create and import packages, use access modifiers that limit your code's visibility, and define interfaces and singletons.
- Unit 3 starts your FP journey by teaching you about pattern matching, one of the most powerful and versatile tools of the Scala language. You'll learn about anonymous and particular functions and how the library http4s uses them to define an HTTP server.
- Unit 4 discusses immutability by introducing you to case classes. It then introduces you to higher order functions and the concept of purity. Option is presented as a tool to indicate that a value may be missing and to avoid those annoying and unpredictable NullPointerExceptions.
- Unit 5 introduces you to List collection as an ordered group of elements of the same kind. It shows you how to perform on it, such as picking, filtering, and sorting its items.
- Unit 6 discusses some of the other collections in the Scala library. You'll learn about Set as an unordered group of unique elements and Map for key-value structures. You'll also see how to use Either for validation and Try for error handling.
- Unit 7 shows you how to code using concurrent asynchronous computations. You'll see how to use Future to represent an asynchronous operation that runs in the background and use the library Quill to connect and query to a Postgres database.
- Finally, Unit 8 teaches you how to use the library circe for JSON serialization and ScalaTest to write tests. It also introduces you to the concept of laziness and IO from the cats-effect library as a tool to control side effects.

Each unit builds on top of the concepts introduced by the previous one, so you should consider reading each of them in succession. Depending on your OOP experience, you may want to skim the first lessons of the book. I strongly recommend not to skip the "Quick Check" and "Try This" exercises, even if they may seem easy, because they are designed to consolidate your understanding and highlight unexpected behavior that newcomers to the language tend to struggle with.

About the code

Throughout the book, you will see lots of code examples and quizzes to help you master the topics of each unit. The source code is formatted in a `fixed-width font like this` to separate it from ordinary text. Sometimes code is also **in bold** to highlight code that has changed from previous steps in the chapter, such as when a new feature adds to an existing line of code.

In many cases, the original source code has been reformatted; we've added line breaks and reworked indentation to accommodate the available page space in the book. In rare cases, even this was not enough, and listings include line-continuation markers (➡). Additionally, comments in the source code have often been removed from the listings when the code is described in the text. Code annotations accompany many of the listings, highlighting important concepts.

Source code, exercises, and solutions are available for download from the Manning website at https://www.manning.com/books/get-programming-with-scala and from GitHub at https://github.com/DanielaSfregola/get-programming-with-scala.

liveBook discussion forum

Purchase of *Get Progamming with Scala* includes free access to a private web forum run by Manning Publications where you can make comments about the book, ask technical questions, and receive help from the author and from other users. To access the forum, go to https://livebook.manning.com/book/get-programming-with-scala/welcome/v-10/. You can also learn more about Manning's forums and the rules of conduct at https://livebook.manning.com/#!/discussion.

Manning's commitment to our readers is to provide a venue where a meaningful dialogue between individual readers and between readers and the author can take place. It is not a commitment to any specific amount of participation on the part of the author, whose contribution to the forum remains voluntary (and unpaid). We suggest you try asking the author some challenging questions lest her interest stray! The forum and the archives of previous discussions will be accessible from the publisher's website as long as the book is in print.

About the author

 Daniela Sfregola is a senior software engineer based in London (UK), and a Scala user since 2013. She is an active contributor to the Scala community, a public speaker at Scala conferences and meetups, and a maintainer of open source projects at github .com/DanielaSfregola. In her blog at danielasfregola.com, she discusses common challenges developers can encounter when coding in Scala. You can also find her on Twitter at twitter.com/ DanielaSfregola.

Hello Scala!

Welcome to *Get Programming with Scala*! In Unit 0, you'll have an overview of Scala and everything you need to know to set up your development environment and start coding. In particular, you'll see the following subjects:

- Lesson 1 illustrates the key Scala features and why it is such a great programming language to learn. You'll discover the typical execution flow of a Scala program, and you'll get a glance at some Scala code.
- Lesson 2 shows you how to install and run the Scala REPL, a crucial tool to play and experiment with. You'll write code snippets and see how the compiler interprets them.
- Lesson 3 introduces you to sbt—the Scala Build Tool. You'll install it and write your first Scala program by organizing your folders and source files according to the sbt standard.

After setting your environment up, you'll continue with unit 1, where you'll review the basics of object-oriented programming in Scala.

WHY SCALA?

After reading this lesson, you'll be able to

- Discuss the advantages of adopting Scala
- Describe the execution flow of a typical Scala program
- Define the key features of the Scala language

In this lesson, you'll discover why Scala is an excellent language to learn and why its adoption is increasing so rapidly. You'll see how Scala relates to the JVM and the key features that make it unique. You'll also start looking at snippets of Scala code to get an idea of its appearance. After giving you an overview of the Scala language, you'll continue with the next lesson, in which you'll install the Scala REPL and use it to interpret snippets of code.

 ## 1.1   Why Scala?

Why should you spend time and effort in learning Scala? Why is it becoming so popular? What are the advantages of adopting it? Let's discuss its main selling points.

> **THE JVM**   The JVM is the standard platform for running Scala programs. Sun Microsystems introduced it in 1994—more than 25 years ago. Since then, the industry has been extensively relying on it. The Java community has also been extremely active, and it has produced an impressive amount of libraries. Thanks

to its integration with Java, you can use all these libraries in your Scala programs; this is also true for any Java legacy code you or your company may have.

A HYBRID LANGUAGE Scala manages to combine two programming techniques that are considerably different: the object-oriented style with the functional one. When executing code on the JVM, the object-oriented approach can be more performant but prone to errors. When using mutable state, your program will re-allocate its memory: every time a change occurs, it will change the data in place. However, sharing state can cause your application to suffer from data inconsistency issues due to multiple processes accessing and modifying the same portion of data.

A functional approach can be more readable and reusable but not as performant. Thanks to immutable data and structures, you can guarantee your program's correctness when dealing with concurrency: your data never changes, so it is safe to share it. Your code will also be easier to understand and reuse because all its components will be independent of external factors outside its control. But recreating data rather than updating could be a memory-expensive operation, even though it has massively improved thanks to numerous optimizations and efficient garbage collection strategies in recent years.

In Scala, you do not have to stick to a particular style, but you can take advantage of one or the other paradigm depending on the specific task you are solving. Look at figure 1.1 for a comparison of how the two approaches tackle different programming tasks.

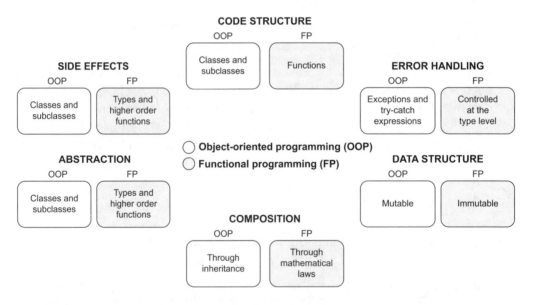

Figure 1.1 Comparison of the object-oriented and functional programming styles and how they handle different programming tasks

CONCISE SYNTAX   Scala's programming style is relatively concise, particularly when compared to other languages like Java. Having a compact syntax can increase both the productivity and readability of your program. At the beginning of your journey with Scala, you may find it quite overwhelming. In this book, syntax diagrams will help you master new topics and make your learning path smoother.

FLEXIBILITY   Scala is extremely flexible: you can achieve the same goal in more than one way, making the language extremely fun and exciting to use. The opportunity to choose between different programming paradigms allows you to gradually shift your mindset from one approach to another without committing to a specific style since day one. For example, you can dip your toe in the functional programming world without any long-term commitment. In this book, you'll start writing Scala code using an object-oriented style and then gradually move to a more functional one.

CONCURRENCY   Thanks to its use of immutable data structures and expressive type system, dealing with concurrency is less prone to errors than in other languages. As a result, Scala programs tend to utilize resources more efficiently, and they usually perform better under pressure.

BIG DATA AND SPARK   Thanks to Scala's features and optimizations at its compile level, the community has developed new performant tools for big data processing. Apache Spark is the most popular of these tools. Thanks to Scala's lazy evaluation, which is a topic you are going to discover in unit 8, Spark can perform optimizations at compile time that have huge impacts on its runtime performance:

"Run programs up to 100× faster than Hadoop MapReduce in memory, or 10× faster on disk."

Source: https://spark.apache.org

 ## 1.2   Scala and the JVM

Scala takes its name from the word *scalable*. Martin Odersky and his team designed it in 2004 with the intent of creating a language for the Java Virtual Machine (JVM) that can easily handle high volumes of requests.

To understand the execution of a Scala program, let's compare it with the typical execution flow of a Java program; figure 1.2 provides a visual representation of the two processes. The JVM is a machine to perform tasks by executing a well-defined set of operations, called *bytecode*. A JVM language aims to translate its code into executable JVM bytecode, usually formed by multiple files with extension *.class. When coding in Java, you save your source files with extension *.java and use the compiler javac to produce a jar file containing the generated bytecode. When writing Scala code, your source files have extension *.scala. The Scala compiler called scalac is in charge of translating the code into bytecode. You can seamlessly add Java sources and depend on Java libraries in your Scala codebase. The Scala compiler fully integrates with the byte-code that the Java compiler produces, making the integration between the two languages straightforward.

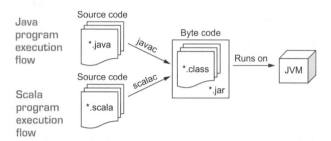

Figure 1.2   Comparison between the execution of a Java program with a Scala one. The Java source code has extension *.java, and javac translates it into bytecode files with extension *.class. You save Scala code in files with extension *.scala, and scalac is the compiler responsible for converting them into bytecode. The JVM is now ready to run the bytecode, usually conveniently grouped in a *.jar file.

Scala as a multiplatform language

Odersky and his team designed Scala for the JVM. A few open source projects (some more experimental than others) are trying to develop new compilers so that you can use the language in other platforms too.

scala-js is a well-established open source project that allows you to compile Scala code to JavaScript. It is a framework to build applications that run in your browser. It enables you to share code between the front and the backend of your application. Visit https://www.scala-js.org for more information.

scala-native (see http://www.scala-native.org) is another project targeting Scala for the Low-Level Virtual Machine (LLVM) compiler. Its development is in progress but looks promising; running Scala programs on the LLVM would optimize their speed and memory.

Finally, if you are looking for an alternative (more fun?) way of writing CSS code, look at scalacss (see https://github.com/japgolly/scalacss) for a "super type-safe CSS" in Scala.

1.3 Scala's key features

Since 2004, Scala has evolved a lot, but its fundamental features have not changed. In this section, you'll glance at a few fragments of Scala code, and you'll learn about each of these topics in this book.

> **SCALA IS OBJECT-ORIENTED** An object-oriented programming language has a structure based on classes and subclasses. They have well-defined behaviors, and they exchange information through methods.

Listing 1.1 MyClass example

```
// our first Scala example          ◄─────── This is a comment.
class MyClass(name: String) {       ◄─────
  def sayHello(otherName: String) =            This is a class with a
    s"Hi $otherName, my name is $name!"  ◄─    parameter "name" and
}                                              a method "sayHello."
```

Example of string interpolation: s"..." is the operator for string interpolation; it replaces $otherName and $name with their value.

In unit 1, you'll learn how to define classes and subclasses. In unit 4, you'll also discover *case classes* to present data in an immutable manner.

Singleton instances are instances that you should initialize at most once. Scala offers a dedicated syntax for them: you usually refer to them as objects. Do not be confused by the term *object*, as it can refer to an instance rather than a singleton in other languages. In unit 2, you'll learn about singleton objects in Scala and how not to be confused by the terminology.

Listing 1.2 MySingleton example

```
object MyObject {                      ◄─────── This is a singleton.
  val a = new MyClass("Scala")         ◄─────
  println(a.sayHello("Martin"))               This is an instance of
}                                             the class MyClass.
```

Exceptions are another typical feature of an object-oriented language. They represent code anomalies: you can throw and catch them to control your program's execution flow. In Scala, exceptions are similar to those in languages such as Java, Python, and C++.

Listing 1.3 Example of throwing and catching exceptions

```
try {
  throw new IllegalStateException("ERROR!")        ←──  Example of throwing a
} catch {                                                java.lang.IllegalState-
  case ex: RuntimeException =>      ←──                  Exception
    println("Something went bad...")                 Example of catching and handling
}                                                    any RuntimeException. Note that
                                                     an IllegalStateException is a
                                                     subclass of RuntimeException.
```

You'll learn about try-catch expressions in detail in unit 3, in which you are also going to discover partial functions. In unit 6, you'll master how to handle errors without throwing exceptions using a more functional and safe approach that uses types.

Mutable data structures and assignments are also part of the language. The language's design discourages their use, but you can still take advantage of them when needed. In lesson 4, you'll learn about the difference between a value and a variable. In units 5 and 6, you'll also discover what the Scala Collections have to offer.

Listing 1.4 Example of mutable assignments

```
var a = "hello"              Prints hello
println(a)          ←──
a = "Scala"
println(a)          ←──      Prints Scala
```

> **SCALA IS FUNCTIONAL** FP languages base their entire structure on functions. Functions play a big part in Scala as its first-class citizens. In lesson 6, you'll learn their basics and how to define them. In unit 4, you'll discover functional purity and its several advantages and how you can use functions as parameters or return values: you refer to them as higher order functions. They allow you to create powerful abstractions that simplify and remove code duplication in a way that is usually not so easily achievable in an object-oriented approach.

Listing 1.5 Example of Higher Order Function

```
                                                     A function that takes an
def divideByTwo(n: Int): Int = n / 2     ←──         Int and returns an Int

def addOne(f: Int => Int): Int => Int =  ←──         A function that takes a
  f andThen(_ + 1)                                   function from Int to Int as a
                                                     parameter and that returns a
                                                     new function from Int to Int
  def divideByTwoAndAddOne = addOne(divideByTwo)

   A function defined by compositing
   two existing functions
```

SCALA HAS A ROBUST TYPE SYSTEM   Scala is a statically typed language. Types define the acceptable range of values for your computation. Thanks to them, the compiler can check at compile time that your code doesn't violate any constraints, which makes your code more reliable and less prone to errors at runtime. Scala has a type inference system, so you do not have to specify the intended type for every expression of your program, making your code less verbose. Languages that do not have a type inference system require you to provide types explicitly and tend to be more verbose. Scala's type system is also quite flexible: you can reuse existing or create custom types to ensure business requirements at the type level. Starting from unit 4, you'll discover the most common types the language has to offer. In unit 7, you'll see how to use type classes and define custom types to enforce requirements at compile time.

SCALA'S INTEGRATION WITH JAVA   Scala is a JVM language that you can easily integrate Java code into your Scala programs. Most IDEs that provide Scala support, such as IntelliJ IDEA, can even rewrite Java code into Scala code automatically.

Listing 1.6 Java to Scala code example

```
// file Snippet.java
String dateAsString = "22.11.2017";
SimpleDateFormat format = new SimpleDateFormat( "dd.MM.yyyy" );
Date date = format.parse(dateAsString);


// file Snippet.scala
import java.text.SimpleDateFormat
import java.util.Date

val dateAsString = "22.11.2017"
val format = new SimpleDateFormat("dd.MM.yyyy")
val date: Date = format.parse(dateAsString)
```

Alternatively, you can also add files with extension *.java directly into your Scala project; Scalac will recognize them as Java and compile them accordingly.

 **Summary**

In this lesson, my objective was to give you an overview of the Scala language.

- You learned about its unique features and why it is a great language to learn.
- You discovered the typical execution flow of a Scala program and looked at Scala code snippets.

THE SCALA ENVIRONMENT

After reading this lesson, you'll be able to

- Execute commands on the Scala REPL
- Use the REPL to evaluate expressions
- Install the git and docker development tools

The Scala REPL (Read-Eval-Print-Loop) is a development tool to interpret Scala code snippets. It will be a crucial tool in learning Scala, and it doesn't require too much setup or infrastructure: you'll be able to play and experiment with the language by typing and evaluating fragments of code. You'll also install the git and docker development tools on your machine, which are not specific to Scala but used in some of the more advanced capstones. In the next lesson, you'll complete your machine's setup by installing sbt—a tool to build and run structured Scala programs.

 ## 2.1 The REPL installation

In this section, you'll learn how to install the Scala REPL on Linux, macOS, and Windows using a package manager. Alternatively, you can also download Scala binaries from its official website (visit https://scala-lang.org/download and its "Download the Scala binaries" section for instructions on how to do this).

First, you need to check that you have installed Java 8+ JDK. Open the terminal and type the command java -version to check your java version. You should see a message similar to the following:

```
$ java —version
openjdk version "15.0.1" 2020-10-20
OpenJDK Runtime Environment (build 15.0.1+9-18)
OpenJDK 64-Bit Server VM (build 15.0.1+9-18, mixed mode, sharing)
```

If you need to install or upgrade your JDK, you can find instructions on how to do so on the OpenJDK's website (https://openjdk.java.net/install).

You are now ready to download and install the Scala REPL; depending on your operating system, you will have different instructions to follow.

LINUX   On Ubuntu and other Debian-based distribution, type the following command in the terminal:

```
$ sudo apt-get install scala
```

If you are using an RPM-based distribution, such as Red Hat Enterprise, type the following instruction:

```
$ sudo yum install scala
```

Use emerge package manager if you are on Gentoo:

```
$ emerge dev-lang/scala
```

MACOS   On macOS, you can install Scala using Homebrew by executing the following command in your terminal:

```
$ brew install scala
```

If you prefer, you can also use MacPorts as follows:

```
$ port install scala
```

WINDOWS   Visit https://scala-lang.org/download to download the MSI installer for Scala and open the file to complete the installation.

Once you have completed the installation, you should be able to execute the command scala and receive a message similar to the following:

```
$ scala
Welcome to Scala 2.13.6 (OpenJDK 64-Bit Server VM, Java 15.0.1).
Type in expressions for evaluation. Or try :help.

scala>
```

The symbol scala> indicates that the Scala REPL is running and ready to receive your commands.

2.2   The REPL commands

A REPL tool can receive instructions and interpret snippets of code. Let's see what the Scala REPL's main commands.

The Scala REPL identifies commands by the prefix ":"; it considers any other instruction as Scala code snippets to compile and evaluate. Lots of commands are available, but you usually remember just a few of them. Here's a list of the most useful commands:

- :quit gracefully exits the interpreter:

```
scala> :quit
```

- :help lists all the commands available with a brief description. Use it to discover new commands or to check the syntax of an existing one:

```
scala> :help
All commands can be abbreviated, e.g., :he instead of :help.
:help [command]          print this summary or command-specific help
:completions <string>    output completions for the given string
// truncated as the list is quite long!
```

- :reset forgets any snippet evaluated so far. In other words, it restores the REPL to its initial state:

```
scala> :reset
Resetting interpreter state.
Forgetting this session history:

val a = "hello world"

Forgetting all expression results and named terms: a
```

- :replay resets the REPL and executes all the commands in the session history:

```
scala> :replay
Replaying: val a = "hello world"
val a: String = hello world
```

- :load <path> interprets snippets of code from a file. Suppose you have started the REPL from a directory containing a file called Test.scala and with text println (1 + 2). You can interpret the instructions in the Test.scala file as follows:

```
scala> :load Test.scala
Loading Test.scala...
3
```

Include the relative and absolute path of your file to load documents from other folders of your machine.

After reviewing the main REPL commands, let's see how you can use it to interpret code fragments.

 ## 2.3 The REPL code evaluation

You are now ready to interpret Scala expressions in the REPL. Let's start by evaluating the arithmetic expression 1 + 2:

```
scala> 1 + 2
val res0: Int = 3
```

Figure 2.1 analyzes the structure of your expression and its interpretation. It sums the integers 1 and 2 using the operator +, resulting in the value 3 of type Int. The REPL automatically saves the result as a value with a name having prefix res followed by an incremental number; in this case, it's res0.

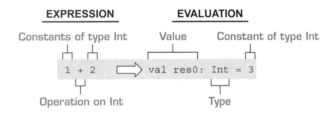

Figure 2.1 Analysis of the REPL's evaluation of an arithmetic expression. The interpretation of the sum of two integers produces a constant of type Int. The REPL saves the result in a value called res0.

You can use the result value res0 in your computations. For example, you can do the following:

```
scala> res0 + 39
val res1: Int = 42
```

You can also request the result to be saved with a specific name:

```
scala> val x = 1 + 2
val x: Int = 3

scala> x
val x: Int = 3
```

Note that you have not specified any type explicitly in all the examples you have seen so far. Thanks to its type inference, the Scala compiler infers that summing two integers returns an integer. When needed, you can provide an explicit return type; if not compatible with the expression provided, the compiler will display an error.

```
scala> val x: Int = 1 + 2
val x: Int = 3

scala> val y: Double = x
val y: Double = 3.0
// the compiler knows how to automatically convert Int to Double!

scala> val z: String = x
                       ^
        error: type mismatch;
         found    : Int
         required: String
```

The compiler knows how to convert an Int into a Double, but it cannot do the same when transforming an Int into a String.

You can define and call functions using the REPL. For example, you can implement a function sayHello that takes one parameter n of type String, and it returns a String. Look at figure 2.2 for a diagram of how the REPL interprets a function.

```
scala> def sayHello(n: String) = s"Hi $n!"
def sayHello: (n: String)String

scala> sayHello("Scala")
val res1: String = Hi Scala!
```

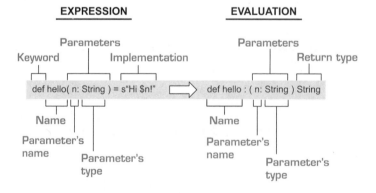

Figure 2.2 Analysis of the REPL's interpretation of a function definition. The REPL identifies the function by its name, parameter, and return type.

In the previous example, you didn't have to specify the return type for the sayHello function; the compiler can correctly infer its type is String. When needed, you can specify the desired return type of a function, and the compiler will see if this is compatible with its implementation:

```
scala> def sayHello(n: String): String = s"Hi $n!"
def sayHello: (n: String)String

scala> def sayHello(n: String): Int = s"Hi $n!"
                                      ^
        error: type mismatch;
         found    : String
         required: Int
```

Let's see how you can define a class and create an instance using the REPL:

```
scala> class MyClass(n: String)
class MyClass

scala> new MyClass("Martin")
val res2: MyClass = MyClass@32cf48b7
```

Finally, you can implement and use singletons or objects as follows:

```
scala> object MyObject
object MyObject

scala> MyObject
val res3: MyObject.type = MyObject$@176d53b2
```

Scala Worksheet

Most IDEs with dedicated support for Scala, such as IntelliJ IDEA, often also support Scala Worksheets. These are files with extension sc that can contain snippets of Scala code. Your IDE will start a REPL session to evaluate each snippet of code within the file and display its results within the text editor itself. Scala Worksheets are a valid alternative to manually starting a Scala REPL session from the command line.

2.4   Other development tools

To complete the environment setup, you'll also need to install other development tools: sbt, Git, and Docker. The next lesson will go into the details of how to install and use sbt. Let's see how to set Git and Docker up in this section.

2.4.1   Git installation

Git is a commonly used open source version control system and is often preinstalled in Unix machines. You'll use it to download existing code and give you a head start in the more advanced lessons. Run the following command in the terminal to check if Git is already installed on your machine:

```
$ git --version
git version 2.21.1
```

If you need to install git, please follow the instructions for your operating system at https://github.com/git-guides/install-git.

2.4.2   Docker installation

Docker is a platform that helps you manage the complexity of your infrastructure using virtual machines. You'll use Docker to run a temporary PostgreSQL database instance to use in your Scala applications. Follow the instructions on how to install Docker at https://docs.docker.com/get-docker. After its installation, you should be able to execute the docker --version command in your terminal and get an output similar to the following:

```
$ docker --version
Docker version 20.10.0, build 7287ab3
```

 ## Summary

In this lesson, my objective was to show you how to use the Scala REPL.

- You learned its most common commands.
- You wrote your first snippets of Scala code, and you have seen their evaluated values in the REPL.
- You installed the git and docker development tools on your machine; you'll use these tools in the more advanced lessons in the book.

Let's see if you got this!

TRY THIS   Perform the following operations in the REPL:

1 Start the REPL and evaluate the following expression: "na" * 3 + 42.
2 Restore the REPL to its initial state using the appropriate REPL command.
3 Quit the REPL gracefully with the :quit command.

SCALA BUILD TOOL (SBT)

After reading this lesson, you'll be able to

- Run commands in sbt
- Create an sbt project
- Describe the structure of the files of a Scala project built with sbt

In the previous lesson, you learned how to evaluate snippets of code using the Scala REPL. Programs have several components: they depend on other modules and libraries, and they are structured in multiple files and folders. In this lesson, you'll discover the basics of the Scala Build Tool, sbt. You'll compile and run your first Scala program on the JVM using sbt. In this book, you'll use sbt to manage dependencies, compile your code, and run your Scala programs.

 ## 3.1   Why sbt?

You can build Scala projects using several build tools such as Maven, Ant, and Gradle, but sbt is the most common build tool in the community. It is a complex but powerful tool that manages your dependencies, and it defines the build cycle of your code. sbt has its syntax and predefined instructions. You can also load plugins, which are programs written using the sbt syntax, to add new commands or modify the build process's existing behaviors. Throughout this book, you are going to write Scala programs that use the default sbt configuration. You are not going to learn about its advance uses and functionalities in this book, but you can look at its documentation at www.scala-sbt.org if you'd like to learn more about it.

Alternatives to sbt

The Scala community has a particular love-hate relationship with sbt: while some people think it is a great tool to work with, others dislike it for its complexity. Although extremely powerful, sbt can become complicated to understand and maintain.

sbt is undoubtedly the most popular choice for Scala projects but not the only one. For example, you could use any build tool with JVM support, such as Maven or Gradle.

Scala also has another community-driven build tool, called Mill. It takes most of its design choices from another build tool called Bazel, and it aims at a syntax that is simple to use and a fast and predictable build. For more information, look at https://github.com/lihaoyi/mill.

 ## 3.2   sbt installation

In this section, you'll discover how to install sbt using a package manager on Linux, macOS, and Windows. You can also install it from its binaries; look at www.scala-sbt.org/download for instructions on how to do so.

Before installing sbt, make sure you have Java 8+ JDK installed on your machine. Execute the command java –version to check which Java version your machine is running. You should see a message similar to the following:

```
$ java –version
openjdk version "15.0.1" 2020-10-20
OpenJDK Runtime Environment (build 15.0.1+9-18)
OpenJDK 64-Bit Server VM (build 15.0.1+9-18, mixed mode, sharing)
```

If missing, look at the previous lesson instructions on installing or upgrading your Java JDK.

Depending on your operating system, you'll need to use a different package manager to install sbt.

LINUX   On Ubuntu and other Debian-based distributions, you can execute the following command in the terminal:

```
$ sudo apt-get install sbt
```

If you are using an RPM-based distribution, such as Red Hat Enterprise, you can use yum:

```
$ sudo yum install sbt
```

If you are on Gentoo, type the following command on the terminal:

```
$ emerge dev-java/sbt
```

MACOS   You can use Homebrew to install sbt by running the following command in your terminal:

```
$ brew install sbt
```

If you prefer, you can also use MacPorts:

```
$ port install sbt
```

WINDOWS   Download the MSI installer for sbt at www.scala-sbt.org/1.x/docs/Installing-sbt-on-Windows. Open the file and follow the instruction on the UI to complete the installation.

After completing the installation, you should be able to open the terminal and execute the command sbt. When running sbt for the first time, it will download some dependencies; this could take a while and display lots of text in the console. It will happen only the first time, as it then saves them in its local cache; the next time you start sbt, it will be a lot faster. Eventually, sbt will be up and ready to receive commands. Your terminal should look similar to the following:

```
$ sbt
[info] Loading project definition from /my/path
// ...
// Lots of output omitted here!
// ...
[info] sbt server started at local://some/other/path
sbt>
```

Congratulations! sbt is now running and ready to accept commands.

 ## 3.3   sbt commands

sbt operates in the folder in which you typed the command. On startup, sbt looks for a specific folder structure (more on this in section 3.5) to tentatively load your project and start its server. Once done, it will wait for commands to execute. The most common and useful ones are the following:

- exit gracefully terminates your session.
- about provides general information on the sbt version that you are running.
- compile triggers the compilation of your code.
- run compiles and runs your program on the JVM.
- help lists each sbt command followed by a brief description of their usage.
- clean deletes any file produced during the compilation.
- reload re-evaluates the configurations provided in the project.
- new creates an sbt project using a Giter8 template (you'll see it in action in the next section).
- console starts the REPL within a sbt project; all your code and dependencies are now accessible from the REPL for you to experiment with them.

Now that you have installed sbt, you are ready to build your first sbt project.

 ## 3.4   Your first sbt project

sbt has dedicated support to Giter8 templates; you can use them to create a skeleton for your Scala project.

> **What is Giter8?**
>
> Giter8 is a project by Foundweekends (see http://www.foundweekends.org) that allows you to host templates on GitHub and apply them to generate skeleton projects: sbt is one of the supported ones. It is becoming more and more popular in the community as one of the quickest ways to get started with many popular Scala libraries.
>
> Visit https://github.com/foundweekends/giter8/wiki/giter8-templates for a list of some of the templates available. Spark, Spark Job Server, Akka, Akka-HTTP, Play, Lagoom, Scala Native, and http4s are just a few projects that have published an official Giter8 template. See http://www.foundweekends .org/giter8 for more information.

Your first application prints "Hello, World!" in the console. Let's create it by applying a Giter8 template called scala/hello-world.g8, using the following sbt command:

```
$ sbt
sbt> new scala/hello-world.g8

A template to demonstrate a minimal Scala application
```

```
name [Hello World template]: //press enter to use the default name

Template applied in ./hello-world-template

[info] shutting down server
```

This command has created a new directory, called hello-world-template, containing the code generated by the template. You can access, compile, and run the code as follows:

```
$ cd hello-world-template
$ sbt
sbt:hello-world> compile
// …
// output omitted here!
// …
[info]   Compilation completed in 13.992s.
[success] Total time: 16 s, completed 8 Jan 2021, 18:27:20

sbt:hello-world> run
[info] running Main
Hello, World!
[success] Total time: 1 s, completed 8 Jan 2021, 18:34:20

sbt:hello-world>
```

Eureka! Congratulations on compiling and running your first Scala program using sbt.

How to change your Scala version using sbt

sbt allows you to change the Scala version of your project on the fly. Imagine you want to change your Scala version from 2.13.6 to 3.0.0; you can achieve this using the following command:

```
sbt> ++3.0.0!
```

You can also use sbt to access the Scala REPL of a specific Scala version by combining its ++..! command with console. For example, if you want to start the REPL for scala 3.0.0, you can execute sbt ++3.0.0! console.

Which IDE to use?

Having the right tool to write code can make you extremely productive. The choice of using or not using an IDE is pretty subjective and often dictated by personal preferences. This book doesn't require you to use an IDE, but it recommends you pick one of the following two options as they make the language easier to learn and use.

Most people in the community use IntelliJ IDEA (see https://www.jetbrains.com/idea). It has dedicated support for Scala: it offers syntax highlighting, code completion, integrated REPL, jump to the source code, debugger, worksheet support, and more. It also has a sbt integration to help you build projects that respect the standard sbt project structure.

IntelliJ IDEA is full of useful features, but it can be demanding on the CPU and slow at times. If you prefer to use a text editor, Metals (https://scalameta.org/metals/) is an excellent alternative. It adds IDE-like features to text editors such as Visual Studio Code, Atom, Vim, Emacs, and Sublime. It has many of the functionalities of an IDE, but it is faster and lighter to run.

 ## 3.5 sbt project structure

sbt Scala projects have a standard structure. Let's see how you should organize your program by looking at the skeleton project you have created using the hello-world giter8 template in the previous section.

> **THE HELLO-WORLD-TEMPLATE FOLDER** By applying the template, you have created a new folder called `hello-world-template`; figure 3.1 shows its content. The `build.sbt` contains everything that sbt needs to know to compile and run your code: its Scala version, your application name, organization and version, and external libraries.

Listing 3.1 build.sbt file

```
// Lots of comments to give you an overview
// of the most common configurations
// sbt has to offer: have a look at them!

scalaVersion := "2.13.3"        ←        Mandatory
                                         settings
name := "hello-world"
organization := "ch.epfl.scala"
version := "1.0"
```

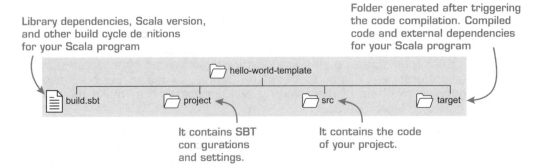

Figure 3.1 Files and directories in the hello-world-template folder. The build.sbt file contains the instructions on how to build your Scala program. The project folder contains sbt configurations and settings, while src contains all your source code. sbt creates the target folder after you compile your code; it includes the JVM bytecode of your application.

In this file, you can add external library dependencies you'd like to use in your code. For example, you can add a dependency to cats, a popular library for functional programming, by adding the following line to your build.sbt file:

```
libraryDependencies += "org.typelevel" %% "cats" % "2.2.0"
```

sbt identifies external dependencies by their organization (i.e., "org.typelevel"), their name (i.e., "cats"), and version (i.e., "2.2.0").

The project directory contains everything that sbt needs to run: its configurations and code (more on this later in this section).

The src folder contains the source code for your project; you'll see how production and test code are separated.

Finally, sbt generates the target folder after compiling your code: it contains its bytecode together with external dependencies and resources so that you can run it on the JVM.

THE PROJECT FOLDER   Look at figure 3.2 for the content of the project folder in the root directory; it contains everything that sbt needs to run.

The build.properties file specifies the desired sbt version.

Listing 3.2 project/build.properties file

```
sbt.version=1.5.2
```

The hello-world Giter8 template doesn't use any sbt plugin, but if you wish to do so, you can add custom functionalities to sbt by creating a file plugins.sbt in

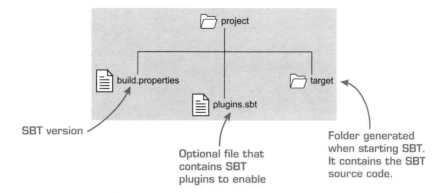

Figure 3.2   The project folder contains the sbt version to use (see build.properties file), the source code for sbt in the target folder, and any sbt plugin that needs to be imported.

the project directory. Listing 3.3 demonstrates how to enable the sbt plugin sbt-scoverage: it measures and produces reports on your test coverage by running a custom command called coverage.

Listing 3.3   Example of plugins.sbt file

```
addSbtPlugin("org.scoverage" % "sbt-scoverage" % "1.6.1")
```

The project/target folder contains all the information that sbt needs to run. sbt parses it, download its source code of the expected version (see build.properties) and plugins (see plugins.sbt). The first time you launch sbt, it is going to take a few minutes to start up. After that, sbt reuses the already downloaded sources, and it will be much faster.

THE SRC DIRECTORY   Figure 3.3 shows the src directory's content in the root folder; it contains all the source code for your project.

While the src/test folder contains code to prove your program's correctness, the src/main folder includes your actual application. Note that the hello-world Giter8 template doesn't have tests, the reason sbt will not create the test folder. Both main and test have three optional folders: scala to store all your *.scala files, java for any Java source code, and resources for any static ones. In src/main/resources you usually collect application and logging configurations files, while src/test/resources is generally reserved for test data, such as JSON and XML files, to load and parse in your tests.

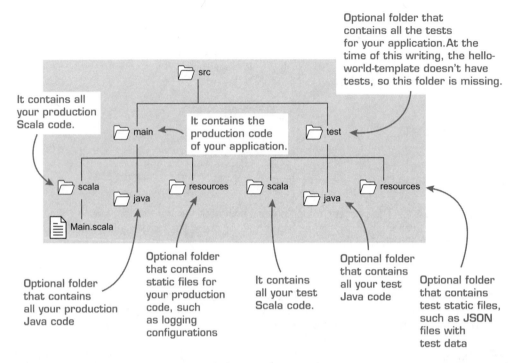

Figure 3.3 The src folder's content: the main directory contains all your production code, while the test folder contains all your tests to verify your application's correctness. The main and test folders have the same structure: the scala and java folders include all the Scala and Java code, respectively. The resources folder contains all the static files needed, such as logging and application configurations.

Let's look at the only *.scala the hello-world Giter8 template has produced: the Main.scala file in the src/main/scala directory.

Listing 3.4 Main.scala

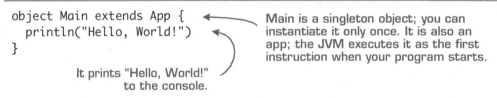

Some code elements will be new to you, but do not worry; you'll learn about each component of this program later on in the book.

Figure 3.4 shows a summary of the entire structure of a sbt project.

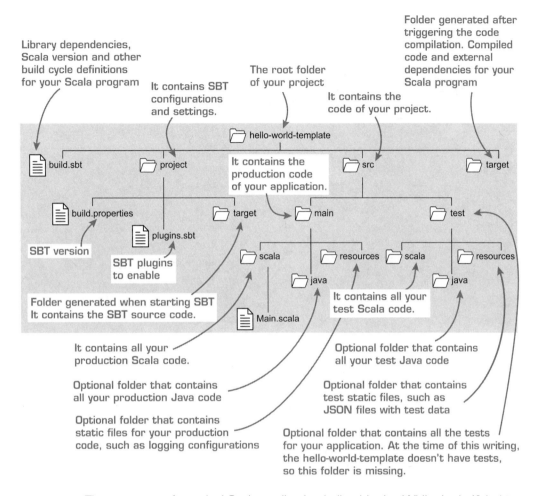

Figure 3.4 The structure of a typical Scala application built with sbt. While the `build.sbt` file and the project directory are specific to sbt, the `src` and `target` folders contain your application source code and bytecode, respectively.

Summary

In this lesson, my objective was to introduce you to sbt, the Scala Build Tool.

- You installed sbt and discovered its main features.
- You created, compiled, and run your first sbt projects.
- You also learned about how sbt expects you to organize your files and folders.

Let's see if you got this!

TRY THIS

1 Modify `Main.scala` in the `hello-world-template` project by removing the following
   instruction: "extends App." What is going to happen? Validate your assumptions by
   running the modified code. HINT: You can use your IDE's "jump to source" functionality to peek at the source code for the app.

2 Change your `hello-world-template` to print your name in the console; compile and
   run it using sbt.

The Basics

In Unit 0, you installed everything you need to start coding in Scala. In this unit, you'll begin writing Scala code. You'll learn how to program a vending machine in Scala using the same OOP principles already familiar to you. In particular, we will discuss the following subjects:

- Lesson 4 illustrates the difference between values and variables and the clear separation between mutable and immutable assignments.
- Lesson 5 introduces conditional constructs to control the execution flow of our program. You'll learn about loops to repeat the same operation multiple times.
- Lesson 6 shows you how to define functions in Scala.
- Lesson 7 demonstrates how to use classes to represent interactions between elements. You'll learn about abstract classes and how to express a class-subclass relation.
- Finally, you'll apply all the principles learned so far to code a vending machine that sells chocolate and granola bars to your customers in lesson 8.

Once comfortable with the basics, you'll continue with unit 2, where you'll learn more about object-oriented fundamentals.

VALUES AND VARIABLES

After reading this lesson, you'll be able to

- Write code that uses values to save and reuse computational results
- Implement programs that carefully take advantage of variables

Scala has a clear separation between mutable and immutable assignments. In Scala, values are immutable: you cannot modify them after creating them. Variables are mutable: they can refer to different instances over time. Deciding when to declare a value rather than a variable is essential for your code to be fast and bug-free. Variables are more straightforward to use in your code because you can modify them. However, they can make your program extremely difficult to maintain and lead to errors when different processes try to do so simultaneously. Values can be challenging to use because you cannot modify them once created. But they can make your program easier to understand: their assignments never change, so you can easily predict and test their evaluation. They also guarantee that your code will not be affected by concurrency issues, such as data inconsistencies, resources starvation, and deadlocks, when accessed by several threads. A fragment of code that multiple processes can access without causing concurrency issues is *thread-safe*. In the capstone for this unit, you'll define both values and variables to name fragments of code and make your program more readable.

Consider this

Consider the other languages you have encountered so far in your career. Do they make a clear distinction between mutable and immutable assignments? If so, how? If not, can you think of the advantages and disadvantages of not having a clear separation between the two?

 ## 4.1   Values

Assignments improve your code's readability by breaking down the computation and assigning meaningful names to it. They can also increase your program's performance by saving intermediate results that you can reuse and share between processes. Values are the most commonly used type of assignments in Scala.

In the next example, you'll see how values can improve your code's readability, particularly when dealing with complex scenarios. Suppose you are performing some calculation to mark exams with the following requirements: each exam has three questions, each with a possible score of 3 points, and its final mark must be between 1 and 10. Several solutions are possible; let's pick one of them. You could calculate the average score for all the questions and then convert it to a number from 1 to 10. For example, you should follow these steps for three questions scoring 1.5, 2, and 2.5:

1 You compute the average score for all the questions: $(1.5 + 2 + 2.5) / 3$ is 2.
2 You scale the average score from 1 to 10. Considering that the maximum score possible for each question is 3, then you can rescale it as follows: $2 * 10 / 3$ is about 6.6.
3 You round 6.6 up to the closest integer and obtain 7.

Let's translate this procedure into code.

Listing 4.1 Marking an exam

```
def markExam(q1: Double, q2: Double, q3: Double) =
  Math.round((((q1 + q2 + q3) / 3) * 10 / 3)
```

The function markExam replicates the calculations described, but it is difficult to identify its objective and computation steps. You can improve the readability of the markExam function by using values with descriptive names.

Listing 4.2 Marking an exam—a more readable version

```
def markExam(q1: Double, q2: Double, q3: Double) = {
  val avgScore = (q1 + q2 + q3) / 3
  val scaledScore = avgScore * 10 / 3      No need for the return key-
  Math.round(scaledScore)          ⟵      word; the last expression is
}                                          the one returned.
```

Values are a fundamental component of your code. In Scala, you declare them by using the keyword *val*. You can only initialize them once because they are immutable; if you try to reassign them, the code will not compile. Consider the following example:

```
scala> val a = 1
val a: Int = 1

scala> a
val res0: Int = 1
                                                You cannot reassign
scala> a = 2                                    a value, which is an
<console>:11: error: reassignment to val  ⟵   immutable assignment.
```

> **Quick Check 4.1** Can you use the += operator with a value of type Int? What about the operator -=?

When declaring a value, its type is optional; the compiler tries to infer it for you. If the compiler infers an unexpected type, you can provide it explicitly; the compiler will check if the type you specified is compatible with the assignment of your value and eventually return a compilation error:

```
scala> val b: Int = 1
val b: Int = 1
                                    The compiler knows
                                    how to fit an Int into
scala> val c: Double = 1      ⟵    a Double.
val c: Double = 1.0

scala> val d: Int = "not-an-int"   ⟵
       error: type mismatch;              You cannot assign
       found   : String("not-an-int")     a String to an Int.
       required: Int
```

```
scala> val d: Any = "not-an-int"
val d: Any = not-an-int
```

Any is the root of the class hierarchy: you can assign any value to it.

Look at figure 4.1 for a syntax diagram on values in Scala.

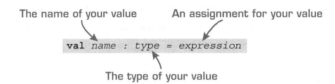

VALUE: IMMUTABLE ASSIGNMENT

The name of your value   An assignment for your value

val *name : type = expression*

The type of your value

Figure 4.1   Syntax diagram of how to define a value in Scala. A value is immutable, so you can assign it only once.

Quick Check 4.2   Which of these expressions are valid? Use the REPL to validate your hypotheses.
1 val test: Double = 2.0
2 val test: Int = 2.0
3 val test: Any = 2.0

4.2   Variables

In the previous section, you wrote a function to mark an exam. Let's expand it so that you can compute the average score of all exams you marked so far. Values are immutable, so you cannot use them to keep track of how your stats evolve, which is the *mutable state* of your program. In these cases, you can use variables.

Listing 4.3 Keeping track of the mark statistics

```
var marksSum = 0
var marksCount = 0

def averageMark: Double =
  marksSum.toDouble / marksCount
```

Example of a variable

When converting marksSum to Double, the result of your division must be a Double. An integer divided by another integer produces an Int while diving a double by an integer returns a double.

```
def markExam(q1: Double, q2: Double, q3: Double): Int = {
  val avgScore = (q1 + q2 + q3) / 3
  val scaledScore = avgScore * 10 / 3
  val mark = Math.round(scaledScore).toInt

  marksSum += mark
  marksCount += 1
  mark
}
```

Math.round results in a constant of type Long, so you need to convert it to Int.

There's no need for the return keyword; the last expression is the one returned.

In Scala, variables are very similar to values: while you can assign values only once, you can reassign variables multiple times. Consider the following example:

```
scala> var a = 1
var a: Int = 1

scala> a
val res1: Int = 1

scala> a = 2
// mutated a
```

You do not need to provide a type for your variable; the compiler will infer it for you. When doing so, the compiler makes sure that the assignment is compatible with it. Look at figure 4.2 for a summary of how to define variables in Scala.

VARIABLE: MUTABLE ASSIGNMENT

The name of your variable   An assignment for your variable

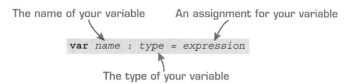

`var` *name* : *type* = *expression*

The type of your variable

Figure 4.2 Syntax diagram of how to define a variable in Scala. A variable is a mutable assignment: you can reassign it more than once.

Think in Scala: val or var?

When in doubt, you should always try to use val instead of var.

Having immutable values makes your programs safe from concurrency inconsistency in exchange for some additional memory allocation; most of the time, you will not notice this extra memory usage thanks to the JVM's garbage collection.

Using mutable structures makes your programs challenging to test and reason about; you need to pay attention to how processes share data and how they evolve. Mutable structures may be more performant, but they also expose your code to complex concurrency issues such as data inconsistency, deadlocks, and resource starvation.

Before choosing to stick with a var, you should make sure you have tried everything else in your book of tricks; variables should be your last and least desirable option.

At this point in your Scala journey, you may think that using mutability is often the only option. But this is not the case: in future units and lessons, you'll discover many tools and techniques, such as case classes, that will allow you to get rid of var from your code.

Quick Check 4.3 Can you use the += operator with a var of type String? What about the operator -=?

 Summary

In this lesson, my objective was to teach about the different types of assignments in Scala.

- You have learned how to declare values and that you can only assign them once.
- You have seen how to define variables and how you can reassign them multiple times.

Let's see if you got this!

TRY THIS Modify your markExam function to keep track of both the lowest and the highest mark computed so far.

Answers to quick checks

Quick Check 4.1 The operators += and -= cannot be used with `val`: a value is immutable and once assigned you cannot reassign it.

Quick Check 4.2 The first and third expressions are valid, while the second one is invalid:

1 Valid: an expression of type `Double` is compatible with `Double`.
2 Invalid: the compiler doesn't know how to fit an expression of type `Double` into an `Int`. Even if the quantity 2.0 is equal to 2 from a mathematical perspective, the compiler doesn't automatically convert a `Double` to `Int` to avoid precision loss; 2.5 is not equivalent to neither 2 or 3. Note that the opposite (i.e., assigning an `Int` expression to a `Double`) is valid.
3 Valid: `Any` is compatible with any type because it is at the root of Scala's class hierarchy.

Quick Check 4.3 You can use the operator += together with a `var` of type `String`; you can reassign a variable, and the class `String` has an implementation for the function +. You cannot use the operator -= with a `var` of type `String` because the class `String` doesn't have a method called "-".

CONDITIONAL CONSTRUCTS AND LOOPS

After reading this lesson, you'll be able to

- Control the execution of your code using an `if-else` construct
- Iterate through instructions using `while` and `for` loops

In lesson 4, you learned how to define values and variables to store computation results. But life is not always so linear; when performing a task, you may also need to make informed decisions by selecting one approach rather than the other. In this lesson, you'll discover how to combine different executions of your code through given conditions. You'll learn how to use the most common conditional constructs and loops in Scala. You'll use if-else constructs to check if the system should allow a requested operation in the capstone.

> **Consider this**
>
> In the previous lesson, you wrote a program to mark exams from 1 to 10. Suppose you need to label a mark as follows: "failed" if the score is lower than 4, "satisfactory" if between 4 and 6 excluded, "good" if between 6 and 9 excluded, "excellent" otherwise. How would you implement this new functionality?

5.1   If-else construct

Suppose you have a list of events; each one has a number representing the day of the week it occurs, starting with 1 for Sunday and ending with 7 for Saturday. You want to write a function that takes an integer representing a day of the week and returns either *weekday* or *weekend* accordingly.

Listing 5.1 Categorizing the day of the week

```
def categorizeDayOfWeek(n: Int) = {
  if (n == 1 || n == 7) {
    "weekend"
  } else if (n > 1 && n < 7 ) {
    "weekday"
  } else {
    "unknown"
  }
}
```

Listing 5.2 shows you another example of using the if-else construct with a function that returns a string to label an integer as positive, negative, or neutral.

Listing 5.2 Labeling a number

```
def label(n: Int) =
  if (n == 0) "neutral"
  else if (n < 0) "negative"
  else "positive"
```

The structure of the if-else construct is similar to other languages; figure 5.1 summarizes its Scala syntax. The keyword *if* is the only one that is mandatory, and it identifies the first condition. You can add more predicates by using the keywords *else if*. Finally, the keyword *else* defines the behavior for the values that don't satisfy any previous criteria.

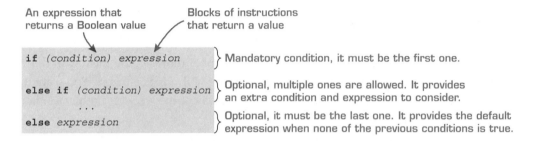

An expression that returns a Boolean value

Blocks of instructions that return a value

`if (condition) expression`	} Mandatory condition, it must be the first one.
`else if (condition) expression`	} Optional, multiple ones are allowed. It provides an extra condition and expression to consider.
`else expression`	} Optional, it must be the last one. It provides the default expression when none of the previous conditions is true.

Figure 5.1 Syntax diagram of how to define an `if`-`else` construct in Scala. The `if` component is mandatory, while the `else if` and `else` ones are optional.

Expressions and curly braces: Omit or not to omit?

Expressions are everywhere in Scala; they are in values, variables, conditional constructs, functions, and more!

Scala uses curly braces to identify expressions; one or more instructions make an expression. When an expression contains only one instruction, you can omit its curly braces. For example, the expressions val a = 42 and val a = { 42 } are equivalent because they both assign the expression 42 to the value a.

Let's look at listing 5.2 again. You could have implemented the `label` function as follows:

```
def label(n: Int) = {
  if (n == 0) { "neutral" }
  else if (n < 0) { "negative" }
  else { "positive" }
}
```

You can omit the curly braces for the expressions associated to each if-condition because they consist of a single expression:

```
def label(n: Int) = {
  if (n == 0) "neutral"
  else if (n < 0) "negative"
  else "positive"
}
```

You can also eliminate the curly braces at the function level: the `if`-`else` construct is a single expression that identifies the body of the function `label`:

```
def label(n: Int) =
  if (n == 0) "neutral"
  else if (n < 0) "negative"
  else "positive"
```

You should omit curly braces where possible but without compromising the readability of your code.

Quick Check 5.1 Write a function called evenOrOdd that takes an integer and prints a message to the console to tell if a number is even or odd. HINT: Use the modulo operator % for the remainder of a division (e.g., 5 % 2 returns 1).

```
def evenOrOdd(n: Int)
```

 ## 5.2   While loop

Imagine you'd like to write a function called echo5 to print a given message on the console five times. You could write a function that has five print instructions:

```
def echo5(msg: String) = {
  println(msg)
  println(msg)
  println(msg)
  println(msg)
  println(msg)
}
```

Your implementation of the function echo5 doesn't scale: what if you need to print 50 messages rather than just 5? What if their number changes according to the parameters passed to the function?

When you need to repeat an instruction until a particular condition is satisfied, you can use a while loop.

Listing 5.3 Repeating using a while loop

```
def echo5(msg: String) = {
  var i = 1
  while(i <= 5) {
```

```
        println(msg)
        i += 1
      }
  }
```

Look at figure 5.2 for a syntax diagram of while loops in Scala: in a while loop, you repeat its instructions until its condition is no longer valid.

An expression that   Blocks of instructions to
returns a Boolean value   perform an operation

Figure 5.2   Syntax diagram of while loops in Scala; you evaluate the expression until the condition is valid.

Think in Scala: while loops as antipatterns

while loops are part of the Scala language, but they are rarely used and often considered antipatterns.

while loops operate on mutable state: they keep track of how it evolves, and they stop once a predicate is respected. Scala discourages the use of mutability, so while loops are relatively rare in the code. In unit 5, you'll learn about how the Standard Scala Collections provides powerful alternatives to while loops through dedicated functions, such as foreach and map, to iterate in a functional and thread-safe way.

Quick Check 5.2   Write a function, called count, to print all the numbers from 1 to 10 using a while loop.

5.3   For loop

In the previous section, you saw how to implement a function called echo5 to print a given message five times using a while loop. In Scala, you can also use a for loop to achieve the same result.

Listing 5.4   Repeating using a for loop

```scala
def echo5(msg: String) = {
    for (i <- 1 to 5) {
        println(msg)
    }
}
```

The expression "1 to 5" returns an iterable data structure called Range containing the numbers 1, 2, 3, 4, and 5 (right end included). You can also use the expression "1 until 6" to generate a range with the right end excluded.

When using a for loop, you repeat an operation over a finite set of values rather than using a stop condition. Look at figure 5.3 for a summary of for loops in Scala.

An iterable structure such as string, range, or list

Blocks of instructions to perform an operation

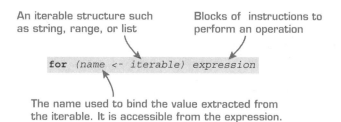

```scala
for (name <- iterable) expression
```

The name used to bind the value extracted from the iterable. It is accessible from the expression.

Figure 5.3   Syntax diagram on for loops in Scala. In a for loop, an expression is repeated for each of a finite set of values.

Scala also offers a more powerful alternative to the classic for loop you have just seen, called for-comprehension. You'll learn about it when discussing the class Option in unit 4.

> **Quick Check 5.3**   Does the following expression compile? If so, what is its output?
>
> ```scala
> for (a <- "hello") println(a)
> ```
>
> Use the REPL to validate your hypothesis.

Summary

In this lesson, my objective was to teach about the basic conditional constructs in Scala.

- You learned how to use an if-else construct to express decision making in your code.
- You learned how to use while and for loops to repeat operations multiple times.

Let's see if you got this!

TRY THIS   Write a function to apply the discount to a given price as follows:

- 0% discount if the price is less than $50
- 10% discount if the price is at least $50 but less than $100
- 15% discount if the price is at least $100

 # Answers to quick checks

Quick Check 5.1   A possible implementation for the function evenOrOdd is:

```scala
def evenOrOdd(n: Int) =
  if (n % 2 == 0) println(s"$n is even")
  else println(s"$n is odd")
```

Quick Check 5.2   You could implement the function count using a while loop as follows:

```scala
def count() = {
  var i = 1
  while(i <= 10) {
    println(i)
    i += 1
  }
}
```

Quick Check 5.3   The expression compiles, and it prints each letter of the word *hello* in a new line of the console:

```scala
scala> for (a <- "hello") println(a)
h
e
l
l
o
```

FUNCTION AS THE MOST FUNDAMENTAL BLOCK OF CODE

After reading this lesson, you will be able to

- Identify the components of a function
- Implement functions in Scala
- Define function parameters with defaults

When coding, functions are the most fundamental block of code. They provide instructions on how to perform a given task; without them, you will not be able to define how your application works. Scala treats functions as its first-class citizens: they are an essential component of your program with different uses and shapes. For example, you can use partial functions, anonymous functions, higher order functions, and more! In this lesson, you'll review the basics of functions in Scala and analyze their different components. You'll also see how to define a function. In the capstone for this unit, you'll use functions to provide instructions on how to operate your vending machine.

6.1   Functions

Suppose you want to determine if a given number is even.

Listing 6.1 The isEven function

```scala
def isEven(n: Int): Boolean = {
    n % 2 == 0
}
```

Listing 6.1 implements a function called isEven. In Scala, a function identifies some computation that takes zero or more parameters, and that may—or may not—return a value. In Scala, a function can throw exceptions or never terminate:

```scala
def myFunc(n: Int): Boolean = {
  if (n < 0) throw new RuntimeException("Error!")
  n % 2 == 0
}
```

```scala
def myFunc2(n: Int): Boolean = {
  if (n < 0) myFunc2(n)
  n % 2 == 0
}
```

For any negative number, the function myFunc throws a runtime exception. The function myFunc2 never terminates as it keeps calling itself (more on this when I introduce you to pure and impure functions).

Figure 6.1 provides an example of the different components of a function in Scala. It has two main parts: a signature that defines what it does and an implementation that details how it does it. You can split a function signature further into its name, parameters, and return type. Let's review each component.

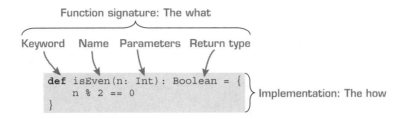

Figure 6.1 The different components of a Scala function. The function signature describes what a function does, and it has the *def* keyword, a name, some parameters, and a return type. The implementation provides detailed instructions on how a function does it.

THE KEYWORD DEF AND A FUNCTION NAME When declaring a basic function, use the keyword *def* followed by a name. When using the keyword *def*, a function must always have a name:

```
def myFunc() = ???
```
← Placeholder for future implementation

The symbol ???

The symbol ??? is one of the most useful and practical features in Scala. It is a placeholder for future code: it tells the compiler that its implementation is currently missing, but you will add it later. If the interpreter evaluates the symbol ??? at runtime, it will throw a NotImplementedError exception.

Scala can infer types so that you can often omit them. When using the symbol ???, you should provide an explicit return type, even if not mandatory; the compiler doesn't have much information, so it can struggle to infer the correct one. Being explicit can also help remind you later on what your intention was and what your implementation should return.

The symbol ??? is a useful tool when designing how the different components of your program interact. It allows you to focus on your code's high-level structure rather than on implementation details.

Starting with an overall design rather than a detailed implementation is an excellent practice to develop programs that are easy to use, maintain, and understand.

PARAMETERS   A function can have zero or more parameters. If present, they are grouped by parentheses and separated by commas. A parameter is identified by a name and a type. The following are valid function declarations:

```
def myFunc = ???
def myFunc() = ???
def myFunc(a: Int) = ???
def myFunc(a: Int, b: String) = ???
```

When invoking a function, you can refer to function parameters by name and change their order:

```
def myFunc(a: Int, b: String) = ???
```

```
myFunc(1, "Scala")              // valid
myFunc("Scala", 1)              // does not compile
myFunc(a = 1, b = "Scala")      // valid
myFunc(b = "Scala", a = 1)      // valid
```

You can also specify default values for its parameters:

```
def myFunc(a: Int, b: String = "Hello") = ???
```

```
myFunc(1, "Scala")              // valid
myFunc(1)                       // valid
myFunc(a = 1)                   // valid
myFunc(b = "Scala")             // does not compile
myFunc(a = 1, b = "Scala")      // valid
myFunc(b = "Scala", a = 1)      // valid
```

You should declare parameters without defaults first; this is common practice but not mandatory. If your function specifies parameters with defaults before others, you must invoke parameters by their name, also called *named parameters*, to trigger the use of their defaults:

```
def myFunc(a: Int = 1, b: String) = ???
```

```
myFunc(1, "Scala")              // valid
myFunc("Scala")                 // does not compile
myFunc(b = "Scala")             // valid
```

The function call myFunc("Scala") does not compile because its first parameter must have type Int. On the other hand, myFunc(b = "Scala") is valid because the compiler understands that the value refers to the second parameter and that it should use the default value for the first one.

RETURN TYPE   A type defines a subset of values. For example, the type Boolean represents the finite set of the values true and false. A function return type tells you the possible values it can return. A function must always have a return type; you can either provide it explicitly or let the compiler infer one for its implementation. If an implementation is missing, the compiler cannot infer its return type, and you must provide it explicitly. If the implementation of your function is not compatible with its return type, the compiler provides an error message explaining the type found and the type requested:

```
def myFunc(a: Int)             // does not compile
                               // Its return type is missing

def myFunc(a: Int): Int        // valid
def myFunc(a: Int) = a + 1     // valid

def myFunc(a: Int): Int = {     // valid
   a + 1
}

def myFunc(a: Int): Boolean = {  // does not compile.
      a + 1                       // found: Int, required: Boolean
}
```

Return type: To omit or not to omit?

You have learned that the compiler can infer the return type of a function from its implementation. You may be wondering when to omit it and when not.

As a rule of thumb, always provide the return type—particularly for public or complex functions.

When providing an explicit return type to your function, you make your code more readable by providing more information about it. You are also taking full advantage of the compiler, and by doing so, you are asking the compiler to confirm that your implementation matches the expected return type.

Unless the function is straightforward and with limited scope, specify the return type, which will allow you to you discover bugs more efficiently and improve your code's readability.

IMPLEMENTATION   The implementation of a function is an ordered sequence of instructions that produces a value that must be compatible with its return type. You do not need to use a *return* keyword in Scala; the value produced by the last expression is the one returned. When a function has no implementation, it is abstract, which the compiler can infer by its lack of implementation, so you do not need to use any keyword for it. In Scala, the *abstract* keyword is for classes only, not functions.

```
def myFunc(a: Int): Boolean              // valid

abstract def myFunc(a: Int): Boolean     // does not compile
                                         // invalid keyword abstract

def myFunc(a: Int): Int = {              // valid
    a + 1
}
```

In lesson 5, you learned about Scala expressions. In particular, you learned that you can omit braces for expressions that are composed of only one instruction; this is still valid in the context of the implementation of a function:

```
def myFunc(a: Int): Int = {              // valid
    a + 1
}

def myFunc(a: Int): Int =  a + 1         // valid

def myFunc(a: Int): Int =                // valid
    a + 1

def myFunc(a: Int): Int = {              // valid
    println("...extra operation here...")
    a + 1
}

def myFunc(a: Int): Int =                // does not compile
    println("...extra operation here...")  // missing parentheses
    a + 1
```

Figure 6.2 shows a summary of the syntax needed for the several components of a function.

> **Quick Check 6.1**   Which of the following functions do not compile? Why?
>   1 def myFunc(x) = x + 1
>   2 def myFunc(x: Int) = x + 1
>   3 def myFunc(x: Int = true): Int
>   4 def myFunc(x: Int)
>   5 def myFunc(x: Int): Int = x == 1
>   6 def myFunc(x: Int) = x == 1

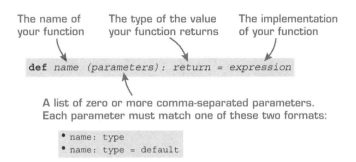

A list of zero or more comma-separated parameters.
Each parameter must match one of these two formats:

- `name: type`
- `name: type = default`

Figure 6.2 Syntax diagram for a function in Scala and its different components

Summary

In this lesson, my objective was to teach you about the basics of functions in Scala.

- You learned that a function has a signature and an implementation.
- You also saw how to define and invoke a function with default parameters.

Let's see if you got this!

TRY THIS

Define a function pow that takes two parameters of type Int and that returns an Int; call the first parameter exponent and the second one base with a default of 2. The function should calculate the power of a number as follows: if the parameter exponent has a value of 3 and base 2, it should compute 2^3. Implement the function using a loop without using the function Math.pow.

Answers to quick checks

Quick Check 6.1

1 It doesn't compile: the parameter x must have a type.
2 It compiles.
3 It doesn't compile: true is a value of type Boolean. The compiler doesn't know how to fit a value of type Boolean into an Int, so you cannot use it as a default for x.
4 It doesn't compile: an abstract function must have a return type.
5 It doesn't compile: its return type is Int, but the expression x == 1 returns a value of type Boolean.
6 It compiles.

CLASSES AND SUBCLASSES TO REPRESENT THE WORLD

After reading this lesson, you will be able to

- Represent real-world elements and their interactions
- Design class-subclass relations

Now that you know the basics of functions in Scala, you'll learn about classes in this lesson. The concept of class is fundamental to the object-oriented paradigm, and it allows you to represent elements and interactions from the real world. Classes, sub-classes, and abstract classes enable you to group entities that have common shapes and behaviors. If you are familiar with other object-oriented programming languages, you'll find similarities with Scala's concept of class. Table 7.1 recaps the different types of classes Scala can offer. In the capstone, you'll use a class to represent your vending machine.

Table 7.1 Summary of the types of classes in Scala, which match the definitions of most other object-oriented languages

Term	Definition
Class	A representation of elements of the same kind from the real world. All its functions have an implementation.
Subclass	A class that inherits behaviors from another class, called superclass. In Scala, a class can have up to one superclass.
Superclass	A class whose methods are inherited by one or more classes, called subclasses.
Abstract class	A class in which one or more methods may be abstract (i.e., they do not have an implementation).

Consider this

Imagine you need to represent the life cycle of the animals of a zoo that hosts cats, dogs, chickens, and lamas. How would you present them? Are there any common behaviors that characterize the life cycle of these animals?

 7.1   Class

Suppose you need to represent a robot with a name in your application. One possible solution is to define a class using the keyword *class*.

Listing 7.1 The class Robot

```scala
class Robot(name: String)
```

You can create two instances of a robot, called Tom and John, by using the keyword *new* followed by the class name and its parameters:

```scala
val tom = new Robot("Tom")
val john = new Robot("John")
```

If you try to access the parameter name of a Robot instance, the compiler will stop you because its parameter is not accessible.

```scala
tom.name    // compiler error:
            // "value name cannot be accessed as a member of" Robot
```

To access the parameter name, you need to declare it as a value (or variable) in the class declaration.

Listing 7.2 **The class Robot: name as val**

```
class Robot(val name: String)          ◄──────────    Name is declared as
                                                       an immutable value.
```

You should now be able to create robots and access their names as follows:

```
val tom = new Robot("Tom")
val john = new Robot("John")

tom.name // returns "Tom"
john.name // returns "John"
```

You can also specify a default value for a class parameter; the compiler will use it when creating an instance of the class without providing a specific value for that parameter. Let's change the class Robot to use the string "Unknown" as the default value for the parameter name:

Listing 7.3 **The class Robot: name with a default value**

```
    class Robot(val name: String = "Unknown")
```

You can now create a robot without providing a name explicitly:

```
    val noName = new Robot
    noName.name // returns "Unknown"
```

In general, a class can have zero or more parameters. You can declare functions in it to define some behavior specific to the class. You can refer to a function defined in a class as *method*. Let's define a method for a robot to produce a greeting message.

Listing 7.4 **The class Robot: a greeting functionality**

```
class Robot(val name: String = "Unknown") {
    def welcome(n: String) = s"Welcome $n! My name is $name"
}
```

Your robots can now greet people as follows:

```
val tom = new Robot("Tom")
tom.welcome("Martin") // returns "Welcome Martin! My name is Tom"
```

Figure 7.1 shows a summary of how to define and initialize a class.

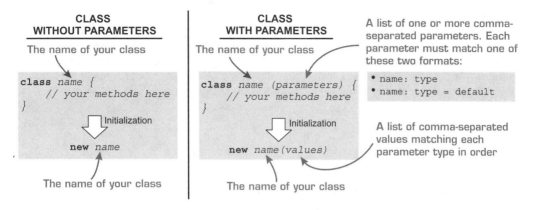

Figure 7.1   Syntax diagram on how to define and initialize a class in Scala

Named parameters

A class can have zero or more parameters. When more than one class of parameters have the same type, you should use named parameters to improve readability and avoid ambiguity.

For example, consider a class to represent coordinates:

```
class Coordinate(latitude: Double, longitude: Double)
```

You can create an instance of the class Coordinate as follows:

```
new Coordinate(42.42, 24.24)
```

When creating an instance of the class Coordinate, you need to remember that the first parameter represents the latitude, while the second represents the longitude. The compiler cannot help you remember their correct order because both the parameters have the same type. A trick to avoid any ambiguity is to use named parameters:

```
new Coordinate(latitude = 42.42, longitude = 24.24)
```

Because you are explicitly naming the parameters, you are free to change their order. The following expression is syntactically valid, and it produces an equivalent result:

```
new Coordinate(longitude = 24.24, latitude = 42.42)
```

As a rule of thumb, you should use named parameters every time it can improve your code's readability and to help avoid mistakes related to the order of the parameters that the compiler cannot detect at compile time.

> **Quick Check 7.1**   Create a class Person with a name of type String and an age of type Int—defaulted to 0. Define a method called presentYourself, for the class Person; it takes no parameters, and it returns a string to communicate the name and age of a person. Create two instances and see what the presentYourself method returns for each of them: Martin is 18, and Bob is 0 years old.

 ## 7.2   Subclass

Suppose you want to represent robots to welcome people in a specific language. For example, you may need an English robot and an Italian one. Your concept of robot now requires a few specializations; some are English, some are Italian. Figure 7.2 illustrates how you could express this relation with a class Robot and the subclasses ItalianRobot and EnglishRobot.

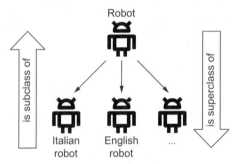

Figure 7.2   Visual representation of hierarchies between robots. Robot is the superclass for ItalianRobot and EnglishRobot, while ItalianRobot and EnglishRobot are subclasses of Robot. The relation has a tree structure: a class can have multiple subclasses, but it can only have one superclass.

Listing 7.5 shows how you can translate this class-subclass relation into code. The class Robot defines a generic robot. The classes ItalianRobot and EnglishRobot extend the class Robot by providing a new implementation for the method welcome.

Listing 7.5 Italian and English robots

```
class Robot(val name: String = "Unknown") {
    def welcome(n: String) = s"Welcome $n! My name is $name"
}
```

```
class ItalianRobot(name: String) extends Robot(name) {

    override def welcome(n: String) =
        s"Benvenuto $n! Il mio nome e' $name"

}

class EnglishRobot(name: String, country: String)
    extends Robot(name) {

    override def welcome(n: String) =
        s"Welcome $n, I am $name from the country of $country!"

}
```

A subclass of Robot

A class can have more parameters than its superclass.

A class can have more parameters than its superclass: EnglishRobot has an additional one called country. You need to specify the keyword *override* because you are redefining a method that already has an implementation. When overriding an abstract function, you can omit the keyword *override*.

In Scala, use the keyword *extends* to express a class-subclass relation. You also use the keyword *override* when redefining a function defined in a superclass, which also tells the compiler that you are deliberately redefining a method: the compiler makes sure that the function you are overriding matches an existing one with the same signature (i.e., the same name, parameters, and return type). Figure 7.3 is a summary of how to express a class-subclass relation in Scala.

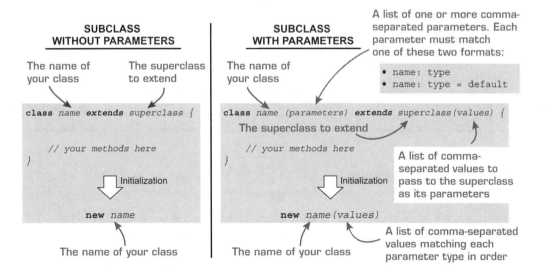

Figure 7.3   Syntax diagram of how to define and initialize a subclass in Scala

A class can only have one superclass. In unit 2, you'll learn how to express multiple inheritance-using traits, which are relatively similar to interfaces in other object-oriented programming languages.

Quick Check 7.2 In Quick Check 7.1, you defined a class Person. Create two subclasses of the class Person: one to represent a teacher; the other to represent a student. A student should have an additional parameter to track its ID.

Scala 3: Optional braces

Scala 3 introduces new indentation rules that make some occurrences of braces optional. For example, consider the following snippet of code:

```
abstract class A {
    def f: Int
}

class B(n: Int) extends A {
    def f: Int = n * 2
}
```

You could rewrite it using optional braces as the following:

```
abstract class A:
    def f: Int

class B(n: Int) extends A:
    def f: Int = n * 2
```

The code examples in this book do not use optional braces to ensure compatibility with previous versions of Scala.

 ## 7.3   Abstract class

In the previous section, you created subclasses for a robot. Because the class Robot already provides an implementation for the method welcome, their subclasses don't have to reimplement it. Suppose you want to ensure that every robot must implement the welcome function from scratch without reusing an existing implementation. You can achieve this by declaring the class Robot as abstract by adding the keyword *abstract* and providing only the function signature for the method welcome.

Listing 7.6 **The abstract class Robot**

```
abstract class Robot(name: String) {        ← An abstract class

    def welcome(n: String): String          ← An abstract function
}                                               has no implementation.
```

If your class is nonabstract, then all its methods must have an implementation. If this is not the case, the compiler provides an error message to remind you what methods you need to implement:

```
scala> class MyRobot(name: String) extends Robot(name)
1 |class MyRobot(name: String) extends Robot(name)
  |      ^
  |class MyRobot needs to be abstract, since def welcome(n: String):
          String in class Robot is not defined
```

Figure 7.4 provides a syntax diagram of abstract classes in Scala.

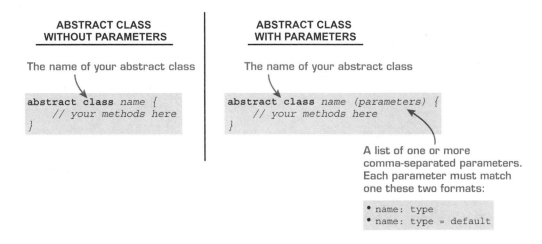

ABSTRACT CLASS
WITHOUT PARAMETERS

The name of your abstract class

```
abstract class name {
    // your methods here
}
```

ABSTRACT CLASS
WITH PARAMETERS

The name of your abstract class

```
abstract class name (parameters) {
    // your methods here
}
```

A list of one or more comma-separated parameters. Each parameter must match one these two formats:

• name: type
• name: type = default

Figure 7.4 Syntax diagram on how to define an abstract class in Scala. Note that you cannot initialize abstract classes.

> **Quick Check 7.3** In Quick Check 7.1, you defined the class Person. Change its implementation to force all its subclasses to implement a method called hello, which takes one String parameter representing a name and returns another String.

 ## Summary

In this lesson, my objective was to teach you about the different kinds of Scala classes, a fundamental component of the object-oriented paradigm.

- You discovered how to use classes to represent elements of the real world.
- You also learned how to use a class-subclass relation to express inheritance and abstract commonalities using abstract classes.

Let's see if you got this!

> **TRY THIS** A bar serves cold and hot beverages. You can request to add more ice to a cold drink or to reheat a hot one. Express these relations using classes and subclasses.

 ## Answers to quick checks

> **Quick Check 7.1** You can define the class Person as follows:
>
> ```scala
> class Person(name: String, age: Int = 0) {
>   def presentYourself = s"My name is $name and I am $age"
> }
> ```
>
> The following code creates two instances of the class Person:
>
> ```scala
> val martin = new Person("Martin", 18)
> martin.presentYourself // returns "My name is Martin and I am 18"
>
> val bob = new Person("Bob")
> bob.presentYourself // returns "My name is Bob and I am 0"
> ```

Quick Check 7.2 The following code creates two subclasses of the class Person:

```
class Person(name: String, age: Int = 0) {
  def presentYourself = s"My name is $name and I am $age"
}

class Teacher(name: String, age: Int)
   extends Person(name, age)

class Student(name: String, age: Int, id: String)
   extends Person(name, age)
```

Quick Check 7.3 You should change the implementation of the class Person as follows:

```
abstract class Person(name: String, age: Int = 0) {

  def presentYourself = s"My name is $name and I am $age"

  def hello(n: String): String
}
```

THE VENDING MACHINE

In this capstone, you will

- Implement functions and classes
- Code using variables and values
- Use if-else constructs

In this capstone, you'll implement a class, load it into the REPL, and interact with it. In particular, you'll represent a vending machine that sells two products: a white chocolate bar for $1.50 and a granola bar for $1.00. Let's keep things simple and assume that your appliance doesn't give any change back.

A customer can buy an item by selecting a specific product and inserting money into the vending machine. Once the vending machine receives the request, it should check that the product is available and the given money is enough; if all the checks are successful, it should collect the money and release the product.

Let's analyze the business requirements and identify the main components of your vending machine.

8.1 Setting up the vending machine

Figure 8.1 summarizes the execution flow of the interaction between a customer and the vending machine. A customer requests a product to buy. Following this operation, the vending machine should check if the product is in stock and if the money is enough to cover its cost. When rejecting the request, it should display a human-readable text explaining what went wrong. When successful, it should collect the money and release the product and a message that acknowledges the purchase.

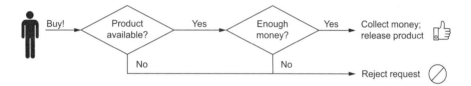

Figure 8.1 Summary of the execution flow for a vending machine. The customer's request to buy a product should be satisfied if and only if the product is available and the inserted money is enough.

Let's first define the API of your vending machine and then focus on its implementation.

8.1.1 The VendingMachine class and its APIs

First, you need to identify the main components of your vending machine, which has a cash register containing the money collected so far and a counter for each product type. Create a new file called VendingMachine.scala and add the code in listing 8.1.

Listing 8.1 The VendingMachine class

```scala
// file VendingMachine.scala

class VendingMachine {

    var chocolateBar = 0          Counter of type Int
    var granolaBar = 0            because 0 is a constant
                                  of type Int.

    var totalMoney = 0.0          Counter of type Double
}                                 because 0.0 is a value
                                  of type Double.
```

A customer can perform one action: request a product by giving money in exchange. Let's define a function called buy that takes two parameters: a `String` for the product and a `Double` for the money. It should return a human-readable message with the outcome of the request.

Listing 8.2 API for VendingMachine

```
class VendingMachine {

    //...

    def buy(product: String, money: Double): String = ???
}
```

The vending machine also needs to perform the following operations:

1 It should check that the requested product is available.
2 It should verify that the inserted money is sufficient.
3 If all the validations are successful, it should complete it by collecting the money and releasing the product.

Let's translate the three operations into code.

Listing 8.3 Main operations for VendingMachine

```
class VendingMachine {

    //...

    def isProductAvailable(product: String): Boolean = ???

    def isMoneyEnough(product: String,
                      money: Double): Boolean = ???

    def completeRequest(product: String,
                        money: Double): String = ???
}
```

You can now implement the function buy.

Listing 8.4 Implementation of function buy for VendingMachine

```
class VendingMachine {

    //...
```

```
def buy(product: String, money: Double): String =
  if (!isProductAvailable(product))
      s"Sorry, product $product not available"
  else if (!isMoneyEnough(product, money))
      "Please, insert more money"
  else completeRequest(product, money)
```

You can omit curly brackets here because the function has an expression that contains only one if-else construct.

```
  def isProductAvailable(product: String): Boolean = ???

  def isMoneyEnough(product: String,
                    money: Double): Boolean = ???

  def completeRequest(product: String,
                      money: Double): String = ???
}
```

All the pieces are connected! You can now replace the occurrences of the symbol ??? with an implementation.

8.1.2   The vending machine and its operations

The vending machine needs to check if the selected product is available and if the money is enough for it to complete a customer request. You have already defined how these functions should look, but you still need to implement them.

Listing 8.5   Implementing checks for VendingMachine

```
class VendingMachine {

  var chocolateBar = 0
  var granolaBar = 0

  //...

  def isProductAvailable(product: String): Boolean = {
    val productQuantity = {
      if (product == "chocolate") chocolateBar
      else if (product == "granola") granolaBar
      else 0
    }
    productQuantity > 0
  }
```

Any unknown product has zero quantity.

```
def isMoneyEnough(product: String, money: Double): Boolean = {
  val cost = if (product == "chocolate") 1.5 else 1
  money >= cost
}
```

If the request is successful, the vending machine should complete it by collecting the money and releasing the selected product.

Listing 8.6 Implementing completeRequest for VendingMachine

```
class VendingMachine {

  var chocolateBar = 0
  var granolaBar = 0

  var totalMoney = 0.0

  //…

  def completeRequest(product: String, money: Double): String = {
    collectMoney(money)
    releaseProduct(product)
    s"There you go! Have a $product bar"
  }

  def collectMoney(money: Double) =
    totalMoney += money

  def releaseProduct(product: String) =
    if (product == "chocolate") chocolateBar -= 1
    else if (product == "granola") granolaBar -= 1

}
```

The implementation of your vending machine is now complete and ready to use!

8.1.3   Let's try it out

Save the code for your VendingMachine class in a file called VendingMachine.scala and load it into the REPL:

```
$> scala
Welcome to Scala 2.13.6 (OpenJDK 64-Bit Server VM, Java 15.0.1).
Type in expressions for evaluation. Or try :help.
scala>
```

First, you need to load the code from the file VendingMachine.scala and create a vending machine:

```
scala> :load /my/path/to/VendingMachine.scala
class VendingMachine

scala> val machine = new VendingMachine
val machine: VendingMachine = VendingMachine@415787d7
```

Let's buy a chocolate bar using $1.50. The vending machine rejects the operation because it contains no products:

```
scala> machine.buy("chocolate", 1.5)
val res0: String = Sorry, product chocolate not available

scala> machine.chocolateBar
val res1: Int = 0

scala> machine.granolaBar
val res2: Int = 0
```

Let's add two chocolate bars and one granola to the machine:

```
scala> machine.chocolateBar += 2

scala> machine.granolaBar += 1
```

You should now be able to buy a chocolate bar:

```
scala> machine.buy("chocolate", 1.5)
val res3: String = There you go! Have a chocolate bar
```

If you try to buy a product with not enough money, the vending machine rejects the request:

```
scala> machine.buy("chocolate", 1)
val res4: String = Please, insert more money
```

Once a product is no longer available, you should no longer be able to buy it:

```
scala> machine.buy("granola", 2)
val res5: String = There you go! Have a granola bar

scala> machine.buy("granola", 2)
val res6: String = Sorry, product granola not available
```

So far, the vending machine should have collected $3.50:

```scala
scala> machine.totalMoney
val res7: Double = 3.5
```

 ## 8.2   Possible improvements to our solution

Congratulations on completing your first capstone! Your vending machine implementation respects the given requirements, but a few improvements are possible. Let's see what these are and what techniques you'll learn to help improve your code.

EVERYTHING IS PUBLICLY ACCESSIBLE   Variables and methods are visible and modifiable without restrictions. Third parties could easily compromise the security of your vending machine by resetting counters and by overriding functions. In unit 2, you'll discover how to use access modifiers to protect your code's sensitive information from unwanted exposure and modifications.

VARS ARE PROBLEMATIC   You should avoid using var in your code; limit their scope and use them only when mutability introduces an impressive performance increase. Your program is incapable of dealing with multiple concurrent requests because of its vars. What would happen if two calls for the same product arrive at precisely the same time? What if your vending machine has the resources to complete only one of them? In unit 4, you'll learn about case classes and how they can help us overcome these issues by representing data in an immutable manner.

STRING AS THE REPRESENTATION OF A PRODUCT   Representing products as string does not provide any information about the products that the machine can offer. Is the product no longer available, or did the user just mistype its name? Is it "choco" or "chocolate"? Is "ChOcOlATe" the same as "chocolate"? In unit 2, you'll see how to represent a finite set of values using sealed traits and objects.

STRING AS RETURN TYPE   Returning String to represent your program's outcome is not expressive enough; using an appropriate type would give you a more explicit indication of the operation's result. Suppose you need to execute some additional computation depending on your program's outcome. The only way to understand if the request was successful is to interpret the returned text using a parser. This approach is error prone and fragile because it is dependent on the specific words used in returned messages. In unit 6, you'll discover the types Try and Either and how they can help you have meaningful return values for your computation.

THE VENDING MACHINE IS NOT CONFIGURABLE   The vending machine is not configurable: if you need to add a new product or change prices, you need the change your code. In unit 4, you'll learn about data structures, such as List and Map, and how you can use them to abstract details like products and prices.

Summary

In this capstone, you implemented a vending machine.

- You designed and implemented an easy-to-use API that respects the given business requirements.
- You also saw which aspects of your implementation are not ideal and which techniques you'll learn in this book to help you overcome its limitations.

Object-oriented fundamentals

In Unit 1, you reviewed the basic concepts of object-oriented programming in Scala. In this unit, you'll keep examining its fundamentals. You'll implement a sbt executable application to return the current date and time for a given time zone using java.time, one of the internal packages available. In particular, you'll learn about the following subjects:

- Lesson 9 demonstrates how to structure your program in logical packages and import internal and external ones into your code.

- Lesson 10 shows you how to use access modifiers to control the scope of your values, functions, and classes, and to prevent your program from exposing sensitive information and unwanted modifications.

- Lesson 11 illustrates objects as built-in singleton support in the language. You'll also discover how to implement static methods and new constructors for a given class through its companion object.

- Lesson 12 introduces traits as a tool to define commonalities between different classes, one of its most popular use cases. You are probably already familiar with this concept; many object-oriented languages refer to it as *interface*.

- Finally, you'll apply these concepts and implement an sbt application to return the current time in a given time zone in lesson 13.

Once you have learned how to create a sbt executable application, you'll continue with unit 3, in which you'll see how to implement a simple HTTP server.

IMPORT AND CREATE PACKAGES

After reading this lesson, you'll be able to

- Import and reuse code from other packages
- Structure your program in logical packages

Now that you've reviewed the basics of object-oriented programming in unit 1, you'll learn about packages. They allow you to organize your software in logical groups to navigate your codebase more easily. By importing them, you can reuse them in several parts of your application. You can also publish them, making their code available online for other people to download and use; you refer to a published package as *library*. In the capstone, you will create a dedicated logical unit for your time application, and you will import and use an internal package called java.time.

> **Consider this**
>
> Suppose you want to create a web service that exposes an API. It should receive data through, for example, a POST request, perform some business validation, and store the information in a database. What are the main components of your service? What package structure would you use to organize your code?

9.1   Import an existing package

Imagine you want to write a program to read the content of a file into a string. This task would be quite challenging and complex without the use of a package or library. You would need to identify the location of the memory cells for each binary file. You would read and convert them to text after applying a particular encoding (e.g., UTF-8). You would also need to handle many edge cases, such as trying to access a file that could be corrupted or missing or uses an unexpected encoding. Luckily, you don't have to deal with such low-level operations, but you find an internal package or library to do all the work for you. The following snippet of code shows how you can do this by exploiting the scala.io module.

Listing 9.1 Implementing readFileIntoString

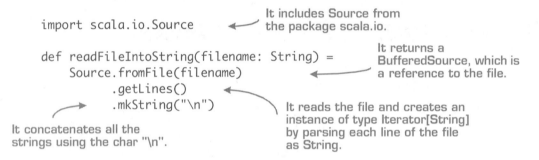

Scala imports are quite versatile: you can import all the code defined inside a package, or you can be extremely selective by including a specific class, function, or value in your scope. You can also specify an alias for the element you imported to make your code more expressive or to resolve clashes between components with the same name.

Listing 9.2 Several uses of import

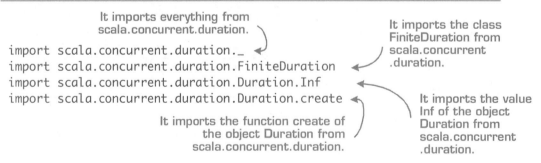

```
import scala.io.{Source => Src}
import scala.math.{BigDecimal, BigInt}
```

It imports the classes BigDecimal and BigInt from scala.math.

It imports the file Source from scala.io, and it creates an alias Src for it.

Try to import just what you require in your scope; it will make your compilation faster and your code more readable by listing all the packages your class requires. You can add imports in a file, a class, an object, a function, and even a value. In the following example, the code for scala.io.Source is accessible only from within the scope of the function readFileIntoString:

```
def readFileIntoString(filename: String) = {
    import scala.io.Source

    Source.fromFile(filename)
        .getLines()
        .mkString("\n")
}
```

Figure 9.1 is a summary of the different usages of Scala imports you have seen so far.

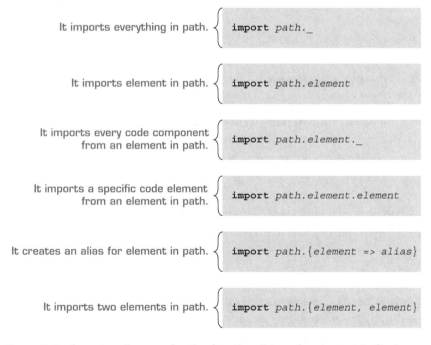

It imports everything in path.
```
import path._
```

It imports element in path.
```
import path.element
```

It imports every code component from an element in path.
```
import path.element._
```

It imports a specific code element from an element in path.
```
import path.element.element
```

It creates an alias for element in path.
```
import path.{element => alias}
```

It imports two elements in path.
```
import path.{element, element}
```

Figure 9.1 A syntax diagram for the functionalities of an import in Scala. Imports allow you to add existing code elements into your scope: you can add all the code in a package, a single class, an object, a function, or even a value.

Scala automatically adds the packages scala, java.lang, and scala.Predef to the scope of your files with extension .scala so that you can use the most common features and classes of the language without using imports.

Scala 3: An alternative import syntax

Scala 3 introduces an alternative syntax for imports: you can use the symbol * instead of _, and as instead of =>. For example, consider the following import instructions:

```
import scala.concurrent.duration._
import scala.io.{Source => Src}
```

You can rewrite them as

```
import scala.concurrent.duration.*
import scala.io.{Source as Src}
```

Quick Check 9.1   Import the package java.sql.Date into your scope and create an alias called "SqlDate."

 9.2   Create a package

In section 9.1 you saw how to write a function to read a file into a string by importing an internal package. Now you will see how you can create a custom package. Because packages are tools to organize an application composed of multiple files, you will not use the REPL, but you will create an sbt project instead. Use your IDE to create an empty sbt project—most of them have dedicated support to do this in just a few clicks. Alternatively, you can reuse the hello-world-template Giter8 template you saw in lesson 3 by typing the following command in your terminal:

```
$ sbt
sbt> new scala/hello-world.g8
```

Suppose you want to create a package called my.example.io so that you can reuse the code shown in listing 9.1 in other parts of your application. First, create a directory with relative path src/main/scala/my/example/io, then create a file called MyExample .scala.

Listing 9.3 Creating a package, my.example.io

```
// File src/main/scala/my/example/io/MyExample.scala

package my.example.io          The class MyExample belongs to
                               a package called my.example.io.

import scala.io.Source
                        You need a class here because
class MyExample {       a function can live only inside a
                        class or singleton object.

  def readFileIntoString(filename: String) =
    Source.fromFile(filename).getLines().mkString("\n")
}
```

A package name doesn't have to match a specific directory structure in your sbt project, but it is a good practice that makes source code easier to find and maintain. Scala automatically includes all the other files that belong to your package in your scope, so you do not need to import them. Figure 9.2 is a summary of how to create packages in Scala.

The name of your package

package *my.package.name*

• The file belongs to the package my.package.name.
• It should be in the directory src/main/scala/my/package/name.

Figure 9.2 Syntax diagram on how to create a Scala package. Ensure your package name matches your directory structure; its files will be easier to find.

> **Quick Check 9.2** Create a new package in an sbt project, called my.quick.check. Add two files to it:
> - TestA.scala contains a class called TestA.
> - TestB.scala contains a class called TestB.

 **Summary**

In this lesson, my objective was to teach you about packages in Scala.

- You discovered how to include code from libraries and internal packages in your scope.
- You also learned how to create packages to logically group code with similar goals and functionality.

Let's see if you got this!

TRY THIS   Create a package in an sbt project, called my.areas, that contains two files: Circle.scala and Square.scala.

 Answers to quick checks

Quick Check 9.1   The following import includes the class java.sql.Date as Sql-Date into your scope:

```
import java.sql.{Date => SqlDate}
```

Quick Check 9.2   The files should have the following path and content:

```
// File src/main/scala/my/quick/check/TestA.scala
package my.quick.check

class TestA

// File src/main/scala/my/quick/check/TestB.scala
package my.quick.check

class TestB
```

SCOPE YOUR CODE WITH ACCESS MODIFIERS

After reading this lesson, you will be able to

- Make your values, variables, functions, and classes accessible only from their class
- Limit your code accessibility to a class and its subclasses

In lesson 9, you learned about packages. Protecting your code by limiting its accessibility is a good practice, especially when creating external modules for third parties. By doing so, you also reduce your code's public entry points, making it easier to use. This approach also prevents external manipulations that could expose sensitive data or introduce undesired behavior in your code. In this lesson, you'll learn about the Scala access modifiers, which are reserved keywords to change your code elements' visibility. You should use them to protect and hide information you should not expose to the public. You'll use access modifiers to implement auxiliary functions accessible within their class in the capstone.

> **Consider this**
> Suppose you are designing a program to manage bank accounts. Your business requirements demand not to expose their balance unless its owner requests it. How would you structure your code to enforce this requirement?

 ## 10.1 Public, the default access modifier

Imagine you need to track the guests and the costs of a party. People registering for the event should be the only publicly accessible functionality. The following snippet provides a possible implementation.

Listing 10.1 The class Party

```
class Party {
    var attendees = 0

    def register(guests: Int) =
        attendees += guests
}
```

Every time your code does not use an explicit access modifier, the compiler applies the default access level, which is the public one. A code element marked as public has no access restrictions: anyone can see its value and modify it. The public access level doesn't have an explicit keyword; if you want to declare an element as public, you don't provide any access modifier keyword.

```
public val a = "hello"        ← It doesn't compile: the keyword public doesn't exist.
val b = "world"               ← It compiles: the value is publicly accessible.
```

> **Quick Check 10.1** In the REPL, declare a value called name, containing the string Scala; make it publicly usable.

10.2 Private

Let's look again at the snippet of code about registering attendees for an event you implemented in listing 10.1:

```scala
class Party {
    var attendees = 0

    def register(guests: Int) =
      attendees += guests
}
```

The variable attendees is publicly accessible: external users can break your application by resetting its assignment to any value of their choice. You can prevent this by marking the variable attendees as private, making it no longer accessible outside the class Party.

Listing 10.2 The class Party, where attendees are private

```scala
class Party {
    private var attendees = 0

    def register(guests: Int) =
      attendees += guests
}
```

In Scala, you use the private access modifier to prevent access to functions, values, and classes that should not be used publicly; when a code element is private, you can only access it from inside its class.

Listing 10.3 Defining a class Test

```scala
class Test {
    val configA = "I am public"
    private val configB = "I am private"
}
```

Let's use the REPL to define a class Test, create an instance for it, and access its values:

```scala
scala> class Test {
     |        val configA = "I am public"
     |        private val configB = "I am private"
     | }
class Test
```

```
scala> val test = new Test
val test: Test = Test@3128213f

scala> test.configA
val res0: String = I am public

scala> test.configB
              ^
        error: value configB in class Test cannot be accessed as a member
   of Test from class
```

 ## 10.3 Protected

After tracking the number of attendees, suppose you need to estimate the cost of an event. You don't want this sensitive information to be public or have external sources making changes to it. At the same time, you'd like to make this functionality reusable for any event to ensure you calculate costs consistently. In this case, you can use the protected access modifier: a protected code element is accessible only from its class and its subclasses. Let's see how you could use the protected access modifier to control the access to the function computing the cost estimation of an event.

Listing 10.4 The class Event

```
class Event {                                    Usage of the protected
                                                  access modifier
    protected def estimateCosts(attendees: Int): Double =
      if (attendees < 10) 50.00 else attendees * 12.34
}

class Party extends Event {          Party is a subclass
                                      of Event.
```

```
    private var attendees = 0

    var cost = estimateCosts(attendees)
```
← Party has access to Event's protected code elements.
```
    def register(guests: Int) =
      attendees += guests
}
```

The protected access modifier allows code to be visible from the current class and any code element that extends it, such as a subclass or interface—a topic that you'll discover in lesson 12.

> **Quick Check 10.3** Can you access the function estimateCosts from outside the class Event? Use the REPL to validate your hypothesis.

 ## 10.4 Which access level to use?

You have now learned several ways to change the visibility of your code. When deciding which access level to use, the temptation of using the public default access level everywhere is quite strong. But this is not a good practice. Exposing your code as public can be confusing for its users because it makes its entry points challenging to identify. By blocking access to portions of your program, you are preventing others from overriding and improperly reusing them. Finally, the more code you expose to the public, the more complicated future changes will be: you will not be able to control what parts of your system you can change without breaking external code that depends on it. As a rule of thumb, pick the most restrictive access modifier that satisfies your needs and avoid using the public access modifier unless strictly necessary. Table 10.1 summarizes the usage of the access modifiers you have seen so far.

Table 10.1 Comparing access modifiers in Scala. A code element is public by default; you can access it from everywhere. You can access it from its class and subclasses when protected, and only from its class when private.

	Private	Protected	Default (Public)
Class	Yes	Yes	Yes
Subclass	No	Yes	Yes
Global	No	No	Yes

 **Summary**

In this lesson, my objective was to teach you about access modifiers in Scala, which are keywords that control the visibility of your code.

- You discovered that your code elements are public by default; anyone can access and modify them.
- You learned that the private access modifier blocks access to your code outside the current scope.
- You also saw that the protected access modifier makes it visible from the current class or any of its subclasses.

Let's see if you got this!

> **TRY THIS**   Define a class `Employee` with three values: a name of type `String`, an age of `Int`, and a salary of type `Double`. While its name should be publicly accessible, its age should be visible only from its class and subclasses, and its salary should be private.

 Answers to quick checks

> **Quick Check 10.1**   Start the Scala REPL and type the following expression:
>
> ```
> scala> val name = "Scala"
> val name: String = Scala
> ```

> **Quick Check 10.2**   The value age is not accessible from the class Student because it is visible only from an instance of the class Person and not from any of its subclasses.
>
> ```
> scala> class Person {
>      |     private val age = 18
>      | }
>      |
>      | class Student extends Person
> class Person
> class Student
>
> scala> val student = new Student
> val student: Student = Student@62d1dc3c
>
> scala> student.age
>              ^
>         error: value age is not a member of Student
> ```

Quick Check 10.3 You cannot publicly access the function estimateCosts of the class Event. You declared estimateCosts as protected; you can access it from either an instance of Event or any of its subclasses, such as the class Party.

```
scala> class Event {
     |
     |       protected def estimateCosts(attendees: Int): Double =
     |           if (attendees < 10) 50.00 else attendees * 12.34
     | }
class Event

scala> val event = new Event
val event: Event = Event@6af78a48

scala> event.estimatedCosts(5)
             ^
        error: value estimatedCosts is not a member of Event
```

SINGLETON OBJECTS

After reading this lesson, you will be able to

- Implement a singleton object
- Use objects as executable programs
- Define static functions in a companion object
- Create factory methods using the `apply` function

The essence of object-oriented programming is representing elements of the real world using classes that describe their behavior through methods. In specific scenarios, such as configurations and main entry points, you need to instantiate a coding element at most once; you usually call it *singleton*. In Scala, you can create singletons using objects elegantly and concisely. You are also encouraged to clearly distinguish between static and non-static methods; the non-static ones act on a specific instance of a class, while the static ones belong to its general definition. In Scala, you implement non-static methods in a class and static methods in an object. In the capstone, you'll use an object to define the main entry point of your application.

> **Consider this**
> Can you think of a few possible use cases for singletons? What about static methods for a class? Can you think of a few examples?

11.1 Object

Consider the following class to represent a robot:

```scala
abstract class Robot(name: String) {

    def welcome: String
}
```

The function `welcome` is abstract, it takes no parameters, and it returns a value of type `String`. Suppose you want to represent a vocabulary of sentences that a robot can use when asked to speak. This vocabulary must be autonomous from any particular implementation of a robot; it must be unique in the whole application and shared between multiple sources.

Listing 11.1 A vocabulary object

```scala
object Vocabulary {

    val sentenceA = "Hi there!"
    val sentenceB = "Welcome!"
    val sentenceC = "Hello :)"
}

Vocabulary.sentenceA        ← It returns "Hi there!"
Vocabulary.sentenceB        ← It returns "Welcome!"
```

When using the object `Vocabulary`, you refer to it by name. Note that you do not use the keyword *new* because you cannot request to instantiate an object explicitly. The compiler guarantees that the JVM instantiates an object no more than once; in other words, it treats it as a singleton. The first time you request access to an object, the JVM allocates it in memory; following references to the same object do not trigger any new instantiation because the JVM reuses its first memory allocation, a model called *singleton pattern*.

Think in Scala: The term object

Many object-oriented languages use the word *object* to indicate an instance of a class. A few examples are Java, Python, JavaScript, and C++.

In Scala, object has a well-defined and specific meaning: it refers to a singleton, not an instance of a class. When referring to Scala code, make sure to use the term *object* correctly to avoid confusion!

The use of singletons is not unique to Scala. Still, its implementation is extremely elegant and convenient to use compared to other languages.

Listing 11.2 Singleton in different languages

```
// Java
public class MySingleton {
    private static MySingleton instance = null;

    private MySingleton() {}

    public static MySingleton getInstance() {
        if(instance == null) {
            instance = new ClassicSingleton();
        }
        return instance;
    }
}

// JavaScript
var MySingleton = (function () {
    var instance;

    function createInstance() {
        var object = new Object("my-instance");
        return object;
    }

    return {
        getInstance: function () {
            if (!instance) {
                instance = createInstance();
            }
            return instance;
        }
    };
})();

// Scala -> only 2 words!
object MySingleton
```

Figure 11.1 shows a syntax diagram on how to define objects in Scala.

The name of the singleton object
you want to create

```
object name {
    // your code here
}
```

Figure 11.1 Syntax diagram on how to implement an object in Scala

Quick Check 11.1 Consider the following snippet of code. Does this code compile? Why? Use the REPL to validate your hypothesis.

```
object MySnippet
new MySnippet
```

 ## 11.2 Executable object

A program usually has at least one entry point to start its execution; you can refer to this as *main* or *executable*. Note that a main for a program is a singleton: you cannot have more than one instance of the same main when running a program.

In Scala, your program's entry point is an object with a main function; this behavior is consistent across the JVM languages. Listing 11.3 demonstrates how to create an executable object that prints the text "Hello World!" in the console.

Listing 11.3 Hello World!

```
object HelloWorld {

  def main(args: Array[String]): Unit = {
    println("Hello world!")
  }
}
```

Scala also offers another more elegant and concise way of defining a program's entry points; you'll discover it in the next lesson when you'll learn about traits.

> **Quick Check 11.2**   When running your program with sbt, what happens if it cannot find its main entry point? What if it finds more than one? Verify your hypothesis by writing two simple programs and executing them with sbt: one with no main, the other with two.

Scala 3: The @main annotation

Scala 3 offers you an alternative way of declaring the entry point of an executable program that uses the annotation @main. For example, you could rewrite the snippet of code from listing 11.3 as follows:

```scala
object HelloWorld {

  @main def hello: Unit = {
    println("Hello world!")
  }
}
```

The @main annotation extracts command line arguments, and it ensures they match the function signature. For example, consider the following @main method:

```scala
object Hello {

  @main def echo(n: Int, word: String): Unit = {
    println(word * n)
  }
}
```

You can save it into a *.scala file and execute it in sbt, using the command run and pass the command line argument to it:

```
$ sbt
..
sbt> run
[info] running echo
Illegal command line: more arguments expected
[success] Total time: 1 s, completed 20 Feb 2021, 13:09:07
// It fails because you didn't provide any command line arguments

sbt> run test
[info] running echo test
```

```
Illegal command line: java.lang.NumberFormatException: For input
       string: "test"
[success] Total time: 0 s, completed 20 Feb 2021, 13:09:40
// It fails because the first parameter is not a number

sbt> run 2 test
[info] running echo 2 test
testtest
[success] Total time: 0 s, completed 20 Feb 2021, 13:09:14
// It prints the text "testtest"
```

11.3 Companion object

In Scala, a *companion object* is an object that has the same name as another existing class. Consider the Robot class you saw in section 11.1 and suppose you want to define a function to return the most talkative robot.

Listing 11.4 The most talkative robot

```
abstract class Robot(name: String) {          ←——   The class Robot

  def welcome: String
}
                                 The companion
                                 object for Robot
object Robot {                 ←
  def mostTalkative(r1: Robot, r2: Robot): Robot = {
    val r1Size = r1.welcome.length        ←——   You are invoking the
    val r2Size = r2.welcome.length              method welcome on r1
    if (r1Size >= r2Size) r1 else r2            and computing the length
  }                                             of its returned value.
}
```

An example usage for mostTalkative and the object Vocabulary implemented in listing 11.1 is the following:

```
val tom = new Robot("Tom") {
  def welcome = Vocabulary.sentenceA
}
```

```
val alice = new Robot("Alice") {
  def welcome = Vocabulary.sentenceB
}
Robot.mostTalkative(tom, alice)
```

The function mostTalkative operates on two robots rather than just one: it doesn't belong
to a specific instance of robot, but it still has to do with the class Robot. The function
mostTalkative is a static function of the class Robot. A *static* method is a function acting
on a class rather than on a specific instance of that class.

Quick Check 11.3 Consider the function welcome defined in the class Robot. Is it a
static method? Why?

In the next section, you'll discover a particular static method dedicated to creating class
instances called *apply*.

 ## 11.4 The apply method

In lesson 7, you learned that a class can have one constructor, and you can use it by
using the keyword *new*. What if you want to specify different ways of creating a class?
How can you do it with only one constructor? The apply function of a companion object
can help in solving your problem.

Assume you have a Person class and that you can create an instance for it by calling the
constructor using the keyword *new* and providing its parameters. You'd also like to
define an alternative way of creating a person by merging two existing ones.

Listing 11.5 The class Person and its companion object

```
class Person(val name: String, val age: Int)

object Person {

  def apply(p1: Person, p2: Person): Person = {          You must provide
    val name = s"Son of ${p1.name} and ${p2.name}"       an explicit return
    val age = 0                                          type for apply.
    new Person(name, age)
  }
}
```

Once you have defined an `apply` method, you can use it in the same way as any other static method implemented in the companion object. You can declare multiple `apply` functions in the companion object, as long as their signature is uniquely identifiable by the compiler. Consider the following snippet of code:

```
object Person {

    def apply(name: String): Person = new Person(name, 0)

    def apply(age: Int): Person = new Person("Mr Unknown", age)

}
```

The two `apply` methods have the same name and return type, but they take different parameters: the first takes a string, while the second an integer. The two implementations can coexist because the compiler can select one or the other by looking at the types of their parameters. You can refer to the concept of having multiple functions with the same name but different parameters with the term *function overloading*.

Developers often use the `apply` function to create class instances. The compiler offers you some syntactic sugar so that you can omit the function name `apply`. When passing a parameter to an object, it looks for an `apply` method defined in that object with parameters that match the ones you have given. Consider the following snippet of code; the two expressions `Person.apply(tom, alice)` and `Person(tom, alice)` are equivalent:

```
val tom = new Person("Tom", 24)
val alice = new Person("Alice", 23)

Person.apply(tom, alice)
Person(tom, alice)
```

The unapply method: A quick preview

You have discovered that the `apply` method is a static function to construct class instances. The method `unapply` is complementary to it: it deconstructs a class into its parameters.

`unapply` is a static function that lives in a class's companion object: it takes an instance class and returns its decomposed representation. For example, you could identify a `Person` class by providing a pair with its name and age. The `unapply` function allows you to use pattern matching, a powerful and expressive tool of the Scala toolbox to match conditions (e.g., age greater than 18) based on the decomposition of a class. You'll learn about this in the next unit.

(continued)
You'll learn about the unapply method later in the book when discussing case classes and the type Tuple in lesson 25.

Figure 11.2 provides a summary of the methods of a companion object that you have seen so far.

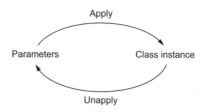

```
The name of the class and companion object to create
They must have the same name.

class name

object name {
    // apply, unapply,
    // and static methods here
}
```

                                    Apply
    Parameters   Class instance
                                    Unapply

Figure 11.2   A syntax diagram for companion objects, their use, and a visual representation of the duality between the apply and unapply methods.

From Scala 3, the compiler automatically generates an apply function for all your classes; you can omit the *new* keyword even if you haven't manually defined an apply method for it.

```
class Test(n: Int)
object Test // a companion object without an apply method

new Test(5) // works in all Scala versions
Test(5)  // works in Scala 3+
```

Quick Check 11.4 Consider this snippet of code. Are the expressions new Dog("Tigger") and Dog("Tigger") equivalent? Why?

```
class Dog(val name: String)

object Dog {
    def apply(name: String): Dog =
        new Dog(s"$name The Dog")
}
```

 **Summary**

In this lesson, my objective was to teach you about objects and their use in Scala.

- You saw that objects are a convenient implementation for singletons.
- You also discovered that companion objects have the same name as an existing class and that you can use them to declare static methods that refer to it.
- Finally, you learned about the apply method as the standard way of creating class instances.

Let's see if you got this!

> **TRY THIS** In listing 11.5, you added an apply method to create an instance of a person given two existing ones. Create new functions for the class Person to
>
> - determine the oldest between two people and
> - create a person by copying the parameters of an existing one.

 Answers to quick checks

Quick Check 11.1 The code doesn't compile. The REPL returns the following output:

```
scala> object MySnippet
object MySnippet

scala> new MySnippet
error: not found: type MySnippet
```

The first expression successfully defines an object called "MySnippet." The second one is incorrect: you cannot request the creation of an object. When using the keyword *new*, the compiler looks for a class or type called MySnippet; an object is neither, so the compiler rejects it with a missing type error.

Quick Check 11.2 When sbt doesn't find any entry point, it will throw a Runtime-Exception with the message "No main class detected." If it detects more than one, it provides a list of the available entry points so that you can choose the one to execute:

```
Multiple main classes detected, select one to run:

 [1] AnotherHelloWorld
 [2] HelloWorld

Enter number: [pick your entry point here]
```

Quick Check 11.3 The method welcome is not static; it acts on a robot's instance, the reason you defined it in the class Robot rather than in its companion object.

Quick Check 11.4 The two expressions are not equivalent. The first returns a Dog instance with the name "Tigger" because it invokes its constructor directly. The second one returns one named "Tigger The Dog" because it calls the apply method defined in its companion object.

TRAITS AS INTERFACES

After reading this lesson, you will be able to

- Declare an interface using a trait
- Implement classes, objects, and traits that conform to one or more interfaces
- Define a closed set of values using sealed traits

Now that you've discovered singleton objects in lesson 11, let's learn about traits. Earlier in this book, you saw that a class can have up to one superclass; you cannot express multiple inheritance using classes and abstract classes. Traits are very similar to abstract classes but with a fundamental difference: a class can inherit from one or more traits. You can use them to express multiple inheritance; you cannot achieve the same with abstract classes. You can use traits to define interfaces to represent a set of features (hence the name *traits*) that your class must have. This is a crucial object-oriented concept that you find in many languages, such as Go, Kotlin, and Java. In future units, you will learn that traits are a lot more than just a way to express an interface: you'll see some of their superpowers and why this makes them a more expressive and powerful tool. In this lesson, you'll discover how to create a trait and implement classes, objects, and other interfaces that conform to one or more interfaces. You'll also learn about sealed traits: they allow you to define a closed set of implementations for your interface that the compiler guarantees at compile time. You'll finally discover the enumeration syntax that Scala 3 introduces as an alternative to sealed traits. In the capstone, you'll use the App trait to implement the entry point of your application.

> **Consider this**
> Consider the programming languages that are already familiar to you. Do they have the concept of interface? How do they express it? Do they support multiple inheritance?

 ## 12.1 Defining traits

Suppose you need to represent a zoo's animals and make sure they all have some common behavior: they all sleep, eat, and move. Let's define an interface to enforce these functionalities.

Listing 12.1 The trait Animal

```
trait Animal {

  def sleep = "ZzZ"

  def eat(food: String): String

  def move(x: Int, y: Int): String
}
```

In Scala, use the keyword *trait* and a name to identify an interface. In Scala 2, a trait can have abstract and fully implemented coding elements, such as functions, values, and variables.

Listing 12.2 The trait Nameable

```
trait Nameable {
  def name: String
}
```

From Scala 3, a trait can also have parameters. For example, in Scala 3 you can redefine the trait Nameable as the following:

```
trait Nameable(name: String) // valid in Scala 3 only!
```

Look at figure 12.1 for a summary of how to define a trait.

The name of the
trait to create

```
trait name {
    // your code here
}
```

Figure 12.1 Syntax diagram of how to define a trait in
Scala; you can use them to implement interfaces.

Quick Check 12.1 Define an interface called Printable that enforces the presence
of a function called print: it takes no parameters, and it returns Unit.

 ## 12.2 Extending traits

After creating an interface, let's see how you can define classes, objects, and other
traits that conform to it. For example, you can implement a class Cat that extends
the trait Animal.

Listing 12.3 The Cat class

```
class Cat extends Animal {

    override val sleep = "sleepy cat!"

    def eat(food: String) = s"the cat is eating $food"

    def move(x: Int, y: Int) = s"the cat is moving to ($x,$y)"

}
```

You are redefining a fully
implemented function, so
you must use the keyword
override.

You can omit the keyword override because
you are providing an implementation
for an abstract function.

You can also extend more than one interface at the same time. For example, you can
define a Dog class to represent an animal with a name.

Listing 12.4 The Dog class

```
class Dog(val name: String) extends Animal with Nameable {

  def eat(food: String) = s"$food $food"

  def move(x: Int, y: Int) = "let's go to ($x, $y)!"
}
```

The keyword val marks the field name of
the class Dog as publicly accessible.

The trait Nameable requires your class to implement def name: String, a method without parameters and without parentheses called name that returns a string. The class Dog defines a publicly accessible field called name, which is considered a valid implementation for def name: String. In Scala, values and variables can implement or override functions with no parameters and no parentheses.

You can now define functionalities that act on any instance that conforms to a given interface:

```
val tiggerTheDog = new Dog("Tigger")
val cat = new Cat

def feedTreat(animal: Animal) =
  animal.eat("treat")

feedTreat(tiggerTheDog)    // compiles
feedTreat(cat)             // compiles


def welcome(nameable: Nameable) =
  println(s"Hi, ${nameable.name}!")

welcome(tiggerTheDog)    // compiles
welcome(cat)             // doesn't compile because
                         // Cat doesn't extend Nameable
```

In Scala, you can define a coding element that inherits from an interface using the keyword *extends*; if you need to conform to more than one trait, you can do so using the keyword *with*. The compiler will guarantee that it respects its interfaces, or it will fail with an error message listing methods and fields that you still need to implement. Figure 12.2 summarizes how to extend traits in Scala.

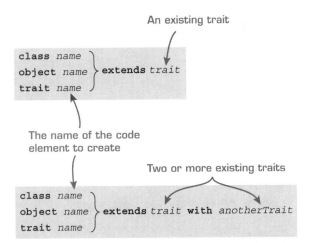

Figure 12.2 Syntax diagram on creating classes, objects, and traits that conform to an interface using the keywords *extends* and *with*.

The trait App

In lesson 11, you learned that Scala identifies a program's entry points by looking for a main function with a specific signature. The following snippet of code provides an example of an executable object:

```scala
object HelloWorld {

  def main(args: Array[String]): Unit =
    println("Hello world!")
}
```

You can achieve the same result by extending App. This trait is part of the standard Scala packages: the compiler automatically adds it into your scope without adding an import instruction. The trait App makes writing application entry points much more straightforward and concise: it automatically includes a main function with the correct signature to ensure that the compiler detects your object as an entry point for your program. Thanks to the trait App, you can rewrite the previous snippet of code as follows:

```scala
object HelloWorld extends App {

  println("Hello world!")
}
```

Extending the trait App, rather than implementing a main function, is the conventional way of creating an executable Scala object.

Quick Check 12.2 Which of the following statements are correct? Use the REPL to validate your hypothesis.

1 A class can extend a class.
2 A class can extend an object.
3 A class can extend a trait.
4 An object can extend a class.
5 An object can extend an object.
6 An object can extend a trait.
7 A trait can extend a class.
8 A trait can extend an object.
9 A trait can extend a trait.

 ## 12.3 Sealed traits

Suppose you want to represent all the suits in a deck of playing cards—the ones you usually use for a game of poker: clubs, diamonds, hearts, spades. You need to express the general concept of a symbol, but you also need to make sure that there are precisely four of its implementations. You can achieve this by using a *sealed* trait.

Listing 12.5 Suits of poker cards

```
sealed trait Suit

object Clubs extends Suit
object Diamonds extends Suit
object Hearts extends Suit
object Spades extends Suit
```

Use a sealed trait to limit the elements that extend it. When using the keyword *sealed*, you inform the compiler that all the components that extend the trait are in the same file where the interface is declared. Thanks to the keyword *sealed*, the compiler knows all the possible implementations for a given trait, and it can warn you if your code forgets to consider all of them (more on this when you learn about pattern matching). In other words, the compiler can infer that a suit is either clubs or diamonds or hearts or spades. You can also refer to this concept as union type or coproduct. Figure 12.3 provides a syntax diagram for sealed traits in Scala.

Quick Check 12.3 Define a trait, called Currency, with only three possible implementations: USD, CAD, and EUR.

The name of the sealed
trait to create

```
sealed trait name {
    // your code here
}
```

• You must declare all its implementations into the same file.

Figure 12.3 Syntax diagram of how to define a sealed trait in Scala. You must declare all the implementations of a sealed trait in that same file.

 ## 12.4 Enumeration in Scala 3

Let's consider your implementation of all the suits in a deck of playing cards using enumeration.

Listing 12.6 Suits of poker cards using enumeration

```
enum Suit {
    case Clubs, Diamonds, Hearts, Spades
}
```

You can now refer to a Hearts suit with the expression Suit.Hearts. You can also perform other operations on it, such as list all its implementations or pick an implementation based on their declaration order:

```
scala> Suit.Hearts
val res0: Suit = Hearts

scala> Suit.values
val res1: Array[Suit] = Array(Clubs, Diamonds, Hearts, Spades)

scala> Suit.fromOrdinal(0)
val res2: Suit = Clubs
```

Scala 3 introduces the keyword *enum* to define an enumeration type. You can then provide implementations for your enumeration using the keyword *case*. You can also have parameters when defining an enumeration type.

Listing 12.7 **A list of countries and codes**

```scala
enum Country(val code: String) {
    case Italy extends Country("IT")
    case UnitedKingdom extends Country("UK")
    case UnitedStates extends Country("US")
    case Japan extends Country("JP")
}
```

Making code a value using the keyword val to make it accessible

You can then refer to Italy's code using the expression Country.Italy.code. Look at figure 12.4 for a summary of how to use enumeration in Scala 3.

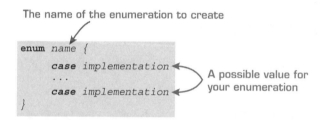

The name of the enumeration to create

```
enum name {
        case implementation
        ...
        case implementation
}
```

A possible value for your enumeration

Figure 12.4   Syntax diagram on how to define enumeration in Scala 3. The keyword *enum* identifies an enumeration type. It can have one or more implementations, which the keyword *case* identifies.

Quick Check 12.4   In Quick Check 12.3, you implemented a sealed trait Currency with three implementations; reimplement it using enumeration syntax for Scala 3.

 **Summary**

In this lesson, my objective was to teach you about traits and enumeration in Scala.

- You discovered how to define interfaces and implement classes, objects, and traits that conform to those interfaces.
- You learned about sealed traits: they can express the concept of union types, which are types defined by the finite set of their possible values.
- Finally, you saw how to define enumeration in Scala 3.

Let's see if you got this!

TRY THIS   Implement an interface to ensure the presence of a field color. Define two classes that conform to your interface: one to represent furniture, the other clothes.

Answers to quick checks

Quick Check 12.1 The implementation of the trait Printable is the following:

```
trait Printable {

    def print(): Unit
}
```

Quick Check 12.2 The answers are the following:
1. True: A class can extend a class.
2. False: A class can extend an object.
3. True: A class can extend a trait.
4. True: An object can extend a class.
5. False: An object can extend an object.
6. True: An object can extend a trait.
7. False: A trait can extend a class.
8. False: A trait can extend an object.
9. True: A trait can extend a trait.

Quick Check 12.3 You can implement the trait Currency and its implementations as follows:

```
sealed trait Currency

object USD extends Currency
object CAD extends Currency
object EUR extends Currency
```

Quick Check 12.4 Your implementation of the enumeration Currency should look similar to the following:

```
enum Currency {
  case USD, CAD, EUR
}
```

WHAT TIME IS IT?

In this capstone, you will

- Create a package for your application
- Import and use the `java.time` package
- Code using classes, objects, and traits together with access modifiers
- Define an executable object

Time zones can be challenging to deal with, particularly in distributed teams and collaborations. In this capstone, you'll implement an executable application that uses sbt to print the current time in a given time zone.

 ## 13.1 What time is it?

The goal of this capstone is to create a small program using sbt: it should start, ask the user to enter a time zone, use the input to compute the current time in it, and display the result in the terminal in a human-readable format, such as RFC 1123 (e.g., "Fri, 27 Apr 2018 11:44:35 +0200"). Let's keep things simple and let the script crash if the user enters an invalid time zone; you'll learn how to handle exceptions in the next unit.

13.1.1 sbt project setup

First, you need to set up the sbt project. There are different ways of achieving this: you can create an sbt project using your IDE or apply the hello-world Giter8 template by typing the command `sbt new scala/hello-world.g8`. When using the hello-world Giter8 template do not forget to delete the `Main.scala` file in the `src/main/scala` folder. Alternatively, you can also create an empty sbt project manually as follows:

1   In your project directory, create a `build.sbt` file containing your Scala version, the name, and your project version.

Listing 13.1 An example of build.sbt file

```
name := "what-time-is-it"

version := "0.1"

scalaVersion := "3.0.0" // this is your scala version
```

2   Create a directory `project` with a `build.properties` file (see listing 13.2) with your sbt version.

Listing 13.2 An example of project/build.properties file

```
sbt.version = 1.5.2 // this is your sbt version
```

3   Finally, create the folder `src/main/scala`; it will contain your application's source code.

You will not need to add any external dependency into your `build.sbt` file for this capstone. You'll use `java.time` to compute the current date and time, which is already accessible as an internal module of the Scala language.

Finally, let's define a package, called `org.example.time`, to contain the code for your application: create a directory with relative path `src/main/scala/org/example/time`.

13.1.2 The business logic layer

The `TimePrinter` class takes care of our business logic. It belongs to the `org.example.time` package, which defines the logic used to compute the current date and time for a given time zone. It uses three elements of the package `java.time`:

- `java.time.ZoneId` lists the time zones supported, and it allows you to perform operations on them.

- java.time.ZonedDateTime represents a date with time and a well-defined time zone.
- java.time.format.DateTimeFormatter converts a temporal event (e.g., date, time, date-time) to and from a string. You can either use one of the already defined formatters or create a custom one.

A TimePrinter has a formatter as its parameter and a publicly accessible method now, which takes one parameter representing a time zone as a string; you do not need to expose its other functions.

Listing 13.3 The TimePrinter class

```scala
// file src/main/scala/org/example/time/TimePrinter.scala
package org.example.time

import java.time.format.DateTimeFormatter
import java.time.{ZoneId, ZonedDateTime}

class TimePrinter(formatter: DateTimeFormatter) {

  def now(timezone: String): String = {
    val dateTime = currentDateTime(timezone)
    dateTimeToString(dateTime)
  }

  private def currentDateTime(timezone: String): ZonedDateTime = {
    val zoneId = ZoneId.of(timezone)
    ZonedDateTime.now(zoneId)
  }

  private def dateTimeToString(dateTime: ZonedDateTime): String =
    formatter.format(dateTime)
}
```

Your implementation works with any formatter.

You are now ready to implement the entry point of your program.

13.1.3 The TimeApp executable object

Your next task is to define an executable object, called TimeApp, containing the logic to ask a time zone in standard input, compute the time zone, and print it in the terminal.

Listing 13.4 The TimeApp object

```
// file src/main/scala/org/example/time/TimeApp.scala

package org.example.time

import java.time.format.DateTimeFormatter
import scala.io.StdIn

object TimeApp extends App {

    val timezone = StdIn.readLine("Give me a timezone:  ")
    val timePrinter =
      new TimePrinter(DateTimeFormatter.RFC_1123_DATE_TIME)
    println(timePrinter.now(timezone))
}
```

It requests a string in input from the terminal.

TimeApp is an executable object because it extends the trait App.

It creates an instance of TimePrinter.

It computes and prints the current time in the time zone.

Your application is now ready to run.

13.1.4 Let's try it out!

It's time to see your program in action. Navigate to the root folder for your project and execute the command sbt run to compile and execute the code. After a few seconds, you should see that the application is waiting for you to provide a time zone:

```
[info] Running org.example.time.TimeApp
Give me a timezone:
```

For example, you can enter the time zone "Asia/Tokyo" and get a result that looks similar to the following:

```
[info] Running org.example.time.TimeApp
Give me a timezone:  Asia/Tokyo
Fri, 24 June 2021 05:50:31 +0900
```

If you enter an invalid or unrecognized time zone, the script will error with an exception:

```
[error] (run-main-0) java.time.zone.ZoneRulesException: Unknown time-
        zone ID: invalid
[error] java.time.zone.ZoneRulesException: Unknown time-zone ID:
        invalid
```

```
[error]        at
java.time.zone.ZoneRulesProvider.getProvider(ZoneRulesProvider.java:272)
[…]
[…more stack trace here…]
[…]
[error]        at java.lang.reflect.Method.invoke(Method.java:497)
[error] Nonzero exit code: 1
[error] (Compile / run) Nonzero exit code: 1
```

Play around with your application. Can you spot any bugs or nonideal behaviors? Let's discuss a few of them in the next section.

 ## 13.2 Possible improvements to our solution

Congratulations on completing your capstone! Your implementation respects the requirements, but a few improvements are possible. Let's see some of them and what techniques you'll learn to overcome them.

ERROR HANDLING If a user enters an invalid time zone, your application crashes with a nasty and difficult-to-understand exception. In unit 3, you'll see how to catch and throw exceptions. You'll also learn how to create custom exceptions to provide your users with a more descriptive message about the error and its cause.

TIME ZONE REPRESENTATION Your application is entirely dependent on the java.time package and its definition of time zone. For example, it considers UTC a valid time zone, while utc is invalid. The time zone Asia/Tokyo is also not equivalent to ASIA/TOKYO. Being dependent on the java.time package has two significant implications:

- A change in the java.time package drastically affects your application, and it can potentially break it without you realizing it.
- In the future, if you wish to migrate to a different time library, it will be excruciating and painful because your definition of valid time zone lives inside the package java.time.

In future units, you'll see how to overcome them thanks to data structures such as Map; they will allow you to have a clear separation between how you represent your data and how you manipulate it.

 **Summary**

In this capstone, you implemented a sbt application that asks the user for a string representing a valid time zone, and it prints the current date and time in a given time zone.

- You created a sbt project, and you used the java.time package to define your business logic.
- You implemented the entry point of your application, and you saw it in action.
- Finally, we discussed possible improvements for your implementation thanks to the techniques you'll see in future units.

HTTP server

In unit 2, you mastered the fundamentals of object-oriented programming in Scala and built an executable sbt application to print the current date and time in the given timezone. In this unit, you'll adapt the code you wrote for the previous capstone to transform your application into an HTTP server. You'll define an HTTP API to return the current date and time for a given country rather than a given time zone using http4s, a popular library to manage HTTP requests and responses. In particular, you'll learn about the following subjects:

- Lesson 14 teaches you about pattern matching, a powerful and useful tool to combine your program's different execution flows based on some predefined condition.
- Lesson 15 shows you what anonymous functions are and how to define them more quickly and concisely.
- Lesson 16 introduces partial functions as a type of anonymous function defined only for some input values. You'll use partial functions when implementing the routing of your HTTP server.
- Lesson 17 illustrates how to use the library http4s to handle GET HTTP requests and responses.

- Finally, you will apply these concepts and implement an HTTP server to return the current date and time of a given country in lesson 18.

Once you have learned how to implement and run an HTTP server, you'll continue your journey with unit 4, where you'll see how to represent your data using immutable structures.

PATTERN MATCHING

After reading this lesson, you'll be able to

- Write code that uses pattern matching as an alternative to an if-else construct
- Pattern match over a closed set of values

After discovering how to express interfaces in Scala using a trait, you'll see how to use pattern matching. You can use pattern matching as an alternative to an if-else construct, which is particularly useful when having many different condition branches. The Scala pattern matching looks similar to the switch/case statement of other languages, such as Java, JavaScript, and C++. It is often more powerful and versatile than in other languages, thanks to its expressive syntax and dedicated support for sealed elements and classes. In this lesson, you'll learn how pattern matching compares to an if-else construct and its base uses. You'll also discover how to define pattern matching over a sealed set of values and how the compiler can warn you if you forget to consider any of them. Pattern matching also has dedicated support for classes, but you'll see how this works later in the book when learning about case classes. In the capstone, you'll use pattern matching to map country names to their time zones.

> **Consider this**
>
> Suppose you need to write a function that takes an integer as the parameter and returns a string representing its corresponding month of the year. If you implement it using an `if-else` construct, how many condition branches (i.e., if/else if/else expressions) will you have to define? Can you think of any alternative and more maintainable solutions?

 ## 14.1 If-else construct vs. pattern matching

Suppose you have to write a function to convert a number into its corresponding day of the week, starting with 1 for Sunday. You could use an `if-else` construct.

Listing 14.1 Converting number to a day of the week

```
def dayOfWeek(n: Int): String =
  if (n == 1) "Sunday"
  else if (n == 2) "Monday"
  else if (n == 3) "Tuesday"
  else if (n == 4) "Wednesday"
  else if (n == 5) "Thursday"
  else if (n == 6) "Friday"
  else if (n == 7) "Saturday"
  else "Unknown"
```

Although this program works as expected, it is not particularly easy to read because of the long list of cases to consider. Its predicate condition always has the same structure: "is n equal to some number?" You are trying to express a one-to-one mapping between numbers and days of the week, and pattern matching is a good fit for some refactoring that makes your code more readable and concise.

Listing 14.2 Mapping numbers with days of the week

```
def dayOfWeek(n: Int): String = n match {
  case 1 => "Sunday"
  case 2 => "Monday"
  case 3 => "Tuesday"
  case 4 => "Wednesday"
  case 5 => "Thursday"
  case 6 => "Friday"
```

```
    case 7 => "Saturday"
    case _ => "Unknown"        ←——— The default case
}
```

You can visualize pattern matching as an expression with a collection of cases and identify it by an expression with a match keyword and one or more case keyword clauses. It considers each case in order of declaration: once it can successfully match a case, it continues the computation by evaluating the corresponding expression.

At first, pattern matching may seem similar to the switch/case statement of other languages like Java or C++. However, it is a lot more powerful because of its expressive syntax and dedicated support for several types, such as sealed traits and case classes.

Imagine you want to write a function that takes a parameter of any type and returns a string depending on its type:

- If its argument is a positive integer or a double, you should return a descriptive string of the represented number.
- If it's the string "ping," you should reply with the string "pong."
- If it's a generic string, you should return a default message.
- If it's none of the previous cases matches, you should return its default standard string representation using the function toString; any class instance has an implementation for it.

Listing 14.3 Implementing objInfo

It matches any double.

Any is the root of the class hierarchy in Scala: param can be of whatever type.

It matches an integer bigger than zero.

```
def objInfo(param: Any) = param match {
    case n: Int if n > 0 => s"$n is a positive integer"
    case d: Double => s"$d is a double"
    case "ping" => "pong"
    case _: String => "you gave me a string"
    case obj => obj.toString
}
```

It matches the string "ping."

It matches any instance; as per Java tradition, any instance always has an implementation for the toString function.

It matches any string. You can use an underscore when you do not need to bind the value to a name.

The function objInfo may not seem extremely useful, but it gives you an example of all the matches that pattern matching can support. Look at figure 14.1 for a summary of the different use pattern matching cases you have seen so far.

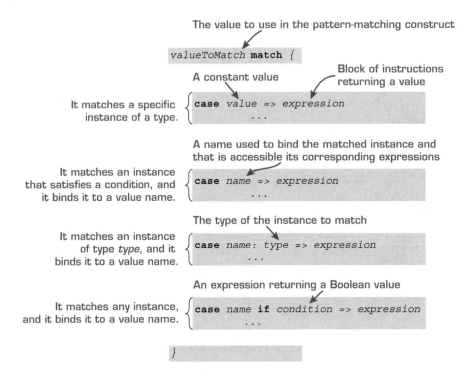

Figure 14.1 Syntax diagram on pattern matching in Scala. When pattern matching, you need to declare at least one case condition.

The many uses of underscore

In lesson 9, you learned about imports: you used the underscore symbol to import all the package components or a specific code element.

In this lesson, you have now encountered another usage of the symbol underscore: you can use it to discard value names. You will soon realize that this symbol has lots of meanings in Scala. But do not be concerned; you'll discover them gradually and become familiar with them relatively quickly.

As a rule of thumb, you state to the compiler that the details are not relevant every time you use an underscore in your code; it will act accordingly.

In listing 14.2, the underscore indicates that you do not care about the value of the parameter n, so the case should always match. In listing 14.3, because you do not refer to the string matched in the case, you can ask the interpreter not to bind it to a value and discard it.

> **Quick Check 14.1** Consider the function objInfo shown in listing 14.3. Guess the type and value that the function returns for the following inputs. Use the REPL to validate your hypotheses.
> - objInfo(-1)
> - objInfo(true)
> - objInfo(200)
> - objInfo(200.00)
> - objInfo("ping")

14.2 Sealed pattern matching

In lesson 12, you discovered how the use of the keyword *sealed* can allow you to define a closed set of possible implementations for a trait; this is particularly useful when combined with pattern matching. Suppose you have the following values to represent several currencies:

```
sealed trait Currency

object USD extends Currency
object GBP extends Currency
object EUR extends Currency
```

You need to define a function, called exchangeRateUSD, to return the USD exchange rate for a given currency.

Listing 14.4 USD exchange rate

```
def exchangeRateUSD(currency: Currency): Double =
  currency match {
    case USD => 1
    case GBP => 0.744
    case EUR => 0.848
  }
```

What happens if you add a new type of currency and forget to update your exchange-RateUSD function accordingly? Let's try it out!

Let's start the REPL and define the existing currencies together with a new one for Canadian dollars, called CAD:

```
scala> sealed trait Currency
     | object USD extends Currency
     | object GBP extends Currency
     | object EUR extends Currency
     | object CAD extends Currency
trait Currency
object USD
object GBP
object EUR
object CAD
```

If you define an exchangeRateUSD function that doesn't consider Canadian dollars, the compiler will provide you with a warning to inform you which implementations of Currency you haven't considered:

```
scala> def exchangeRateUSD(currency: Currency): Double =
     |    currency match {
     |      case USD => 1
     |      case GBP => 0.744
     |      case EUR => 0.848
     |    }
currency match {
         ^
On line 2: warning: match may not be exhaustive.
        It would fail on the following input: CAD
def exchangeRateUSD(currency: Currency): Double
```

If your input doesn't match any of the case clauses, the compiler throws a MatchError exception:

```
scala> exchangeRateUSD(CAD)
scala.MatchError: CAD$@30437e9c (of class CAD$)
   at .exchangeRateUSD(<console>:19)
   ... 28 elided
```

These compiler warnings highlight issues in your code that can potentially be extremely dangerous. Do not ignore them! You can ask the compiler to consider warnings as compilation errors by enabling a feature flag. To do so, add the following line to your build.sbt file:

```
scalacOptions += "-Xfatal-warnings"
```

> **Quick Check 14.2** You now have four possible implementations for the sealed trait Currency. Fix the function exchangeRateUSD so that you no longer see the match-not-exhaustive warning when compiling your code.

 **Summary**

In this lesson, my objective was to teach you about pattern matching.

- You discovered that using if-else is not always the best option, particularly when many condition branches are involved; you should consider using pattern matching instead.
- You learned that pattern matching is more than just an alternative if-else construct; you can match complex conditions that consider many aspects of an expression, such as its value, type, and custom predicates.
- When pattern matching over sealed values, the compiler will warn you if you forget to consider any of them.

Let's see if you got this!

TRY THIS In lesson 5, you wrote a function to apply the discount to a given price as follows:

- 0% discount if the price is less than $50
- 10% discount if the price is at least $50 but less than $100
- 15% discount if the price is at least $100

Reimplement it using pattern matching instead of an if-else construct.

 Answers to quick checks

> **Quick Check 14.1** All the returned values are of type String. The return types and values for the function objInfo are the following:
> - objInfo(-1) returns "-1"
> - objInfo(true) returns "true"
> - objInfo(200) returns "200 is a positive integer"
> - objInfo(200.00) returns "200.0 is a double"
> - objInfo("ping") returns "pong"

Quick Check 14.2   The warning disappears as soon as the function exchangeRateUSD
has a case for Canadian dollars. For example, you could change it as follows:

```
def exchangeRateUSD(currency: Currency): Double =
  currency match {
    case USD => 1
    case GBP => 0.744
    case EUR => 0.848
    case CAD => 1.278
  }
```

ANONYMOUS FUNCTIONS

After reading this lesson, you will be able to

- Implement anonymous functions
- Code using the concise notation for anonymous functions

In lesson 6, you learned the basics of functions in Scala. In this lesson, you'll discover a new type of function: *anonymous*. Anonymous functions are functions that you can define quickly and concisely. At first, they may seem just an alternative to the standard Scala functions you have seen so far, but you'll soon discover that they are particularly handy when combined with another type of function called *higher order*. The concept of an anonymous function is not unique to Scala; other languages, such as Java 8+ and Python, refer to it as *lambda*. In the capstone, you will use a particular kind of anonymous function called *partial* to define your HTTP server's routes.

Consider this

Consider the following two functions to sum and subtract two integers:

```scala
def sum(a: Int, b: Int): Int = a + b

def subtract(a: Int, b: Int): Int = a - b
```

(continued)
Which parts do these two functions have in common? How are they different?
Can you think of a more concise way of achieving the same implementation?

15.1 Function vs. anonymous function

Suppose you implemented a calculator program to perform the standard operations on integers (i.e., sum, subtraction, multiplication, division) together with negation.

Listing 15.1 MyCalculator program

```scala
object MyCalculator {

  def sum(a: Int, b: Int): Int = a + b

  def subtract(a: Int, b: Int): Int = a - b

  def multiply(a: Int, b: Int): Int = a * b

  def divide(a: Int, b: Int): Int = a / b

  def negate(a: Int): Int = subtract(0, a)

}
```

Alternatively, you can also multiply by minus one.

You can use your MyCalculator program as follows:

```scala
import MyCalculator._

sum(3, 5)          // returns 8
subtract(4, 4)     // returns 0
multiply(5, 3)     // returns 15
divide(6, 2)       // returns 3
negate(-5)         // returns 5
```

In Scala, every function has a type; you can represent this by combining its parameters with the arrow "=>" and its return type. For example, let's look at listing 15.1 again. The function sum has the type (Int, Int) => Int, which reads "Int Int to Int" because it takes two integers as parameters and returns an integer. On the other hand, the function negate has type Int => Int, which reads "Int to Int" because it takes an integer as the parameter and returns an integer.

The type notation for functions reflects the syntax used to implement anonymous functions. For example, you can implement the equivalent anonymous functions for sum and negate as follows:

```
def sum(a: Int, b: Int): Int = a + b       // function for sum
{ (a: Int, b: Int) => a + b }              // anonymous function for sum

def negate(a: Int): Int = subtract(0, a)   // function for negate
{ (a: Int) => subtract(0, a) }             // anonymous function for negate
```

When implementing anonymous functions, the function name is no longer needed, while its parameters and body stay the same. Its return type also disappears because the compiler infers it from its implementation. Figure 15.1 shows a syntax summary of how to define anonymous functions.

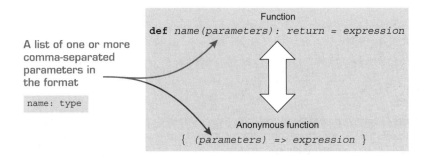

Figure 15.1 Comparison between the syntax for a function and its corresponding anonymous function

Listing 15.2 shows how to reimplement your calculation program using anonymous functions.

Listing 15.2 MySecondCalculator program

```
object MySecondCalculator {

  val sum = { (a: Int, b: Int) => a + b }
```

```
    val subtract = { (a: Int, b: Int) => a - b }

    val multiply = { (a: Int, b: Int) => a * b }

    val divide = { (a: Int, b: Int) => a / b }

    val negate = { (a: Int) => subtract(0, a) }

}
```

In the function negate, you can omit the parenthesis for the parameter a. You can do this when an anonymous function accepts only one parameter. Note that you reused the function names in listing 15.1 to create values that refer to the corresponding anonymous function; this is an optional step that allows you to call the function later on. You can use your MySecondCalculator program by calling the values you defined and by providing parameters as if they were regular functions:

```
import MySecondCalculator._

sum(3, 5)
subtract(4, 4)
multiply(5, 3)
divide(6, 2)
negate(-5)
```

> **Quick Check 15.1**   What is the type for each of the values defined in listing 15.2? Use the REPL to validate your hypothesis.

> **Quick Check 15.2**   Write an anonymous function equivalent to the following function:
>
> ```
>     def hello(n: String): String = s"Hello, $n!"
> ```

 ## 15.2 Concise notation for anonymous functions

Scala offers a more concise notation for anonymous functions. Let's see how it works.

When transforming a function to an anonymous function, its return type is no longer needed because the compiler infers its type, and you can do the same for the parameter type. If you provide the compiler an explicit type for your anonymous function, it will use it to infer the type of your parameters. For example, you can refactor the anonymous functions sum and negate shown in listing 15.2 as follows:

```
val sum = { (a: Int, b: Int) => a + b }          // before
val sum: (Int, Int) => Int = { (a, b) => a + b } // after

val negate = { (a: Int) => subtract(0, a) }      // before
val negate: Int => Int = { a => subtract(0, a) } // after
```

If your anonymous function has an an implementation that consists of a single instruction and your parameters are used in order of declaration, you can even go a step further by removing the parameters completely and replacing them with an underscore:

```
val sum = { (a: Int, b: Int) => a + b }          // before
val sum: (Int, Int) => Int = { (a, b) => a + b } // first refactoring
val sum: (Int, Int) => Int = { _ + _ }           // second refactoring

val negate = { (a: Int) => subtract(0, a) }      // before
val negate: Int => Int = { a => subtract(0, a) } // first refactoring
val negate: Int => Int = { subtract(0, _) }      // second refactoring
```

You can now refactor your calculator program using a more concise notation.

Listing 15.3 MyThirdCalculator program

```
object MyThirdCalculator {

    val sum: (Int, Int) => Int = { _ + _ }

    val subtract: (Int, Int) => Int = { _ - _ }

    val multiply: (Int, Int) => Int = { _ * _ }

    val divide: (Int, Int) => Int = { _ / _ }

    val negate: Int => Int = subtract(0, _)

}
```

You could omit the curly brackets here (e.g., use "_ + _" instead of "{ _ + _ }").

Curly brackets omitted

> **Quick Check 15.3** Are functions funcA and funcB equivalent? In other words, do they return the same output when receiving the same input? Why? Use the REPL to verify your hypotheses.
>
> ```
> val funcA: (Int, Int) => Int = { (a, b) => b / a }
> val funcB: (Int, Int) => Int = { _ / _ }
> ```

> **Readability first!**
>
> In future lessons and units, you'll discover how useful and expressive the concise notation for anonymous functions is, in particular when combined with higher order functions.
>
> Depending on the context you are in, this notation can become quite cryptic and hard to read due to all the information removed and inferred at compile time instead. For example, you could argue that the expression "_ - _" is less expressive and more confusing than "{ (a, b) => a - b }".
>
> Do not compromise the readability of your code. When using the concise notation for anonymous functions, use it only when the omitted information is easy to infer for both the compiler and your fellow developers.

 **Summary**

In this lesson, my objective was to teach you about anonymous functions.

- You can use them to create functions on the fly and without too much boilerplate; you are going to see their full potential when you learn about higher order functions.
- You also discovered their concise notation to remove unnecessary information that the compiler infers from the function's type.

Let's see if you got this!

TRY THIS   Rewrite each of the following functions as anonymous functions; use your concise notation at your discretion.

```
1  def multiply(s: String, n: Int): Int = s.length * n
2  def toDouble(n: Int): Double = n.toDouble
3  def concat(s1: String, s2: String): String = s1 + s2
4  def inverseConcat(s1: String, s2: String): String = s2 + s1
5  def myLongFunc(s: String): String = {
     val length = s.length
     s.reverse * length
   }
```

Answers to quick checks

Quick Check 15.1 The values sum, subtract, multiply, divide have the type (Int, Int) => Int, while the value negate has type Int => Int.

Quick Check 15.2 An implementation of an anonymous function equivalent to the function hello is the following:

```
{ (n: String) => s"Hello, $n!" }
```

Quick Check 15.3 Functions funcA and funcB are not equivalent because of the order of their parameters. Function funcA divides its second parameter called b by its first parameter called a. Function funcB does the inverse: it divides its first parameter by its second one because the compiler substitutes them by following their declaration order.

PARTIAL FUNCTIONS

After reading this lesson, you will be able to

- Implement partial functions to abstract commonalities between functions
- Create new functions by composing partial functions
- Use a try-catch expression to handle exceptions

Now that you've learned about pattern matching, you'll discover partial functions and how they relate to pattern matching in this lesson. Partial functions are functions that are defined only for some input. You'll see how they can be useful to abstract commonalities between functions and how you can compose them to create more complex functionalities. Finally, you'll see how you can use partial functions to catch and handle exceptions. In the capstone, you'll use partial functions to define the routes of your HTTP server.

> **Consider this**
> Suppose you have two pattern matching constructs; they look the same except the last case clause. How would you refactor them so that you can avoid code repetition?

16.1 Partial functions

Suppose you need to compute operations on integers. In particular, you want to calculate the square root of an integer. But this operation is defined only for nonnegative numbers. When dealing with a negative integer, you need to either return the negative value or return zero, depending on your use case. You could use pattern matching and define two functions.

Listing 16.1 Square root of an integer functions

```
def sqrtOrZero(n: Int): Double = n match {
  case x if x >= 0 => Math.sqrt(x)
  case _ => 0
}

def sqrtOrValue(n: Int): Double = n match {
  case x if x >= 0 => Math.sqrt(x)
  case x => x
}
```

The compiler converts the integer into a double because of the function's return type.

The functions sqrtOrZero and sqrtOrValue are very similar: their only difference is the last case clause of their pattern matching constructs. Code duplication makes code difficult to maintain and keep consistent. Let's see how you can avoid repeating yourself using partial functions.

16.1.1 Implementing a partial function

A partial function is a function that you can define only for some instances of a type. You have already encountered examples of partial functions when discussing pattern matching: you can consider each case clause as a partial function. For example, you can define a partial function to compute the square root of a nonnegative integer.

Listing 16.2 The sqrt partial function

```
val sqrt: PartialFunction[Int, Double] =
  { case x if x >= 0 => Math.sqrt(x) }
```

You can read PartialFunction[Int, Double] as "partial function from int to double."

You can view partial functions as a particular anonymous function with one or more case clauses as their body. The compiler cannot infer their type, so you need to specify

their argument and return types. In Scala, the type PartialFunction[A, B] identifies a
partial function of a parameter of type A that returns an instance of type B.

Listing 16.3 A toPrettyString function

```scala
val toPrettyString: PartialFunction[Any, String] = {      ⟵    Partial
    case x: Int if x > 0 => s"positive number: $x"             function for
    case s: String => s                                        any type to
  }                                                            string
```

After you define a partial function, you can perform function calls using the same syntax you learned for anonymous functions. But do not forget that your function is now
partial; if your input doesn't match any of its case clauses, you will receive a MatchError
exception at runtime:

```scala
scala> val toPrettyString: PartialFunction[Any, String] = {
     |      case x: Int if x > 0 => s"positive number: $x"
     |      case s: String => s
     |  }
     |
val toPrettyString: PartialFunction[Any,String] = <function1>

scala> toPrettyString(1)
val res0: String = positive number: 1

scala> toPrettyString("hello")
val res1: String = hello

scala> toPrettyString(-1)
scala.MatchError: -1 (of class java.lang.Integer)
  at scala.PartialFunction$$anon$1.apply(PartialFunction.scala:255)
  at scala.PartialFunction$$anon$1.apply(PartialFunction.scala:253)
  at $anonfun$1.applyOrElse(<pastie>:14)
  at scala.runtime.AbstractPartialFunction.apply(
AbstractPartialFunction.scala:34)
    ... 28 elided
```

Figure 16.1 summarizes how to implement partial functions in Scala.

> **Quick Check 16.1** Define a partial function called transform that reverses strings
> starting with an "a" and converts to uppercase all those beginning with an "s." Use
> the startsWith, reverse, and toUpperCase functions of the class String.

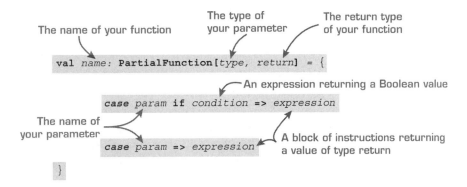

Figure 16.1 Syntax diagram on how to implement partial functions in Scala. Ensure to specify your partial function's type using PartialFunction[A, B]: A is the type of your parameter, while B is its return type.

16.1.2 Function composition

When talking about the composition of functions, you usually refer to chaining two functions together by passing the result of the first function as the parameter to the second one. For example, consider the following two functions:

```
val f: String => Int = _.size
val g: Int => Boolean = _ > 2
```

You can create a new function by calling f and then g:

```
val gof: String => Boolean = { s => g(f(s)) }
```

Alternatively, you can use the andThen function as follows:

```
val gof: String => Boolean = f.andThen(g)
```

The concept of composition may have a different meaning in the context of partial functions. Instead of chaining functions together, you may want to combine partial functions as fallbacks if the previous partial function couldn't match the given input. In Scala, you can compose partial functions as fallbacks using the function orElse. Listing 16.4 shows you how you can refactor your square root functions to remove the code duplication.

Listing 16.4 Two square root functions

```
val sqrt: PartialFunction[Int, Double] =
    { case x if x >= 0 => Math.sqrt(x) }
```

```
val zero: PartialFunction[Int, Double] = { case _ => 0 }

val value: PartialFunction[Int, Double] = { case x => x }

def sqrtOrZero(n: Int): Double = sqrt.orElse(zero)(n)

def sqrtOrValue(n: Int): Double = sqrt.orElse(value)(n)
```

First, you create a new function using orElse. Then you apply the parameter to it.

> **Quick Check 16.2** Consider the partial functions sqrt and zero in listing 16.4. Is the partial function sqrt.orElse(zero) equivalent to zero.orElse(sqrt)?

16.2 Use case: Exception handling

You first encountered partial functions in lesson 14 when discussing pattern matching. You are now ready to discover another popular use of partial functions: the try-catch expression.

Scala's exception handling comes directly from the Java world. In Scala, any class that extends java.lang.Exception is an exception. An exception interrupts your code's execution flow: you need to intercept it or it will terminate your program.

The java.lang package offers a few types of exceptions ready for you to use. A few of them are RuntimeException, NullPointerException, IllegalStateException, IllegalArgument-Exception, and NumberFormatException. Alternatively, you can define a custom exception by extending the java.lang.Exception class:

```
scala> class MyException(msg: String) extends Exception(msg)
class MyException
```

You can use an instance of an exception to interrupt your program using the keyword *throw*:

```
scala> throw new MyException("BOOM!")
MyException: BOOM!
  ... 28 elided
```

After raising an exception, you'll need to catch it before it terminates your program. To do so, you can use a try-catch expression.

Listing 16.5 An exception handling example

```scala
def n(): Int =
  try {
    throw new Exception("BOOM!")
    42
  } catch {
    case ex: Exception =>
      println(s"Ignoring exception $ex. Returning zero instead")
      0
  }
```

When evaluating n, the console will display a message and return the integer zero:

```scala
scala> n()
Ignoring exception java.lang.Exception: BOOM!. Returning zero instead
val res0: Int = 0
```

The *catch* keyword follows partial functions that identify which exceptions it should handle: if an exception doesn't match, it will not intercept it.

Think in Scala: Avoid exceptions

Scala reuses Java code that heavily uses exceptions. Some of its standard libraries and functions also throw them; knowing how to deal with them is crucial. However, you should avoid using exceptions in your code.

Exceptions are the equivalent of ticking bombs: they will explode and kill the whole program unless someone is ready to defuse them!

Exceptions are unpredictable. Identifying which exceptions a function could throw is particularly challenging. Its signature doesn't give you this information. You could document and annotate which exceptions it could throw, but this is not controlled or enforced at compile time, so you have no guarantee that they are still accurate or correct. Often, your only option is to look at its implementation while hunting for exceptions, but this is not an easy task as they can hide in any of its inner function calls.

Exceptions are a drastic solution. If you do not catch an exception, it will terminate your program. Unless you are writing a simple script, your application's crash is probably not the behavior you desire.

In future lessons, you'll see how you can represent possible errors using types (i.e., the absence of a value using the type Option). In doing so, you will have specific information on the possible errors just by looking at your function

(continued)

signature. The compiler will also make sure that you handle them correctly by considering both the positive and negative case scenarios.

Partial functions can be dangerous: they will throw an exception if your input doesn't match any case. You should convert all their possible inputs when composing them. When introducing Option, you'll see how to rewrite any partial function as a total function returning an instance of Option and avoid the inconvenience of dealing with a MatchError exception.

Quick Check 16.3 The following expression throws an IllegalArgumentException exception:

```
val b = "hello".toBoolean
```

Write a try-catch expression to default any non-parsable value to false.

 ## Summary

In this lesson, my objective was to teach you about partial functions.

- You discovered how you can implement partial functions and compose them to abstract commonalities between functions.
- You also learned how to use partial functions in a try-catch expression to handle exceptions.

Let's see if you got this!

TRY THIS Implement a function to parse a string into an integer. If you cannot parse it, return its length instead. HINT: Use the toInt function on an instance of String.

Answers to quick checks

Quick Check 16.1 A possible implementation for the function transform is as follows:

```scala
val transform: PartialFunction[String, String] = {
  case s if s.startsWith("a") => s.reverse
  case s if s.startsWith("s") => s.toUpperCase
}
```

Quick Check 16.2 The two partial functions are not equivalent because of the different composition order: zero.orElse(sqrt) returns zero for any input.

```scala
sqrt.orElse(zero)(4)    // returns 2.0
zero.orElse(sqrt)(4)    // returns 0.0
```

Quick Check 16.3 You could change the expression val b = "hello".toBoolean as follows:

```scala
val b = try {
    "hello".toBoolean
  } catch {
    case _: IllegalArgumentException => false
  }
```

HTTP API WITH HTTP4S

After reading this lesson, you will be able to

- Run an HTTP server using sbt
- Implement an API to handle GET requests

After learning about partial functions, you'll use them as part of your implementation of an HTTP server. Building an HTTP server without the help of an external library would require lots of extra time and code. Thankfully, the Scala ecosystem offers a few external libraries to help you handle HTTP communication in an efficient and performant way. In this lesson, you'll learn about http4s, a popular library to manage HTTP requests and responses. You'll discover how to implement an HTTP server that replies to a GET /ping request with a response with status code 200 – Ok and the text "pong". Finally, you'll see how to run it using sbt. In the capstone, you'll use http4s to create an HTTP server and define its API.

> **Consider this**
> Suppose you are building an HTTP server that provides a REST API for retrieving and storing data. What are the main components of your server? How would you structure your code?

17.1 An overview of http4s

Typelevel is a nonprofit organization to promote purely functional open source Scala projects together with an inclusive and welcoming environment (typelevel.org). http4s (http4s.org) is a Typelevel project and one of the most popular Scala libraries to handle HTTP requests and responses. It is particularly accessible to newcomers to the language, thanks to its extensive documentation and numerous examples.

Even though http4s does offer a Giter8 template (see sidebar), you'll see how to build an HTTP server from scratch in this lesson.

A Giter8 template for http4s

The library http4s offers a Giter8 template to generate a simple HTTP server that replies to an /hello/world endpoint, an ideal skeleton for any new project that deals with an HTTP API. To apply the template, type the following sbt command:

```
$ sbt new http4s/http4s.g8
```

The terminal prompt will ask you to provide some information about your project, such as its name, organization, and package; when in doubt, choose the provided default value.

After applying the template, navigate to the newly created folder and execute the command sbt run to start the HTTP server. You can now send HTTP requests to it:

```
$ curl -i http://localhost:8080/hello/scala
HTTP/1.1 200 OK
Content-Type: application/json
Date: Tue, 29 Dec 2020 15:24:52 GMT
Content-Length: 26

{"message":"Hello, scala"}
```

Pick at its code; it should look reasonably similar to the one you'll see in this lesson. It also provides examples of testing an HTTP application and deserializing from JSON—a topic you'll master in unit 8.

Before explaining how to implement an HTTP server using http4s, let's go over its architecture. First, you need to link your routes to their business logic through instances of `org.http4s.HttpRoutes`. Each `HttpRoutes` uses partial functions to match an incoming HTTP request, and it produces an HTTP response together with a side effect (e.g., an IO read/write, a connection to a third party). At this point, you may not be familiar with the concept of side effects, but do not worry, as you'll learn about them in the next unit. Most applications use `cats.effect.IO` as a generic representation of both synchronous and asynchronous side effects (in unit 8, you'll learn about side effects and why this is crucial). Finally, you define a singleton object that extends `cats.effect.IOApp` and provide instructions on the port and host to bind and services to mount. Your executable object also uses `Blaze` (https://github.com/http4s/blaze) together with streams as the backend for network IO. Figure 17.1 provides a visual summary of the components of an http4s application.

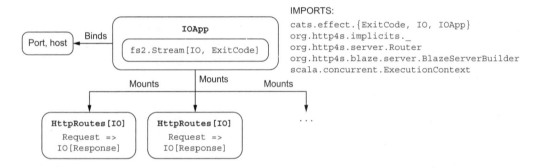

Figure 17.1 Summary of the main components of an http4s application. An HttpRoutes[IO] matches a request, and it produces a response wrapped around an IO instance to represent possible side effects. Your executable object extends IOApp and uses a BlazeServerBuilder to bind to a given port and host and to mount multiple instances of HttpRoutes[IO] to define the API of an HTTP server using an f2.Stream instance.

17.2 A ping server using http4s

Now that you have an overview of http4s, let's see how you can use it to code an HTTP server. Your goal is to implement an HTTP server that runs on localhost:8000 and that replies to a GET /ping request with a response with status code 200 – OK and the string "pong"; look at figure 17.2 for a visual summary of your server's requirements.

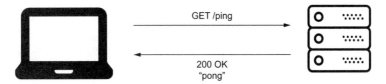

Figure 17.2 Functionalities of your HTTP server: when receiving a GET /ping request, it should reply with status code 200 - OK and body "pong."

17.2.1 Initial setup

Let's create an empty sbt project: use your IDE or a Giter8 template. Alternatively, you can create one manually as follows:

1 Create a build.sbt file in the directory of your project; it should contain the name and version of the project together with the Scala version you'd like to use:

```
// file build.sbt

name := "ping-app"
version := "0.1"
scalaVersion := "3.0.0"
```

2 Create a project directory and create a build.properties file that includes your sbt version:

```
// file project/build.properties

sbt.version = 1.5.2
```

3 Create the directories src/main/scala and src/main/resources to store your source code and static configuration files.

Next, you need to add the http4s modules you'll use for your HTTP server to your build.sbt file. You are also going to add the logback library; http4s uses it as its logging engine.

```
// append to build.sbt

val Http4sVersion = "0.22.0"

libraryDependencies ++= List(
  "org.http4s"       %% "http4s-blaze-server" % Http4sVersion,
  "org.http4s"       %% "http4s-dsl"          % Http4sVersion,
  "ch.qos.logback"   %  "logback-classic"     % "1.2.3"
)
```

logback is a popular Java library to customize your logs' behavior and appearance via a configuration file, usually called logback.xml. Let's create one in the src/main/resources folder. (See https://logback.qos.ch for more information and how to configure it.)

```xml
<!-- file src/main/resources/logback.xml -->

<configuration>
    <appender name="STDOUT" class="ch.qos.logback.core.ConsoleAppender">
        <encoder>
            <pattern>%msg %n</pattern>
        </encoder>
    </appender>
    <root level="INFO">
        <appender-ref ref="STDOUT" />
    </root>
</configuration>
```

Finally, let's define a package that will include all the code for your HTTP ping route by creating the folder src/main/scala/org/example/ping.

17.2.2 Implementing the API

Let's define a class called PingApi to define the routes of your API. PingApi should extend Http4sDsl, a trait that introduces a more intuitive DSL to match HTTP requests and produce HTTP responses.

Listing 17.1 The ping API

```scala
// file src/main/scala/org/example/ping/PingApi.scala

package org.example.ping

import cats.effect.IO
import org.http4s.HttpRoutes
import org.http4s.dsl.Http4sDsl

class PingApi extends Http4sDsl[IO] {

  val routes = HttpRoutes.of[IO] {
    case GET -> Root / "ping" => Ok("pong")
  }
}
```

org.http4s.dsl.Http4sDsl provides an intuitive DSL for matching HTTP requests.

You need to provide a function from a request to a response wrapped in IO to define an instance of HttpRoutes[IO].

It matches a GET request with path /ping and returns a response with status code 200 – OK and body "pong." You do not need to wrap the response as an IO type; the compiler does it for you at compile time automatically.

Quick Check 17.1   Suppose you'd like your `PingApi` to match a request with path/ ping, but with any HTTP method (i.e., `GET`, `POST`, `PUT`, `DELETE`, `PATCH`). How would you change your code?

Quick Check 17.2   Add a new endpoint to your `PingApi` to match a `GET` request with a path `/ping/<name>`; it should return a string containing "pong" followed by the value passed in the path.

17.2.3 Building a server

The only missing component for your HTTP server is your executable application that extends IOApp. It defines your server, so you should instantiate it only once by declaring it as an object.

```
// file src/main/scala/org/example/ping/PingApp.scala

package org.example.ping

import cats.effect.{ExitCode, IO, IOApp}
import org.http4s.server.Router

import org.http4s.implicits._
import org.http4s.blaze.server.BlazeServerBuilder
import scala.concurrent.ExecutionContext

object PingApp extends IOApp {

  private val httpApp = Router(
    "/" -> new PingApi().routes
  ).orNotFound

  override def run(args: List[String]): IO[ExitCode] =
    stream(args).compile.drain.as(ExitCode.Success)

  private def stream(args: List[String]): fs2.Stream[IO, ExitCode] =
    BlazeServerBuilder[IO](ExecutionContext.global)
    .bindHttp(8000, "0.0.0.0")
    .withHttpApp(httpApp)
    .serve
}
```

The org.http4s .implicits._ import adds the orNotFound function to your scope; it returns a 404 error code if a request doesn't match any route.

IOApp is an interface that provides requires to implement a function.

BlazeServerBuilder defines an HTTP server with an address, port, and routes using a stream to process requests. Execution.global indicates the thread pool to use while streaming; you'll learn more about this when discussing concurrency and the type Future.

IOApp is an interface that requires you to define a run function. Use BlazeServer-Builder[IO] together with the function bindHttp to provide a port and host. The function withHttpApp attaches a group of routes with a prefix to your server. Finally, the function serve transforms your Blaze definition into a stream that represents your HTTP server.

> **Quick Check 17.3**   Change your code not to provide a host or port for your server by invoking the function bindHttp without parameters. What happens when you start your application using the command sbt run?

17.2.4 Let's try it out!

The implementation of your HTTP ping server is now complete; it's time to see it in action! Open your terminal, navigate to your project's root directory, and execute the command sbt run. sbt will download the dependencies, compile your code, and start your application. After a few seconds, you should see a message similar to the following in your console:

```
$sbt run
[info] Running org.example.ping.PingApp
Service bound to address /0:0:0:0:0:0:0:0:8000

  _   _   _       _ _
 | |_| |_| |_ _ __| | | ___
 | ' \ _| _| '_ \_  _(_-<
 |_||_\__|\__| .__/ |_|/__/
             |_|
http4s v0.22.0 on blaze v0.15.1 started at
http://[0:0:0:0:0:0:0:0]:8000/
```

Your HTTP server is now running and listening on localhost:8000.

If you send a GET /ping request, you will get back a response with status code 200 - Ok and body "pong":

```
$ curl -i localhost:8000/ping
HTTP/1.1 200 OK
Content-Type: text/plain; charset=UTF-8
Date: Wed, 30 Dec 2020 19:16:18 GMT
Content-Length: 4

pong
```

On the other hand, if you send a POST /ping request rather than a GET /ping request, the server will reply with a 404 – Not Found response:

```
$ curl -i -X POST localhost:8000/ping
HTTP/1.1 404 Not Found
Content-Type: text/plain; charset=UTF-8
Date: Wed, 30 Dec 2020 19:16:35 GMT
Content-Length: 9

Not found
```

 Summary

In this lesson, my objective was to teach you how to build a server that provides an HTTP API to handle GET requests.

- You discovered http4s, a purely functional library to handle HTTP communication.
- You reviewed its main components, and you applied them to implement an HTTP ping server.

Let's see if you got this!

> **TRY THIS** Implement a server that exposes an API that successfully replies to any request with a response with status code 200 – Ok and its body with a message that provides the request method and path. For example, when receiving a request POST /this/is/an/example, it should reply with a response with status code 200 – Ok and a body method is POST; path is /this/is/an/example.

 Answers to quick checks

> **Quick Check 17.1** You can change your partial function to match any HTTP method of an incoming request by using the underscore symbol as follows:
>
> ```
> case _ -> Root / "ping" => Ok("pong")
> ```

> **Quick Check 17.2** Implement an additional case clause for the partial function that defines your HttpRoutes instance:
>
> ```
> case GET -> Root / "ping" / name => Ok(s"pong $name")
> ```

Quick Check 17.3 The function bindHttp uses predefined defaults when invoked with no parameters. It binds the server to host 127.0.0.1 and port 8080:

```
[info] running org.example.ping.PingApp
Service bound to address /127.0.0.1:8080


  _   _   _       _ _
 | |_| |_| |_ _ __| | | ___
 | ' \ _|  _| '_ \_  _(_-<
 |_||_\__|\__| .__/ |_|/__/
             |_|
http4s v0.22.0 on blaze v0.15.1 started at http://127.0.0.1:8080/
```

THE TIME HTTP SERVER

In this capstone, you will

- Define partial functions and pattern matching constructs
- Handle exceptions using a try-catch expression
- Implement an HTTP server using http4s

In this lesson, you'll adapt the code you wrote in the previous capstone to implement an HTTP server to provide the current date and time for a given country (e.g., "Italy" or "Japan"). In particular, you'll expose and an HTTP API to return a representation of the current date and time, or a human-readable error message.

 ## 18.1 What time is it?

Let's define an API that reflects the business requirements. Your server should be able to handle GET requests to the URI /datetime/<country> and return a string representing the current date and time in the correct time zone for the given country. For example, GET /datetime/italy should respond with a status code 200 – Ok and a string with the current date and time in Rome using a human-readable format, such as RFC 1123 (e.g., "Fri, 30 Apr 2021 11:44:35 +0200"). If the given country is not valid or not supported, your application should error with an explicative message. For example, GET /datetime/invalid should return a response with status code 404 - Not Found and the body "Unknown timezone for country invalid". Figure 18.1 provides a summary of the expected behavior of this API.

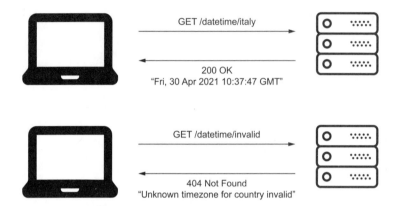

Figure 18.1   Overview of the API for your time HTTP server. When recognizing the country, the application should respond successfully with a string representing its current date and time. Otherwise, it should error with an explicative human-readable message.

18.1.1 Setting your sbt project up

In the capstone for unit 2, you created an empty sbt project with an org.example.time package for your application. Feel free to refer to section 13.1.1 to refresh your memory on how to do this.

You now need to add your external dependencies; you'll use http4s and logback to handle HTTP requests and log messages in the terminal. You'll also need java.time to compute the current date and time, but you do not need to include it as an external library because it is already accessible as an internal module.

Listing 18.1 Adding dependencies to build.sbt

```
// append to build.sbt

val Http4sVersion = "0.22.0"

libraryDependencies ++= List(
  "org.http4s"      %% "http4s-blaze-server" % Http4sVersion,
  "org.http4s"      %% "http4s-dsl"          % Http4sVersion,
```

```
    "ch.qos.logback"  %  "logback-classic"      % "1.2.3"
)
```

You also need to create a directory src/main/resources for your logback.xml file and any other static configuration. The logback.xml file contains the settings and formats for your application's logger.

Listing 18.2 An example of a logback.xml file

```
<!-- file src/main/resources/logback.xml -->

<configuration>
    <appender name="STDOUT" class="ch.qos.logback.core.ConsoleAppender">
        <withJansi>true</withJansi>
        <encoder>
            <pattern>
                %d{HH:mm:ss.SSS} %highlight(%-5level) - %msg %n
            </pattern>
        </encoder>
    </appender>
    <root level="INFO">
        <appender-ref ref="STDOUT" />
    </root>
</configuration>
```

If you have done everything right, you should be about to execute the command sbt compile or sbt update from the root directory of your project; sbt will download all the external dependencies you requested.

18.1.2 The TimePrinter class

In unit 2's capstone, you implemented the TimePrinter class to get the current date and time in a given time zone (see section 13.1.2). Originally, you used the class to compute the date and time in a given time zone, but now the business requirements demand that you do this using a country instead. Let's modify the existing code of the TimePrinter class so that the function now takes a country as the parameter, and let's define a function to match a country to its time zone.

Listing 18.3 The TimePrinter class

```
// file src/main/scala/org/example/time/TimePrinter.scala
package org.example.time
```

```
import java.time.format.DateTimeFormatter
import java.time.{ZoneId, ZonedDateTime}

class TimePrinter(formatter: DateTimeFormatter) {

  def now(country: String): String = {
    val timezone = countryToTimezone(country)
    val dateTime = currentDateTime(timezone)
    dateTimeToString(dateTime)
  }

  private def countryToTimezone(country: String): String =
    country.toLowerCase match {
      case "italy" => "Europe/Rome"
      case "uk" => "Europe/London"
      case "germany" => "Europe/Berlin"
      case "japan" => "Asia/Tokyo"
      case _ =>
        val msg = s"Unknown timezone for country $country"
        throw new IllegalArgumentException(msg)
    }

  private def currentDateTime(timezone: String): ZonedDateTime = {
    val zoneId = ZoneId.of(timezone)
    ZonedDateTime.now(zoneId)
  }

  private def dateTimeToString(dateTime: ZonedDateTime): String =
    formatter.format(dateTime)
}
```

It matches a country with its time zone.

If the country is not recognized, it throws an IllegalArgumentException; you'll need to handle it later.

Now that the business logic is ready, you can define the routes of your API.

18.1.3 The API routes

After implementing your business logic, you need to define your API. Let's create a class, called TimeApi, with a service to handle requests in the shape of GET /datetime/ <timezone>. If successful, you should reply with a 200 - Ok status code and a body containing the current date and time in format RFC 1123. Otherwise, you should return a response with the status code 404 – Not Found and a body containing a human-readable error message.

Listing 18.4 The TimeApi class

```scala
// file src/main/scala/org/example/time/TimeApi.scala

package org.example.time

import java.time.format.DateTimeFormatter

import cats.effect.IO
import org.http4s.HttpRoutes
import org.http4s.dsl.Http4sDsl

class TimeApi extends Http4sDsl[IO] {

  private val printer =
    new TimePrinter(DateTimeFormatter.RFC_1123_DATE_TIME)

  val service = HttpRoutes.of[IO] {
    case GET -> Root / "datetime" / country =>
      try {
        Ok(printer.now(country))
      } catch {
        case ex: IllegalArgumentException =>
          NotFound(ex.getMessage)
      }
  }
}
```

There's no need to expose the printer value outside its class.

The function now throws an exception if the country is invalid or not supported.

It handles an IllegalArgumentException by returning a response with status code 404 – Not Found and a body containing its error message.

The function call printer.now(timezone) throws an exception if it doesn't recognize the country as valid; it inherits this behavior from the contryToTimezone function of the Time-Printer class. You need to remember to handle this implementation detail correctly or your server will error with a cryptic and unhelpful 500 – Internal Server Error.

18.1.4 The HTTP server

The final step is to define a server using an executable object called TimeApp. You need to bind it to a port and host and mount the HTTP service you implemented in the previous section.

Listing 18.5 The TimeApp object

```scala
// file src/main/scala/org/example/time/TimeApp.scala

package org.example.time

import cats.effect.{ExitCode, IO, IOApp}
import org.http4s.implicits._
import org.http4s.server.Router
import org.http4s.blaze.server.BlazeServerBuilder

import scala.concurrent.ExecutionContext

object TimeApp extends IOApp {

  private val httpApp = Router(
    "/" -> new TimeApi().routes
  ).orNotFound

  override def run(args: List[String]): IO[ExitCode] =
    stream(args).compile.drain.as(ExitCode.Success)

  private def stream(args: List[String]) =
    BlazeServerBuilder[IO](ExecutionContext.global)
    .bindHttp(8000, "0.0.0.0")       ◄─────
    .withHttpApp(httpApp)   ◄────
    .serve                                It binds the server to
}                          It mounts the API   http://localhost:8000.
                           routes to the server.
```

18.1.5 Let's try it out!

Your HTTP server is now complete and ready to run. Navigate to your project's root folder to compile and run your application using the command sbt run. After a few seconds, you should see that the server is up and ready to process HTTP requests:

```
[info] Running org.example.time.TimeApp
20:36:31.979 INFO  - Service bound to address /0:0:0:0:0:0:0:0:8000
20:36:31.982 INFO  -    _    _    _       _ _
20:36:31.983 INFO  -   | |_| |_| |_ _ __| | | ___
20:36:31.983 INFO  -   | ' \ _|  _| '_ \_  _(_-<
20:36:31.983 INFO  -   |_||_\__|\__| .__/ |_|/__/
20:36:31.983 INFO  -                |_|
20:36:32.047 INFO  - http4s v0.22.0 on blaze v0.15.1 started at
http://[0:0:0:0:0:0:0:0]:8000/
```

If you perform a GET request to http://localhost:8000/datetime/italy, you should get the current date and time in the correct time zone and the expected format:

```
$ curl -i http://localhost:8000/datetime/Italy
HTTP/1.1 200 OK
Content-Type: text/plain; charset=UTF-8
Date: Sun, 25 Apr 2021 20:45:59 GMT
Content-Length: 29


Sun, 25 Apr 2021 22:45:59 +0200
```

On the other hand, if you call http://localhost:8000/datetime/invalid, you should receive a 404 – Not Found response with an error message:

```
$ curl -i http://localhost:8000/datetime/invalid
HTTP/1.1 404 Not Found
Content-Type: text/plain; charset=UTF-8
Date: Sun, 25 Apr 2021 20:52:33 GMT
Content-Length: 36


Unknown timezone for country invalid
```

Play around with your server and add support for more countries. Can you spot any bugs or implementation issues? You'll discover some of them in the next section.

 ## 18.2 Possible improvements to our solution

Congratulations on completing your HTTP server! Your implementation respects the requirements, but you could improve a few of its aspects. Let's see some of them and what techniques you'll learn to overcome them.

> **EXCEPTIONS ARE DANGEROUS** Exceptions are equivalent to ticking bombs: you throw them and hope that someone will catch them before your program explodes. When coding, you cannot identify which functions throw which exceptions by looking at their signature; you need to look at their (reliable?) documentation or its full implementation most of the time. Forgetting about them is extremely easy, and often you end up writing code wrapped around a preventing try-catch expression. In future lessons, you will learn how to represent error using types rather than exceptions. For example, you'll learn about the type Option as the representation of a possible missing value in the next unit.

> **COUNTRY-TIME ZONE MAPPING** According to Google, there are 195 countries in the world. Your server supports only 4 of them. You also have countries that people identify with multiple names; for example, UK, United Kingdom, and United Kingdom of Great Britain and Northern Ireland are different names for

the same entity. Having a function with 195+ case clauses is not realistic. Your API also has another serious limitation: it assumes that a country has only one time zone, but this is not true for many of them, such as the United States, India, Australia, and Russia. A possible solution is to change your API to return a list of current dates and times for a given country. Later you'll learn about the List and Map data structures, and you'll discover how to generalize this country–time zone relation more efficiently.

DATA REPRESENTATION   Your server responds with plain text, which is the way humans prefer to process data, but machines struggle to process data in plain text: they need to tokenize the string correctly to understand it correctly. When exchanging data over HTTP, you can more efficiently parse and interpret structured data formats, such as JSON and XML. In unit 8, you will learn how to serialize/deserialize JSON objects from/to Scala classes so that a machine can quickly and reliably process the exchanged data.

 Summary

In this capstone, you implemented a fully working HTTP server to determine the current date and time in a given country.

- You have created an sbt project, added some external dependencies, and set a logback logging configuration up.
- You implemented an HTTP API for your server using http4s, and you used the java.time module and pattern matching to define your business logic.
- Finally, you discovered some of the not-so-ideal aspects of your implementation and saw which techniques will help you overcome them.

Immutable data and structures

In unit 3 you learned how to create an HTTP server that consumes GET requests. In this unit, you'll discover how to implement an HTTP server with POST requests to play the game "Paper, Rock, Scissors, Lizard, Spock!" In particular, we will discuss the following subjects:

- Lesson 19 illustrates what case classes are and how to use them to make your data representations immutable. You'll also learn how pattern matching supports case classes thanks to their unapply function.

- Lesson 20 teaches you about higher order functions, one of the most useful types of functions in Scala. You'll see how you can use functions both as parameters and return values of other functions.

- Lesson 21 introduces you to the notion of purity, one of the fundamental concepts of functional programming. You'll also learn about referential transparency and how to differentiate between pure and impure functions.

- Lesson 22 shows you how to model nullable values using the type Option. You'll learn how to represent an optional value and pattern match on it.

- Lesson 23 teaches you about the `map`, `flatten`, and `flatMap` functions: they are fundamental operations you can perform on `Option` to transform and combine optional values.
- Lesson 24 introduces you to `for-comprehension` as a tool to reduce boilerplate code when combining instances of `Option`. I'll also give you an overview of what other operations you can perform on nullable values.
- Lesson 25 teaches you about the structure tuple as a way to quickly group elements together. You'll also learn how to implement an `unapply` function for a generic class.
- Finally, you'll apply everything you learn to implement an HTTP server and play the game "Paper, Rock, Scissors, Lizard, Spock!" in lesson 26.

After learning how to represent data in an immutable manner, you'll continue with unit 5, in which you'll discover the `List` collection.

CASE CLASSES TO STRUCTURE YOUR DATA

After reading this lesson, you'll be able to

- Represent immutable structured data using case classes
- Decide when to use case objects rather than regular objects
- Use case classes together with pattern matching

In the previous unit, you mastered how to create a simple HTTP server. In this lesson, you'll discover an essential tool in your Scala's toolbox called *case class*. When coding, dealing with data is a fundamental and recurring task. A case class provides a convenient and efficient way to represent your data in an immutable way that allows you to share data between multiple threads safely. Being able to express data efficiently and conveniently is essential to make sure our program works correctly. You'll also learn about case objects and how they can be useful when serialization is involved. Finally, you'll see how pattern matching provides dedicated support for case classes thanks to the unapply function. In the capstone, you'll use case classes and case objects to represent the core elements of the game "Paper, Rock, Scissors, Lizard, Spock!"

Consider this
Think of the languages you have encountered in your coding experience. How do they represent data? Are there methods that you must implement? Do you create both setters and getters? Do you have support from either the language itself or your IDE to reduce any potential boilerplate?

 ## 19.1 Case class

Representing data is a crucial part of writing programs, but it is also often mechanical: you need to define your fields, setters, getters, and so on. When coding in languages a bit more verbose such as Java, you usually take advantage of tools, such as your IDE, to generate code automatically. What if the compiler could do this for you instead of relying on your IDE?

A case class is a class with an arbitrary number of parameters for which the compiler automatically adds ad hoc code. In Scala's early versions, you couldn't specify a case class with more than 22 parameters, but this limitation no longer exists since Scala 2.11. Case classes are the ideal data containers because they encourage the use of immutability. The implementation of a case class looks very similar to a regular class, but it has an additional *case* keyword.

Listing 19.1 The case class Person

```
case class Person(name: String, age: Int)
```

You can also think of a case class as a class that is characterized by its parameters. For example, you could identify an instance of person by its name and its age. For this reason, you can also refer to this as *product type*. As a result of the keyword *case*, the compiler automatically adds a few convenience methods to it. Here's an overview considering the following instance of the class Person:

```
val personA = new Person("Tom", 25)
```

> **GETTERS** For each parameter, the compiler adds a getter function so that you can easily access it. For example, you can access the name and age of personA as follows:
>
> ```
> personA.name // returns "Tom"
> personA.age  // returns 25
> ```

COPY FUNCTION You do not have setter functions for parameters because a case class represents data in an immutable way. When changing one of the case class's values, you should use the copy function to create a new data representation. Suppose you want to change the age of you instance personA to be 35:

```
val personB: Person = personA.copy(age = 35)
personA.age        // returns 25
personB.age        // returns 35
```

You can also change more parameters at the same time. For example, if you want to change both its name and age you can just provide more parameters to the copy function:

```
val mark = personA.copy(name = "Mark", age = personA.age + 1)
mark.name // returns "Mark"
mark.age  // returns 26
```

The copy function is effectively equivalent to initializing a new class. Using the copy function is particularly convenient when a case class has lots of fields, but you only need to change one. Consider the following snippet of code:

```
case class Test(a: Int, b: Int, c: Int, d: Int)
val test = Test(1,2,3,4)

val testA = Test(a = 0, b = test.b, c = test.c, d = test.d)
val testB = test.copy(a = 0)
```

The instances testA and testB are equivalent: you initialized testA using the apply function, while you initialized testB using the copy function. Hopefully, you'll agree that the copy function approach is more readable than using the apply one in this case.

TOSTRING, HASHCODE, EQUALS FUNCTIONS Every class has the functions toString, hashCode, and equals; their implementation comes directly from the Java world. In Java, java.lang.Object is the superclass of all the classes, and it provides an implementation for several functions inherited by all the other classes. A case class redefines the implementation for some of these functions inherited from java.lang.Object. Let's see how:

- toString: By default, a toString function returns a string representing the class's name, followed by the hexadecimal representation of the instance's memory address (e.g., Person@1e04fa0a). A case class redefines this method to return a string that is descriptive of the data it contains:

  ```
  personA.toString() // returns "Person(Tom,25)"
  ```

- hashCode: The hashCode function returns an integer that represents an instance of a class. The JVM uses this number in data structures and hash tables when storing objects in a more performant way. While a hash code of an instance usually considers both its internal structure and memory allocation, a case class overrides its hash code so that it considers only its internal structure. The compiler makes sure that two case classes with the same type and structure have the same hash code.

```
class C(x: Int)
new C(5).hashCode == new C(5).hashCode // returns false

case class A(x: Int)
new A(5).hashCode == new A(5).hashCode // returns true
```

- equals: According to the implementation of equals defined in java.lang .Object, equality holds if two instances are the same. In other words, they are equal if they point to the same memory allocation. When working with case classes, the compiler provides a different implementation for equals in which case classes that belong to the same type and structure are considered equal.

```
class C(x: Int)
new C(5).equals(new C(5)) // returns false

case class A(x: Int)
case class B(n: Int)
new A(5).equals(new B(5)) // returns false
new A(5).equals(new A(5)) // returns true
```

Scala 3: Strict equality

Scala 2 uses universal equality: you can always compare two instances for equality, even if they have different types. For examples, the following expression comparing a Boolean and a String is considered valid (with a compiler warning):

```
scala> true == "true"
            ^
        warning: comparing values of types Boolean and String
          using
`==` will always yield false
val res0: Boolean = false
// it compiles in Scala 2 with a warning
```

Scala 3 adopts strict equality: you can only compare instances that have the same type. The previous expression no longer compiles:

```
scala> "true" == true
1 |"true" == true
  |^^^^^^^^^^^^^^^
  |Values of types String and Boolean cannot be compared
with == or !=
    // it doesn't compile in Scala 3
```

COMPANION OBJECT: APPLY AND UNAPPLY FUNCTIONS When declaring a case class, the compiler generates its companion object with implementations for the apply and unapply functions. You can use such methods to construct and deconstruct an instance of a case class, respectively. Let's see how they work:

- apply: thanks to the generated apply method, you can create an instance of your case class by providing parameters for it. You have already encountered the apply function when discussing singleton objects; let's quickly recap how it works. For example, to create an instance of Person, you can use the apply method rather than directly invoking its constructor. All the following expressions are equivalent:

```
new Person("Tom", 25)
Person.apply("Tom", 25)
Person("Tom", 25)
Person(age = 25, name = "Tom")
```

- unapply: you can use the unapply method to decompose a class. In a case class, the compiler implements the unapply to return the class fields. For example, you can decompose a Person to obtain an optional grouping containing a name and an age:

```
Person.unapply(Person("Tom", 25))
// returns Some((Tom, 25))
// which has type Option[(String, Int)]
```

You may not be able to fully understand its return type and implementation yet. You'll learn about the unapply method in detail when discussing optional values and tuples. In the next section, you'll see how having an implementation for the unapply function allows you to pattern match over the fields of a case class.

Through the use of case classes, the compiler saves us from writing lots of potentially buggy code. Listing 19.2 shows the amount of boilerplate that you would have to define to implement a class that is equivalent to a case class.

Listing 19.2 Class vs. case class

```scala
class Person(n: String, a: Int) {

  val name: String = n
  val age: Int = a

  def copy(name: String, age: Int) =
    new Person(name, age)


  override def toString(): String = s"Person($n,$a)"

  override def hashCode(): Int = ???

  override def equals(obj: Any): Boolean = ???
}
object Person {

  def apply(name: String, age: Int): Person =
    new Person(name, age)

  def unapply(p: Person): Option[(String, Int)] =
    Some((p.name, p.age))
}
```

Implementation omitted

Figure 19.1 shows a summary of how to declare a case class and the functionalities the compiler generates for it.

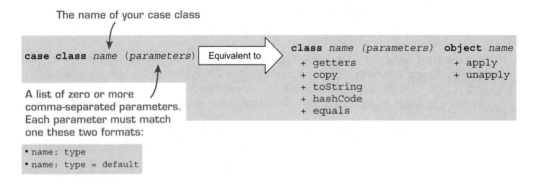

Figure 19.1 A syntax diagram for a case class. A case class is equivalent to a regular class with its companion object that the compiler has enriched with a set of useful functions.

19.2 Pattern matching and case classes

In the previous section, you discovered that the compiler provides an implementation for the unapply function for a case class. This function decomposes a case class into its parameters, and it enables pattern matching to analyze them. This process is entirely transparent; you do not need to invoke the unapply function explicitly. The compiler will look for an unapply function in the companion object for the class and the number of parameters you use in your pattern matching construct.

Consider again the case class Person in listing 19.1:

```
case class Person(name: String, age: Int)
```

Suppose that you want to write a function, called welcome, that returns a different message depending on the name and age of a person.

Listing 19.3 Pattern matching of a case class Person

It matches a person
with the name Tom.

It matches a person with an
age higher than 18.

```
def welcome(person: Person): String = person match {
    case Person("Tom", _) => "Hello Mr Tom!"
    case Person(name, age) if age > 18 => s"Good to see you $name"
    case p @ Person(_, 18) => s"${p.name}, you look older!"
    case Person(_, _) => "Hi bro!"
}
```

It matches a person with
any name and any age.

It matches a person
with age 18, and it
binds it to a value p.

You saw a new way of patterning using value binding in listing 19.3:

```
case p @ Person(_, 18) => s"${p.name}, you look older!"
```

When pattern matching a class, you can also bind the entire class instance to a value by providing a name and the symbol @.

Quick Check 19.2   What happens to the implementation of the function welcome if you declare Person as a regular class rather than a case class—that is, you remove the *case* keyword from its declaration?

 ## 19.3 Case object

Now that you understand what case classes are, you may wonder if an equivalent scenario exists for singleton objects: you refer to them as *case objects*. Let's look at an example of a case object for currency.

Listing 19.4 USD currency

```
case object USD
```

A case object is a regular singleton object for which the compiler automatically overrides some useful methods; it redefines the implementation of toString to produce a human-readable string representation. For a regular object, toString returns its name followed by the hexadecimal encoding of its memory address. This looks similar to "USD@7b36aa0c." When dealing with a case object, the compiler changes the definition for toString to return only the object name:

```
USD.toString      // returns "USD"
```

Figure 19.2 shows a summary of the syntax for case objects.

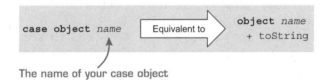

The name of your case object

Figure 19.2   A syntax diagram for a case object in Scala. A case object is equivalent to an object with a redefined toString function.

Quick Check 19.3   Consider the code in listing 19.4. Modify the implementation of USD to define three more currencies using case objects: GBP, CAD, and EUR. Use a sealed trait to group them all as currency.

 **Summary**

In this lesson, my objective was to teach you about case classes, how they differ from regular classes, and why they are beneficial when representing data.

- You learned how to use pattern matching with a case class and use the symbol @ to bid an entire instance to a value.
- We also discussed case objects and why they are ideal for representing singleton objects using strings.

Let's see if you got this!

TRY THIS   Use case classes and case objects to represent the following data:

- An author has a forename and a surname.
- A genre has only three possible values: drama, horror, romantic.
- A book has a title, an author, and a genre.

 Answers to quick checks

Quick Check 19.1   The following code describes the relations between brewery and beer:

```
case class Brewery(name: String)
case class Beer(name: String, brewery: Brewery)
```

Quick Check 19.2   The function welcome no longer compiles. The compiler complains that it cannot find a value Person; a companion object with the name Person containing an implementation for the unapply function no longer exists because you declared Person as a regular class rather than a case class. Also, its fields name and age are no longer accessible.

Quick Check 19.3   A representation for currencies using case objects and a sealed trait is the following:

```
sealed trait Currency
case object USD extends Currency
case object GBP extends Currency
case object CAD extends Currency
case object EUR extends Currency
```

HIGHER ORDER FUNCTIONS

After reading this lesson, you will be able to

- Define functions that have functions as parameters
- Implement functions that return functions
- Build powerful abstractions that remove code duplication

Functions are first-class citizens in Scala: you can use them as parameters or return them as the result of some computation. *Higher order functions* are functions that accept other functions as parameters, return functions, or both. Their use allows you to create powerful abstractions that reduce duplication and increase the reusability of your code. In the capstone, you'll use higher order functions to extract information on the winner of the game "Paper, Rock, Scissors, Lizard, Spock!"

> **Consider this**
>
> Suppose you want to compute some calculations and perform some input/output operation on them. For example, you may need to express two case scenarios. You should display the result of your computation into the console in the first, while you should append it to an existing file in the second. How would you design your functions to avoid code duplication and ensure their implementation is consistent everywhere in your program? How efficiently can you add support for other IO operations, such as querying a database?

20.1 Functions as parameters

Suppose you want to perform some simple statistics on a string to calculate its length and how many letters or digits it has.

Listing 20.1 Stats on a string

```
def size(s: String): Int   =
    s.length

def countLetters(s: String): Int =
    s.count(_.isLetter)

def countDigits(s: String): Int =
    s.count(_.isDigit)
```

count is a function defined in the class String to calculate how many chars of a string respect a specific property.

The solution shown in listing 20.1 works, but it is not ideal. Adding new types of statistics to your program drastically increases the number of functions you need to write and maintain. The functions countLetters and countDigits are very similar; the only difference is the predicate used to determine if you should count a char. How can you design functions so that you can avoid code duplication? How can you also ensure you define them so that you can support new operations easily?

Let's look again at the statistics you need to perform: compute its length, count its letters, and count its digits. In other words, you need to determine if you should consider a character. You should include each one when calculating the length of a string. At the same time, you should consider only those with a particular property (i.e., being a letter, being a digit, etc.) for the other two operations.

Listing 20.2 Stats on a string 2

```
def stats(s: String, predicate: Char => Boolean): Int =
    s.count(predicate)
```

predicate is a function that takes a char as its parameter and returns a Boolean.

After defining the function stats, you can compute the requested statistics needed as follows by removing any code duplication:

```
def size(s: String): Int   = stats(s, _ => true)

def countLetters(s: String): Int = stats(s, _.isLetter)

def countDigits(s: String): Int = stats(s, _.isDigit)
```

You can also support custom statistics by calling the function stats directly. For example, you can count the number of uppercase letters or how many chars "x" it contains as follows:

```
val text = "This is my Text Example"
stats(text, _.isUpper)  // count of upper letters
stats(text, _ == 'x')   // count of chars equal to "x"
```

> **Quick Check 20.1** Write a function called foo that takes a function f of type Int => Double as its parameter and returns a Double; apply 42 to the function parameter and then add 2 to its result.

You can specify defaults for function parameters. For example, you can change the implementation of your stats function so that it counts all the chars by default—in other words, to be equivalent to the length of a string.

Listing 20.3 Stats on a string with default

```
def stats(s: String,
     predicate: Char => Boolean = { _ => true } ): Int =
   s.count(predicate)
```

predicate is the name of the function parameter. Char => Boolean is the type of the function parameter. { _ => true } is an anonymous function used as default value.

Once you have provided a default for the function parameter, you can call the function without providing the parameter predicate:

```
stats(s) // count of all the chars
```

Figure 20.1 shows a summary of the Scala syntax for function parameters.

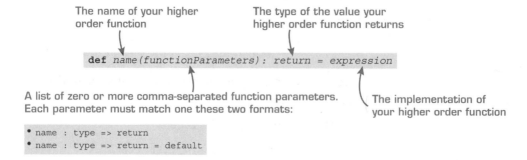

The name of your higher order function

The type of the value your higher order function returns

```
def name(functionParameters): return = expression
```

A list of zero or more comma-separated function parameters. Each parameter must match one these two formats:

The implementation of your higher order function

```
• name : type => return
• name : type => return = default
```

Figure 20.1 A syntax diagram for function parameters in Scala and their use of defaults

20.2 Functions as return values

In the previous section, you implemented a function called stats to perform statistics on a string (see listing 20.3). In particular, you represented each of the predefined options with three functions called size, countLetters, countDigits. This solution works for a small set of alternatives, but it will quickly become quite verbose once your program needs to provide more and more preferences. You will need to define a function with shape String => Int for each possible alternative. This approach can cause the number of functions in your program to explode. If you need to express 20 different alternatives, you will have 20 functions with a very similar structure. Another solution is to represent all the available selections with a set of well-defined values (or union types) and write a function to select the predicate filter to use for your stats function.

Listing 20.4 PredicateSelector function

```
sealed trait Mode                          ←—— A finite set of
case object Length extends Mode                 values to define
case object Letters extends Mode                all the options
case object Digits extends Mode

def predicateSelector(mode: Mode): Char => Boolean =
  mode match {
    case Length  => _ => true               It selects a
    case Letters => _.isLetter              predicate based
    case Digits  => _.isDigit               on a given mode.
  }
```

Now that you have defined the predicateSelector function, you can use it to call the stats function:

```
val text = "This is my Text Example"
stats(text, predicateSelector(Length))   // count of all chars
stats(text, predicateSelector(Letters))  // count of upper letters
```

Thanks to this solution, you can support additional predefined statistics by adding a case object for the trait Mode and a case clause in the predicateSelector function rather than defining a new function from scratch.

Figure 20.2 provides a summary of how to implement higher order functions that return functions in Scala.

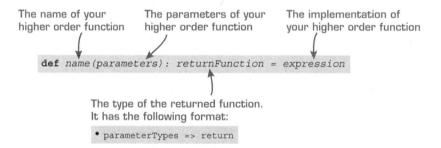

Figure 20.2   A syntax diagram of higher order functions that return functions as result type

> **Quick Check 20.3**   Change the code in listing 20.4 to support a new kind of statistics to count the whitespaces in a string; use the function isWhitespace defined in the class Char.

 **Summary**

In this lesson, my objective was to teach you about higher order functions and how to use them to build powerful abstractions.

- You saw how to create functions that accept other functions as parameters.
- You discovered how to implement functions that return functions.

Let's see if you got this!

TRY THIS   Write a function, called operationWithFallback, that returns an Int and has three parameters:

- n is an integer.
- operation is a function from Int to Int.
- fallback is an integer.

The function operationWithFallback should be implemented as follows: compute the value of operation applied to n and return it if more than zero; otherwise, compute the fallback. Make sure to evaluate fallback only if needed.

Answers to quick checks

Quick Check 20.1 An implementation for the function foo is the following:

```
def foo(f: Int => Double): Double = f(42) + 2
```

Quick Check 20.2 The implementation is modified as follows:

```
def foo(f: Int => Double = _.toDouble): Double = f(42) + 2
```

Quick Check 20.3 The implementation shown in listing 20.4 should be modified as follows:

```
sealed trait Mode
case object Length extends Mode
case object Letters extends Mode
case object Digits extends Mode
case object Whitespaces extends Mode


def predicateSelector(mode: Mode): Char => Boolean =
    mode match {
        case Length => _ => true
        case Letters => _.isLetter
        case Digits => _.isDigit
        case Whitespaces => _.isWhitespace
    }
```

WHAT IS PURITY?

After reading this lesson, you will be able to

- Differentiate between pure and impure functions
- Provide code examples in which impure functions cause unpredicted code behavior

In this lesson, you'll learn about purity, a fundamental principle of functional programming. In particular, you'll see that a pure function is total and has no side effects. Distinguishing between pure and impure functions can help you identify and prevent bugs in your code. For example, consider the following scenario:

Suppose you are developing the software for a smart thermostat. Your business requirements dictate your thermostat never to reach temperatures below the freezing point of 0°C (equivalent to 32°F) because it could damage its mechanical parts. If this happens, your program should trigger an emergency recovery plan that changes the target temperature to a default value the user can configure. You could translate this with the following function:

```
def monitorTemperature(current: Double, recovery: Double): Double =
  if (current >= 0) current else recovery
```

This function monitorTemperature behaves in different ways depending on the *purity* of its parameters. Consider the following function invocations:

```
scala> monitorTemperature(current = 5, recovery = 10)
val res0: Double = 5.0

scala> monitorTemperature(
     |   current = 5,
     |   recovery = { println("EMERGENCY! Triggering recovery"); 10 }
     | )

EMERGENCY! triggering recovery
val res1: Double = 5.0
```

Both function calls are valid, but the second one behaves unpredictably: even when the current temperature is above the freezing threshold, an unexpected (and confusing!) message appears in the console.

Later in the book you'll learn about lazy evaluation and how to handle these use cases in which you'd like to evaluate a given function parameter only if needed. For now, let's discuss purity and how it differs from impurity. In the capstone, you will use pure functions to determine the winner of the game "Paper, Rock, Scissors, Lizard, Spock!"

> **Consider this**
> Can you think of another example in which your function may suffer from some unexpected behavior because of the possibly impure values you passed as parameters?

 ## 21.1 A definition of purity

A pure function is total and has no side effects. Let's see what each of these terms mean.

> **TOTALITY** A function is total if it is well-defined for every input: it must terminate for every parameter value and return an instance that matches its return type.

Let's consider the following functions:

```
def plus2(n: Int): Int = n + 2                      // total

def div(n: Int): Int = 42 / n                       // non-total

def rec(n: Int): Int = if (n > 0) n else rec(n - 1) // non-total
```

The function plus2 is total because for every possible integer passed as its parameter, it terminates and returns an integer value as the result of its evaluation. The div function is not total because even if it always ends, it doesn't always return a value of type Int. It throws an ArithmeticException, its parameter n equal to zero. A thrown exception is an unexpected value not represented in its return type. Finally, the rec function is not total because it never terminates for any integer less or equal to zero.

Quick Check 21.1   Which of the following functions are total? Why?

```
1  def opsA(n: Int): Int = if(n <= 0) n else n + 1
2  def opsB(n: Int): Int = if(n <= 0) n else opsB(n + 1)
3  def selectException(predicate: Boolean): Exception =
     if (predicate) new IllegalStateException("msg here")
     else new ArithmeticException("another msg here")
4  def anotherToString(obj: AnyRef): String = {
     Thread.sleep(1000) // measured in millis
     obj.toString
   }
5  def validateDistance(dist: Double): Double =
     if (dist < 0) {
       throw new IllegalStateException("Distance cannot be negative")
     } else dist
```

SIDE EFFECTS   A side effect is an operation that has an observable interchange with elements outside its local scope. It affects (i.e., writes side effect) or is affected by (i.e., reads side effect) the state of your application by interacting with the outside world. Here are a few examples:

```
def negate(predicate: Boolean): Boolean = !predicate
                                       // no side effect


class Counter {
  private var counter = 0

  def incr(): Unit = counter += 1      // (write) side effect
  def get(): Int = counter             // (read) side effect
 }

def hello(name: String): String = {
  val msg = s"Hello $name"
  println(msg)                         // (write) side effect
  msg
 }
```

The function negate has no side effects; its only instruction acts on its parameter to produce a return value. The function Counter.incr contains a (write) side effect: every time you invoke the function, it changes the assignment for the variable counter, which is a code element that lives outside of its local scope. Counter.get also has a (read) side effect: given the same input, it returns a different integer depending on the variable counter's current assignment. The function hello has a (write) side effect because its println instruction produces a message in the console, a component shared across your application that lives independently from its local scope.

Quick Check 21.2   Which of the following functions have side effects? Why?

```
1 def div(a: Int, b: Int): Int = {
    if (b == 0) throw new Exception("Cannot divide by zero")
    else a / b
  }
2 def getUserAge(id: Int): Int = {
    val user = getUser(id) // gets data for a database
    user.id
  }
3 def powerOf2(d: Double): Double = Math.pow(2, d)
4 def anotherPowerOf2(d: Double): Double = {
    println(s"Computing 2^$d...")
    Math.pow(2, d)
  }
5 def getCurrentTime(): Long = System.currentTimeMillis()
```

Quick Check 21.3   A pure function is total and has no side effects. Consider the code snippets provided in Quick Checks 21.1 and 21.2: which ones are pure?

21.2 Differentiating between pure and impure functions

In the previous section, you discovered that a function is pure if total and without side effects. You can describe this concept in a less formal way as follows: a function is pure if only its parameters determine its behavior, which its return type describes (figure 21.1).

A pure function guarantees that it always returns the same output given the same input parameters. In other words, you can replace its invocation with its return value and obtain the same outcome: This concept is called *referential transparency*, and it has several practical implications.

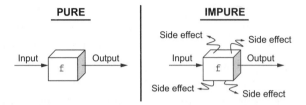

Figure 21.1   A visual representation of the differences between pure and impure functions. Given an input, a pure function returns an output. An impure one produces additional effects not represented in its return value.

Suppose you have the following two functions, called pureF and impureF, that take a string as their parameter and return another string as the result of some computation:

```
def pureF(name: String): String = s"Hi $name!"

def impureF(name: String): String = {
  println("...doing something here...")
  s"Hi $name!"
}
```

The function pureF is pure, while the function impureF is impure.

You can substitute the function call pureF("Bob") with the string "Hi Bob!". However, swapping the function call impureF("Bob") with the string "Hi Bob!" would not produce the same result because the print instruction in the console would be missing.

Functions with no parameters: Parentheses or no parentheses?

When declaring a function with no parameters, you should omit the parentheses if the function is pure (i.e., def f = ???) and vice versa; specify them if the function is impure (i.e., def f() = ???).

This rule is a style suggestion rather than a law imposed by the compiler.

Quick Check 21.4   Which of the following statements are true?

1 Pure functions do more than just compute a value.
2 You can replace calls to impure functions with their return value without losing functionalities.
3 Pure functions are total.
4 A function that throws exceptions is pure.
5 A function with side effects is impure.

 **Summary**

In this lesson, my objective was to teach you about the functional concept of purity.

- You learned that pure functions are total and have no side effects.
- You also discovered referential transparency and how you can use it to differentiate between pure and impure functions.

Let's see if you got this!

TRY THIS   Which of the following functions are pure? Which are impure?

```scala
1 def welcome(n: String): String = s"Welcome $n!"
2 def printWelcome(n: String): Unit =
    println(s"Welcome $n!")
3 def slowMultiplication(a: Int, b: Int): Int = {
    Thread.sleep(1000) // 1 second
    a * b
  }
4 def saveUser(user: User): User = {
    insertUser(user) // inserts in a database
    user
  }
5 def getUser(id: Int): User = {
    selectUser(id) // searches in a database
  }
```

 Answers to quick checks

Quick Check 21.1

1   The function opsA is total because it always terminates and returns an integer for every integer passed as its parameter.
2   The function opsB is not total: it calls itself recursively and never terminates for positive integers.
3   The function selectException is total because it returns an exception: it computes a value that matches its return type for every input. The keyword *throw* is missing, so the function does not throw the exception, but it returns it as a class instance.
4   The function anotherToString is total: for every input, it eventually terminates after sleeping for 1 second (or 1,000 milliseconds) and returning a string. What if the function was to block for a much more extended period (e.g., 10 years); would you still consider it total?
5   The function validateDistance is not total because it throws an exception for any negative double number.

Quick Check 21.2

1 The function `div` has no side effects; throwing exceptions is not a side effect because it does not change the state of components external to the function.
2 The function `getUserAge` returns different results depending on which objects are in the database, which is a (read) side effect.
3 The function `powerOf2` has no side effects as its return value depends entirely on its input.
4 The function `anotherPowerOf2` has a (write) side effect: every time you call it, it produces a new message to the console, changing its state.
5 The function `getCurrentTime` returns a value that depends on your machine's internal clock, which is a (read) side effect.

Quick Check 21.3 In Quick Check 21.1, the functions `opsA`, `selectException`, `anotherToString` are pure. In Quick Check 21.2, there is only one pure function: `powerOf2`.

Quick Check 21.4

1 False
2 False
3 True
4 False
5 True

OPTION

After reading this lesson, you will be able to

- Represent a nullable value using `Option`
- Use pattern matching on instances of the type `Option`

Now that you've mastered higher order functions, you'll learn about the type `Option`. Using `null` to represent nullable or missing values in Scala is an antipattern; use the type `Option` instead. The type `Option` ensures that you deal with both the presence or the absence of an element. Thanks to the `Option` type, you can make your system safer by avoiding nasty `NullPointerExceptions` at runtime. Your code will also be cleaner as you will no longer preventively check for `null` values; you will be able to clearly mark nullable values and act accordingly only when effectively needed. The concept of an optional type is not exclusive to Scala. If you are familiar with another language's `Option` type, such as Java, you will recognize a few similarities between them. You'll analyze the structure of the `Option` type. You'll also discover how to create optional values and analyze them using pattern matching. In the capstone, you will use `Option` to represent that a winner for the game "Paper, Rock, Scissors, Lizard, Spock!" may be missing in case of a tie.

> **Consider this**
> Suppose you need to design a structure to represent nullable values: how would you indicate that an element may or may not be there?

22.1 Why Option?

Suppose you defined the following function to calculate the square root of an integer:

```
def sqrt(n: Int): Double =
    if (n >= 0) Math.sqrt(n) else null
```

This function has a fundamental problem. Its signature (i.e., *what* a function does) does not provide any information about its return value being nullable: you need to look at its implementation (i.e., *how* a function computes a value) and remember to deal with a potentially null value. This approach is particularly prone to errors as you can easily forget to handle the null case, causing a NullPointerException at runtime, and it forces you to write a lot of defensive code to protect against null:

```
val x: Int = ???
val result = sqrt(x)
if (result == null) {
    // protect from null here
} else {
    // do things here
}
```

The type Option is equivalent to a wrapper around your value to provide the essential information it may be missing. Thanks to the use of Option, you no longer need to look at the specific implementation of a function to discover if its return value is nullable because this information will be in its signature. The compiler will also make sure that you handle both cases when Option is present and when it is absent, making your application safer at runtime.

 ## 22.2 Creating an Option

Now that we've discussed how the use of the type Option can improve your code's quality, let's see how you can create instances for it. A nullable value either exists or is missing.

Listing 22.1 The Option type

```
package scala

sealed abstract class Option[A]
```

```
case class Some[A](a: A) extends Option[A]
case object None extends Option[Nothing]
```

Let's analyze its definition line by line.

- package scala

  The Option type lives in the scala package, so it is already available in your scope and there is no need for an explicit import.

- sealed abstract class Option[A]

  Option is an abstract class, so you cannot initialize it directly. It is sealed: it has a well-defined set of possible implementations (i.e., Some of a given value and None). For the first time, you also encountered the Scala notation for generics: Option[A]. An optional type works independently from the actual instance it contains. You would expect an optional value to behave in the same way as an optional integer, an optional string, or any other optional value. With the notation Option[A], you tell the compiler that you will associate Option with a type that you will provide during initialization; in other words, Option has a type parameter. Scala has a convention of using uppercase letters of the alphabet for type parameters, the reason Option uses A, but you can provide any other name for it.

- case class Some[A](a: A) extends Option[A]

  Some is case class and a valid implementation of Option that represents the presence of a value. It has a type parameter A that defines the type of the value it contains. Some[A] is an implementation of Option[A], which implies that Some[Int] is a valid implementation for Option[Int] but not for Option[String]:

  ```
  scala> val optInt: Option[Int] = Some(1)
  val optInt: Option[Int] = Some(1)

  scala> val optString: Option[String] = Some(1)
          error: type mismatch;
          found   : Int(1)
          required: String
  ```

  Scala's type inference is about to infer type parameters. For this reason, you can write Some(1) instead of Some[Int](1).

- case object None extends Option[Nothing]

  None is the other possible implementation for Option, and it represents the absence of a value. It is a case object, which means it is a serializable singleton object. You can apply the concept of a missing value to any instance independently from its type. For this reason, None doesn't have a type parameter, but it extends

Option[Nothing]. Nothing has a special meaning in Scala: it is the subclass of every other class, and it is at the bottom of the class hierarchy (figure 22.1).

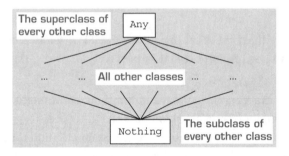

Figure 22.1   In Scala, the types Any and Nothing have a special meaning. Any is the superclass of every other class; in other words, it is the root of the class hierarchy. Nothing is at the bottom of the class hierarchy; it is the subclass of every other class.

Because None extends Option[Nothing], you can use None as a valid implementation for Option independently of its type parameter. Thanks to its special meaning, Nothing will always be compatible with the type parameter you provided:

```
scala> val optInt: Option[Int] = None
val optInt: Option[Int] = None

scala> val optString: Option[String] = None
val optString: Option[String] = None
```

The terms None, Nothing, and null can be confusing here, so let's recap what each of them means. None is an instance of the class Option, and it represents a missing nullable value. Nothing is a type that you can associate with every other Scala type. The term null is a keyword of the language to indicate a missing reference to an object.

You can now reimplement your sqrt function to use the type Option.

Listing 22.2 The sqrt function with Option

```
def sqrt(n: Int): Option[Double] =
  if (n >= 0) Some(Math.sqrt(n)) else None
```

Think in Scala: class vs. type

This lesson considers the terms *class* and *type* as synonymous for simplicity; however, this is not always the case.

A class represents a code element with a particular behavior that you can instantiate through its constructor. A type uniquely identifies a much broader category of items you can use in your programs. Let's use the Scala REPL to see a few examples in action.

String has the same class and type:

```
scala> import scala.reflect.runtime.universe._
import scala.reflect.runtime.universe._

scala> classOf[String]
val res0: Class[String] = class java.lang.String

scala> typeOf[String]
val res1: reflect.runtime.universe.Type = String
```

This is not the case when comparing Option[Int] with Option[String]. They both belong to the class Option but have different types:

```
scala> classOf[Option[Int]]
val res2: Class[Option[Int]] = class scala.Option

scala> classOf[Option[Int]] == classOf[Option[String]]
val res3: Boolean = true

scala> typeOf[Option[Int]]
val res4: reflect.runtime.universe.Type = scala.Option[Int]

scala> typeOf[Option[String]]
val res5: reflect.runtime.universe.Type = scala.Option[String]

scala> typeOf[Option[Int]] == typeOf[Option[String]]
val res6: Boolean = false
```

Figure 22.2 provides a visual summary of Scala's Option type.

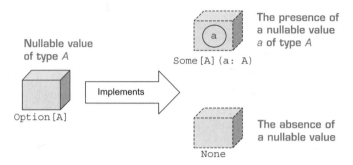

Figure 22.2   Visual summary of the structure of the Scala's Option type. An Option[A] is either a Some[A] of a value *a*, or None, which represents its absence.

Quick Check 22.1   Write a function called `filter` that takes two parameters of type String, called text and word, and returns an Option[String]. It should return either the original string if text contains word or no value.

Convert partial functions to total functions returning Option

In lesson 16, you learned about partial functions as a tool to abstract common-alities between functions. An example of a partial function is the following:

```scala
val log: PartialFunction[Int, Double] =
  { case x if x > 0 => Math.log(x) }
```

When you call a partial function on an input that is not defined, it will throw a MatchError exception, which is not ideal, as exceptions are unpredictable. Instead of using a partial function, you can define a total function that returns an optional value which will protect your code from an unexpected MatchError exception at runtime. For example, you could reimplement the function log as a total function as follows:

```scala
def log(x: Int): Option[Double] = x match {
  case x if x > 0 => Some(Math.log(x))
  case _ => None
}
```

Unless you are using an API or library that is explicitly requesting you to use partial functions, consider redefining your partial functions as total functions to make your code safer at runtime by avoiding possible unpredicted exceptions.

22.3 Pattern matching on Option

After looking at the structure of an Option, let's see how you can handle it.

In lesson 13, you learned that when pattern matching on a sealed item the compiler will warn you if you haven't considered all its possible implementations, as this could cause a MatchError exception. In lesson 19, you also saw how to pattern match case classes and case objects. Let's put everything together and see how you can pattern match on an optional value.

When handling an optional value, one possibility is to use pattern matching to consider both the presence and the absence of a value.

Listing 22.3 Pattern Matching over Option

```scala
def sqrt(n: Int): Option[Double] =
  if (n >= 0) Some(Math.sqrt(n)) else None


def sqrtOrZero(n: Int): Double =
  sqrt(n) match {
    case Some(result) => result
    case None => 0
  }
```

sqrt(n) returns a value with type Option[Double].

If the value is present, return it.

If the value is missing, return 0.

Note that pattern matching is not the only way to handle an optional value. In the next lesson, you'll discover how to achieve the same result using predefined higher order functions such as map and flatMap.

> **Quick Check 22.2** Write a function called greetings that takes an optional custom message as its parameter and returns a string. Use its optional parameter as its greeting message when defined (i.e., it contains a value); use the predefined message "Greetings, Human!" when missing. For example, greetings(Some("Hello Scala")) should return the string "Hello Scala", while greetings(None) should return "Greetings, Human!"

 **Summary**

In this lesson, my objective was to teach you about Scala's Option type:

- You discovered how you can use it to represent nullable values and improve the quality of your code.
- You learned how to create instances of Option and how to handle them using pattern matching.

Let's see if you got this!

> **TRY THIS** Define a case class Person to represent a person with a first name, an optional middle name, and a last name. Write a function that takes an instance of Person as its parameter and returns a string describing its full name. For example, when representing a person with first name George, middle name Watson, and last name Lucas, it should return the string "George Watson Lucas". On the other hand, when representing a person with first name Martin, no middle name, and last name Odersky, it should return "Martin Odersky".

 Answers to quick checks

> **Quick Check 22.1** A possible implementation for the function filter is the following:
>
> ```
> def filter(text: String, word: String): Option[String] =
>   if (text.contains(word)) Some(text) else None
> ```

> **Quick Check 22.2** You could implement the function greetings as follows:
>
> ```
> def greetings(customMessage: Option[String]): String =
>   customMessage match {
>     case Some(message) => message
>     case None => "Greetings, Human!"
>   }
> ```

WORKING WITH OPTION:
MAP AND FLATMAP

After reading this lesson, you will be able to

- Transform an element contained in an Option using the map operation
- Simplify a nested optional structure using flatten
- Chain optional values together using flatMap

In the previous lesson, you discovered the type Option and how to pattern match on it. After working with optional types for some time, you will realize that some of its operations are particularly recurrent. The class Option offers you a set of higher order functions for them to be more productive, and you do not have to use pattern matching every time. This lesson will introduce you to some of the most common and useful predefined functions on Option. You'll discover how to transform an optional value using map. You'll see how to simplify a nested optional structure using flatten. Finally, you'll learn how to combine optional values in an order sequence using flatMap. These functions describe patterns common to many Scala types other than Option: understanding them is crucial as you'll encounter them in many different contexts. In the capstone, you will use the functions map on Option to extract data from the winner (if any) of the game "Paper, Rock, Scissors, Lizard, Spock!"

Consider this
What are the fundamental operations you can perform on an optional value?
What if you have more optional values that need to be combined?

 ## 23.1 Transforming an Option

Let's start by showing you how you can transform the content of an optional value using the map, flatten, and flatMap methods, which are among the most fundamental and recurrent helper functions defined on Option.

Suppose you need to represent the following scenario involving a car and its owner:

- A car has a model, and it may have an owner and a registration plate.
- A person has a name and age and may have a driver's license.
- A car may have no owner (e.g., when it is brand-new).
- A car may have no registration plate if its owner hasn't registered the vehicle with the local authorities yet.
- A person without a driving license is still entitled to purchase a car.

You can translate these requirements using two case classes, called Car and Person.

Listing 23.1 The Car and Person case classes

```
case class Car(model: String,
               owner: Option[Person],
               registrationPlate: Option[String])

case class Person(name: String,
                  age: Int,
                  drivingLicense: Option[String])
```

Let's see how the functions map, flatten, and flatMap can help you extract information on your data set.

23.1.1 The map function

Suppose that you'd like to find the name of the owner of a particular car. You could use pattern matching as follows:

```
def ownerName(car: Car): Option[String] =
  car.owner match {
```

```
        case Some(p) => Some(p.name)
        case None => None
    }
```

You can rewrite this function using the function map rather than pattern matching.

Listing 23.2 Example usage of map on Option

```
def ownerName(car: Car): Option[String] =
    car.owner.map(p => p.name)
```

In Scala, you refer to the operation of applying a function to the content of an optional value as map. The function map is a higher order function defined on Option that takes a function f as its parameter:

- If the optional value is present, it will apply the function f to it and return it wrapped as optional value.
- If the optional instance is None, it will return it without applying any function.

Listing 23.3 The function map on Option

```
def map[B](f: A => B): Option[B] =
    this match {                          ←——— This is a keyword that
        case Some(a) => Some(f(a))             refers to the current
        case None => None                      instance of the class.
    }
```

Compare the implementation of map with your implementation of the function ownerName using pattern matching: they look very similar and have the same structure. Look at the signature of the map function for the abstract class Option[A]:

```
def map[B](f: A => B): Option[B]
```

You do not need to remember what a map function does, as its signature informs you of that. If you have an instance of Option[A] and you have a function f that transforms an A into a B, you can apply the map operation to obtain a value of type Option[B]. Figure 23.1 provides a summary of how the higher order function map operates on an instance of Option.

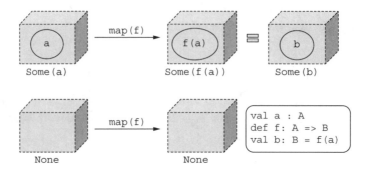

Figure 23.1   Visual representation of the map operation on Option. If the optional value is present, map will apply the function f to it and wrap its result in a Some instance. It will return None without applying the function f if the optional value is absent.

Quick Check 23.1   Consider the case class Car shown in listing 23.1. Write a function called extractRegistrationPlate that takes an instance of Car and returns an optional registration plate with its text all uppercase. Use the function map on Option:

```
def extractRegistrationPlate(car: Car): Option[String]
```

23.1.2 The flatten function

Suppose you need to retrieve the driver's license of an owner of a car, if there is one. You could achieve this using map as follows:

```
def ownerDrivingLicense(car: Car): Option[Option[String]] =
  car.owner.map(_.drivingLicense)
```

The ownerDrivingLicense returns a value of type [Option[String]]: the first optional type indicates if an owner exists; the second, if the owner has a driving license. You may want to keep this distinction in a particular business context, but it doesn't seem natural in a general case. As a human, you expect the value either to be there or not; you do not say that a value "may may be there" but that a value "may be there."

You can use the flatten function to combine two nested optional values.

Listing 23.4 Example usage of flatten on Option

```
def ownerDrivingLicense(car: Car): Option[String] =
  car.owner.map(_.drivingLicense).flatten
```

The function flatten acts on an instance of Option[Option[A]], and it returns an Option[A]:

- If the outer optional value is a Some of a value, return the inner instance of Option.
- If the other optional value is None, return it.

Here's a possible implementation of the function flatten on an instance of Option[Option[A]].

Listing 23.5 The function flatten on Option

```
def flatten: Option[A] =
  this match {
    case Some(opt) => opt
    case None => None
  }
```

The function flatten merges two optional values into one; if you need to flatten more than two values, you can reapply it multiple times.

> **Quick Check 23.2**   Write a function called superFlatten that takes an instance of Option[Option[Option[String]]] and returns a value of type Option[String] using the function flatten:
>
> ```
> def superFlatten(
>         opt: Option[Option[Option[String]]]
>     ): Option[String]
> ```

23.1.3 The flatMap function

In listing 23.4, you implemented a function to extract the driver's license of a car owner using the function map with the flatten function:

```
def ownerDrivingLicense(car: Car): Option[String] =
  car.owner.map(_.drivingLicense).flatten
```

These combined operations are so common that Scala has created an ad hoc function for it called flatMap. Listing 23.6 shows you how to rewrite the ownerDrivingLicense function using flatMap rather than combining map and flatten operations.

Listing 23.6 Example usage of flatMap on Option

```
def ownerDrivingLicense(car: Car): Option[String] =
  car.owner.flatMap(_.drivingLicense)
```

In Scala, the function flatMap is a higher order function on Option[A] that applies a function f, which returns an optional value itself—in other words, f has type A => Option[B]:

- It will apply the function f to it if the optional value is present. The function f returns an instance of Option, so you do not need to wrap the result in an optional value.
- It will return it without applying any function if the optional instance is None.

Listing 23.7 The function flatMap on Option

```
def flatMap[B](f: A => Option[B]): Option[B] =
  this match {
    case Some(a) => f(a)
    case None => None
  }
```

Figure 23.2 shows a representation of the flatMap function on Option.

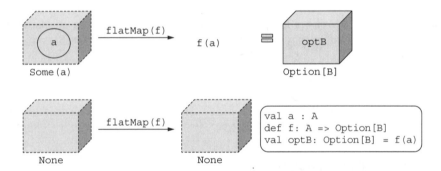

Figure 23.2 Visual representation of the flatMap operation on Option. If the value is present, flatMap will apply the function f to it, which will produce a new optional value. It will return None without applying any function f if absent.

Quick Check 23.3 Write a function called ownerBelowAge that takes two parameters: an instance of Car and an age parameter of type Int. It returns an optional string containing the car owner's name if younger than the given age. Use the flatMap function on Option.

```
def ownerBelowAge(car: Car, age: Int): Option[String]
```

Look at the flatMap function again to understand why it is so powerful. Consider you have an optional car, and you'd like to extract the driver's license of its owner, if there is one. Its implementation using pattern matching could be similar to the following:

```
def ownerDrivingLicense(optCar: Option[Car]): Option[String] =
  optCar match {
    case None => None
    case Some(car) =>
      car.owner match {
        case None => None
        case Some(person) =>
          person.drivingLicense
      }
  }
```

Having two nested pattern matching constructs makes your code extremely difficult to read. You could get rid of the nested pattern matching by taking advantage of the fact that both Car and Person are case classes, so you can easily decompose them:

```
def ownerDrivingLicense(optCar: Option[Car]): Option[String] =
  optCar match {
    case Some(Car(_, Some(Person(_, _, drivingLicense)), _)) =>
      drivingLicense
    case None => None
  }
```

This second version of your code is a bit more readable but strictly coupled with your case classes' structure. You'll need to remember the order of their fields when implementing the function, and you'll need to modify it every time you add, remove, or reorder any of them. Finally, let's try to use the flatMap function.

Listing 23.8 Chaining optional values with flatMap

```
def ownerDrivingLicense(optCar: Option[Car]): Option[String] =
  optCar.flatMap { car =>
    car.owner.flatMap { person =>
      person.drivingLicense
    }
  }
```

The code is more readable and independent from the specific structure of the involved case classes. In the next lesson, you'll discover another and even more readable way of implementing this function using *for-comprehension*.

Because of its unique structure, the flatMap function allows you to chain multiple optional operations together. Figure 23.3 provides a visual summary of how you can use flatMap to combine multiple optional values in an ordered sequence. Consider you have an instance of Option[A] and due functions f: A => Option[B] and g: B => Option[C]; by calling flatMap(f) you can transform your instance into Option[B] and then apply flatMap(g) to it and obtain Option[C].

Figure 23.3   Example of chaining optional operations using flatMap. First, you apply flatMap(f) to an instance of Option[A] to produce Option[B]. Then, you apply flatMap(g) to it and obtain Option[C].

 **Summary**

In this lesson, my objective was to teach you about transforming an optional value.

- You saw that the map function applies a function to the element of an Option.
- You discovered that you can use the flatten function to unify nested optional structures.
- You learned that the flatMap operation is the composition of a map followed by a flatten function to combine optional values in an ordered sequence.

Let's see if you got this!

TRY THIS   Consider the following scenario:

- A student has an ID and a name.
- A student may have a professor assigned as a tutor.
- A professor has an ID and a name.
- A professor may have the help of an assistant.
- An assistant has an ID and a name.

You can translate this to code with the following case classes:

```
case class Student(id: Long,
                   name: String,
                   tutor: Option[Professor])
```

```
case class Professor(id: Long,
                     name: String,
                     assistant: Option[Assistant])
case class Assistant(id: Long, name: String)
```

Write functions to extract the following information:

1 Retrieve the name of the tutor of a given student.
2 Find the ID of a professor's assistant who is tutoring a given student.
3 Return a given student only if they have a tutor with a given ID.

 # Answers to quick checks

Quick Check 23.1 A possible implementation for the function extractRegistration-Plate is the following:

```
def extractRegistrationPlate(car: Car): Option[String] =
  car.registrationPlate.map(_.toUpperCase)
```

Quick Check 23.2 You can implement the superFlatten function by applying the flatten function twice as follows:

```
def superFlatten(
      opt: Option[Option[Option[String]]]
    ): Option[String] =
  opt.flatten.flatten
```

Notice how much simpler this implementation is compared to its equivalent using pattern matching.

Quick Check 23.3 A possible implementation for the function ownerBelowAge is the following:

```
def ownerBelowAge(car: Car, age: Int): Option[String] =
  car.owner.flatMap { p =>
    if (p.age < age) Some(p.name)
    else None
  }
```

WORKING WITH OPTION: FOR-COMPREHENSION

After reading this lesson, you will be able to

- Chain optional values together using `for-comprehension`
- Introduce conditions within `for-comprehension` constructs
- Code using the most common operations defined on `Option`

In the previous lesson, you learned how to use the functions `map`, `flatten`, and `flatMap` to manipulate optional values. In this lesson, you are also going to discover a more readable and elegant way of combining instances of `Option` thanks to a new type of construct called `for-comprehension`. You'll also see how to integrate Boolean conditions to control how values are chained together. Finally, you'll discover other useful operations implemented for `Option`, such as `isDefined`, `getOrElse`, `find`, and `exists`. In the capstone, you will use the function `getOrElse` on `Option` to provide an alternative message for your HTTP request when a draw of the game "Paper, Rock, Scissors, Lizard, Spock!" occurs.

> **Consider this**
>
> Assume you implemented a function to combine many (e.g., five or more)
> optional values in an ordered sequence using flatMap. Can you think of any
> aspect of your implementation that could make your code difficult to maintain
> and read?

 ## 24.1 For-comprehension on Option

In the previous lesson, you discovered the flatMap function and how you can use it to
concatenate optional operations. Review the code from listing 23.8:

```
def ownerDrivingLicense(optCar: Option[Car]): Option[String] =
  optCar.flatMap { car =>
    car.owner.flatMap { person =>
      person.drivingLicense
    }
  }
```

The code is fairly readable, but it requires you to nest many flatMap function calls
together. If you have to chain five or more optional operations together, your code will
look something like the following:

```
opA().flatMap{ a =>
  opB(a).flatMap { b =>
    opC(b).flatMap { c =>
      opD(c).flatMap { d =>
        opE(d)
      }
    }
  }
}
```

We like to refer to this as *rocket coding*: you write so many nested operations that force
you to indent your code many times, making it difficult to read. Scala introduced some
syntactic sugar (i.e., an alternative syntax to simplify verbose operations) for the map and
flatMap functions called for-comprehension.

24.1.1 For-comprehension as syntactic sugar for nested map and flatMap calls

Listing 24.1 shows you how you can reimplement your ownerDrivingLicense function using for-comprehension.

Listing 24.1 Example of for-comprehension

```
def ownerDrivingLicense(optCar: Option[Car]): Option[String] =
  for {
    car <- optCar
    person <- car.owner
    drivingLicense <- person.drivingLicense
  } yield drivingLicense
```

The expressions optCar, car.owner, and person.drivingLicense are all producing an optional value: they have type Option[Car], Option[Person], Option[String], respectively. The values car, person, and drivingLicense are their corresponding extracted values: type Car, Person, and String. You also encountered a new keyword, *yield*, which returns a value you can compute using the extracted values wrapped into an Option. In this case, it returns the value of drivingLicense as an optional value. As soon as the for-comprehension finds an absent optional value (e.g., car.owner is None), it evaluates the entire expression as None.

You can use for-comprehension on every class with a flatMap function. You'll soon discover that this applies to types other than Option, so your code can avoid an excessive nested structure, which makes it easier to read and understand. You can rewrite the earlier example of chained five or more operations as follows:

```
for {
  a <- opA()
  b <- opB(a)
  c <- opC(b)
  d <- opD(c)
  e <- opE(d)
} yield e
```

Quick Check 24.1   Consider the following snippet of code:

```scala
def f(n: Int): Option[Int] =
  if (n < 5) Some(n * 2)
  else None

def foo(optA: Option[Int]) =
  for {
    a <- optA
    b <- f(a)
    c <- Some(5 * b)
  } yield c
```

What is the value returned by each of the following function calls? Verify your hypothesis using the Scala REPL.

1 foo(Some(1))
2 foo(Some(5))
3 foo(None)

24.1.2 Filtering values within for-comprehension

Assume that you have to modify your ownerDrivingLicense function to return the drivingLicense all uppercase and only for an owner with a given name. You could implement it using flatMap as follows:

```scala
def ownerDrivingLicense(
      optCar: Option[Car],
      ownerName: String): Option[String] =
  optCar.flatMap { car =>
    car.owner.flatMap { person =>
      if (person.name == ownerName)
        person.drivingLicense.map(_.toUpperCase)
      else None
    }
  }
```

Listing 24.2 Example of for-comprehension with if condition

```scala
def ownerDrivingLicense(
      optCar: Option[Car],
      ownerName: String): Option[String] =
  for {
    car <- optCar
```

```
    person <- car.owner
    if person.name == ownerName
    drivingLicense <- person.drivingLicense
} yield drivingLicense.toUppercase
```

When the condition is false, the chain will stop and cause the expression to return None.

You can modify the yield value before returning it.

You can modify the yield values in for-comprehension (e.g., drivingLicense.toUppercase) and add conditions to stop the combination of values by adding the keyword *if* followed by a Boolean expression (e.g., if person.name == ownerName). Figure 24.1 shows a syntax diagram on for-comprehensions in Scala.

The value contained in the optional value

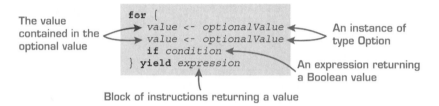

```
for [
    value <- optionalValue
    value <- optionalValue
    if condition
} yield expression
```

An instance of type Option

An expression returning a Boolean value

Block of instructions returning a value

• It returns the expression wrapped into a Some instance only if all Option instances contain a value.

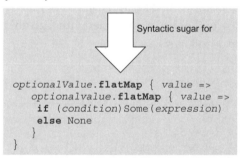

Syntactic sugar for

```
optionalValue.flatMap { value =>
    optionalvalue.flatMap { value =>
    if (condition) Some (expression)
    else None
    }
}
```

Figure 24.1 Summary of for-comprehension on Option, which allows you to chain optional operations thanks to their syntactic sugar to rewrite nested map and flatMap function calls.

Quick Check 24.2 In the previous lesson, you implemented a function, ownerBelow-Age, that returns the car owner's name if younger than a given age; reimplement it using for-comprehension.

```
def ownerBelowAge(car: Car, age: Int): Option[String]
```

24.2 Other operations on Option

The functions map, flatten, and flatMap are some of the available operations you can perform on an optional value. Other commonly used functions defined for an instance of Option[A] are as follows:

- isDefined returns true if an optional instance has a value, false otherwise.

  ```
  def isDefined: Boolean
  ```

  ```
  Some(1).isDefined      // returns true
  None.isDefined         // returns false
  ```

- The function isEmpty is the opposite of isDefined: it returns true if an optional instance is absent, false otherwise.

  ```
  def isEmpty: Boolean
  ```

  ```
  Some(1).isEmpty        // returns false
  None.isEmpty           // returns true
  ```

- getOrElse returns the optional value if present; otherwise, it will execute the provided default operation.

  ```
  def getOrElse(default: A): A
  ```

  ```
  Some(1).getOrElse(-1)   // returns 1
  None.getOrElse(-1)      // returns -1
  ```

- find returns an optional value if its element satisfies a given predicate.

  ```
  def find(predicate: A => Boolean): Option[A]
  ```

  ```
  Some(10).find(_ > 5)    // returns Some(10)
  Some(1).find(_ > 5)     // returns None
  None.find(_ > 5)        // returns None
  ```

- The function exists combines find with isDefined: it returns true if the value is present and satisfies a given predicate, false otherwise.

  ```
  def exists(predicate: A => Boolean): Boolean
  ```

  ```
  Some(10).exists(_ > 5)   // returns true
  Some(1).exists(_ > 5)    // returns false
  None.exists(_ > 5)       // returns false
  ```

Think in Scala: Do not use the function get on Option

You may have noticed that Option has an implementation for a function called get, which returns the value if present and throws a java.util.NoSuchElement- Exception if absent. Because it throws an exception, you should consider it unsafe to use and an antipattern because the compiler will no longer be able to guarantee that your implementation does not throw exceptions at runtime.

Do not use the function get on Option. When tempted to do so, you should ask yourself if that type should be optional in the first place. Maybe you should consider resolving the optional wrapper using pattern matching. Perhaps you need to reevaluate the operations you are performing on an optional value.

For example, consider the following function foo:

```scala
def foo(a: Option[Int]): Int = if (a.isDefined) a.get else 0
```

It would be best if you rewrote it using the getOrElse operation on Option as follows:

```scala
def foo(a: Option[Int]): Int = a.getOrElse(0)
```

Quick Check 24.3 Implement a function called carWithLicensedOwner that takes and returns an optional car instance if its owner has a driving license.

```scala
def carWithLicensedOwner(optCar: Option[Car]): Option[Car]
```

 Summary

In this lesson, my objective was to teach you about for-comprehension in Scala.

- You learned that for-comprehension is an alternative, more readable way to rewrite nested flatMap expressions to chain optional values together.
- You saw how to use if conditions to filter the values to consider in a for-comprehension construct.
- You had a quick tour of other useful functions available on an instance of Option.

Let's see if you got this!

TRY THIS   Let's reconsider the scenario at the end of lesson 23 that describes a student-professor-assistant relation:

You can translate the code with the following case classes:

```scala
case class Student(id: Long,
                   name: String,
                   tutor: Option[Professor])
case class Professor(id: Long,
                     name: String,
                     assistant: Option[Assistant])
case class Assistant(id: Long, name: String)
```

Reimplement the following functions using for-comprehension and the other operations on Option you saw in this lesson:

1 Retrieve the name of the tutor of a given student.
2 Find the ID of a professor's assistant who is tutoring a given student.
3 Return a given student only if they have a tutor with a given ID.

 Answers to quick checks

Quick Check 24.1

1 The expression foo(Some(1)) evaluates to Some(10): all the optional values are present, so the chain of operations is completed and its value returned.
2 The function call foo(Some(5)) returns None: op(5) returns None, causing the chain to break.
3 foo(None) returns None because the first value of the for-comprehension expression is None.

Quick Check 24.2 You can reimplement the function ownerBelowAge as follows:

```scala
def ownerBelowAge(car: Car, age: Int): Option[String] =
  for {
    person <- car.owner
    if person.age < age
  } yield person.name
```

Quick Check 24.3 A possible implementation of the function carWithLicensedOwner is the following:

```scala
def carWithLicensedOwner(optCar: Option[Car]): Option[Car] =
  optCar.find { car =>
    car.owner.flatMap(_.drivingLicense).isDefined
  }
```

TUPLE AND UNAPPLY

After reading this lesson, you'll be able to

- Group elements using tuples
- Retrieve data from tuples
- Extract information from an instance of a class using the unapply method

In the previous lessons, you discovered how to handle nullable values using Option. In this lesson, you'll learn about tuples, one of the most basic data structures Scala offers to quickly group data in a given order. You'll then combine what you have seen about tuples and the type Option to discuss the unapply method. The function unapply is complementary to apply: you use the apply function to create a class instance and unapply to extract information from it.

Pattern matching is one of the most powerful tools you can use. So far, you have seen that you can pattern match over raw values (e.g., string, integers, doubles), objects, and case classes. By defining an unapply method for a class, you'll also be able to pattern match on them. In the capstone, you'll use tuples to group data together, and you'll define unapply methods to pattern match over classes without exposing sensitive information.

> **Consider this**
> Suppose you need to represent the concept of a debit card in your application. It must contain the name of its owner, its number, and its security code. For security reasons, you must ensure never to expose its owner's name and security code. How would you implement it so that you respect its business requirements, but without using the opportunity to pattern match on it?

 ## 25.1 Tuples

Suppose you have a website, and you'd like to know its number of visits for the previous day and month. You can use a third-party API to retrieve several statistics about your website. You call an existing function that looks similar to the following:

```
def get3rdPartyStats(): WebsiteStats = ???
```

```
case class WebsiteStats(
        lastHour: Long,
        lastDay: Long,
        lastMonth: Long,
        lastQuarter: Long,
        lastYear: Long
        /* many more fields here!*/)
```

The API offers this service for free for a limited number of requests, and it is not particularly performant. For these reasons, you would like to minimize your calls to it.

A first possible implementation could be calling the function and wrapping the information you need in a new case class.

Listing 25.1 Website stats using a case class

```
case class MyStats(lastDay: Long, lastMonth: Long)

def lastDayAndMonthStats(): MyStats = {
  val allStats = getStats()
  MyStats(allStats.lastDay, allStats.lastMonth)
}
```

Suppose you then discover that you need to write another function to extract the stats on your website for the last quarter and the last year. You could decide to write a similar function returning a new case class, MyStats2, containing last quarter and last year's data. This approach is not sustainable as it will cause you to create lots of classes to represent the same data many times.

When all you need is to group data without creating a specific representation for it, you can use tuples.

Listing 25.2 Website stats using tuples

```
def lastDayAndMonthStats(): (Long, Long) = {        The return type is a
  val allStats = getStats()                         tuple containing
  (allStats.lastDay, allStats.lastMonth)            two elements, both
}                                                    of type Long.

                    It builds a tuple of two
                    instances of type Long.
```

After defining the function lastDayAndMonthStats, you can either refer to its tuple or decompose it to save its elements:

```
val stats = lastDayAndMonthStats()
// stats refers to the entire tuple
```

```
val (lastDay, lastMonth) = lastDayAndMonthStats()
// lastDay refers to the first element of the tuple
// lastMonth refers to the second element of the tuple
```

In Scala, a tuple is a tool that allows you to quickly group data that can have a minimum of 1 item and a maximum of 22. You can define it by using round brackets to wrap its items, separated by a comma. Tuples have one or more elements. The compiler automatically decomposes a tuple containing only one element, the reason it evaluates the following expression to true:

```
scala> (1) == 1
val res0: Boolean = true
```

The compiler will not simplify tuples with two or more elements. Here are a few examples:

```
scala> (1,2,3) // tuple with 3 items of type Int
val res1: (Int, Int, Int) = (1,2,3)

scala> val a = "hello"
val a: String = hello

scala> (a, 1) // tuple with 2 item of type String and Int respectively
val res2: (String, Int) = (hello,1)
```

Scala also has an alternative constructor for tuples containing two elements, called the *arrow* constructor:

```
scala> 1 -> 2 // tuple with two elements of type Int
val res3: (Int, Int) = (1,2)

scala> 1 -> 2 -> 3
val res4: ((Int, Int), Int) = ((1,2),3)
// tuple of two elements: a tuple of two Int, and an Int
```

You can use pattern matching to deconstruct a tuple:

```
scala> val t = ("hello", "scala", "!")
val t: (String, String, String) = (hello,scala,!)

scala> t match {
     |    case (_, _, c) if c == "!" => "?"
     |    case (a,b,c) => s"$a-$b-$c"
     | }
val res5: String = ?
```

You can also use getters for each of its elements based on their order: the function _1 returns the first one, _2 the second one, _3 the third one, and so on.

```
scala> t._1
val res6: String = hello

scala> t._2
val res7: String = scala

scala> t._3
val res8: String = !
```

Using the getter functions defined for tuples is not particularly elegant. It doesn't provide any information about the structure. The item's position in the tuple is usually not indicative of what it represents. A more readable option is to assign the items of tuples to values using value decomposition:

```
scala> val (a, b, c) = ("hello", "scala", "!")
val a: String = hello
val b: String = scala
val c: String = !
```

Suppose you are interested in only extracting some items. In that case, you can use the underscore symbol to tell the compiler to discard the corresponding value and not bind it to any value:

```
scala> val (a, b, _) = ("hello", "scala", "!")
val a: String = hello
val b: String = scala
```

Figure 25.1 summarizes the different ways you can create and decompose a tuple.

2 elements: `(a, b)` or `a -> b`
3+ elements: `(a, b, ..., n)`

To extract data from a tuple t:

1) Pattern matching

```
t match {
    case (a, b) => ???
    case (a,b, ..., n) => ???
}
```

2) Getters

```
val a = t._1
val b = t._2
...
val n = t._n
```

3) Decomposition

```
val (a, b) = t
val (a, b, ..., n) = t
```

Figure 25.1 A summary of how to define a tuple and extract information from it. You can decompose a tuple using pattern matching or its predefined getters or value decomposition.

Think in Scala: When to use tuples?

Tuples are a great way to group data quickly, but they have several problems related to their lack of expressiveness. Use tuples in functions for temporary grouping of data but try to avoid using them outside of this context.

Every time you find yourself using tuples as return types of a function, especially if the tuple contains three or more items, you should ask yourself: is this function doing too many things? Try to refactor it by using a more expressive data structure, such as a case class.

Try to use tuples only in short and concise fragments in your program, which will make your code more readable and easier to maintain.

Quick Check 25.1 Define a tuple with three elements: the number 5, the string "Jane," and the integer 3. Extract the second and third items and multiply them together using the multiplier operator "*."

25.2 Implementing the unapply method

So far, you have discovered several advantages of having an unapply method, but you haven't seen how to implement it. Let's recap what it is before seeing how you can code it.

The unapply function is a static method defined in the companion object of a class. It is complementary to apply to extract information from a class instance. When declaring a case class, the compiler automatically adds an unapply method to its companion object. A pattern matching construct uses it to determine which parameters it should consider. You cannot use pattern on a class's parameters if it doesn't have an unapply method in its companion object.

Suppose you need to analyze the nutrition facts of a drink. To keep things simple, let's assume that your application uses the metric system: it measures all the liquids in milliliters and other amounts in grams. Your task consists of labeling a drink based on its saturated fat and sugar intake. Somewhere in your code you have already represented the concept of a drink and its nutrition facts as follows:

```
case class NutritionFacts(
  totalFat: Double /* grams */,
  saturatedFat: Double /* grams */,
  sugars: Double /* grams */,
  salt: Double /* grams */
)

class Drink(
  name: String,
  brand: String,
  size: Double /* milliliter */) {

  def loadNutritionFacts(): NutritionFacts = ???
  // it retrieves the data from a database or third party
}
```

One possible solution is to define a function to associate a Label to an instance of Drink.

Listing 25.3 Analyzing an instance of Drink

```
sealed trait Label
case object LowSaturatedFatAndSugar extends Label
case object LowSaturatedFat extends Label
```
The representation of all the possible labels for a drink

```
case object LowSugar extends Label
case object HighSaturatedFatAndSugar extends Label

val saturatedFatThreshold: Double = ???
val sugarThreshold: Double = ???
```

The threshold value
for saturated fat
and sugar

```
def analyze(drink: Drink): Label = drink.loadNutritionFacts() match {
  case NutritionFacts(_, saturatedFat, sugar, _)
    if saturatedFat < saturatedFatThreshold &&
       sugar < sugarThreshold => LowSaturatedFatAndSugar
  case NutritionFacts(_, saturatedFat, _, _)
    if saturatedFat < saturatedFatThreshold  => LowSaturatedFat
  case NutritionFacts(_, _, sugar, _)
    if sugar < sugarThreshold  => LowSugar
  case _   => HighSaturatedFatAndSugar
}
```

The function analyze respects the given requirements, but it is difficult to read due to the numerous instances of "_" to represent the discarded information and the long variable names. You need to distinguish between the concept of total and saturated fat, as both data is available during pattern matching.

Let's see how defining an unapply method for an instance of Drink could improve the readability of your code.

Listing 25.4 Analyzing an instance of Drink using unapply

```
/* Defining a companion object */

object Drink {

  def unapply(drink: Drink): Option[(Double, Double)] = {
    val nutritionFacts = drink.loadNutritionFacts()
    Some((nutritionFacts.saturatedFat, nutritionFacts.sugars))
  }
}
```

Implementing of a
companion object
for the class Drink

Adding an implementation
for unapply for an
instanceof Drink

```
sealed trait Label
case object LowSaturatedFatAndSugar extends Label
case object LowSaturatedFat extends Label
case object LowSugar extends Label
case object HighSaturatedFatAndSugar extends Label
```

```
val fatThreshold: Double = ???
val sugarThreshold: Double = ???

def analyze(drink: Drink): Label = drink match {
  case Drink(fat, sugar)
          if fat < fatThreshold &&
            sugar < sugarThreshold => LowSaturatedFatAndSugar
  case Drink(fat, _) if fat < fatThreshold   => LowSaturatedFat
  case Drink(_, sugar) if sugar < sugarThreshold  => LowSugar
  case _   => HighSaturatedFatAndSugar
}
```

Pattern matching only on the field (saturated) fat and sugar of a drink

The unapply method in the companion object Drink defines that the compiler should consider only its values for saturated fat and sugar when decomposing a Drink instance. This technique allows you to forget many unnecessary details when pattern matching, which simplifies your code greatly. For example, you do not need to remember that your program needs to load the nutritional facts from another source or that your instance contains many other fields. You can also refer to saturated fat as fat, as the ambiguity between total fat and saturated fat is no longer possible.

You usually define the unapply method in the companion object of a class. It always returns a nullable tuple: the tuple represents the information to extract, while Option allows you to select no data for specific instances of a type.

The compiler automatically implements an unapply method for case classes by extracting all its fields in order of declaration. For example, consider the following case class:

```
case class Person(name: String,  age: Int)
```

Listing 25.5 The unapply method of Person

```
object Person {

  def unapply(p: Person): Option[(String, Int)] =
    Some((p.name, p.age))
}
```

> **Quick Check 25.2** Reimplement the unapply method for an instance of Person so that it is not possible to extract information when pattern matching on any person with the name "James Bond."

Summary

In this lesson, my objective was to teach you about tuples and how to implement the unapply method.

- You saw how to create a tuple and the different ways you can extract information from it.
- You learned how to implement an unapply method for a class by combining the concepts of optional values and tuples.

Let's see if you got this!

TRY THIS Suppose you are writing a program to represent all the books in a public library. Represent a book to have the following information: its title, author, publication date, editor, an ISBN (i.e., a code that uniquely identifies it), and its total page number. You can search a book either by title, author, ISBN, or a combination of the three in the library search engine. Also, all the books in the search engine should have at least 10 pages. Implement a book representation for the library and define an unapply method to reflect your search engine's requirements.

Answers to quick checks

Quick Check 25.1 The following code multiples the second and third items of a tuple:

```
val (_, name, n) = (5, "Jane", 3)
name * n // returns "JaneJaneJane"
```

Quick Check 25.2 A possible implementation is the following:

```
object Person {

  def unapply(p: Person): Option[(String, Int)] = {
    if (p.name.equalsIgnoreCase("James Bond")) None
    else Some((p.name, p.age))
  }
}
```

ROCK, PAPER, SCISSORS, LIZARD, SPOCK!

In this capstone, you will

- Implement the main components of your game using case classes and case objects
- Manipulate immutable data using higher order and pure functions
- Represent nullable values using Option
- Use tuples to group elements together
- Define unapply methods to pattern match on classes

In this capstone, you'll implement an HTTP server to play a popular variation of the classic game "Paper, Rock, Scissors!" called "Rock, Paper, Scissors, Lizard, Spock!" Two players each pick a symbol randomly, and the selected symbols determine who the winner is. The allowed moves are paper, rock, scissors, lizard, Spock, and they interact as follows:

> *Scissors cut paper, paper covers rock, rock crushes lizard, lizard poisons Spock, Spock smashes scissors, scissors decapitate lizard, lizard eats paper, paper disproves Spock, Spock vaporizes rock, rock crushes scissors.*

If both players pick the same symbol, your application will not select a winner and declare the game a tie. Figure 26.1 shows a visual representation of the rules.

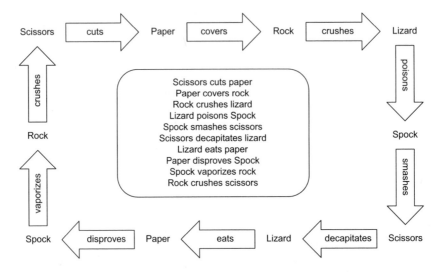

Figure 26.1   "Rock, Paper, Scissors, Lizard, Spock!" has five symbols: scissors, paper, rock, lizard, Spock. The diagram summarizes the interaction between its symbols. You will use them in your implementation to determine the winner (if any).

 26.1 Implementing Rock, Paper, Scissors, Lizard, Spock!

Let's define the API's behavior for your HTTP server to play the game. Your application should be able to consume an HTTP POST request to the URI /play. The body of the POST request should provide information about the name and selected symbol of both players using the following format:

nameA: symbolA – nameB: symbolB

For example, if the player Daniela selects Spock and the player Martin picks paper, the HTTP request should have the body "Daniela: Spock – Martin: Paper." Your application should parse it and reply with a successful response that provides information about the game's outcome (e.g., "Player Martin with symbol Paper wins!"). Figure 26.2 provides an example of the expected behavior of the API of your HTTP server.

26.1.1 sbt project setup and packages

The first step is to set an empty sbt project up with the external dependencies and logging configurations you need to implement an HTTP server with http4s. This process is the same as the capstone project for unit 3. To refresh your memory, follow the instructions in section 18.1.1.

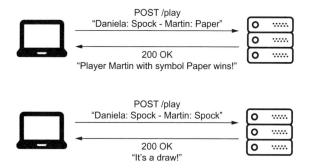

Figure 26.2 Overview of the API for your HTTP server. After parsing the message, the server should respond successfully with a human-readable message containing the game's outcome.

Create a package: org.example.game. All the files for your application will belong to it. You should also add another package, called org.example.game.entities, to contain your game's rationale, which allows you to have a clear separation between business logic and server definition.

26.1.2 Defining a symbol

The first key component of the game is the concept of symbol: a player uses it to represent a selected move. You should compare the current symbol to another to determine if it is the winning one. One possible solution is to represent this with a trait.

Listing 26.1 Definition of a Symbol

```scala
// file src/main/scala/org/example/game/entities/Symbol.scala
package org.example.game.entities

trait Symbol {

  protected def beats: List[Symbol]

  def wins(other: Symbol): Boolean =
    beats.contains(other)

}
```

There's no need to expose the list of symbols that beat the current move; you want to force external users of your code to use the wins function.

The method contains belongs to the class List, and it returns true if a list contains the given element, false otherwise.

After defining the generic rules of a symbol, let's define specific instances for it. The symbols available in our game are rock, paper, scissors, lizard, Spock.

Listing 26.2 Creating instances for Symbol

```scala
// file src/main/scala/org/example/game/entities/Symbol.scala
package org.example.game.entities

sealed trait Symbol {
  protected def beats: List[Symbol]

  def wins(other: Symbol): Boolean =
    beats.contains(other)
}

/**
  * Rock crushes Lizard
  * Rock crushes Scissors.
  */
case object Rock extends Symbol {
  protected val beats = List(Lizard, Scissors)
}

/**
  * Paper covers Rock
  * Paper disproves Spock
  */
case object Paper extends Symbol {
  protected val beats = List(Rock, Spock)
}

/**
  * Scissors cuts Paper
  * Scissors decapitates Lizard
  */
case object Scissors extends Symbol {
  protected val beats = List(Paper, Lizard)
}

/**
  * Lizard poisons Spock
  * Lizard eats Paper
  */
case object Lizard extends Symbol {
  protected val beats = List(Spock, Paper)
}
```

Symbol is now a sealed trait: you want to prevent your users from defining new instances.

You are using case objects rather than objects because you need to provide a human-readable text representation of each symbol.

```
/**
  * Spock smashes Scissors
  * Spock vaporizes Rock
  */
case object Spock extends Symbol {
  protected val beats = List(Scissors, Rock)
}
```

You are using case objects rather than objects because you need to provide a human-readable text representation of each symbol.

Finally, let's define how to parse a string into an instance of Symbol. Let's create an object to define this logic.

Listing 26.3 The object Symbol

```
// file src/main/scala/org/example/game/entities/Symbol.scala
package org.example.game.entities

[...]

object Symbol {

  def fromString(text: String): Symbol =
    text.trim.toLowerCase match {
      case "rock" => Rock
      case "paper" => Paper
      case "scissors" => Scissors
      case "lizard" => Lizard
      case "spock" => Spock
      case unknown =>
       val errorMsg = s"Unknown symbol $unknown. " +
        "Please pick a valid symbol [Rock, Paper, Scissors, Lizard,
          Spock]"
        throw new IllegalArgumentException(errorMsg)
    }
}
```

It binds the matched text to a value called unknown rather than discarding it because it displays it in the error message.

The name of the object in this snippet of code has no particular relevance; you could also rename it to SymbolUtils and obtain the same result. You can have an object and a trait with the same name because the Scala compiler is smart enough to understand when referring to one rather than the other.

26.1.3 Representing a player

Another fundamental concept of your game is the player. A player has a name and a symbol to represent a valid move. You could represent this using a case class, but this would expose its name and its symbol. Avoid exposing a player's name, as you need to prevent your application from using it when selecting a winner to guarantee that your program doesn't have any biases based on a player's name. You could represent a player using a class.

Listing 26.4 The class Player

```scala
// file src/main/scala/org/example/game/entities/Player.scala
package org.example.game.entities

class Player(name: String, val symbol: Symbol) {

  override def toString: String = s"Player $name with symbol $symbol"
}
```

Because you declared Player as a class, not as a case class, only its fields marked as val are publicly accessible. Do not forget to override the function toString. Your program should always produce a human-readable representation when converting an instance of Player to text. If you fail to do so, the compiler will use toString's default definition and return a string similar to Player@12345.

You now need to define how to parse text into a player. One possible solution is to define a companion object for the class Player and define an apply function for it.

Listing 26.5 The object Player and the apply method

```scala
// file src/main/scala/org/example/game/entities/Player.scala
package org.example.game.entities
```

It splits a text into up to two tokens using ":" as the delimiter and returns an array.

```scala
object Player {

  // valid example: "Daniela: Spock"
  def apply(text: String): Player =
    text.split(":", 2) match {
      case Array(name, symbol) =>
    new Player(name.trim, Symbol.fromString(symbol))
      case _ =>
        val errorMsg = s"Invalid player $text. " +
```

It matches an instance of Array that has exactly two elements. You are going to see more of this when you learn about collections.

```
"Please, use the format <name>: <symbol>"
        throw new IllegalArgumentException(errorMsg)
    }
}
```

Finally, let's also define an *unapply* method for Player to use pattern match on players.

Listing 26.6 The object Player and the unapply method

```
// file src/main/scala/org/example/game/entities/Player.scala
package org.example.game.entities

object Player {

  [...]

  def unapply(player: Player): Option[Symbol] = Some(player.symbol)

}
```

The expressions Option[Symbol] and Option[(Symbol)] are equivalent because you can always omit tuples that contain only one element.

26.1.4 Defining a game

You are now ready to represent the concept of a game. A game must have two players, and it must provide an outcome. You could represent a game using a case class.

Listing 26.7 The Game case class

```
// file src/main/scala/org/example/game/entities/Game.scala
package org.example.game.entities

case class Game(playerA: Player, playerB: Player) {

  private val winner: Option[Player] =
    (playerA, playerB) match {
      case (pA @ Player(sA), Player(sB)) if sA.wins(sB) => Some(pA)
      case (Player(sA), pB @ Player(sB)) if sB.wins(sA) => Some(pB)
      case _ => None // it's a draw!
    }

  val result: String = winner.map(player => s"$player wins!")
                             .getOrElse("It's a draw!")
}
```

Game is a case class, so all its fields are publicly accessible.

Using tuples to pattern match on both players

It provides a human-readable message to describe the game's outcome.

You can pattern match on Player instances because its companion object has an unapply function for it.

Finally, you can now define how to parse an instance of Game from a string. Let's define another apply method in its companion object.

Listing 26.8 The Game companion object

```scala
// file src/main/scala/org/example/game/entities/Game.scala
package org.example.game.entities

[...]

object Game {

  // valid example: "Daniela: Spock - Martin: Paper"
  def apply(text: String): Game =
    text.split("-", 2) match {
      case Array(playerA, playerB) =>
        apply(Player(playerA), Player(playerB))
      case _ =>
        val errorMsg = s"Invalid game $text. " +
        s"Please, use the format <name>: <symbol> - <name>: <symbol>"
        throw new IllegalArgumentException(errorMsg)
    }
}
```

Calling apply method that the compiler automatically adds in the companion object Game

Note that you can have multiple definitions of the apply and unapply methods in a companion object, as long as they have different signatures. In this code snippet, Game is a case class, so its companion object has two apply methods: one takes a String as its parameter (i.e., the one you have implemented), and the other takes two parameters of type Player (i.e., the one the compiler generates at compile time).

26.1.5 The API routes

After coding your business logic, you define the API of your HTTP server. Let's create a class called GameApi to describe the shape of the requests it should handle. It should process any POST request to the URI /play, parse its body as raw text into a game and reply with code 200 - Ok containing the game's outcome.

You are now defining your HTTP layer, so you are going to add files to the package org.example.game instead of org.example.game.entities.

Listing 26.9 The GameApi class

```
// file src/main/scala/org/example/game/GameApi.scala
package org.example.game

import cats.effect.IO
import org.example.game.entities.Game
import org.http4s.HttpRoutes
import org.http4s.dsl.Http4sDsl

class GameApi extends Http4sDsl[IO] {

  val routes = HttpRoutes.of[IO] {
    case req @ POST -> Root / "play" =>
      for {
        text <- req.as[String]
        response <- Ok(Game(text).result)
      } yield response
  }

}
```

You need to return an expression of type IO[Response[IO]].

Using for-comprehension over the type IO

Extracting the body of the request as String

Creating a successful reply containing the game's outcome

The assignment response has type Response[IO].

The type IO represents computations that may have side effects. Because it has an implementation for the functions map and flatMap, you can use for-comprehension to manipulate and combine values (more about this later when you discover the type IO).

26.1.6 The HTTP server

The last step of your implementation consists of associating the API routes you defined to an HTTP server. Let's create a class GameApp in the org.example.game package.

Listing 26.10 The GameApp class

```
// file src/main/scala/org/example/game/GameApp.scala
package org.example.game

import cats.effect.{ExitCode, IO, IOApp}
import org.http4s.implicits._
import org.http4s.server.Router
import org.http4s.blaze.server.BlazeServerBuilder

import scala.concurrent.ExecutionContext
```

```
object GameApp extends IOApp {

  private val httpApp = Router(
    "/" -> new GameApi().routes
  ).orNotFound

  override def run(args: List[String]): IO[ExitCode] =
    stream(args).compile.drain.as(ExitCode.Success)

  private def stream(args: List[String]) =
    BlazeServerBuilder[IO](ExecutionContext.global)
    .bindHttp(8080, "0.0.0.0")         ◄────────   The server runs
    .withHttpApp(httpApp)                           on localhost on
    .serve                                          port 8080.
}
```

The implementation of your game HTTP server is now complete and ready to run.

26.1.7 Let's try it out!

Congratulations on completing the implementation of "Rock, Paper, Scissors, Lizard, Spock!" It's now time to try to run your server and play. Navigate to the run folder and execute the command sbt run; it will compile and run your server. If everything goes according to plan, you should see that your server is now running on http://localhost:8080 after a few seconds:

```
[info] Done packaging.
[info] Running org.example.game.GameApp
08:49:33.981 INFO  - Service bound to address /0:0:0:0:0:0:0:0:8080
08:49:33.999 INFO  -   _   _   _       _ _
08:49:34.001 INFO  -  | |_| |_| |_ _ __| | | ___
08:49:34.001 INFO  -  | ' \ _|  _| '_ \_  _(_-<
08:49:34.001 INFO  -  |_||_\__|\__| .__/ |_|/__/
08:49:34.001 INFO  -              |_|
08:49:34.211 INFO  - http4s v0.22.0 on blaze v0.15.1 started at
            http://[0:0:0:0:0:0:0:0]:8080/
```

Let's send a few POST requests to your server and see if it reflects the given business requirements. For example, suppose you have two players: Leonard and Sheldon. The first time Leonard selects rock, while Sheldon picks Spock. Sheldon should win because Spock vaporizes rock:

```
$ curl -i -d "Leonard: Rock - Sheldon: Spock" \
  -X POST http://localhost:8080/play
```

```
HTTP/1.1 200 OK
Content-Type: text/plain; charset=UTF-8
Date: Mon, 08 Feb 2021 09:07:47 GMT
Content-Length: 38

Player Sheldon with symbol Spock wins!
```

If both players select Spock, the server should show that is a tie:

```
$ curl -i -d "Leonard: Spock - Sheldon: Spock" \
 -X POST http://localhost:8080/play
HTTP/1.1 200 OK
Content-Type: text/plain; charset=UTF-8
Date: Mon, 08 Feb 2021 09:09:06 GMT
Content-Length: 12

It's a draw!
```

Play a few more rounds of "Rock, Paper, Scissors, Lizard, Spock!" and see if you can spot any bugs or possible improvements to your server.

 ## 26.2 Possible improvements to our solution

Congratulations on implementing your game! Your implementation respects the requirements, but it suffers from a few defects. Let's see what these are and what techniques can help you overcome them.

> **NO ERROR HANDLING** If you try to send a POST request containing a message that the server cannot parse, the server will reply with status code 500 – Internal Server Error because it doesn't handle exceptions correctly:
>
> ```
> $ curl -i -d "Leonard - Sheldon" \
>  -X POST http://localhost:8080/play
> HTTP/1.1 500 Internal Server Error
> Connection: close
> Date: Mon, 08 Feb 2021, 18:42:06 GMT
> Content-Length: 0
> ```
>
> Your application should reply with a response with status code 400 – Bad Request containing a message that hints at the reason for the failure. Exceptions are unpredictable and surprisingly simple to forget. A better approach is to rely on the compiler to stop your mistakes. Later in the book you'll learn about the type Try; it marks computations that can fail and it ensures that your program handles them correctly.

DATA FORMAT   Your application does not use a standard format to transmit information between machines. Clients that want to use your server need to learn its data format. Having a custom format also requires some heavy lifting to ensure your application can correctly parse text; you need to trim it, convert it to all lowercase, and split it into tokens. Using a standard data format, such as JSON and XML, makes your server more straightforward to use. It also makes your code simpler to write because you can rely on external libraries to parse your data. Later in the book you will learn how to use circe, a popular library to serialize and deserialize data to and from JSON.

Summary

In this capstone, you implemented an HTTP server to play the game "Rock, Paper, Scissors, Lizard, Spock!"—a variation of the game "Rock, Paper, Scissors!"

- You represented the main components of the game using case classes and case objects.
- You defined pure functions to determine a winner using the Option type.
- You used tuples to group elements and defined apply and unapply methods to compose and decompose classes.
- You saw your code in action and learned about a few possible improvements to your implementation.

List

In unit 4, you discovered how to code data with immutable structures and handle nullable values using the Option type. In this unit, you'll use the functionalities of the List collection to query a publicly accessible data set called "The Movies Dataset" by Rounak Banik, which provides information on more than 45,000 films. In particular, you are going to learn about the following subjects:

- Lesson 27 teaches you how to define an instance of List and add elements to it. You'll also see how to use pattern matching to traverse it and manipulate its items.
- Lesson 28 shows you how to transform its elements and chain multiple sequences using the map, flatten, and flatMap functions.
- Lesson 29 demonstrates how you can query on a list's fundamental properties, such as its size or the characteristics of its items.
- Lesson 30 teaches you different strategies to select a single element from it. You are going to discover how to pick one, either by its position or by its features. You are also going to find the minimum/maximum item based on specific criteria.
- Lesson 31 shows you how to filter elements of a list either by position or by feature. You are also going to see how to remove duplicates from a sequence.

- Lesson 32 introduces you to different sorting strategies for a list and how to produce a human-readable representation for it. You are also going to learn how to group elements per feature and how to sum numerical sequences.
- Finally, you'll use all the operations you discover on List to query a movie data set and display your results in a consistent and human-readable manner in lesson 33.

After learning about the List collection, you'll continue with unit 6, in which you'll discover other useful collections in the standard Scala collection and different strategies of error handling.

LIST

After reading this lesson, you will be able to

- Define an ordered sequence of items
- Adding elements to an existing list
- Traverse and transform its items using pattern matching

Now that you have discovered the Option type in the previous unit, you'll learn about List in this lesson; many of the concepts you have mastered for optional values are also applicable to lists but in a slightly different context. The type List allows you to represent an immutable ordered sequence of elements. This concept is not exclusive to the Scala language. For example, you use an ArrayList or a LinkedList in Java, a list in C++, a list literal in Python, and an array in Javascript. You'll find that lists in Scala are relatively similar to many other languages, with a fundamental difference: they are immutable by default. Using mutable lists is still possible but discouraged. In this lesson, you'll learn how to create a list and add elements to it. You'll also see how to pattern match on lists. In the capstone, you'll use lists to represent the information presented in the movies data set.

> **Consider this**
> Suppose you need to represent all the books you own. What data structure would you use?

 ## 27.1 Creating a list

Imagine you want to write a program to keep track of your contacts. You could present your data using a list data structure.

Listing 27.1 Creating a list of contacts

```
case class Contact(name: String, surname: String, number: String)    ⟵ Representation
                                                                         of a contact
val alice = Contact(name = "Alice",
                    surname = "Abbott",
                    number = "+123456789")

val bob = Contact(name = "Bob",
                  surname = "Brown",
                  number = "+987654321")
                                           The value contacts has
val contacts = List(alice, bob)    ⟵      type List[Contact].
```

A list is a data structure representing a sequence of items of the same kind in a given order. Figure 27.1 shows you its typical recursive structure in which you have the head as its first element, followed by all the others represented as its tail; you can refer to it as a linked list.

"Head" represents the value of an element in the sequence.

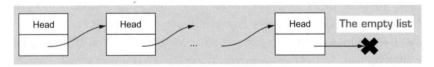

"Tail" is a pointer to the next element in the sequence.

Figure 27.1   The typical structure of a sequence in a given order. Zero or more elements define a list. Each has a head containing a value and a tail pointing to the next. A symbol for the empty list identifies its end.

In Scala, List provides you with a collection that reflects this particular head-tail data structure.

Listing 27.2 The List type

```
package scala

sealed abstract class List[A] {          ←──  It represents the gen-
  def head: A                                 eral structure of a list.
  def tail: List[A]
}
                                                    It represents
                                                    an empty list.
case object Nil extends List[Nothing] {  ←──
  def head = throw new NoSuchElementException("head of empty list")
  def tail: List[Nothing] =
  throw new UnsupportedOperationException("tail of empty list")
}

case class ::[A](head: A, tail: List[A]) extends List[A]    ←
                                                                 )
                             It represents a list that          /
                         contains at least one element.
```

This implementation has many commonalities, including the one for Option you saw in section 22.2. Let's analyze each component of the Scala's List implementation:

- package scala

  The class List lives in the scala package, so it's ready for you to use without the need to add an import statement.

- sealed abstract class List[A]

  List is a class with a well-defined set of possible implementations (i.e., Nil for an empty list, and :: for a nonempty list). It also has one type parameter that identifies the type of instances it can contain. Note that you cannot initialize an instance of List directly because it is declared as abstract. However, you can write expressions such as List(1,2,3) thanks to an apply method defined into a companion object List:

  ```
  object List {

      def apply[A](xs: A*): List[A] = xs.toList
  }
  ```

  The expression A* uses a special syntax called *varargs*, a short name for "variable arguments." Scala has inherited this concept from Java, which indicates that a method can accept zero or more arguments assigned to a named value (e.g., in this specific example, the value xs). The class List has one type parameter: all the elements in the list must be of the same kind. When defining a list, Scala will infer its type parameter by selecting the closest type compatible with all its elements. Let's see a few examples:

```
scala> List(1, 2, 3)
val res0: List[Int] = List(1, 2, 3)
// The inferred type is List[Int] as all the elements are of type Int

scala> List("Hello", "Scala", "!")
val res1: List[String] = List(Hello, Scala, !)
// The inferred type is List[String]

scala> List(1, 2, 42.24)
val res2: List[Double] = List(1.0, 2.0, 42.24)
// The inferred type is List[Double] because the compiler can
// automatically convert elements of type Int to Double,
// but not the other way around: Double "wins"

scala> List(42, "Scala")
val res3: List[Any] = List(42, Scala)
// The inferred type is List[Any] because the first common type
// between an Int and a String is Any (i.e., the root of the
// Scala class hierarchy)
```

- case object Nil extends List[Nothing]
  Nil is one of the possible implementations of List, and it represents the concept of an empty sequence. It is a case object, which means it is a singleton with a meaningful string representation (i.e., the string Nil). The concept of an "emptiness" can be associated with any List, independently from the type of elements it contains. Nil extends List[Nothing], which makes it compatible with any list thanks to Nothing being the subclass of any other class:

  ```
  scala> val ints: List[Int] = Nil
  val ints: List[Int] = List()

  scala> val strings: List[String] = Nil
  val strings: List[String] = List()
  ```

An empty list does not have any element or a tail, the reason Nil's implementations for the methods head and tail throw NoSuchElementException exceptions when called.

- case class ::[A](head: A, tail: List[A]) extends List[A]

  The class ::, which some developers refer to as *the Cons class*, is the implementation of List to represent a nonempty list. It is a case class, which means the compiler will automatically generate getters for its fields head and tail. You can create a nonempty list by invoking its apply method as follows:

  ```
  scala>  new ::(1, ::(2, Nil))
  val res0: scala.collection.immutable.::[Int] = List(1, 2)
  ```

  Building a list by calling the apply method on the class :: can make your code difficult to read: Scala developers rarely use it. Thanks to a cleverly named method defined in the abstract class List, you can use an alternative and more concise way to obtain the same result:

  ```
  scala> 1 :: 2 :: Nil
  val res1: List[Int] = List(1, 2)
  ```

Figure 27.2 provides a visual representation of all the possible implementations of the type List.

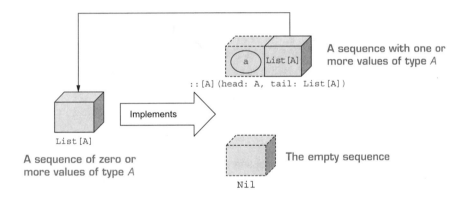

Figure 27.2 Visual summary of the structure of List in Scala. You have two possible implementations: Nil identifies the empty list, while :: represents the nonempty list with a head and a tail.

Quick Check 27.1 Using the Scala REPL, create a list containing the number 42 and the nullable string "scala." What is the type of your List instance? Why?

27.2 Adding elements to a list

Now that you've learned how to create a list in Scala, let's discover how you can add elements to it.

Return to the example scenario you saw at the beginning of section 27.1 and imagine that you have a new contact to add to your address book.

Listing 27.3 Adding a new contact

```
val charlie = Contact(name = "Charlie",
                      surname = "Clarke",
                      number = "+43 3544665 3434")

val moreContacts = contacts :+ charlie
```

The value moreContacts contains a new list of all the elements in contacts together with the charlie contact.

By design, Scala encourages the use of immutable data structures. You'll obtain a new list rather than modify your existing instance when adding new elements because the class List is immutable.

PREPEND TO LIST *Prepend* is the operation that adds an element to the beginning of a sequence. It is a particularly efficient operation for List as it happens in constant time. It is independent of its size and requires only to create a new instance containing the new element as head and the existing list as its tail. In Scala, you can prepend an element using the method "+:":

```
scala> 42 +: List(1 ,2, 3)
val res0: List[Int] = List(42, 1, 2, 3)
```

APPEND TO LIST *Append* is the process of adding an element to the end of a list. This operation is more expensive than prepending. Its complexity is proportional to its size: you need to traverse the entire sequence to find its end before adding the new element. In Scala, you can append an element to the operator ":+":

```
scala> List(1 ,2, 3) :+ 42
val res1: List[Int] = List(1, 2, 3, 42)
```

CONCATENATING LISTS You can also merge two lists and refer to this operation as *concatenation*. You can achieve this thanks to the method "++":

```
scala> List(1, 2, 3) ++ List(42)
val res2: List[Int] = List(1, 2, 3, 42)

scala> List(1, 2, 3) ++ Nil
val res3: List[Int] = List(1, 2, 3)
```

Think in Scala: "+:" versus ":+"

The operators to prepend (+:) and append (:+) are easy to confuse. A simple trick can help you select the correct symbol without relying on the compiler: the character ":" is always pointing toward its collection component. A few examples are the following:

```
List(1) +: 3   // does not compile!
List(1) :+ 3   // correct

3 :+ List(1)   // does not compile!
3 +: List(1)   // correct
```

Quick Check 27.2 Use the Scala REPL to prepend the number 42 to the list containing the string "scala."

 ## 27.3 Pattern matching on a list

After learning the structure of List and its implementations, let's discover how you can use pattern matching on it.

Imagine you need to define a function to ensure you always have at least two contacts in your address book. Two possible solutions using pattern matching are the following.

Listing 27.4 Pattern matching on List

```
case class Contact(name: String, surname: String, number: String)

def validateContacts(contacts: List[Contact]): List[Contact] =
  contacts match {
    case List() =>                            It matches an
      throw new IllegalStateException(         empty list.
        "Invalid empty address book! " +
        "Please provide at least two contacts")
    case List(a) =>                           It matches a list with
      throw new IllegalStateException(        exactly one element.
        s"Only contact ${a.name} ${a.surname} found. " +
        s"Please provide at least another one")
    case cs => cs                  It matches any list.
  }
```

Listing 27.5 Pattern matching using the "::" operator

```
case class Contact(name: String, surname: String, number: String)

def validateContacts(contacts: List[Contact]): List[Contact] =
  contacts match {
    case Nil =>                          It matches any
      throw new IllegalStateException(   empty list.
        "Invalid empty address book! " +
        "Please provide at least two contacts")
    case a :: Nil =>                     It matches a list with
      throw new IllegalStateException(   exactly one element.
        s"Only contact ${a.name} ${a.surname} found. " +
        s"Please provide at least another one")
    case cs => cs                        It matches any list.
```

When pattern matching on a list, you can use two different notations: you can either use the unapply method on List (e.g., "List()" and "List(a)") or use the "::" operator (e.g., "Nil" and "a :: Nil"). The two notations are generally equivalent, and you can mix them within the same pattern matching construct. The unapply method on List is usually more readable, but the "::" operator allows you to express more complex conditions. For example, let's assume you need to match any list that has at least three elements. You can write the following condition thanks to the "::" operator:

```
case a :: b :: c :: tail => ???
```

When using the unapply method on List, you need to use the help of an if condition to your case clause to achieve the same result:

```
case list if list.size >= 3 => ???
```

Let's look at more complex examples of using pattern matching on a sequence. Another common task consists of using pattern matching to traverse all the list elements and modify them. For example, imagine you need to extract the surnames of all the contacts in your address book. You can achieve this using pattern matching.

Listing 27.6 Traversing a list with pattern matching

```
case class Contact(name: String, surname: String, number: String)

def getSurnames(contacts: List[Contact]): List[String] =
  contacts match {
```

```
    case Nil => Nil
    case head :: tail => head.surname :: getSurnames(tail)
  }
```

The function getSurnames returns the empty list if there are no contacts. It extracts the surname for its head element and repeats the getSurnames operation on its tail otherwise. This technique of calling the same function but with different parameters is called *recursion*.

Quick Check 27.3 Use pattern matching to define a function sum that takes a list of integers as its parameter and returns an integer representing the sum of all its elements.

 ## Summary

In this lesson, my objective was to teach you about the basics of the collection List.

- You saw that it has an immutable head-tail structure. In particular, you discovered Scala provides an implementation for an empty list called Nil and a non-empty one called ":: ".
- You learned how to add elements to a sequence and how to concatenate two lists.
- You saw the different ways you can pattern match on List and use it to manipulate its elements.

Let's see if you got this!

TRY THIS Define a function to filter all the even numbers of a sequence of integers: pass the list as its parameter and use pattern matching on it.

Answers to quick checks

Quick Check 27.1 You can create the list by typing the following instruction in the Scala REPL:

```
scala> 42 :: Some("scala") :: Nil
val res0: List[Any] = List(42, Some(scala))
```

Or alternatively

```
scala> List(42, Some("scala"))
val res1: List[Any] = List(42, Some(scala))
```

The list has type List[Any] because Any is the most specific type to represent both Int and Option[String].

Quick Check 27.2 The following expressions prepends the number 42 to a list containing the word "scala":

```
scala> 42 +: List("scala")
val res0: List[Any] = List(42, scala)
```

Alternatively, you can also do the following:

```
scala> List(42) ++ List("scala")
val res1: List[Any] = List(42, scala)
```

Quick Check 27.3 A possible implementation for the function sum is the following:

```
def sum(numbers: List[Int]): Int = numbers match {
  case Nil => 0
  case head :: tail => head + sum(tail)
}
```

WORKING WITH LIST: MAP AND FLATMAP

After reading this lesson, you will be able to

- Transform the elements of a sequence using the map function
- Simplify a nested structure using the flatten method
- Manipulate and combine lists using the flatMap operation
- Chain instances of List using for-comprehension

In the previous lesson, you learned the basics of the type List of the Scala standard collection library. In this lesson, you'll learn about the basic operations you can perform on lists similar to those you have seen for the class Option. You will see how to use the map operation to apply a function to a sequence's elements, unify nested lists using flatten, and chain them together using flatMap. You'll learn how to use for-comprehension to combine and manipulate multiple lists into one. In the capstone, you will use operations to extract information from the movies data set.

> **Consider this**
> Imagine you need to traverse and apply a function to every element of a list. How would you implement it?

28.1 The map, flatten, and flatMap operations

In the previous lesson, you represented the contacts of your address book using the following representation:

```
case class Contact(name: String, surname: String, number: String)
```

Suppose you now need to change your program to include extra information about each of your contacts. For example, you could track multiple phone numbers for the same contact and label them with a category, as well as store any email address or company name.

Listing 28.1 Representation of a contact

```
case class Contact(name: String,
                   surname: String,
                   numbers: List[ContactNumber],
                   company: Option[String],
                   email: Option[String])

sealed trait Label
case object Work extends Label
case object Home extends Label

case class ContactNumber(number: String, label: Label)
```

Let's see how you can use the map, flatten, and flatMap higher order functions to query your address book's contacts.

28.1.1 The map function

Suppose the first operation you need to implement requires you to extract all the surnames of your contacts:

```
def getSurnames(contacts: List[Contact]): List[String] =
  contacts match {
    case Nil => Nil
    case head :: tail => head.surname :: getSurnames(tail)
  }
```

However, a more elegant way of achieving the same is using the map higher order function.

Listing 28.2 Getting all the contact surnames

```
def getSurnames(contacts: List[Contact]): List[String] =
    contacts.map(contact => contact.surname)
```

For each contact in contacts, it extracts its surname. You can omit the variable contact and write "contacts.map(_.surname)."

In Scala, you use the map function to iterate through each element of a list and apply a given transformation. The map operation on List has a very similar signature to the one defined on Option.

```
def map[B](f: A => B): List[B]
```

It is a higher order function that takes a parameter f, and it behaves as follows:

- If the list has at least an element, it applies the function f to its head, and it recursively invokes the same operation to its tail.
- If empty, it returns Nil.

> **Quick Check 28.1** Define a function plus5 that adds five to each element of a given list of integers using the map function.
>
> ```
> def plus5(ns: List[Int]): List[Int]
> ```

28.1.2 The flatten function

Suppose you now need to extract the numbers of all the contacts. You could use the map operation as follows:

```
def getNumbers(contacts: List[Contact]): List[List[ContactNumber]] =
    contacts.map(_.numbers)
```

The function getNumbers return type is List[List[ContactNumber]]. However, rather than having an unnecessary nested structure, you would like to return an instance of List[ContactNumber]. You can use the flatten function to combine two sequences into one.

Listing 28.3 **Getting all the contact numbers**

```
def getNumbers(contacts: List[ContactNumber]): List[ContactNumber] =
  contacts.map(_.numbers).flatten
```

You can invoke the function flatten on nested collections, such as List[List[A]]: it concatenates the inner sequences in order to produce a non-nested structure. A few examples are the following:

```
scala> List(List(), List(1, 2), List(3)).flatten
val res0: List[Int] = List(1, 2, 3)

scala> List(List()).flatten
val res1: List[Nothing] = List()
```

> **Quick Check 28.2** Can you apply the function flatten on an instance of List[Double]? Why?

28.1.3 The flatMap function

The flatMap function combines the map and flatten operations. You can reimplement your getNumbers method from listing 28.3.

Listing 28.4 **Getting all the contact numbers with flatMap**

```
def getNumbers(contacts: List[Contact]): List[ContactNumber] =
  contacts.flatMap(_.numbers)
```

The flatMap function on List[A] is a higher order function that applies a function f of type A => List[B] to produce an instance of List[B]:

- If the list has at least one element, it applies the function f to its head, and it recursively invokes the same operation on its tail.
- If empty, it returns the object Nil.

Listing 28.5 **The flatMap function on List**

```
def flatMap[B](f: A => List[B]): List[B] =
  this match {
    case Nil => Nil
    case head :: tail => f(head) ++ tail.flatMap(f)
  }
```

Quick Check 28.3 Define a method triple that takes a list of integers as its parameter and returns a new list with each element from the original sequence repeated three times. For example, when invoking it with List(1, 2, 3) it should return List(1, 1, 1, 2, 2, 2, 3, 3, 3). Use the flatMap function.

```
def triple(ns: List[Int]): List[Int]
```

Table 28.1 provides a summary of the signature and usage of the basic operations on List.

Table 28.1 Summary of the three fundamental operations on List. The function map applies a given function to each element of the sequence, while the function flatten creates a list by combining two nested structures. The flatMap operation combines the map and flatten operations to chain sequences together.

	Acts on	Signature	Usage
map	List[A]	map(f: A => B): List[B]	It applies a function to each element of the list.
flatten	List[List[A]]	flatten: List[A]	It merges two nested lists into one.
flatMap	List[A]	flatMap(f: A => List[B]): List[B]	The combination of map followed by flatten. It chains sequences together.

28.2 For-comprehension

Let's go back to your address book program. Imagine you now need to select your contacts based on a given list of emails.

Listing 28.6 Selecting contacts by email

```
def selectByEmails(contacts: List[Contact],
                   emails: List[String]): List[Contact] =
  contacts.flatMap { contact =>
    emails.flatMap { email =>
      if (contact.email.exists(_.equalsIgnoreCase(email)))
        List(contact)
      else List()                        Emails are case
    }                                    insensitive.
  }
```

A more elegant way of expressing the same is using `for-comprehension`.

Listing 28.7 Selecting contacts by email using for-comprehension

```
def selectByEmails(contacts: List[Contact],
                   emails: List[String]): List[Contact] =
  for {
    contact <- contacts
    email <- emails
    if contact.email.exists(_.equalsIgnoreCase(email))
  } yield contact
```

Emails
are case
insensitive.

You encountered `for-comprehension` when learning about `Option`, and you have now seen that `List` is another Scala type that supports it. In future lessons, you'll discover there are many others! You can rewrite your code to use `for-comprehension` for every type with a `flatMap` function.

> **Quick Check 28.4** In quick check 28.3, you implemented a function, called `triple`, using `flatMap`; reimplement it, using `for-comprehension`.

Summary

In this lesson, my objective was to teach you about the basic operations on `List`.

- You learned that you can use the `map` function to apply some transformation to all the elements of a sequence.
- You saw that the `flatten` method allows you to merge two nested lists into one.
- You discovered the `flatMap` function as the combination of the `map` and `flatten` operations to chain sequences together.
- You also mastered how to manipulate lists using `for-comprehension`, which is syntactic sugar for one or more nested `flatMap` and `map` operations.

Let's see if you got this!

> **TRY THIS** Define a function that takes a list of people and extract their names if they are 18 years or older. Use the following case class to represent a person:
>
> ```
> case class Person(name: String, age: Int)
> ```

Answers to quick checks

Quick Check 28.1 A possible implementation for the function plus5 is the following:

```
def plus5(ns: List[Int]): List[Int] = ns.map(_ + 5)
```

Quick Check 28.2 You cannot apply the function flatten on an instance of List[Double] because it operates on nested structures only. When trying to do so, the compiler will complain that it cannot convert Double to a type that is compatible with List (i.e., an instance of IterableOnce).

```
scala> List(12.34).flatten
        error: No implicit view available from Double =>
            scala.collection.IterableOnce[B].
```

Quick Check 28.3 An implementation for the function triple using flatMap is the following:

```
def triple(ns: List[Int]): List[Int] =
  ns.flatMap(n => List(n, n, n))
```

Quick Check 28.4 You can implement the function triple using for-comprehension as follows:

```
def triple(ns: List[Int]): List[Int] =
  for {
    n <- ns
    i <- List(n, n, n)
  } yield i
```

WORKING WITH LIST: PROPERTIES

After reading this lesson, you will be able to

- Inquire over the size of a list
- Check if a sequence contains a specific item
- Count the number of elements that respect a given predicate

In the previous lesson, you learned how to use the map and flatMap functions over an instance of List. These are two of its fundamental operations: when combined with pattern matching, they allow you to define the vast majority of operations you can perform for a sequence. However, implementing the same procedures over and over may not be performant and may be challenging to maintain. For these reasons, the class List provides you with many ready-to-use and performant functions for common transformations and queries. In this lesson, you'll discover which methods you can use to analyze the properties of a sequence. You'll learn how to get the size of a list and check if it contains a given element. You'll also investigate how many of its items respect a given predicate. In the capstone, you will use these operations to query and analyze the movies data set.

> **Consider this**
> Suppose you have a list representing the exam results of a class, and you need to provide statistics to describe the percentage of students who failed, those who passed, and those who excelled. How would you implement it?

 29.1 Size of a list

In the previous lesson, you represented the contacts in your address book using an instance of List[Contact], where each contact has a name, surname, a list of numbers, and potentially an email and company.

Listing 29.1 Representation of a contact

```
case class Contact(name: String,
                   surname: String,
                   numbers: List[ContactNumber],
                   company: Option[String],
                   email: Option[String])

sealed trait Label
case object Work extends Label
case object Home extends Label

case class ContactNumber(number: String, label: Label)
```

Suppose you need to implement a function to ensure your address book respects the following library requirements:

- It cannot be empty.
- It cannot contain more than 1,000 contacts.

Listing 29.2 Property Operations on List

```
private def reject(msg: String) = throw new IllegalStateException(msg)

private def validateNonEmpty(contacts: List[Contact]): List[Contact] =
  if (contacts.isEmpty) reject("Address book cannot be empty!")
  else contacts
```

The function isEmpty returns true if the list has size zero, false otherwise.

```
private val maxCollSize = 1000
private def validateWithinSize(contacts: List[Contact]): List[Contact] = {
  val size = contacts.size                    ←──────────  The method size returns
  if (size > maxCollSize)                                  the number of elements
    reject(s"Address book collection too big! " +         in the sequence.
    s"Found $size contacts, maximum allowed is $maxCollSize")
  else contacts
}

def validateAddressBook(contacts: List[Contact]): List[Contact] = {
  validateNonEmpty(contacts)
  validateWithinSize(contacts)
}
```

The first set of operations you'll discover allows you to inquire about the size of a list. These are the following:

- size—The function size takes no parameters, and it returns the number of elements in the list:

```
scala> List().size
val res0: Int = 0

scala> List(1,2,3).size
val res1: Int = 3
```

- isEmpty—The method isEmpty requires no parameters, and it returns true if a sequence has no elements, false otherwise:

```
scala> List().isEmpty
val res2: Boolean = true

scala> List(1,2,3).isEmpty
val res3: Boolean = false
```

- nonEmpty—The function nonEmpty is the negation of the function isEmpty. It has no parameters, and it returns true for all the lists that have at least one element, false for the empty list:

```
scala> List().nonEmpty
val res4: Boolean = false

scala> List(1,2,3).nonEmpty
val res5: Boolean = true
```

Table 29.1 shows a summary of the methods regarding the size of a collection.

Table 29.1 The methods to investigate the size of an instance of List

Signature	Description	Example
def size: Int	The size of the sequence	List(1,2).size // it returns 2
def isEmpty: Boolean	It asserts if the list is empty.	List(1,2).isEmpty // it returns false
def nonEmpty: Boolean	It states if the list has at least one element.	List(1,2).nonEmpty // it returns true

> **Quick Check 29.1** What is the value returned by the following snippet of code?
>
> ```
> List("").isEmpty
> ```

29.2 Properties of the elements in a list

Let's imagine you now need to provide functionalities so that you can perform the following queries on your address book:

- Verify if a specific contact is present.
- Check if a contact with a given name exists.
- Count the number of contacts from a given company.

Listing 29.3 Inquiring of the elements of a list

```
def isPresent(addressBook: List[Contact], contact: Contact): Boolean =
    addressBook.contains(contact)
```
← The function contains returns true if a given element is in the list, false otherwise.

```
def isPresentByName(addressBook: List[Contact], name: String): Boolean =
    addressBook.exists(_.name == name)
```
← The method exists returns true if at least one item in the list satisfies a given predicate. It returns false otherwise.

```
def countByCompany(addressBook: List[Contact], company: String): Int =
    addressBook.count(_.company.contains(company))
```
The method count counts for how many list elements respect a given predicate.

When inquiring about the elements contained in a list, you can use the following methods:

- contains—The method contains takes one element as its parameter, and it asserts if it equals to any of the items in the sequence:

```scala
scala> List().contains("scala")
val res0: Boolean = false

scala> List(1, 2, 3).contains("scala")
val res1: Boolean = false

scala> List(1, 2, 3).contains(3)
val res2: Boolean = true
```

- exists—For an instance of List[A], the function exists takes a function of type A => Boolean. It returns true if any of the elements in the list respects the given predicate:

```scala
scala> List(1,2,3).exists(_ > 42)
val res3: Boolean = false
// Is there an element bigger than 42?

scala> List(1,2,3).exists(e => e > 2 && e < 5)
val res4: Boolean = true
// Is there an element bigger than 2, and smaller than 5?
```

- count—For an instance of List[A], the method count returns the number of elements that respect a given predicate of type A => Boolean.

```scala
scala> List(1,2,3).count(_ > 1)
val res5: Int = 2

scala> List(1,2,3).count(_ > 3)
val res6: Int = 0
```

Table 29.2 summarizes all the functions you can use to verify if or how many items in the sequence have specific characteristics.

Table 29.2 Recap of the methods you can use to investigate the properties of the elements in an instance of List[A]. Where necessary, the method signatures have been simplified to hide non-relevant implementation details.

Signature	Description	Example
def contains(elem: A): Boolean	It verifies if the sequence contains a given element.	List(1,2).contains(3) // it returns false
def exists(p: A => Boolean): Boolean	It asserts if the list contains at least one element that respects a given predicate.	List(1,2).exists(_ > 1) // it returns true

Quick Check 29.2 What is the return value of the following snippets of code? Use the REPL to validate your hypothesis.

```
1  List("Welcome", "to", "Scala").contains("scala")
2  List("Welcome", "to", "Scala").exists(_.endsWith("me"))
3  List("Welcome", "to", "Scala").count(_.contains("o"))
4  class A(i: Int); List(new A(1)).contains(new A(1))
5  case class B(i: Int); List(new B(1)).contains(new B(1))
```

Create an empty list for a given type

When creating an empty list, the compiler struggles to infer its type correctly since it has no elements to help it in its guessing. Without any hint or cast on its intended type, the compiler infers the expression List() to be of type List[Nothing]:

```
scala> List()
val res0: List[Nothing] = List()
// The compiler has no type information
// so it infers the type List[Nothing]

scala> val myList: List[Int] = List()
val myList: List[Int] = List()
// The compiler assigns it the type List[Int]

scala> List().asInstanceOf[List[Int]]
val res1: List[Int] = List()
// Explicit casting from List[Nothing] to List[Int]
```

For a type A, you can use the method List.empty[A] to create an empty list of type List[A] in a more compact and elegant way:

```
scala> List.empty
val res2: List[Nothing] = List()
// The compiler has no type information
// so it creates an empty list of type List[Nothing]

scala> List.empty[Int]
val res3: List[Int] = List()
// The compiler creates a list of type List[Int]
```

Summary

In this lesson, my objective was to teach you some of the common operations on a list.

- You learned how to inquire about the size of a sequence.
- You saw how to check if it contains a given element or an element with determined characteristics.
- You discovered how to count how many list items have certain features.

Let's see if you got this!

TRY THIS   Given a list of people, write a function to ensure an individual with a given name is in it. You should use the following case class to represent a person:

```
case class Person(name: String, age: Int)
```

Answers to quick checks

Quick Check 29.1   The expression returns false because the list contains one element: the empty string.

```
scala> List("").isEmpty
val res0: Boolean = false
```

Quick Check 29.2   The answers are the following:

1. The compiler evaluates the expression to false because the sequence does not contain the word "scala." String equality is case sensitive, so "scala" and "Scala" are considered different.
2. The snippet of code returns true because the word "Welcome" ends with "me."
3. The expression returns the integer 2: the words "Welcome" and "to" are the ones containing the string "o."
4. It returns false because class equality requires two classes to be the same, if and only if their memory allocation address is the same. For this reason, the following expression returns false:

   ```
   scala> new A(1).equals(new A(1))
   val res0: Boolean = false
   ```

5. It returns true because case class equality requires two classes to be the same if they have the same structure. The following expression returns true because B is a case class:

   ```
   scala> new B(1).equals(new B(1))
   val res1: Boolean = true
   ```

WORKING WITH LIST: ELEMENT SELECTION

After reading this lesson, you will be able to

- Select the first element of a sequence
- Pick the nth item of a list
- Find the first element of a sequence that respects a given predicate
- Find the minimum/maximum item in a list according to some criteria

In the previous lesson, you learned how to analyze the properties of a sequence. In this lesson, you'll discover how to select one item in a list by its position. You'll also learn how to find an item that has specific characteristics. Finally, you'll see how to select the minimum or maximum element in a list based on natural ordering or custom ordering criteria. In the capstone, you'll analyze the movies data set to determine which movie has the highest profit.

> **Consider this**
> You have a list of exam scores. How will you find the highest and the lowest ones?

30.1 Selecting an element by its position

Let's continue to expand the functionalities of your address book program.

Listing 30.1 Representation of a contact

```
case class Contact(name: String,
                   surname: String,
                   numbers: List[ContactNumber],
                   company: Option[String],
                   email: Option[String])

sealed trait Label
case object Work extends Label
case object Home extends Label

case class ContactNumber(number: String, label: Label)
```

Imagine you now need to select a contact based on its position in you address book.

Listing 30.2 Get contact by position

```
def getByPosition(addressBook: List[Contact], n: Int): Contact =
  addressBook.apply(n)
```
Alternatively, you can also use the equivalent expression addressBook(n). If the index you provide is invalid, it throws an IndexOutOfBoundsException.

When selecting an element in a sequence by its position, you can use the following functions on an instance of the class List:

- apply—The method apply takes the index of the element in a sequence to return. In Scala, indexes always start from zero: the first element will have index 0, the second one index 1, and so on. It is an impure function because it throws IndexOutOfBoundsException if no item is available for the given index.

  ```
  scala> List(1,2,3).apply(0)
  val res0: Int = 1
  // expression equivalent to List(1,2,3)(0)

  scala> List(1,2,3).apply(3)
  java.lang.IndexOutOfBoundsException: 3
    at scala.collection.LinearSeqOptimized.apply(
      LinearSeqOptimized.scala:63)
    ... 28 elided
  // expression equivalent to List(1,2,3)(3)
  ```

- headOption—The function head and its equivalent apply(0) are impure functions as they throw exceptions for empty sequences. The method headOption is their pure alternative. When selecting the first element in a list, it returns its first element wrapped in a Some if present, or None if missing.

```scala
scala> List().headOption
val res0: Option[Nothing] = None

scala> List(1, 2, 3).headOption
val res1: Option[Int] = Some(1)
```

Table 30.1 provides a summary of the methods apply and headOption for the class List.

Table 30.1 Summary of the functions for an instance of List[A] to select an element by its position

Signature	Description	Example
def apply(n: Int): A	It returns the element of the sequence at position n. It throws an exception if the index is invalid.	List(0,1,2).apply(3) // it throws an IndexOutOfBoundsException
def headOption: Option[A]	It returns a nullable value containing the first element of the sequence, if any.	List(0,1,2).headOption // it returns Some(0)

> **Quick Check 30.1** The method apply is impure because it throws an exception when the given index does not conform to the sequence's length. Implement a method called safeApply as its pure equivalent. Your function should return an optional value other than throwing an exception:
>
> ```scala
> def safeApply[A](list: List[A], n: Int): Option[A]
> ```

30.2 Finding an element with given features

Imagine you'd like to find the first contact with a name starting with a specific text. You can achieve this thanks to the function find.

Listing 30.3 Finding contact by name

```scala
def findByName(addressBook: List[Contact],
              name: String): Option[Contact] =
    addressBook.find(contact => contact.name.startsWith(name))
```
Assuming here that name is case sensitive

When you need to find an element by its feature rather than its position, you can use the find method. For an instance of List[A], the function find optionally returns the first element in a sequence that respects a given predicate with shape A => Boolean. It returns an item as soon as it finds one, so it can avoid having your program traversing the entire list.

```
scala> List(1,2,3).find(_ > 1)
val res0: Option[Int] = Some(2)

scala> List(1,2,3).find(_ > 3)
val res1: Option[Int] = None
```

Table 30.2 summarizes when and how to use the function find on an instance of List.

Table 30.2   When working with a sequence and needing to find an element with specific properties, you should use the function find.

Signature	Description	Example

def find(
  p: A => Boolean): Option[A]
	It returns the first element in the collection for which the predicate p is true, if any.	List(0,1,2)
		  .find(_ <= 1)
		// it returns Some(0)

> **Quick Check 30.2**   Using your address book program, implement a function find-ByCompany to find one contact from a given company:
>
> ```
> def findByCompany(addressBook: List[Contact],
>                   company: String): Option[Contact]
> ```
>
> Consider the company name case insensitive.

30.3 Picking the minimum or maximum item

Let's consider your address book program again. Suppose you need to find the contact with the shortest full name (i.e., surname and name) and the last one in alphabetical order.

Listing 30.4 Selecting minimum and maximum elements

```
def shortestFullName(addressBook: List[Contact]): Contact =
  addressBook.minBy { contact =>          ⟵  Ordering per length of
                                             surname and name
```

```
      contact.surname.length + contact.name.length  ←
  }

def lastContactByFullName(addressBook: List[Contact]): Contact =
  addressBook.maxBy { contact =>
    s"${contact.surname} ${contact.name}"  ←
  }
```

If addressBook is empty, it throws an Unsupported-OperationException.

Ordering per alphabetical order
of surname and name

You can use the following function to select the minimum or maximum element in a list:

- max—For an instance of List[A] where A is a type with a given ordering, the method max returns the maximum element in the sequence. In Scala, you define an ordering for a type A by providing an implementation for Ordering[A] (you'll learn how to specify a custom order for any given type when discussing the implicit language feature). When the list is empty, it throws an Unsupported-OperationException. In Scala, many types have a predefined order: String, Int, BigDecimal, Char, Byte, and Boolean are some of them.

  ```
  scala> List(1, 2, 3).max
  val res0: Int = 3

  scala> List(1.4, 2.5, 3.6).max
  val res1: Double = 3.6

  scala> List.empty[Float].max
  java.lang.UnsupportedOperationException: empty.max
     ... 28 elided

  scala> List("scala", "hello").max
  val res2: String = scala
  // By default, Scala compares strings in alphabetical order
  ```

- min—The function min is complementary to the method max. For an instance of List[A] where A is a type with a given ordering, the method min returns the minimum element in the sequence. If the list is empty, it throws an Unsupported-OperationException.

  ```
  scala> List(1, 2, 3).min
  val res0: Int = 1

  scala> List(1.4, 2.5, 3.6).min
  val res1: Double = 1.4
  ```

```
scala> List.empty[Float].min
java.lang.UnsupportedOperationException: empty.min
   ... 28 elided

scala> List("hello", "scala").min
val res2: String = hello
// By default, Scala sorts strings in alphabetical order
```

- maxBy—The method maxBy returns the maximum element according to a given parameter. For an instance of List[A], it takes a function f with type A => B. The type B must have a given ordering. In other words, it needs to have an implementation for Ordering[B]. The function maxBy will use the function f: A => B to select the maximum element in the sequence. It throws an UnsupportedOperationException exception when the list is empty.

```
scala> case class Foo(n: Int, text: String)
case class Foo

scala> List(Foo(1, "z"), Foo(9, "a")).maxBy(_.n)
val res0: Foo = Foo(9,a)

scala> List(Foo(1, "z"), Foo(9, "a")).maxBy(_.text)
val res1: Foo = Foo(1,z)

scala> List.empty[Foo].maxBy(_.n)
java.lang.UnsupportedOperationException: empty.maxBy
   ... 28 elided
```

When defining a custom ordering rule, you can also use tuples to provide multiple criteria with different priorities. For example, you could pick the maximum element for a sequence of Foo instances by looking at their text field's length first and then at their alphabetical order:

```
scala> List(Foo(1, "zz"), Foo(9, "a"), Foo(8, "aa")).maxBy { foo =>
   // ordering by the size of text
   // and then by its alphabetical order
   (foo.text.size, foo.text)
}
val res2: Foo = Foo(1, "zz")
```

- minBy—The function minBy is complementary to maxBy. For an instance of List[A], it takes a function f with type A => B, where B has a given ordering. The function minBy will apply the function f: A => B to determine the minimum element in the sequence. When there are no elements, it throws an instance of Unsupported-OperationException.

```
scala> case class A(n: Int, text: String)
case class A

scala> List(A(1, "z"), A(9, "a")).minBy(_.n)
val res0: A = A(1,z)

scala> List(A(1, "z"), A(9, "a")).minBy(_.text)
val res1: A = A(9,a)

scala> List.empty[A].minBy(_.n)
java.lang.UnsupportedOperationException: empty.minBy
    ... 28 elided
```

Table 30.3 provides a summary of the functions to pick the minimum and maximum item in a sequence.

Table 30.3 Summary of the methods to select the minimum or maximum element in an instance for List[A] by natural or given ordering criteria. A valid custom ordering predicate is a function that transforms an item of type A to a type B, where B has a known natural ordering. When necessary, I have simplified the signature to hide unnecessary implementation details.

Signature	Description	Example
def max(implicit ord: Ordering[A]): A	It returns the maximum element in a sequence based the element's natural ordering type.	List(0,1,2).max // it returns 2
def min(implicit ord: Ordering[A]): A	It picks the minimum item in a list according to the element's natural ordering type.	List(0,1,2).min // it returns 0
def maxBy[B](f: A => B) (implicit ord: Ordering[B]): A	It selects the maximum item in a sequence given custom order criteria.	List(0,1,2) .maxBy(_ * -12.34) // it returns 0
def minBy[B](f: A => B) (implicit ord: Ordering[B]): A	It returns the minimum element in a list according to custom ordering criteria.	List(0,1,2) .minBy(_ * -12.34) // it returns 2

Quick Check 30.3 Consider your address book program and the following snippet of code:

```
def topContact(addressBook: List[Contact]): Contact =
  addressBook.max
```

Does it compile? What does it return? Why? Use the REPL to validate your hypothesis.

Summary

In this lesson, my objective was to teach you about different approaches to select an item in a sequence.

- You saw how to pick an element based on its position.
- You discovered how to find an item with specific properties.
- You learned how to select the minimum or maximum element based on different ordering criteria.

Let's see if you got this!

> **TRY THIS**   Imagine you are developing a rating system program for movies. Each movie has a title, a director, a publication year, a short description, and a list of awards it received. Write a function to find the most recent production with the most awards.

Answers to quick checks

Quick Check 30.1   A possible implementation for the function safeApply is the following:

```
def safeApply[A](list: List[A], n: Int): Option[A] =
  if (0 < n &&  n < list.size) Some(list.apply(n))
  else None
```

Quick Check 30.2   You can implement the method findByCompany:

```
def findByCompany(addressBook: List[Contact],
                company: String): Option[Contact] =
  addressBook.find { contact =>
    contact.company.exists(_.equalsIgnoreCase(company))
  }
```

Quick Check 30.3   The code does not compile because the compiler does not know that it should order a sequence of contacts. It errors with the following message: "No implicit Ordering defined for Contact." You can solve this by using the maxBy function and providing an explicit ordering rule. You could also define a natural ordering for contacts. You'll see how to do this in unit 7.

WORKING WITH LIST: FILTERING

After reading this lesson, you will be able to

- Remove or select items from a sequence based on their position
- Filter elements of a list that respect a given predicate
- Remove duplicated items in a sequence

In the previous lesson, you learned how to select a single element in a sequence based on its position or features. In this lesson, you'll continue to discover other operations you can perform on an instance of List. You'll see how to create a new list from an existing one by selecting one of its subsections. You'll discover how to pick elements that have specific characteristics. Finally, you'll learn how to create a new sequence that contains no duplicated items. In the capstone, you'll use these operations to create a subset of movies that have specific characters.

> **Consider this**
> Suppose you need to define a function to select all the even numbers in a given sequence of integers. How would you implement it?

31.1 Dropping and taking elements

In the previous lessons, you developed a program to store your contacts. Let's recall that your program represents a contact record.

Listing 31.1 Representation of a contact

```
case class Contact(name: String,
                   surname: String,
                   numbers: List[ContactNumber],
                   company: Option[String],
                   email: Option[String])

sealed trait Label
case object Work extends Label
case object Home extends Label

case class ContactNumber(number: String, label: Label)
```

Let's imagine you need to select the first n contacts in your address book.

Listing 31.2 First n contacts

```
def firstN(addressBook: List[Contact], n: Int): List[Contact] =
  addressBook.take(n)
```
⟵ If you have less than n contacts, it returns the address book unchanged.

When working with lists, you can drop and take elements based on different criteria:

- drop—The function drop takes an integer n as its parameter, and it creates a new list without its first n items. If the sequence has less than n elements, it returns the empty list.

```
scala> List(1,2,3).drop(1)
val res0: List[Int] = List(2, 3)

scala> List(1,2,3).drop(0)
val res1: List[Int] = List(1, 2, 3)

scala> List(1,2,3).drop(4)
val res2: List[Int] = List()
```

- take—The method take is complementary to drop: it takes an integer n as its parameter, and it creates a new list containing its first n items. If the sequence has less than n elements, it returns the given parameter.

```scala
scala> List(1,2,3).take(1)
val res0: List[Int] = List(1)

scala> List(1,2,3).take(0)
val res1: List[Int] = List()

scala> List(1,2,3).take(4)
val res2: List[Int] = List(1, 2, 3)
```

- dropWhile—For an instance of List[A], the method dropWhile creates a new list by removing elements starting from its head until a given predicate A => Boolean is respected.

```scala
scala> List(1,2,3,-1,-2,-3).dropWhile(_ < 2)
val res0: List[Int] = List(2, 3, -1, -2, -3)

scala> List(1,2,3,-1,-2,-3).dropWhile(_ < 0)
val res1: List[Int] = List(1, 2, 3, -1, -2, -3)
```

- takeWhile—The method takeWhile is complementary to dropWhile. For an instance of List[A], the function takeWhile creates a new sequence by selecting elements from its head until a given predicate A => Boolean is verified.

```scala
scala> List(1,2,3,-1,-2,-3).takeWhile(_ < 2)
val res0: List[Int] = List(1)

scala> List(1,2,3,-1,-2,-3).takeWhile(_ < 0)
val res1: List[Int] = List()
```

Table 31.1 provides a recap of the drop and take operations on a sequence.

Table 31.1 The functions to take and drop elements either by position or feature for the class List[A]. Where necessary, the method signature has been simplified to hide nonrelevant implementation details.

Signature	Description	Example
def drop(n: Int): List[A]	It creates a new list by selecting all elements but the first n.	List(0,1,2).drop(1) // it returns List(1,2)
def take(n: Int): List[A]	It creates a new list by picking the first n elements.	List(0,1,2).take(1) // it returns List(0)

Table 31.1 The functions to take and drop elements either by position or feature for the class List[A]. Where necessary, the method signature has been simplified to hide nonrelevant implementation details. *(continued)*

Signature	Description	Example

def dropWhile(
    p: A => Boolean): List[A]
	It creates a new list by selecting elements until the predicate p is true.	List(0,1,2)
		  .dropWhile(_ < 2)
		// it returns List(2)

def takeWhile(
    p: A => Boolean): List[A]
	It creates a new list by picking elements until the predicate p is true.	List(0,1,2)
		  .takeWhile(_ < 2)
		// it returns List(0,1)

Quick Check 31.1 Using the functions drop and take, implement the following method to paginate a sequence of strings:

```
def paginate(data: List[String],
             pageN: Int,
             pageSize: Int): List[String]
```

To simplify, you can assume that the parameters pageN and pageSize are positive numbers. If the sequence is not big enough for the requested pagination, an empty list is returned. For example, given a page size of 10, page 1 should return the first 10 elements, while page 2 should return from the 11th element to the 20th.

 ## 31.2 Filtering Items of a list

Let's consider your book address program again, and let's imagine you now need to identify all the contacts that belong to a given company.

Listing 31.3 All contacts from a given company

```
def fromCompany(addressBook: List[Contact],
                             corp: String): List[Contact] =
  addressBook.filter(contact =>
    contact.company.exists(_.equalsIgnoreCase(corp))
  )
```

Assuming here that the company name is case insensitive

The class List has two functions that allow you to filter elements based on a given criterion:

- filter—For an instance of List[A], the method filter takes a function of type A => Boolean as its parameter, and it returns a new list with all the elements that respect the predicate.

```scala
scala> List(1,2,3).filter(_ > 0)
val res0: List[Int] = List(1, 2, 3)

scala> List(1,2,3).filter(_ > 2)
val res1: List[Int] = List(3)
```

- filterNot—This is the complementary of the filter method. For an instance of List[A], the function filterNot returns a new list containing all the elements that do not respect a given predicate of type A => Boolean.

```scala
scala> List(1,2,3).filterNot(_ > 0)
val res0: List[Int] = List()

scala> List(1,2,3).filterNot(_ > 2)
val res1: List[Int] = List(1, 2)
```

Table 31.2 summarizes the methods on a sequence to filter elements based on their features.

Table 31.2 The functions filter and filterNot allow you to filter items of an instance of class List[A based on given criteria. Some method signatures are simplified to hide nonrelevant implementation details.

Signature	Description	Example

def filter(
    p: A => Boolean): List[A]
	It returns a new sequence containing all the elements for which the predicate p is true.	List(0,1,2)
		  .filter(_ <= 1)
		// it returns List(0,1)

def filterNot(
    p: A => Boolean): List[A]
	It returns a new sequence containing all the elements for which the predicate p is false.	List(0,1,2)
		  .filterNot(_ <= 1)
		// it returns List(2)

Quick Check 31.2 Implement a function that, given a list of double, returns a new sequence containing only its nonnegative numbers:

```scala
def filterNonNegative(numbers: List[Double]): List[Double]
```

31.3 Removing duplicates

You want to remove any duplicated contact from your address book. Let's assume that two contacts are the same if and only if they contain the same information.

Listing 31.4 All contacts with no duplicates

```
def removeDuplicates(addressBook: List[Contact]): List[Contact] =
  addressBook.distinct
```

When in need of removing duplicated elements in a list, you can use the method distinct: it operates on a sequence by creating a new one containing the same items but without duplicates.

```
scala> List(1,2,3,3,3).distinct
val res0: List[Int] = List(1, 2, 3)

scala> List(1,2,3).distinct
val res1: List[Int] = List(1, 2, 3)
```

Table 31.3 provides a description of the distinct function for a list.

Table 31.3   The method distinct removes duplicates from an instance of class List[A].

Signature	Description	Example

def distinct: List[A]	It returns a new collection without duplicate elements.	List(1,0,0,1)
		  .distinct
		  // it returns List(1,0)

Quick Check 31.3   Consider the following snippet of code:

```
class A(i: Int)
val myList = List(new A(1), new A(2), new A(1))
```

What is the value returned by the expression myList.distinct? Why? Use the REPL to validate your hypothesis.

Summary

In this lesson, my objective was to teach you about creating a sequence by filtering elements of an existing one.

- You learned how to take or drop elements based on their position or until your program meets one with a particular feature.
- You discovered how to select items based on a given predicate.
- You saw how to remove duplicates from a list.

Let's see if you got this!

> **TRY THIS** Represent a collection of books, in which each book has a title, a list of authors, and a genre. Possible genres are action, comic, and drama. Implement a function to return all its drama authors and ensure there are no duplicates in the sequence.

Answers to quick checks

> **Quick Check 31.1** A possible implementation for the function paginate is the following:
>
> ```
> def paginate(data: List[String],
>              pageN: Int,
>              pageSize: Int): List[String] = {
>   val toSkip = (pageN - 1) * pageSize
>   data.drop(toSkip).take(pageSize)
> }
> ```

> **Quick Check 31.2** You can implement the function filterNonNegative using the filter function:
>
> ```
> def filterNonNegative(numbers: List[Double]): List[Double] =
>   numbers.filter(_ >= 0)
> ```
>
> Alternatively, you can also use the filterNot method:
>
> ```
> def filterNonNegative(numbers: List[Double]): List[Double] =
>   numbers.filterNot(_ < 0)
> ```

Quick Check 31.3 The expression myList.distinct returns the sequence myList. You have declared A a regular class rather than a case class; class equality requires two classes to be the same if and only if their memory allocation address is the same. Notice that the following expression returns false:

```
scala> (new A(1)).equals(new A(1))
val res0: Boolean = false
```

On the other hand, case class equality only requires two classes to be the same if they have the same structure. If you change the code to declare A a case class, you will receive a sequence containing only two elements when invoking the distinct function.

WORKING WITH LIST: SORTING AND OTHER OPERATIONS

After reading this lesson, you will be able to

- Sort a list
- Produce a string representation of a sequence
- Sum all the numerical elements of a list
- Group items according to given criteria

In the previous lesson, you mastered how to filter elements of a sequence. In this lesson, you'll learn about a variety of operations you can perform on lists. You'll discover different approaches to sorting the items of a sequence. Also, you'll learn how to produce a text representation for it. Finally, you'll see how to restructure your list into a dictionary-like structure that groups elements with common features. In the capstone, you'll use these operations to rank the films in the movies data set and display your data analysis in a human-readable form.

> **Consider this**
> Imagine you have a numerical list, and you'd like to sort its elements from its largest number to its smallest one. How would you implement it?

32.1 Sorting elements

In this unit, you have developed a software program to manage an address book to represent each contact.

Listing 32.1 Representing a contact

```scala
case class Contact(name: String,
                   surname: String,
                   numbers: List[ContactNumber],
                   company: Option[String],
                   email: Option[String])

sealed trait Label
case object Work extends Label
case object Home extends Label

case class ContactNumber(number: String, label: Label)
```

So far, you have been storing your contacts in no particular order. However, you may want to sort them so that people can easily consult them. Imagine you'd like to sort them alphabetically by surname and name.

Listing 32.2 Sorting the contacts alphabetically

```scala
def sort(addressBook: List[Contact]): List[Contact] =
  addressBook.sortBy { contact =>
    (contact.surname, contact.name)        ←——— Sorting in alphabetical
  }                                               order by surname first,
                                                  then by name
```

You have several different options when sorting a sequence. The most popular functions to do so are the following.

- sorted—For an instance of List[A] where A is a type with a given order, the function returns a new sequence with its elements ordered accordingly. Let's recall that type A has a given order if it has an implementation for Ordering[A].

  ```scala
  scala> List(0.4, -2, 3).sorted
  val res0: List[Double] = List(-2.0, 0.4, 3.0)

  scala> List("my", "example").sorted
  val res1: List[String] = List(example, my)
  ```

```
scala> List.empty[Double].sorted
val res2: List[Double] = List()
```

- sortBy — The method sortBy sorts the elements of a sequence according to a given criterion. For an instance of List[A], the function sortBy takes a function f with type A => B as its parameter, where the type B must a defined ordering. You can combine multiple criteria by using a tuple. The first criteria in the tuple will have priority over the second one, and so on.

```
scala> List(0.4, -2, 3).sortBy(i => -i)
val res0: List[Double] = List(3.0, 0.4, -2.0)
// Ordering doubles in descending order

scala> case class A(n: Int, text: String)
case class A

scala> List(A(1, "z"), A(9, "a"), A(1, "a"))
     |          .sortBy(e => (e.text, e.n))
val res1: List[A] = List(A(1,a), A(9,a), A(1,z))
// Ordering by the field text first, then by n
```

- reverse — The method reverse returns a new list containing elements in reverse order.

```
scala> List(1, 3, 2).reverse
val res0: List[Int] = List(2, 3, 1)

scala> List.empty[String].reverse
val res1: List[String] = List()
```

How to shuffle items in a list

Imagine you have a sequence and you'd like to change the order of its elements randomly. You can achieve this thanks to the scala.util.Random class as follows:

```
scala> import scala.util.Random
import scala.util.Random

scala> Random.shuffle(List(1, 2, 3))
val res0: List[Int] = List(2, 1, 3)

scala> Random.shuffle(List(1, 2, 3))
val res1: List[Int] = List(3, 2, 1)
// calling Random.shuffle multiple times returns a different result!
```

Table 32.1 provides a summary of the methods you can use to sort the elements of a list.

Table 32.1   The different functions you can use to sort an instance of the class List[A].

Signature	Description	Example

`def sorted(implicit ord: Ordering[A]): List[A]`	It sorts a list according to its elements' natural ordering type. Type A must have a natural ordering, that is an implementation of `Ordering[A]`.	`List(1,0,2).sorted`
		`// it returns`
		`// List(0,1,2)`

`def sortBy[B](f: A => B) (implicit ord: Ordering[B]): List[A]`	It sorts the sequence according to a given custom ordering criteria.	`List(1,0,2)`
		`  .sortBy(_ * -10)`
		`// it returns`
		`// List(2,1,0)`

`def reverse: List[A]`	It returns a new list in which its elements are in reverse order.	`List(1,0,2)`
		`  .reverse`
		`// it returns`
		`// List(2,0,1)`

Quick Check 32.1   Consider the following snippet of code:

```
List().sorted
```

Does it compile? If so, what does it return? Why? Use the REPL to validate your hypothesis.

32.2 Converting a list to a string

Now that you have seen how to sort your contacts, you may want to display a summary representation for them. For example, you may want to produce a text to list the first n contacts' surname and name.

Listing 32.3 Pretty representation of contact

```
case class Contact(name: String,
                   surname: String,
                   numbers: List[ContactNumber],
                   company: Option[String],
                   email: Option[String]) {

  def toPrettyString: String = s"$surname $name"
}
```

Rather than using the default implementation of toString for the case class Contact, you define an alternative string conversion.

```
def describeFirstN(n: Int, addressBook: List[Contact]): String =
  addressBook.take(n).map(_.toPrettyString).mkString("\n")
```

Invoking toPrettyString for each
contact and concatenating the
results with \n

When building a string that represents a sequence and its items, you can use the function mkString. It returns a string representing the list and its elements; converts each element into text by invoking the toString method, which the compiler ensures it exists for every instance; and concatenates them using a separator, set by default to the empty string. You can also provide strings to use as prefix and suffix of the produced string:

```
scala> List("Hello", "Scala").mkString
val res0: String = HelloScala
// Using the default separator ""
```

```
scala> List("Hello", "Scala").mkString(", ")
val res1: String = Hello, Scala
// Using the separator ", "
```

```
scala> List("Hello", "Scala").mkString("[", "-", "]")
val res2: String = [Hello-Scala]
// Using the separator "-", "[" as prefix, and "]" as suffix
```

```
scala> List().mkString("[", "-", "]")
val res3: String = []
// Using the separator "-", "[" as prefix, and "]" as suffix
```

Table 32.2 shows a technical summary for the function mkString on an instance of List[A].

Table 32.2   The function mkString produces a string representation of a sequence.

Signature	Description	Example

def mkString(
    start: String,
    sep: String,
    end: String): String
	It produces a string representing the list, starting with the string start and ending with the string end. It converts its elements by invoking the method toString on each of them and concatenating the results using the string sep.	List(0,1,2)
		    .mkString(
		        "{", ",", "}")
		// it returns
		// "{0,1,2}"

def mkString(
    sep: String): String
	The equivalent of invoking the function mkString(start, sep, end) as mkString("", sep, "").	List(0,1,2)
		    .mkString(",")
		// it returns
		// "0,1,2"

Table 32.2   The function mkString produces a string representation of a sequence. *(continued)*

Signature	Description	Example
def mkString: String	It produces the same effect of invoking the function mkString(start, sep, end) as mkString("","", "").	List(0,1,2).mkString // it returns "012"

Quick Check 32.2   Consider the following two snippets of code; what value does each of them produce? Use the REPL to confirm your hypotheses.

1   class A(i: Int)
    List(new A(0), new A(1), new A(2)).mkString(",")

2   case class B(i: Int)
    List(new B(0), new B(1), new B(2)).mkString(",")

 ## 32.3 Sum elements of numerical sequences

Let's consider your address book program again. Suppose you need to compute many numbers stored in your device, keeping in mind that each contact may have zero or more phone numbers.

Listing 32.4 Total phone numbers stored

```
def totalNumbers(addressBook: List[Contact]): Int =
    addressBook.map(_.numbers.size).sum
```
← Counting how many numbers each contact has and summing all of them up

When working with numerical sequences, you can sum its elements using the function sum. For an instance of List[A] where A is a numeric type, the method sum returns a value of type A representing the sum of its numbers. In Scala, a type A is numeric if it has an implementation for Numeric[A]. You'll revisit this concept in unit 7, in which you'll learn about the keyword *implicit*, and you'll show you how to create your custom numeric type. The types Byte, Short, Int, Long, Float, Double, and BigInt are examples of numeric types in Scala.

```
scala> List(1, 2, 3).sum
val res0: Int = 6
```

```
scala> List(1.4, 2.5, 3.6).sum
val res1: Double = 7.5

scala> List.empty[Float].sum
val res2: Float = 0.0

scala> List("hello", "scala").sum
       error: could not find implicit value for parameter num:
           scala.math.Numeric[String]
// The compiler could not find an implementation for Numeric[String]
// since String is not a numeric type
```

Table 32.3 provides a summary of the method sum for an instance of List[A].

Table 32.3 You can use the method sum to sum the elements of a numerical sequence.

Signature	Description	Example
def sum(implicit num: Numeric[A]): List[A]	It sums the elements of a numerical list. A type A is numerical if it has an implementation for Numeric[A].	List(0,1,2).sum // it returns 3

Quick Check 32.3 Write a function sumOfFirstN to sum all numbers for 0 to n inclusive:

```
def sumOfFirstN(n: Int): Int
```

For example, sumOfFirstN(10) should return 55, and sumOfFirstN(-10) should return 0. HINT: You can generate a sequential structure containing all numbers from 0 to n inclusive using the operator to. For example, the expression 0 to 3 returns a range containing the numbers 0, 1, 2, and 3.

32.4 Grouping elements by feature

Imagine you now need to display contacts per company.

Listing 32.5 Contacts per company

```
def perCompany(
  addressBook: List[Contact]): Map[Option[String], List[Contact]] =
  addressBook.groupBy(_.company)
```

The function returns a key-value structure called map where the key is the nullable company name (i.e., "Option[String]"), and the value is the list of contacts with that company value (i.e., "List[Contact]").

You can use the method groupBy on a sequence to group elements based on their characteristics by producing a key-value structure called map. For an instance of List[A], the function groupBy takes a parameter f with type A => B, and it returns a value of type Map[B, List[A]] (you'll learn about the type Map in the next unit). The function groupBy uses the function f to determine each key of the dictionary and its corresponding values.

```scala
scala> case class A(n: Int, text: String)
case class A

scala> List(A(1, "z"), A(9, "a")).groupBy(_.text)
val res0: scala.collection.immutable.Map[String,List[A]] =
  Map(z -> List(A(1,z)), a -> List(A(9,a)))
// A dictionary with two keys: "z" and "a"

scala> List("hello", "world", "scala").groupBy(_.length)
val res1: scala.collection.immutable.Map[Int,List[String]] =
  Map(5 -> List(hello, world, scala))
// A dictionary containing the key 5

scala> List("hello", "world", "scala").groupBy(_.contains('a'))
val res2: scala.collection.immutable.Map[Boolean,List[String]] =
  Map(false -> List(hello, world), true -> List(scala))
// A dictionary with two keys: false and true

scala> List.empty[String].groupBy(_.contains('a'))
val res3: scala.collection.immutable.Map[Boolean,List[String]] =
  HashMap()
// The empty dictionary
```

Option and string as special implementations of list

The Scala List collection is full of useful functions that make it versatile to use. Many of the methods you have seen are defined for several other types, not just List. For example, you will see that both Set and Map have a filter operation.

The compiler makes these functionalities available for all the types that can automatically convert to a sequence-like structure. You can consider the type String as a sequence of characters and perform the following operations:

```scala
scala> "scala".max
val res0: Char = s
// 's' is the char with the highest ASCII code
```

```
scala> "scala".min
val res1: Char = a
// 'a' is its char with the lowest ASCII code
```

You can also see an Option type as a special case of List that has either zero or one element:

```
scala> Some(5).filter(_ < 3)
val res2: Option[Int] = None

scala> Some(5).size
val res3: Int = 1
```

Table 32.4 provides a summary of the groupBy function for an instance of List[A].

Table 32.4 The method groupBy groups list elements based on their features.

Signature	Description	Example

def groupBy[K](
    f: A => K): Map[K, List[A]]
	It groups the items of a sequence according to the computation of a value K.	List(0,1,2)
		  .groupBy(_ % 2)
		// it returns
		// Map(
		// 0 -> List(0,2),
		// 1 -> List(1))

Quick Check 32.4 Implement a function perLetter to group your address book contacts according to the first letter of their surname:

```
def perLetter(addressBook: List[Contact]): Map[Char, List[Contact]]
```

You should add those contacts with an empty surname to a category identified by the space char ''.

Summary

In this lesson, my objective was to teach you about operations you can perform on a list.

- You discovered different strategies to sort its elements.
- You mastered how to use the mkString function to produce a more expressive string representation for your sequence.
- You learned how to sum numerical lists.

- You saw how to group elements with features in common thanks to the *groupBy* function.

Let's see if you got this!

> **TRY THIS** Imagine you are building a program to mark exams. Assume that a mark has an exam name, a score, and a student ID. Write a function that takes a sequence of marks and prints a human-readable message to the console containing the top five scores' student ID.

 ## Answers to quick checks

> **Quick Check 32.1**   The snippet of code List().sorted does not compile:
>
> ```
> scala> List().sorted
>        error: diverging implicit expansion for type Ordering[B]
>        starting with method Tuple9 in object Ordering
> ```
>
> The snippet List() has type List[Nothing]. When invoking the function sorted on it, the compiler looks for an instance of Ordering[Nothing] to use in the ordering; the compiler cannot find exactly one, so it rejects the expression as valid.

> **Quick Check 32.2**   The first snippet produces a string value similar to the following:
>
> ```
> val res0: String = A@ed2f2f6,A@7c281eb8,A@65f40689
> ```
>
> The second one produces a more readable text:
>
> ```
> val res1: String = B(0),B(1),B(2)
> ```
>
> The function mkString invokes the function toString for each element in the list. Class B is a case class: the compiler changes its toString implementation to describe its structural composition. On the other hand, A is a regular class: its toString method refers to its default implementation in java.lang.Object, which returns a text containing the class name and the memory address of the instance.

Quick Check 32.3 A possible implementation for the function sumOfFirstN is the following:

```scala
def sumOfFirstN(n: Int): Int = (0 to n).sum
```

The expression 0 to n produces a sequence-like structure called *inclusive range*, which contains all the numbers from 0 to n inclusive. You can invoke the toList function to convert a range to a list:

```scala
scala> val range = 0 to 10
val range: scala.collection.immutable.Range.Inclusive = Range 0 to 10
scala> range.toList
val res0: List[Int] = List(0, 1, 2, 3, 4, 5, 6, 7, 8, 9, 10)
```

Quick Check 32.4 You can implement the function perLetter as the following:

```scala
def perLetter(
        addressBook: List[Contact]): Map[Char, List[Contact]] =
  addressBook.groupBy(_.surname.headOption.getOrElse(' '))
```

THE MOVIES DATASET

In this capstone, you will

- Define ordered sequences of elements
- Transform and count the items of a list
- Find the minimum and maximum elements according to specific features
- Filter items based on their characteristics and selecting them based on their position
- Sort lists and produce string representation for them

In this capstone, you'll analyze data for more than 45,000 movies. The information is a subset of a popular and publicly accessible dataset called "The Movies Dataset" by Rounak Banik. On its website, you can find its latest version as well as an extensive description of its content:

> *These files contain metadata for all 45,000 movies listed in the Full MovieLens Dataset. The dataset consists of movies released on or before July 2017. Data points include cast, crew, plot keywords, budget, revenue, posters, release dates, languages, production companies, countries, TMDB vote counts and vote averages.*
>
> *This dataset also has files containing 26 million ratings from 270,000 users for all 45,000 movies. Ratings are on a scale of 1–5 and have been obtained from the official GroupLens website.*
>
> From https://www.kaggle.com/rounakbanik/the-movies-dataset

For this capstone, you'll focus on a subset of its data contained in a file called movies_metadata.csv. Its rows provide information on movies, such as their title, language, release date, vote average, and popularity. Table 33.1 is a list of the properties you'll consider for this capstone.

Table 33.1 Summary of the features for a movie from "The Movies Dataset" by Rounak Banik that you'll consider for this capstone

Feature	Description	Format	Nullable
budget	Budget in USD for the movie	Int	No
genres	The list of genres the movie belongs to	JSON	No
id	Its unique identifier	Int	No
imdb_id	External reference for the IMDB data set	String	No
original_language	The original language of the movie	String	No
original_title	Its original title	String	No
overview	A short description of the plot	String	No
popularity	Popularity score for the movie	Float	Yes
release_date	Its release date	Local Date	Yes
revenue	Revenue in USD for the movie	Int	Yes
runtime	Its duration in minutes	Double	Yes
title	Its English title	String	Yes
vote_average	Average vote from reviewers	Float	Yes
vote_count	Number of reviewers who rated the film	Float	Yes

In this capstone, you will interrogate the data set to discover information about these movies. In particular, you'll find answers to the following questions:

1 How many movies are there in the data set?
2 How many of them were released in 1987?
3 Find the top five productions per vote average and count with at least 50 votes.
4 Find the top five movies per popularity.
5 Select five non-English movies.
6 Which movie made the most profit?

33.1 Download the base project

Rather than creating an empty sbt project from scratch, let's use `git` to look at code that you'll use as the starting point for your capstone. You can ensure that `git` is available on your machine by executing the following command in your terminal:

```
$ git --version
git version 2.21.1 (Apple Git-122.3)
```

If needed, look at section 2.4.1 for instructions on installing `git` on your machine. You can now navigate to an empty folder of your choosing and download the code from its remote branch:

```
$ git init
$ git remote add get-prog-with-scala https://github.com/DanielaSfregola/
        get-programming-with-scala.git
$ git fetch get-prog-with-scala
$ git checkout -b my_lesson33 get-prog-with-scala/baseline_unit5_lesson33
```

The code you've downloaded is an sbt project with a few files ready to use. The files project/build.properties and build.sbt provide information on the sbt and Scala versions on which external dependencies to use. The src/main/resources/movies_metadata.csv is the resource containing the movie data you'll analyze. It provides many fields for each movie, but you'll only focus on some of them. Finally, the src/scala folder contains some useful implementations:

- `org.example.movies.MoviesDataset` uses an external dependency, called `scala-csv`, to read the file and parse each line into a `Movie` instance by invoking the `org.example.movies.entities.Movie.parse` function.
- `org.example.movies.entities.Parsers` contains several functions to parse string values. Each parse function tries to convert some text into a specific type value. It returns `None` in case of failure, and it wraps the parsed value into a `Some` otherwise. These parser functions take advantage of the `Map` and `Try` types and the `circe` library to parse JSON objects, which are topics you'll learn about in subsequent units of the book.
- `org.example.movies.entities.Movie` provides the structure of a movie and its fields you should consider in your analysis. You will provide an implementation for its `parse` function by combining the provided base parse functions.

Let's compile your project by executing the command `sbt compile` to download all its external dependencies and ensure the correctness of the code you have so far. You are now ready to start coding!

33.2 Parsing a movie entity

Let's begin by completing the implementation for the movie entity.

Listing 33.1 The initial content of Movie.scala

```scala
package org.example.movies.entities

import java.time.LocalDate
import org.slf4j.LoggerFactory

case class Genre(id: Int, name: String)

case class Movie(genres: List[Genre],
                 id: Int,
                 imdbId: String,
                 originalLanguage: String,
                 originalTitle: String,
                 title: String,
                 overview: String,
                 popularity: Option[Float],
                 releaseDate: Option[LocalDate],
                 revenue: Int,
                 budget: Int,
                 duration: Option[Double],
                 voteAverage: Float,
                 voteCount: Float)

object Movie {
  import Parsers._

  private val logger = LoggerFactory.getLogger(this.getClass)

  def parse(row: Map[String, String]): Option[Movie] = ???
}
```

A genre has an ID and a name.

Fields of a movie you'll consider

The parse function to implement

The scala-csv library will convert each line of the movies_metadata.csv file into a dictionary-like structure called Map, in which it associates each movie feature with its corresponding string value. You'll now implement the function Movie.parse, which converts the row parameter into a Movie instance. It will rely on the parse functions already implemented in Parsers. Their signatures are as follows:

```
def parseInt(row: Map[String, String], key: String): Option[Int]

def parseDouble(row: Map[String, String], key: String): Option[Double]

def parseString(row: Map[String, String], key: String): Option[String]

def parseFloat(row: Map[String, String], key: String): Option[Float]

def parseLocalDate(row: Map[String, String],
                   key: String): Option[LocalDate]

def parseGenres(row: Map[String, String],
                key: String): Option[List[Genre]]
```

These functions will try to find the value associated with a given key/feature and create an instance for their specific type. If a value exists and is compatible with the expected type, it will produce an instance of that type wrapped into a Some. For all the other cases, it will return None. A few example usages are the following:

```
parseInt(Map("id" -> "1"), "id")
// returns Some(1)

parseInt(Map("id" -> "1"), "myId")
// returns None because a value for key myId does not exist

parseInt(Map("id" -> "test"), "id")
// returns None because the string "test" cannot be converted to an Int
```

You can combine the existing parse function to parse a Movie instance.

Listing 33.2 The Movie.parse function

```
def parse(row: Map[String, String]): Option[Movie] = {

    val movie = for {                           Mandatory fields
      /* MANDATORY FIELDS */           ◄─────   requested to create
      genres <- parseGenres(row, "genres")      an instance of Movie
      id <- parseInt(row, "id")
      imdbId <- parseString(row, "imdb_id")
      originalLanguage <- parseString(row, "original_language")
      originalTitle <- parseString(row, "original_title")
      overview <- parseString(row, "overview")
      budget <- parseInt(row, "budget")
    } yield {
```

```
/* NULLABLE FIELDS */
val popularity = parseFloat(row, "popularity")
val releaseDate = parseLocalDate(row, "release_date")
val runtimeInMinutes = parseDouble(row, "runtime")

/* NULLABLE FIELDS WITH DEFAULTS */
val revenue = parseInt(row, "revenue").getOrElse[Int](0)
val title = parseString(row, "title").getOrElse(originalTitle)
val voteAverage = parseFloat(row,
    "vote_average").getOrElse[Float](0)
val voteCount = parseFloat(row,
    "vote_count").getOrElse[Float](0)

Movie(genres,
      id,
      imdbId,
      originalLanguage,
      originalTitle,
      title,
      overview,
      popularity,
      releaseDate,
      revenue,
      budget,
      runtimeInMinutes,
      voteAverage,
      voteCount)
  }

  if (movie.isEmpty) logger.warn(s"Skipping malformed movie row")
  movie
}
```

Features of a movie that may be missing

Optional properties of a film that have a reasonable default value

Warning to making visible when an entire row cannot the parsed

Although the data set documents that every movie has a unique identifier under the label ID, this is missing for three films in the CSV file. Rather than failing at runtime, your program gracefully handles it by logging a warning and skipping the row.

33.3 Printing query results

When querying the data set, you'll print human-readable messages containing the question you asked and its answer. Let's ensure that this is done consistently in your program by creating a few helper functions. Add the following file to the org.example.movie package.

Listing 33.3 The print helper functions

```scala
// file src/main/scala/org/example/movies/PrintResultHelpers.scala
package org.example.movies

object PrintResultHelpers {

  def printResult(question: String, answer: String): Unit =
    printResult(question, answers = List(answer))

  def printResult(question: String, answer: Option[String]): Unit =
    printResult(question: String, answers = answer.toList)

  def printResult(question: String, answers: List[String]): Unit = {
    println()
    println("==============")
    println(s"$question")

    if (answers.isEmpty) println("NOT FOUND")
    else println(answers.map(a => s"- $a").mkString("\n"))
  }
}
```

It prints a message when no answers are available.

It prints one or more answers.

After implementing these helper functions, you can now define the main class to query the data set.

 ### 33.4 Querying the movie data set

The components of your program are now ready for you to analyze the data set. Let's define the main application that loads the data set and parse it to produce an instance of List[Movie].

Listing 33.4 The movie application

```scala
// file src/main/scala/org/example/movies/MovieApp.scala
package org.example.movies

import PrintResultHelpers._

object MovieApp extends App {
```

This is needed to print questions and answers consistently.

```
val dataset = new MoviesDataset("movies_metadata.csv")
val movies = dataset.movies

private val unknown = "--"

// add your queries here!

}
```

It loads and parses the CSV file to produce an instance of List[Movie].

You'll use this for empty nullable values, rather than displaying the text "None."

You can now execute the command sbt run to run your main application to load and parse the data. In the terminal, you should see an output similar to the following:

```
$sbt run
[info] running org.example.movies.MovieApp
21:11:10.645 [run-main-0] INFO org.example.movies.MoviesDataset -
          Processing file movies_metadata.csv...
21:11:14.120 [run-main-0] INFO org.example.movies.MoviesDataset -
          Completed processing of file movies_metadata.csv! 45466
          records loaded
21:11:15.550 [run-main-0] WARN org.example.movies.entities.Movie$ -
          Skipping malformed movie row
21:11:15.764 [run-main-0] WARN org.example.movies.entities.Movie$ -
          Skipping malformed movie row
21:11:15.905 [run-main-0] WARN org.example.movies.entities.Movie$ -
          Skipping malformed movie row
[success] Total time: 21 s, completed 20-Jan-2021 21:11:16
```

Notice three expected warnings in the logs; the three movies without a value for ID are causing them. Your program can load and parse the movie information from the data set, and it is ready for you to query.

HOW MANY MOVIES ARE THERE IN THE DATA SET? You can use the function size to count the movies in the data set.

Listing 33.5 Amount of movies in the data set

```
printResult(
  question = "How many movies are there in the dataset?",
  answer = {
    val totCount = movies.size
    s"$totCount movies"
  }
)
```

You'll see that there are 45,463 films in the data set when executing the sbt run command:

```
===============
How many movies are there in the dataset?
 - 45463 movies
```

This result is consistent with the 45,466 records in the CSV file and the three skipped movie rows.

HOW MANY OF THEM WERE RELEASED IN 1987? Thanks to the count method, you can compute the numbers of movies in the data set that have a release date of 1987.

Listing 33.6 Amount of movies released in 1987

```
printResult(
  question = "How many movies were released in 1987?",
  answer = {
    val countFrom1987 = movies.count(
            _.releaseDate.exists(_.getYear == 1987))    ←——  The field
    s"$countFrom1987 movies"                                  releaseDate
  }                                                           is optional.
)
```

Executing your main class will produce the following output:

```
===============
How many movies were released in 1987?
 - 462 movies
```

The message shows that 462 movies were released in 1987. How would you count how many movies had no release date?

TOP FIVE MOVIES PER VOTE AVERAGE AND COUNT Let's find the five films with the highest vote average and count. However, you want to penalize those with a low vote count, so discard all movies with less than 50 votes.

Listing 33.7 Top five movies per vote average and count

```
printResult(
  question = "TOP 5 movies per vote average and count",
  answers = {
    val topPerVote =
      movies.filter(_.voteCount >= 50)
        .sortBy { movie =>
          (- movie.voteAverage, - movie.voteCount)
```

```
      }.take(5)
    topPerVote.map { movie =>
      s"[AVG: ${movie.voteAverage}, COUNT: ${movie.voteCount}] " +
      s"${movie.title}"
    }
  }
)
```

Executing the command sbt run will produce the following message:

```
================
TOP 5 movies per vote average and count
 - [AVG: 9.5, COUNT: 50.0] Planet Earth II
 - [AVG: 9.1, COUNT: 661.0] Dilwale Dulhania Le Jayenge
 - [AVG: 8.8, COUNT: 176.0] Planet Earth
 - [AVG: 8.7, COUNT: 68.0] Sansho the Bailiff
 - [AVG: 8.6, COUNT: 98.0] Human
```

Notice how the movie with the highest score, titled *Planet Earth II*, barely survived the vote count selection: it has 50. Simply discarding movies with an arbitrary low count may not be good enough. Can you think of a better strategy?

FIND THE TOP FIVE MOVIES PER POPULARITY   Let's now compute a movie ranking per popularity and select the top five.

Listing 33.8 Top five movies per popularity

```
printResult(
  question = "TOP 5 movies per popularity",
  answers = {
    val topPerPopularity =
      movies.sortBy { movie =>
            -movie.popularity.getOrElse(0f)
      }.take(5)
    topPerPopularity.map { movie =>
      s"[POPULARITY: ${movie.popularity.getOrElse(unknown)}] " +
      s"${movie.title}"
    }
  }
)
```

Popularity is an optional field, so you should provide a reasonable default.

You can produce the following by running your executable object:

```
================
TOP 5 movies per popularity
 - [POPULARITY: 547.4883] Minions
```

```
- [POPULARITY: 294.33704] Wonder Woman
- [POPULARITY: 287.25366] Beauty and the Beast
- [POPULARITY: 228.03275] Baby Driver
- [POPULARITY: 213.84991] Big Hero 6
```

The result shows a clear winner: the film *Minions* has a much higher popularity score than any other movie in the data set.

SELECT FIVE NON-ENGLISH MOVIES   So far, all the movies you selected are movies in English. Are there any movies that are not in English?

Listing 33.9 Selection of five non-English movies

```
printResult(
  question = "5 non-english movies",
  answers = {
    val topNonEnglishPerPopularity =
      movies.filterNot(_.originalLanguage == "en")          The field
            .take(5)                                        releaseDate
    topNonEnglishPerPopularity.map { movie =>               is optional.
      s"[LANG: ${movie.originalLanguage}, " +
      s"RELEASE DATE: ${movie.releaseDate.getOrElse(unknown)}] " +  ⤶
      s"${movie.title} (${movie.originalTitle})"
    }
  }
)
```

Executing the command sbt run reveals the following output:

```
=================
5 non-english movies
- [LANG: fr, RELEASE DATE: 1995-05-16] The City of Lost Children
      (La Cité des Enfants Perdus)
- [LANG: zh, RELEASE DATE: 1995-04-30] Shanghai Triad (?????????)
- [LANG: fr, RELEASE DATE: 1996-09-18] Wings of Courage
      (Guillaumet, les ailes du courage)
- [LANG: it, RELEASE DATE: 1994-01-01] Lamerica (Lamerica)
- [LANG: it, RELEASE DATE: 1994-09-22] The Postman (Il postino)
```

The list shows movies from French, Italian, and Chinese productions. Can you count how many Italian movies it contains? What about German films?

WHICH MOVIE MADE THE MOST PROFIT?   Let's now find which movie the most profit. Although profit is not a property in our movie data set, you can derive it from its revenue and budget.

Listing 33.10 **Movie with the most profit**

```
printResult(
  question = "Which movie made the most profit?",
  answer = {
    val mostProfit = movies.maxBy(
      movie => movie.revenue - movie.budget)
    val formattedProfit = {
      val formatter = java.text.NumberFormat.getInstance()
      formatter.format(mostProfit.revenue - mostProfit.budget)
    }
    s"[PROFIT: USD $formattedProfit] ${mostProfit.title}"
  }
)
```

Using a formatter to make monetary amounts easier to read

When running your executable object MovieApp, you will see the following result:

```
===============
Which movie made the most profit?
- [PROFIT: USD 1,823,223,624] Star Wars: The Force Awakens
```

The Disney production *The Force Awakens* is the most profitable movie with a return of $1.8 billion USD.

Try a few more queries and see if you can find any unexpected answers. For example, can you list all the genres available in the data set? Which movie is the most recent one? What is the duration of the longest film? Which of them made the smallest profit?

Summary

In this capstone, you queried a subset of the movie data set.

- You created a parser for the movie entity by chaining optional values.
- You created helper functions to consistently display your query results by creating lists and producing a custom string representation for them.
- You selected elements based on their features and positions.
- You filtered and sorted items in a sequence according to different criteria.
- You determined minimum and maximum elements based on given features.

Other collections and error handling

In unit 5, you learned about the structure List and its most common operations. In this unit, you'll discover other collections that Scala has to offer and how to handle errors in a more functional style. In the capstone, you'll parse data from the goodbooks-10k data set to define a book collection for your library and manage book loans. In particular, we will discuss the following subjects:

- Lesson 34 introduces you to the class Set to represent an unordered group of distinct values. You'll also learn how to traverse its elements and manipulate them using its map, flatten, and flatMap operations.
- Lesson 35 shows you how to perform the union, difference, and intersection operations on two sets. You'll see how inquiry about the property of an instance of Set and select one or more of its elements according to given criteria.
- Lesson 36 teaches you about a key-value structure called Map. You'll add and remove entries from it, as well as manipulate its content using its map, flatten, and flatMap functions.
- Lesson 37 gives you an overview of the operations you can perform on Map. You'll inquire

about its size and the properties of the entries it contains, as well as filter them based on their features.

- Lesson 38 introduces you to the class Either to represent a value that can have one of two possible types, an approach particularly useful when performing validation tasks. You'll also learn how to manipulate its content using its map, flatten, and flatMap operations.
- Lesson 39 teaches you how to handle Either instances by checking their kind and extracting their value.
- Lesson 40 shows you how to use the class Try to handle errors without throwing exceptions. You'll use pattern matching on it, as well as retrieve its value.
- Finally, you'll parse book information to define a book collection and use it to represent a library in which users can search, reserve, and return books in lesson 41.

After learning more about collections and handling errors without relying on exceptions, you'll continue with unit 7, in which you'll master how to handle asynchronous computations.

SET

After reading this lesson, you will be able to

- Define an unordered group of distinct values called Set
- Add and remove items from Set
- Manipulate a set's elements using the map, flatten, and flatMap methods
- Chain multiple Set instances using for-comprehension

In the previous unit, you have learned about List and the operations you can perform on it. In this lesson, you'll discover the collection Set as an immutable representation of a group of elements. Sets and lists have many features in common and similar syntax, with a fundamental difference: the items of a set are unique and have no order. You'll see how to create a set and add and remove elements from it. You'll discover how to manipulate its items using the map, flatten, and flatMap operations. Finally, you'll chain multiple instances of Set using for-comprehension. In the capstone, you'll use sets to store the book loans of a library.

> **Consider this**
> Suppose you'd like to convert the list of your favorite movies to a list of your favorite genres. You should consider each genre once. How would you ensure there are no duplicates?

34.1 Creating a set

Suppose you are writing a program to track which topics a student has selected, and each of them must be unique.

Listing 34.1 The Student and Exam classes

```
case class Student(id: Int, name: String, topics: Set[String])

val alice = Student(
  id = 1,
  name = "Alice Abbott",
  topics = Set("History", "Math")
)
```

The field topics has type Set[String].

Initializing a set containing two elements

In Scala, you should use the collection Set to represent a group of unique elements that have no specific order. A few examples of how to create a set in Scala are the following:

```
scala> Set(1, 2, 3)
val res0: scala.collection.immutable.Set[Int] = Set(1, 2, 3)
// A set containing the numbers 1, 2, and 3

scala> Set("hello", "hi", "hello")
val res1: scala.collection.immutable.Set[String] = Set(hello, hi)
// A set contains no duplicates, so it contains
// the word "hello" only once

scala> Set(1, "scala")`
val res2: scala.collection.immutable.Set[Any] = Set(1, scala)

scala> Set()
val res3: scala.collection.immutable.Set[Nothing] = Set()
// An empty set for instances of Nothing

scala> Set.empty[Double]
val res4: scala.collection.immutable.Set[Double] = Set()
// The empty function allows you to create an empty Set for a given type
```

The elements of a Set are unordered. You can iterate through a set, but the order of its items is not guaranteed. When typing the expression Set(1,2), the REPL produces a message showing its elements in the same order: 1,2. This is a coincidence that is dependent on the underlying implementation, and it can change depending on the Scala version you are using.

> **Quick Check 34.1** Define a set containing the numbers 3 and 12.34 using the Scala REPL. What is the type of your Set instance? Why?

 ## 34.2 Adding and removing elements

Imagine that you'd like to update the topics a student has selected by removing and adding elements to the set

Listing 34.2 Adding and removing exam records

```scala
val updatedTopics = alice.topics + "Chemistry" - "Math"
alice.copy(topics = updatedTopics)
```
Adding "Chemistry" and removing "Math"

In Scala, Set is an immutable collection: your program will create a new set every time you add or remove an element from it. You can add an element to a set using the + operator:

```scala
scala> Set() + 1
val res0: scala.collection.immutable.Set[Int] = Set(1)
// Adding 1 to the empty set

scala> Set(1) + 2
val res1: scala.collection.immutable.Set[Int] = Set(1, 2)
// Adding 2 to a set containing one element

scala> Set(1) + 1
val res2: scala.collection.immutable.Set[Int] = Set(1)
// A set contains no duplicates
```

When removing an element from a set, use the - operator:

```scala
scala> Set(1, 2) - 2
val res3: scala.collection.immutable.Set[Int] = Set(1)
// Removing the element 2 from the set

scala> Set(1, 2) - 3
val res4: scala.collection.immutable.Set[Int] = Set(1, 2)
// Removing an element not in the set returns the same set
```

```
scala> Set() - 2
val res5: scala.collection.immutable.Set[Int] = Set()
// Removing an element from the empty set returns the empty set
```

Adding and removing elements from a Set are efficient operations that happen in constant time. This is not the case for List: prepending an element is performant, but appending is not because it requires traversing the entire sequence.

> **Quick Check 34.2** Consider the following two expressions. What value do they return? Are they equivalent?
>   1 Set(2) + 1
>   2 1 + Set(2)
> Use the Scala REPL to validate your hypothesis.

 ## 34.3 The map, flatten, and flatMap operations

When working with Option and List, you learned that you can use the methods map, flatten, and flatMap to manipulate their elements. You can also use these operations with Set.

34.3.1 The map function

Suppose that your program needs to extract the names of a group of unordered students.

Listing 34.3 Extracting the names of a set of students

```
case class Student(id: Int, name: String, topics: Set[String])

def getIds(students: Set[Student]): Set[String] =
    students.map(_.name)
```
For each student, extract the field name.

The map function for a Set behaves similarly to the one for List and Option. It allows you to iterate over each element of a set and apply a transformation to it. In particular, the map operation on Set[A] is a higher order function that takes a parameter f of type A => B to produce a value of type Set[B]. It behaves as follows:

- It returns the empty set if it contains no elements.
- If not empty, it traverses each value, and it applies the function f to each of them.

A few examples for the function map on an instance of Set are the following:

```scala
scala> Set(0, 2, 4).map(_ * 3)
val res0: scala.collection.immutable.Set[Int] = Set(0, 6, 12)
// Multiplying each element by 3

scala> Set.empty[Int].map(_ * 3)
val res1: scala.collection.immutable.Set[Int] = Set()
// The set is empty, no elements to multiply by 3!
```

> **Quick Check 34.3** Define a function called allUpper that takes a set of words and returns a new one in which each element is now uppercase.
>
> ```scala
> def allUpper(words: Set[String]): Set[String]
> ```

34.3.2 The flatten function

Imagine you want to extract all the topics a group of students is following. You could use the map operation, but you would obtain a return type of Set[Set[String]]:

```scala
def getTopics(students: Set[Student]): Set[Set[String]] =
  students.map(_.topics)
```

This solution is not what you'd like, as this will contain a set for each student rather than the group of all topics. You can simplify a nested structure thanks to the flatten function.

Listing 34.4 Extracting topics of a group of students using flatten

```scala
def getTopics(students: Set[Student]): Set[String] =
  students.map(_.topics).flatten
```

When you have a nested set structure, you can simplify it using the flatten method. Its behavior and usage match the one for List and Option. A few examples are the following:

```scala
scala> Set(Set(1), Set(2)).flatten
val res0: scala.collection.immutable.Set[Int] = Set(1, 2)

scala> Set(Set(1), Set(1)).flatten
val res1: scala.collection.immutable.Set[Int] = Set(1)
// Duplicated element 1 is shown once

scala> Set(Set(), Set()).flatten
val res2: scala.collection.immutable.Set[Nothing] = Set()
```

> **Quick Check 34.4** Consider the snippet of code Set(3).flatten. What does it return? Why? Use the Scala REPL to validate your hypothesis.

34.3.3 The flatMap function

Let's consider the function you implemented in listing 34.4 to extract the topics a group of students has selected.

Listing 34.5 Extracting the topics of a group of students using flatMap

```
def getTopics(students: Set[Student]): Set[String] =
  students.flatMap(_.topics)
```

The method flatMap combines the behavior of the map and flatten operations. The flatMap method on Set[A] is a higher order function that takes a parameter f of type A => Set[B] to produce an instance of Set[B]. It behaves as follows:

- It returns the empty set if it contains no elements.
- If not empty, it extracts each value, and it applies the parameter f to it. Then, it combines all the results in one Set.

Here are a few examples of what you can achieve using the flatMap function:

```
scala> Set(1, 2, 3).flatMap(n => Set("a", "b").map(_ * n))
val res0: scala.collection.immutable.Set[String] = Set(a, b, bbb, aa,
          bb, aaa)
// Repeating the strings "a" and "b" a number of times
// equal to the corresponding set element.

scala> Set.empty[Int].flatMap(n => Set("a", "b").map(_ * n))
val res1: scala.collection.immutable.Set[String] = Set()
// The set is empty, so it returns a group with no strings.
```

> **Quick Check 34.5** Using the flatMap operation, define a function called cross-Multiplier that takes two sets of integers as its parameters and returns a new one containing all the numbers produced by multiplying each element of the first one for the second.
>
> ```
> def crossMultiplier(groupA: Set[Int],
>                     groupB: Set[Int]): Set[Int]
> ```

For example, when applying the crossMultiplier function to two sets containing the numbers 1,3 and 2,4,6, respectively, it should return a new one containing the numbers 2, 4, 6, 12, 18.

Table 34.1 provides a summary of the map, flatten, and flatMap functions acting on a Set.

Table 34.1 Technical recap of the three fundamental operations on Set. The function map applies a given function to each element in the group, while the function flatten creates a set by unifying two nested structures. The flatMap operation combines the map and flatten operations to chain values together.

	Acts on	Signature	Usage
map	Set[A]	map(f: A => B): Set[B]	It applies a function to each value in the set.
flatten	Set[Set[A]]	flatten: Set[A]	It merges two nested sets into one.
flatMap	Set[A]	flatMap(f: A => Set[B]): Set[B]	The combination of map followed by flatten. It chains sets together.

 ## 34.4 For-comprehension

Let's consider your program to track students and their selected topics and imagine that you now need to return the group of topics that a selected group of students are following. You could achieve this using the flatMap operation.

Listing 34.6 Retrieving topics for student IDs using flatMap

```
def getTopicsForStudentIds(students: Set[Student],
                           ids: Set[Int]): Set[String] =          Iterating
  students.flatMap { student =>                                   through each
    ids.flatMap { id =>                                           student
      if (student.id == id) student.topics
      else Set.empty                                              Looping through
    }                                                             each ID
  }
```

If the student ID doesn't match, return no topics.

If the student ID matches, return the student's topics.

A more elegant way of rewriting the same code is to use for-comprehension.

Listing 34.7 **Retrieving topics for student IDs using for-comprehension**

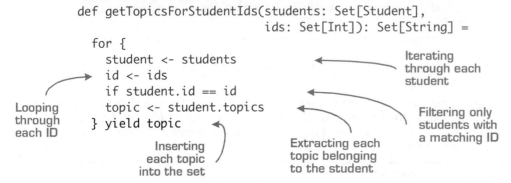

The function getTopicsForStudentIds has Set[String] as its return type. You need to iterate through each topic a student has. Suppose you were to yield the value student .topics rather than a single topic; the for-comprehension construct would return an instance of Set[Set[String]] rather than the desired Set[String].

Every time your code has nested calls to flatMap and map functions, you should consider rewriting it using for-comprehension to improve its readability.

For example, consider the following snippet of code you saw in the previous subsection on flatMap:

```scala
scala> Set(1, 2, 3).flatMap(n => Set("a", "b").map(_ * n))
val res0: scala.collection.immutable.Set[String] = Set(a, b, bbb, aa,
        bb, aaa)
```

You can refactor it using for-comprehension as follows:

```scala
scala> for {
    |   n <- Set(1, 2, 3)
    |   s <- Set("a", "b")
    | } yield s * n
val res1: scala.collection.immutable.Set[String] = Set(a, b, bbb, aa,
        bb, aaa)
```

Quick Check 34.6 Rewrite the function crossMultiplier you implemented in Quick Check 34.5 using for-comprehension.

 **Summary**

In this lesson, my objective was to teach you about the Set collection.

- You learned how to create a set.
- You saw how to add and remove elements from a set using the + and - operators.
- You discovered how to manipulate a set's values using the `map`, `flatten`, and `flatMap` functions.
- You mastered how to chain multiple set instances using `for-comprehension`.

Let's see if you got this!

TRY THIS   Define a function that takes a set of books to return the set of genres a given author has written. Use the following case class to represent a book:

```
case class Book(title: String,
                authors: List[String],
                genres: Set[String])
```

 Answers to quick checks

Quick Check 34.1   You can define a set as follows:

```
scala> Set(3, 12.4)
val res0: scala.collection.immutable.Set[Double] = Set(3.0, 12.4)
```

Your instance has type `Set[Double]` because the compiler can unify both integers and doubles under the type `Double`.

Quick Check 34.2   The two expressions are not equivalent. The first snippet of code creates a set containing the numbers 1 and 2. You can rewrite the expression `Set(2) + 1` as `Set(2).+(1)`; you are calling the method called + defined in the class Set. The second expression does not compile. The expression `1 + Set(2)` corresponds to `1.+(Set(2))`; you are calling the method + in the class Int. For this reason, the compiler thinks you are trying to add the set to the number 1, which is an illegal operation.

Quick Check 34.3 A possible implementation for the function allUpper is the following:

```
def allUpper(words: Set[String]): Set[String] =
  words.map(_.toUpperCase)
```

Quick Check 34.4 The expression Set(3).flatten does not compile. You can use the flatten function only on nested structures; Set(3) is not.

```
scala> Set(3).flatten
        error: No implicit view available from Int =>
          scala.collection.IterableOnce[B].
```

Quick Check 34.5 You can implement the crossMultiplier function as follows:

```
def crossMultiplier(groupA: Set[Int],
                    groupB: Set[Int]): Set[Int] =
  groupA.flatMap { a =>
    groupB.map(b => a * b)
  }
```

Quick Check 34.6 You can rewrite the crossMultiplier function using for-comprehension as the following:

```
def crossMultiplier(groupA: Set[Int],
                    groupB: Set[Int]): Set[Int] =
  for {
    a <- groupA
    b <- groupB
  } yield a * b
```

WORKING WITH SET

After reading this lesson, you will be able to

- Perform union, intersection, and difference operations on sets
- Inquire about the properties of a set
- Select one of a set's elements based on its features
- Filter its items according to their characteristics

In the previous lesson, you learned about the structure of a set and how to transform its elements. In this lesson, you'll discover other methods that the class Set has to offer. You'll apply the operations of union, intersection, and difference on two sets. Then, I'll introduce you to more complex transformations. You'll notice a lot of overlap with the concepts you discovered for the List collection in unit 5. You'll inquire about the properties of a set, such as its size or the presence of an item. You'll select one of its elements based on its characteristics and determine its minimum and maximum. You'll filter its values based on their features. In the capstone, you'll use these operations to analyze the book loans of your library.

> **Consider this**
> Imagine you have a group of books, and you'd like to check if a given title is present. Your application performs this operation often, and it needs to be as efficient as possible. How would you implement it?

35.1 The Union, Intersection, and Difference operations

Let's consider the program to track students and their selected topics you saw in the previous lesson. Suppose you want to identify students based on their topic selection.

Listing 35.1 Student selection based on their topics

```scala
case class Student(id: Int, name: String, topics: Set[String])

def eitherTopics(topicA: Set[Student],
            topicB: Set[Student]): Set[Student] =
  topicA.union(topicB)

def bothTopics(topicA: Set[Student],
            topicB: Set[Student]): Set[Student] =
  topicA.intersect(topicB)

def topicAnoTopicB(topicA: Set[Student],
                topicB: Set[Student]): Set[Student] =
  topicA.diff(topicB)

def topicBnoTopicA(topicA: Set[Student],
                topicB: Set[Student]): Set[Student] =
  topicB.diff(topicA)
```

The students taking topicA or topicB ⟵

Those who have selected topicA and topicB ⟵

Those following topicA but not topicB ⟵

Students who have picked topicB but not topicA ⟵

In Scala, the class Set mimics the concept of a mathematical set. In this section, you'll learn how to apply the operations of union, intersection, and difference. Figure 35.1 shows the Venn diagram of their mathematical meaning.

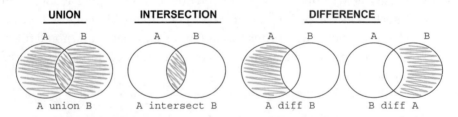

Figure 35.1 The fundamental operations on sets. The operation union merges them, while the intersection selects only the elements they have in common. Finally, the difference includes the values in one but not the other.

When working with two or more sets, you can perform the following operations to combine their elements and analyze their commonalities and differences:

- union—For an instance of Set[A], the method union takes another Set[A] as its parameter. It returns a new set that contains all the values from any of them. You can also use the operator ++ as an alias for the method union.

```
scala> Set(1, 2, 3).union(Set(1, 4))
val res0: scala.collection.immutable.Set[Int] = Set(1, 2, 3, 4)
// The following two expressions are also equivalent:
// Set(1, 2, 3) union Set(1, 4)
// Set(1, 2, 3) ++ Set(1, 4)

scala> Set(1, 2, 3).union(Set())
val res1: scala.collection.immutable.Set[Int] = Set(1, 2, 3)
// Alternatively, you can also write:
// Set(1, 2, 3) union Set()
// Set(1, 2, 3) ++ Set()
```

- intersect—For an instance of Set[A], the method intersect takes another Set[A] as its parameter. It returns a new set with only the values they both contain. It also has an alias: the method &.

```
scala> Set(1, 2, 3).intersect(Set(1, 4))
val res0: scala.collection.immutable.Set[Int] = Set(1)
// You can also write:
// Set(1, 2, 3) intersect Set(1, 4)
// Set(1, 2, 3) & Set(1,4)

scala> Set(1, 2, 3).intersect(Set())
val res1: scala.collection.immutable.Set[Int] = Set()
// Or alternatively:
// Set(1, 2, 3) intersect Set()
// Set(1, 2, 3) & Set()
```

- diff—For an instance of Set[A], the function diff takes Set[A] as its parameter. It returns a new set containing all the elements in the original set but not in the given one. You can also use the operator -- as its alias.

```
scala> scala> Set(1, 2, 3).diff(Set(1, 4))
val res0: scala.collection.immutable.Set[Int] = Set(2, 3)
// The following two expressions are also equivalent:
// Set(1, 2, 3) diff Set(1, 4)
// Set(1, 2, 3) -- Set(1, 4)
```

```scala
scala> Set(1, 4).diff(Set(1, 2, 3))
val res1: scala.collection.immutable.Set[Int] = Set(4)
// Or you can write:
// Set(1, 4) diff Set(1, 2, 3)
// Set(1, 4) -- Set(1, 2, 3)
```

Table 35.1 shows a summary of the union, intersect, and difference operations for two sets.

Table 35.1 Summary of the functions to perform basic operations on two instances of Set[A]. Where necessary, I have simplified their signatures to hide nonrelevant implementation details.

Signature	Description	Example

def union(
   other: Set[A]): Set[A]
	It unifies the elements of the two sets.	Set(1,0,2)
		  .union(Set(1,3))
		// it returns
		// Set(0,1,2,3)

def ++(other: Set[A]): Set[A]	It behaves the same as union.	Set(1,0,2) ++ Set(1,3)
		// it returns
		// Set(0,1,2,3)

def intersect(
   other: Set[A]): Set[A]
	It selects the values present in both groups,	Set(1,0,2)
		  .intersect(Set(1,3))
		// it returns
		// Set(1)

def &(other: Set[A]): Set[A]	It aliases intersect.	Set(1,0,2) & Set(1,3)
		// it returns
		// Set(1)

def diff(
   other: Set[A]): Set[A]
	It returns a new set containing the items present in this set but not in other.	Set(1,0,2)
		  .diff(Set(1,3))
		// it returns
		// Set(0,2)

def --(other: Set[A]): Set[A]	It behaves the same as diff.	Set(1,0,2) -- Set(1,3)
		// it returns
		// Set(0,2)

Quick Check 35.1 Consider these two snippets of code. Are they equivalent? Use the Scala REPL to validate your hypotheses.

1 Set(1, 2, 3).diff(Set(3,4))
2 Set(3,4).diff(Set(1,2,3))

35.2 Other operations on Set

Suppose you need to analyze certain features of the group of students and their topics. In particular, you'd like to

- check if a student with a specific ID is in the group,
- filter those who have selected a given class, and
- find the one that is following the most topics.

Listing 35.2 Analyzing a group of students

It checks if a value with the
given characteristic exists.

```scala
case class Student(id: Int, name: String, topics: Set[String])

def existsById(students: Set[Student], id: Int): Boolean =
  students.exists(_.id == id)

def filterByTopic(students: Set[Student],
                  topic: String): Set[Student] =
  students.filter { student =>
    student.topics.contains(topic)
  }

def maxByTopics(students: Set[Student]): Student =
  students.maxBy { student =>
    student.topics.size
  }
```

It filters elements
based on a specific
feature.

It checks if the
set contains a
value.

It returns the maximum
item according to a
given criterion.

It returns the
size of a set.

In Scala, both List and Set implement a common interface called Iterable. Thanks to this design choice, they share a consistent group of methods for you to use. You can apply the operations you have discovered for List on an instance of Set, with the following exceptions:

- You cannot sort a set because their elements are unordered by design. You cannot invoke the methods sorted or sortedBy on it.
- You cannot remove duplicates from it, as its items are already unique. It doesn't have a distinct function.

List and Set also differ in performance when checking if an element exists. The element lookup time in a list is proportional to its size, while it is constant for a set.

> **Quick Check 35.2** Define a function called sumInRange that takes a set of doubles and returns the sum of all its values with those between 0 and 100 excluded. For example, given the numbers 0.5, -1, 0 50.5, 99, and 100, it should return the double 150.00.
>
> ```
> def sumInRange(numbers: Set[Double]): Double
> ```

 ## Summary

In this lesson, my objective was to teach you about the operations to perform on a set.

- You saw how to merge, intersect, and subtract two sets
- You learned how to check the size of a set and the properties of its elements.
- You mastered how to select one of its elements based on a given criterion.
- You saw how to filter a set's values according to its features.

Let's see if you got this!

> **TRY THIS**   Implement a function that takes a group of students and a set of topics as its parameters. It returns a new set containing the students who are taking any of the given topics. Use the student representation you used in this lesson:
>
> ```
> case class Student(id: Int, name: String, topics: Set[String])
> ```

 ## Answers to quick checks

> **Quick Check 35.1**   The two expressions are not equivalent. The difference between sets is not commutative, which means that its parameters' order does change the result. While the first expression returns the instance Set(1, 2), the other evaluates to Set(4).

> **Quick Check 35.2**   A possible implementation for the function sumInRange is the following:
>
> ```
> def sumInRange(numbers: Set[Double]): Double =
>   numbers.filter(d => d > 0 && d < 100).sum
> ```

MAP

After reading this lesson, you will be able to

- Define a key-value structure, called Map
- Add and remove entries to Map
- Compute the union and difference of two Maps
- Manipulate the elements of a key-value structure using the map and flatMap functions
- Chain multiple instances using for-comprehension

In the previous lesson, you mastered the operations you can perform on a set. In this lesson, you'll discover a new data structure called Map. In Scala, Map is an immutable data structure to store a set of keys, each of them associated with a value. The concept of mapping keys to values is not unique to the Scala language; some languages, such as Java, refer to it using the term *hashmap*; others, such as Python, call it *dictionary*. You'll create an instance of Map and add and remove elements to it. You'll merge and subtract the keys of two maps to create a new one. You'll manipulate and transform its entries using the map and flatMap functions. You'll also combine multiple values using for-comprehension. In the capstone, you'll use Map to read the data from a CSV file.

> **Consider this**
> Imagine you have a list of books that you'd like to group per genre. Which data structure would you use to represent it?

 ## 36.1 Creating Map

Consider the program to track the students and their selected topics you developed in previous lessons. Imagine you want to modify it so that you can record the students registered for an exam session.

Listing 36.1 Tracking students registered to each exam session

```scala
import java.time.LocalDate

// Representing our data...
case class Student(id: Int, name: String)
case class ExamSession(title: String, localDate: LocalDate)

// Instances of ExamSession
val historySession = ExamSession(
  "History", localDate = LocalDate.now.plusDays(30))
val chemistrySession = ExamSession(
  "Chemistry", localDate = LocalDate.now.plusDays(45))

// Instances of Student
val alice = Student(id = 1,  name = "Alice Abbott")
val bob = Student(id = 2, name = "Bob Brown")
val charlie = Student(id = 3,  name = "Charlie Clarke")

val registrations: Map[ExamSession, List[Student]] =
  Map(
    historySession -> List(alice, bob),
    chemistrySession -> List(alice, charlie)
  )
```

It creates a map with key ExamSession and List[Student] as its value.

It creates a tuple of type (ExamSession, List[Student]).

A Map is a key-value data structure. It has a set of keys that are unordered and unique and that have values linked to each of them. Scala represents each key-value association, called *entry*, with a tuple. Its keys and values have specific types. Each instance of a Map has type Map[K, V], in which K is the type of its keys and V the type of their values. Figure 36.1 shows a visual summary of the structure of a Map.

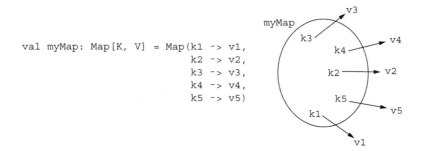

```
val myMap: Map[K, V] = Map(k1 -> v1,
                           k2 -> v2,
                           k3 -> v3,
                           k4 -> v4,
                           k5 -> v5)
```

Figure 36.1 Visual representation of the key-value structure of Map. Its keys are unordered, unique, and of a given type K. Each of them has an associated value of a given type V. You can create a key-value structure Map[K,V] by invoking its constructor with zero or more tuples of the type (K,V).

When creating a map of type Map[K,V], you represent each of its entries using tuples of type (K,V) and pass them to its constructor:

```
scala> Map((1,"hi"), (2,"scala"))
val res0: scala.collection.immutable.Map[Int,String] = Map(1 -> hi,
        2 -> scala)
// A Map containing two entries of type (Int, String)
```

```
scala> Map((42.31, 42))
val res1: scala.collection.immutable.Map[Double,Int] = Map(42.31 -> 42)
// A Map containing one entry of type (Double, Int)
```

```
scala> Map()
val res2: scala.collection.immutable.Map[Nothing,Nothing] = Map()
// The empty Maap
```

```
scala> Map.empty[String, Double]
val res3: scala.collection.immutable.Map[String,Double] = Map()
// The empty Map with key of type String, and values of type Double
```

Scala offers an alternative syntax to create tuples. When creating a tuple, you can also use the -> operator. The following expressions are equivalent:

```
scala> ("hello", "world")
val res0: (String, String) = (hello,world)
// Creating a tuple

scala> "hello" -> "world"
val res1: (String, String) = (hello,world)
// Equivalent creation of tuple using the -> operator
```

This can improve your code's readability, especially in certain contexts such as the creation of instances of Map:

```
scala> Map(1 -> "hi", 2 -> "scala")
val res0: scala.collection.immutable.Map[Int,String] = Map(1 -> hi,
          2 -> scala)
// Equivalent to Map((1,"hi"), (2,"scala"))

scala> Map(42.31 -> 42)
val res1: scala.collection.immutable.Map[Double,Int] = Map(42.31 -> 42)
// An alternative to Map((42.31, 42))
```

> **Quick Check 36.1**   Create a key-value structure of type Map[Int, String] to associ-
> ate a number to its corresponding day of the week. For example, you should associ-
> ate the number 1 to Monday and 2 to Tuesday.

 ## 36.2 Adding and removing elements

Imagine you need to add a new exam session for math and remove one for chemistry in your exam tracking program.

Listing 36.2 Adding and removing exam sessions

```
val mathSession = ExamSession("Math", localDate = LocalDate.now)
registrations + (mathSession -> List(bob))
              - chemistrySession
```

Adding the entry
for math and the
student Bob

Removing the entry
associated with
chemistry

A Map is an immutable structure: adding or removing elements to it creates a new
instance rather than modifying the existing one. To create a new instance with an added
entry, you can use the invoke the method + with the entry to add. For example, you can
do the following:

```scala
scala> Map(1 -> "hello") + (2 -> "scala")
val res0: scala.collection.immutable.Map[Int,String] = Map(1 -> hello,
        2 -> scala)

scala> Map() + (1 -> "scala")
val res1: scala.collection.immutable.Map[Int,String] = Map(1 -> scala)
```

A Map has unique keys by keys, so if you add an entry for an existing key, its corresponding value will also be replaced:

```scala
scala> Map(1 -> "hello") + (1 -> "scala")
val res2: scala.collection.immutable.Map[Int,String] = Map(1 -> scala)
// The value "hello" is no longer in the map.
```

When removing the entry, you can use the method - with the key of the entry for
removal:

```scala
scala> Map(1 -> "hello", 2 -> "scala") - 1
val res0: scala.collection.immutable.Map[Int,String] = Map(2 -> scala)
// Removing entry with key 1

scala> Map(1 -> "hello", 2 -> "scala") - 3
val res1: scala.collection.immutable.Map[Int,String] =
Map(1 -> hello, 2 -> scala)
// Removing a non-existing key returns the original Map.
```

The operation of adding and removing elements are fast because they happen in constant time independently from the size of your dictionary.

Quick Check 36.2 Consider the following snippet of code. What does it return?
Why? Use the Scala REPL to validate your hypothesis:

```scala
Map(42 -> "hi") + 3
```

36.3 Merge and remove multiple entries

Let's consider your program to track the exam sessions and the students registered to them. Imagine you have two separate key-value structures to represent two different exam registrations in the year and you'd like to merge them.

Listing 36.3 Merging two exam registrations

```scala
def merge(
    regA: Map[ExamSession, List[Student]],
    regB: Map[ExamSession, List[Student]]
  ): Map[ExamSession, List[Student]] =
  regA ++ regB
```

Merging the two registrations together ←

In Scala, you can consider a Map as a set of keys, each linked to a value. You can perform operations on them similar to the ones you learned for Set. You can merge the entries of two maps using the operator ++. For the keys in common, the entries of the second map override those of the first. A few examples are the following:

```scala
scala> Map(1 -> "hello") ++ Map(2 -> "scala")
val res0: scala.collection.immutable.Map[Int,String] =
Map(1 -> hello, 2 -> scala)
// Merging two key-value structures

scala> Map(1 -> "hello") ++ Map()
val res1: scala.collection.immutable.Map[Int,String] = Map(1 -> hello)
// Merging a Map with the empty one

scala> Map(1 -> "hello") ++ Map(1 -> "scala")
val res2: scala.collection.immutable.Map[Int,String] = Map(1 -> scala)
// The entry (1, "scala") overrides (1, "hello")
```

You can also use the method -- to remove multiple entries by providing their keys. Its parameter has type Iterable, which indicates you can use any list-like structure, such as Set or List.

```scala
scala> Map("Rome" -> "Italy", "London" -> "UK") -- Set("Rome", "Paris")
val res3: scala.collection.immutable.Map[String,String] = Map(London
          -> UK)
// Removing the keys "Rome" and "Paris" using Set as Iterable

scala> Map("Rome" -> "Italy", "London" -> "UK") -- List("Berlin")
val res4: scala.collection.immutable.Map[String,String] =
                  Map(Rome -> Italy, London -> UK)
```

```
// Removing a non-existing key, returns the original data structure
// using List as Iterable.
```

Quick Check 36.3 In Quick Check 36.1, you defined a key-value data structure of type Map[Int, String] to represent the numbers and their corresponding days of the week. Use the operator -- to create a new map containing only weekdays (i.e., all but Saturday and Sunday).

36.4 The map and flatMap operations

A Map is a key-value data structure that you can see as an iterable of tuples. As you discovered previously, Iterable is a shared interface between Set and List. For this reason, the map and flatMap operations on Map behave similarly to the iterable collections you have seen so far. Let's see them in action in the following subsections.

36.4.1 The map function

Let's consider your program to track the exam sessions and the students registered to them and imagine you'd like to create a key-value data structure that links each exam session to the number of students enrolled for it.

Listing 36.4 Number of registrations for each exam session

```
def registrationsCountPerSession(
          registrations: Map[ExamSession, List[Student]]
    ): Map[ExamSession, Int] =
registrations.map { case (examSession, students) =>      ←——  Iterating
    examSession -> students.size    ←——                        through each
}                                                              entry in the Map
                          Using a partial function to
                          decompose the elements
                          of each tuple
```

When applying the function map over an instance of Map, you are iterating through each tuple. For example, given a capital to country mapping, you can swap it so that it becomes a country to capital one:

```
scala> Map("Rome" -> "Italy", "London" -> "UK").map {
     |    tuple => tuple._2 -> tuple._1
     | }
val res0: scala.collection.immutable.Map[String,String] =
                    Map(Italy -> Rome, UK -> London)
```

Although the methods ._1 and ._2 on a tuple work as expected, you often want to improve your code's readability by providing a more descriptive name to each element of the tuple. You can achieve this by using a partial function on each tuple as follows:

```scala
scala> Map("Rome" -> "Italy", "London" -> "UK").map {
     |     case (capital, country) => country -> capital
     | }
val res1: scala.collection.immutable.Map[String,String] =
Map(Italy -> Rome, UK -> London)
```

Scala 3 compiler is more capable than the Scala 2 when inferring types. You do not need a partial function to decompose each entry tuple in Scala 3 because the compiler can do this for you automatically. You can omit the *case* keyword by writing the following if you are using Scala 3:

```scala
scala> Map("Rome" -> "Italy", "London" -> "UK").map {
     |        (capital, country) => country -> capital
     | }
val res2: Map[String, String] = Map(Italy -> Rome, UK -> London)
```

You can also transform each entry into a type rather than a tuple. In such a case, the compiler will not build a key-value structure and return an iterable of that type:

```scala
scala> Map("Rome" -> "Italy",
     |       "London" -> "UK").map { case (capital, country) =>
     |          s"$capital is the capital of $country"
     | }
val res3: scala.collection.immutable.Iterable[String] =
List(Rome is the capital of Italy, London is the capital of UK)
```

The Map collection and the flatten function

You cannot flatten a key-value data structure. In Scala, the compiler can consider an instance of type Map[K, V] equivalent to Iterable[(K, V)]; this structure is not nested because a tuple is not an iterable. If you try to invoke the method flatten on Map, the compiler will complain that it doesn't know how to transform your tuple into an Iterable:

```scala
scala> Map("hello" -> "world").flatten
                    ^
       error: No implicit view available from (String, String) =>
           scala.collection.IterableOnce[B].
```

> **Quick Check 36.4** Consider the following snippet of code. What does it return? Why? Use the Scala REPL to validate your hypothesis.
>
> ```
> Map("hello" -> 1, "scala" -> 1).map { case (w, n) => n -> w }
> ```

36.4.2 The flatMap function

Imagine that in your program to track exam registrations you'd like to return data specific to a given group of student IDs. You can implement this using the flatMap function.

Listing 36.5 Filtering exam registrations by student IDs using flatMap

```
def filterByStudentId(
    registrations: Map[ExamSession, List[Student]],
    ids: List[Int]
  ): Map[ExamSession, List[Student]] =
  registrations.flatMap { case (examSession, students) =>      ⟵
    val matches = students.filter(student =>
      ids.contains(student.id))
    if (matches.nonEmpty) List(examSession -> matches)
    else List.empty
}                                                              You can omit the
      ⟵                                                        keyword case in
            Map and List are both                              Scala 3.
            implementations of Iterable, so you
            can mix them when using flatMap.
```

When using a flatMap on a Map, the compiler transforms it into an iterable of tuples. It will return a value of type Map if the structure of the returned value allows it to do so. For example, you can filter the entries containing positive numbers:

```
scala> Map(1 -> 2, 0 -> 2, 2 -> 0).flatMap { case (a, b) =>
     |    if (a > 0 && b > 0) Some(a -> b) else None
     | }
val res0: scala.collection.immutable.Map[Int,Int] = Map(1 -> 2)
// Option is automatically converted to List,
// which is an implementation of Iterable
```

Also, you can multiply the two numbers in the tuple and return an instance of type Iterable[Int]:

```
scala> Map(1 -> 2, 0 -> 2, 2 -> 0).flatMap { case (a, b) =>
     |    if (a > 0 && b > 0) Some(a * b) else None
     | }
val res1: scala.collection.immutable.Iterable[Int] = List(2)
```

> **Quick Check 36.5** Consider the following snippet of code. What does it return? Why? Use the Scala REPL to validate your hypothesis.
>
> ```
> Map("hello" -> 1, "scala" -> 10).flatMap { case (w, n) =>
>    if (w.length > n ) Some(w -> n) else None
> }
> ```

 ## 36.5 For-comprehension

Let's consider your implementation to filter your exam registrations based on given student IDs in listing 36.6. You can refactor it using for-comprehension.

Listing 36.6 Filter exam registration by student IDs using for-comprehension

```
def filterByStudentId(
      registrations: Map[ExamSession, List[Student]],
      ids: List[Int]
   ): Map[ExamSession, List[Student]] =
  for {
    (examSession, students) <- registrations
    matches = students.filter(student => ids.contains(student.id))
    if matches.nonEmpty
  } yield examSession -> matches
```

You can omit val here.

You can refactor any expressions using flatMap on Map with a for-comprehension construct. For example, you can rewrite the examples you have seen for it as the following:

```
scala> for {
     |    (a, b) <- Map(1 -> 2, 0 -> 2, 2 -> 0)
     |    if a > 0 && b > 0
     | } yield a -> b
val res0: scala.collection.immutable.Map[Int,Int] = Map(1 -> 2)

scala> for {
     |    (a, b) <- Map(1 -> 2, 0 -> 2, 2 -> 0)
     |    if a > 0 && b > 0
     | } yield a * b
val res1: scala.collection.immutable.Iterable[Int] = List(2)
```

Quick Check 36.6 Reimplement the following snippet of code using for-comprehension:

```
Map("hello" -> 1, "scala" -> 10).flatMap { case (w, n) =>
  if (w.length > n ) Some(w -> n) else None
}
```

 ## Summary

In this lesson, my objective was to teach you about the `Map` collection.

- You mastered how to create a `Map` using both the tuple constructor and its -> operator.
- You saw how to add and remove single and multiple entries from a key-value structure.
- You learned how to transform its entries and combine its elements using the `map` and `flatMap` operations.

Let's see if you got this!

TRY THIS Suppose you have two key-value structures representing a capital to its country and a country to its continent. Combine the two instances of `Map` to link each capital to its continent.

36.6 Answers to quick checks

Quick Check 36.1 You can define your instance of `Map` as the following:

```
Map(
    1 -> "Monday",
    2 -> "Tuesday",
    3 -> "Wednesday",
    4 -> "Thursday",
    5 -> "Friday",
    6 -> "Saturday",
    7 -> "Sunday"
)
```

Alternatively, you can also use the standard constructor for tuples:

```
Map(
    (1, "Monday"),
    (2, "Tuesday"),
```

continued
```
   (3, "Wednesday"),
   (4, "Thursday"),
   (5, "Friday"),
   (6, "Saturday"),
   (7, "Sunday")
)
```

Quick Check 36.2 The snippet of code doesn't compile because an integer is not a valid representation for the entry of a dictionary:

```
scala> Map(42 -> "hi") + 3
       error: type mismatch;
        found   : Int(3)
        required: (Int, ?)
```

Quick Check 36.3 You can create a new map representing the weekdays as the following:

```
val days = Map(
  1 -> "Monday",
  2 -> "Tuesday",
  3 -> "Wednesday",
  4 -> "Thursday",
  5 -> "Friday",
  6 -> "Saturday",
  7 -> "Sunday"
)

val weekdays = days -- Set(6,7)
```

Alternatively, you can use List rather than Set to indicate the group of keys to remove:

```
val weekdays = days -- List(6 ,7)
```

Quick Check 36.4 The expression returns a key-value data structure containing one entry rather than two. Your output may change slightly depending on the Scala version you are using:

```scala
scala> Map("hello" -> 1, "scala" -> 1).map { case (w, n) => n -> w }
val res0: scala.collection.immutable.Map[Int,String] = Map(1 ->
          scala)
```

The snippet of code creates a new Map by swapping keys with values. Because its keys must be unique, the compiler overrides new entries with the same key without warnings. You should be careful when transforming a Map's data, or you may discard it without realizing it!

Quick Check 36.5 The snippet of code evaluates to a key-value data structure containing the entry ("hello", 1):

```scala
scala> Map("hello" -> 1, "scala" -> 10).flatMap { case (w, n) =>
     |    if (w.length > n ) Some(w -> n) else None
     | }
val res0: scala.collection.immutable.Map[String,Int] = Map(hello
          -> 1)
```

The compiler can return its resulting value of type Iterable[(String, Int)] as an instance of Map[String, Int].

Quick Check 36.6 You can refactor the snippet of code using for-comprehension as follows:

```scala
for {
  (w, n) <- Map("hello" -> 1, "scala" -> 10)
  if w.length > n
} yield w -> n
```

WORKING WITH MAP

After reading this lesson, you will be able to

- Retrieve the value associated with a key
- Get all keys and all values stored in a Map
- Check its size and the feature of its entries
- Filter its elements based on given criteria

In the previous lesson, you learned about the basics of Map. In this lesson, you'll master the most common operations you can apply to it. You'll use different strategies to retrieve a value linked to a given key. You'll get the keys and the values in an instance of a Map. Finally, you will get its size, inquire about its entries' properties, and filter its elements according to their characteristics by reusing the same methods you saw for List and Set. In the capstone, you will apply these operations to extract the book information from a CSV file and create your library's book collection.

> **Consider this**
> Imagine that you have a key-value structure representing a sequence of books per genre, and you'd like to retrieve books with the genre *drama*. How would you implement it?

37.1 Retrieving a value for a given key

Consider the program to track the exam registration that you are implementing. Imagine you now need to retrieve the students who have enrolled for a given exam session.

Listing 37.1 Getting students for an exam session

```scala
import java.time.LocalDate

case class Student(id: Int, name: String)
case class ExamSession(title: String, localDate: LocalDate)

def getStudents(registrations: Map[ExamSession, List[Student]],
            session: ExamSession): List[Student] =
  registrations.getOrElse(session, List.empty)
```

It returns the students for the session if present, an empty list otherwise.

Retrieving the value associated with a key in a dictionary is a fast operation that is constant in time. Scala offers several strategies to do so:

- get—For an instance of Map[K, V], the method get takes one parameter of type K and returns an Option[V], its value wrapped in a Some if the given key exists, None if missing.

```scala
scala> Map(1 -> "a", 2 -> "b").get(2)
val res0: Option[String] = Some(b)

scala> Map(1 -> "a", 2 -> "b").get(3)
val res1: Option[String] = None
```

- getOrElse—For an instance of Map[K,V], the function getOrElse takes two parameters: an element of type K and an expression to produce a value of type V. If a key equal to the given K parameter exists, it returns its associated value. If missing, it will evaluate the provided expression to produce a value of type V. Your program will do this only if the key is missing, so it can contain side effects.

```scala
scala> def defaultValue: String = {
         |   println("Missing Key!!!")
         |   "N/A"
         | }
def defaultValue: String

scala> Map(1 -> "a", 2 -> "b").getOrElse(2, defaultValue)
val res0: String = b
```

```
scala> Map(1 -> "a", 2 -> "b").getOrElse(3, defaultValue)
Missing key!!!
val res1: String = N/A
```

- apply—For an instance of Map[K, V], the method apply takes one parameter of type K and returns a value of type V: its value if a key equal to the given one exists, a NoSuchElementException exception otherwise.

```
scala> Map(1 -> "a", 2 -> "b").apply(2)
val res0: String = b
```

```
scala> Map(1 -> "a", 2 -> "b").apply(3)
java.util.NoSuchElementException: key not found: 3
  at scala.collection.immutable.Map$Map2.apply(Map.scala:135)
  ... 28 elided
```

This method is unsafe because it throws an exception if the key is missing. You either must be confident that the given key exists or add an ad hoc error handling strategy to it. Try to use the safe functions get and getOrElse instead.

Table 37.1 shows a summary of the different methods you can use to retrieve a value associated with a given key.

Table 37.1   Recap of the functions to retrieve a value for a given key for an instance of Map[K,V]. The notation => V indicates that your program will evaluate the expression only when needed, which you can also refer to as *lazy evaluation*.

Signature	Description	Example

def get(key: K): Option[V]	It returns the value associated with the given key if the key exists. Otherwise, it returns None.	Map("hi" -> 5).get("hi")
		// it returns
		// Some(5)

def getOrElse(
    key: K,
    default: => V): V
	It returns the value associated with the given, if the key exists. Otherwise, it evaluates the default value.	Map("hi" -> 5)
		 .getOrElse("hello", -1)
		// it returns
		// -1

def apply(K): V	It returns the value associated with the given key if present. It throws a NoSuchElementException otherwise.	Map("hi" -> 5)
		 .apply("hello")
		// it throws a
		//NoSuchElementException

Quick Check 37.1 Implement a function called getCountry that takes two parameters: a key-value data structure representing a set of capitals matched to their countries and a capital. It returns either the capital's country or the text "Unknown."

```
def getCountry(capitalToCountry: Map[String, String],
               capital: String): String
```

37.2 Getting all keys and values

Let's consider your program to track exam registrations and imagine that you need to get its exam sessions and registered students.

Listing 37.2 Getting the exam sessions

```
def getExamSessions(
      registrations: Map[ExamSession, List[Student]]
   ): Iterable[ExamSession] =
   registrations.keys                    ⟵——— It returns the
                                                keys in a Map.
def getStudents(
      registrations: Map[ExamSession, List[Student]]
   ): Iterable[Student] =
   registrations.values    ⟵——— It returns the
            .flatten               values in a Map.
```

When working with a Map, you can retrieve all its keys and values using the following methods:

- keys—You can apply the function keys on an instance of Map[K, V]. It returns a value of type Iterable[K] containing the keys in your key-value structure.

  ```
  scala> Map(1 -> "a", 2 -> "b").keys
  val res0: Iterable[Int] = Set(1, 2)

  scala> Map.empty[String, Int].keys
  val res1: Iterable[String] = Set()
  ```

- values—For an instance of Map[K, V], the method values takes no parameters and returns an Iterable[V] containing all its values.

  ```
  scala> Map(1 -> "a", 2 -> "b").values
  val res0: Iterable[String] = MapLike.DefaultValuesIterable(a, b)

  scala> Map.empty[String, Int].values
  val res1: Iterable[Int] = MapLike.DefaultValuesIterable()
  ```

Table 37.2 provides a technical summary of the methods you can apply on a key-value structure to retrieve its keys and its values.

Table 37.2 Summary of the functions to retrieve the keys and the values of an instance of Map[K,V]

Signature	Description	Example

def keys: Iterable[K]	It returns the keys of a key-value structure.	Map("hi" -> 5).keys
		// it returns
		// Set("hi")

def values: Iterable[V]	It returns the values of a Map.	Map("hi" -> 5).values
		// it returns
		// Iterable(5)

Quick Check 37.2 Implement a function called getCapitals that returns a list of the capitals in a key-value data structure representing a group of capitals and their countries.

```
def getCapitals(
        capitalToCountry: Map[String, String]
    ): List[String]
```

 ## 37.3 Other operations on Map

Imagine that you'd like to analyze your exam registrations. In particular, you'd like to

- check the number of scheduled exam sessions,
- filter the exam sessions on a given date, and
- find the exam sessions with the most registrations.

Listing 37.3 Analyzing exam registrations

```
def totExamSessions(registrations: Map[ExamSession, List[Student]]): Int =
    registrations.size          ←——— It returns the number of keys
                                      in the key-value structure.

def getExamSessions(registrations: Map[ExamSession, List[Student]],
                date: LocalDate): Map[ExamSession, List[Student]] =
    registrations.filter { case (session, _) =>      ←——— It filters the entries
        session.localDate == date                          based on some of
    }                                                      their characteristics.
```

```
def getStudents(
      registrations: Map[ExamSession, List[Student]]
   ): (ExamSession, List[Student]) =
   registrations.maxBy{ case (_, students) => students.size }
```

It selects a maximum element
according to given criteria.

The Map collection implements the Iterable interface, so it shares many functionalities with List. You can reuse the methods you discovered in unit 5. You can inquire about its size and the properties of its elements. You can find one of its entries with specific characteristics and pick the minimum/maximum one according to the given criteria. You can filter its keys and values. However, it has the following differences with List:

- You cannot sort a Map; its keys are unordered by design. You cannot apply the sorted and sortBy methods on it.
- A key-value structure doesn't have a distinct function because its elements are already unique.
- It has a contains function, but with a slightly different signature: it takes a key rather than a tuple to represent an entry. For an instance of type Map[K,V], the method contains takes one parameter of type K. It returns true if a key equal to the given one exists, false otherwise.

  ```
  scala> Map(1 -> "a", 2 -> "b").contains(2)
  val res0: Boolean = true

  scala> Map(1 -> "a", 2 -> "b").contains(3)
  val res1: Boolean = false
  ```

  Checking if a given key exists in a dictionary is an efficient operation, which completes in a constant time that is independent from its size.

> **Quick Check 37.3** Implement a function called longestCapitalName that takes a capital-to-country key-value structure and returns the capital with the longest name.
>
> ```
> def longestCapitalName(
>       capitalToCountry: Map[String, String]
>    ): String
> ```

 **Summary**

In this lesson, my objective was to teach you about the most common operations you can perform on a Map.

- You mastered how to retrieve a value associated with one of its keys.
- You discovered how to get all its keys and all its values.
- You learned how to inquire about its size and the feature of its entries.
- You saw how to select one entry based on its characteristics.
- You discovered how to filter Map's elements according to the given criteria.

Let's see if you got this!

TRY THIS   Suppose you have two key-value structures representing a capital and its country, and a country to its continent. Combine the two instances of Map to link each capital to its continent, using the retrieve value strategies you saw in this lesson.

 ## Answers to quick checks

Quick Check 37.1   A possible implementation of the function getCountry is the following:

```
def getCountry(capitalToCountry: Map[String, String],
            capital: String): String =
  capitalToCountry.getOrElse(capital, "Unknown")
```

Quick Check 37.2   You can implement the function getCapitals as the following:

```
def getCapitals(
      capitalToCountry: Map[String, String]
    ): List[String] =
  capitalToCountry.keys.toList
```

The return type of your function is List[String] rather than Iterable[String]; you need to use the methods toList to convert the generic iterable value into a list.

Quick Check 37.3   A possible implementation for the function longestCapitalName is the following:

```
def longestCapitalName(
      capitalToCountry: Map[String, String]
    ): String = {
  val (capital, _) = capitalToCountry.maxBy { case (c, _) =>
    c.length
  }
  capital
}
```

EITHER

After reading this lesson, you will be able to

- Define a value that can have one of two possible types, called `Either`
- Decompose it using pattern matching
- Transform its content using the `map` and `flatMap` functions
- Chain multiple instances of `Either` using `for-comprehension`

In the previous lesson, you mastered the operations you can perform on a `Map`. In this lesson, you'll discover a new Scala type called `Either`. You can use it to represent a value with one of two possible types. You'll learn about its structure and how to define an instance for it. You'll use pattern matching to handle all its possible implementations. You'll transform its values using the `map` and `flatMap` function, and you'll chain multiple values using `for-comprehension`. You'll use the class `Either` to validate if your library can accept a given book request in the capstone.

> **Consider this**
> Imagine you have a list of values representing an online form. You should process it if its items are valid or reject it by explaining why this happened. What type would you use to implement this?

38.1 Why Either?

Imagine you want to write a function to validate a phone number. You do not want to throw exceptions because they are difficult to control and too risky, so you decide to use the type Option. You return the phone number wrapped in a Some if valid, None otherwise. It looks similar to the following:

```
private def containsOnlyDigits(phoneNumber: String): Boolean = ???
private def hasExpectedSize(phoneNumber: String): Boolean = ???

def validatePhoneNumber(phoneNumber: String): Option[String] =
  if (!containsOnlyDigits(phoneNumber)) None
  else if (!hasExpectedSize(phoneNumber)) None
  else Some(phoneNumber)
```

Alternatively, you could also achieve similar results by returning a Boolean value. Although these approaches work, they don't provide information on *why* a phone number may be considered invalid. Is it because of its size? Is it because it contains characters that shouldn't be there? Is it because it cannot contain spaces? If you want to find more information, you must read its full implementation and all its checks to find the one that applies to your input. Boolean and Option are often not expressive enough for validation purposes.

The type Either has many uses, but its most popular is validation. It allows you to return a value that can have one of two possible types. The word *right* is a synonym for *correct* in the English language, so the right side is often mapped to the happy case, the left to the unhappy one. An instance of Either[A, B] can represent either a failure outcome by returning an instance of type A or a successful one by returning type B. You are going to learn more about this later in this lesson. You can reimplement your validatePhoneNumber function using Either as the following:

```
private def containsOnlyDigits(phoneNumber: String): Boolean = ???
private def hasExpectedSize(phoneNumber: String): Boolean = ???

def validatePhoneNumber(phoneNumber: String): Either[String, String] =
  if (!containsOnlyDigits(phoneNumber))
    Left("A phone number should only have digits")
  else if (!hasExpectedSize(phoneNumber))
    Left("Unexpected number of digits! A number has 10 digits")
  else Right(phoneNumber)
```

Your function will now provide information on why a given phone number isn't valid. For example, when invoking validatePhoneNumber("hello"), it returns the Either instance Left("A phone number should only have digits").

 ## 38.2 Creating an Either

Let's consider your program to track exam registrations and imagine you now want to register the outcome of an exam. A mark is either a fail or a pass for ratings between 60 and 100. Your program should not reveal the score of a failed exam but provide a message for the student.

Listing 38.1 Marking exams using Either

```scala
case class Pass(score: Int) {
  require(score >= 60 && score <= 100,
          "Invalid pass: score must be between 60 and 100")
}

def mark(score: Int,
         msg: Option[String] = None): Either[String, Pass] =
  if (score >= 60) Right(Pass(score))
  else Left(msg.getOrElse("Score below 60"))
```

If score is out of range, the instance will throw an exception.

Creating the right instance if it is a pass.

Creating the left instance if it is a fail.

In Scala, Either is an immutable structure to indicate one of two possible values.

Listing 38.2 The structure of Either

```scala
sealed abstract class Either[A, B]

case class Left[A, B](value: A) extends Either[A, B]

case class Right[A, B](value: B) extends Either[A, B]
```

You cannot initialize the class Either directly, as it is abstract. Instead, you need to use one of its two implementations: Left and Right. For an instance of Either[A, B], provide a value of type A to create a Left[A, B] and a value of type B for Right[A, B]. A few examples of how to create an instance of Either are the following:

```
scala> val a: Either[String, Int] = Left("scala")
val a: Either[String,Int] = Left(scala)

scala> val b1: Either[String, Int] = Left(42)
      error: type mismatch;
       found    : Int(42)
       required: String
// Left must contain a value of type String

scala> val b2: Either[String, Int] = Right(42)
val b2: Either[String,Int] = Right(42)

scala> val c: Either[String, Int] = Right("scala")
      error: type mismatch;
       found    : String("scala")
       required: Int
// Right must contain a value of type Int
```

Figure 38.1 provides a visual summary of the structure of an Either.

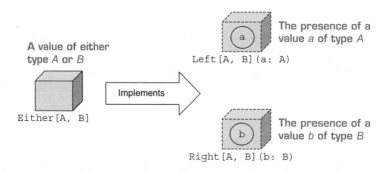

Figure 38.1   The class Either[A,B] represents an instance with one of two types. It has two possible implementations: Left[A,B] containing a value of type A and Right[A, B] representing one of type B.

Quick Check 38.1   Implement a function called sqrt that takes an integer. It returns the square root of the given number if nonnegative, a message otherwise explaining that this operation for negative numbers is not supported.

```
def sqrt(n: Int): Either[String, Double]
```

38.3 Pattern matching on Either

Let's consider your marking program and imagine you now want to produce a message to the display according to their exam outcome.

Listing 38.3 Transforming an exam outcome to a message

```
def toMessage(outcome: Either[String, Pass]): String =        It matches
  outcome match {                                              an instance
    case Left(msg) => s"Fail: $msg"                            of Left.
    case Right(pass) => s"Pass with score ${pass.score}"
  }                                        Evaluated for an
                                           instance of Right
```

You need to provide case clauses for both the implementations Left and Right because the class Either is marked as sealed. If you forget to provide any of its implementations, the compiler shows you a warning at compile time that suggests which of its matches is not exhaustive:

```
scala> def toMessage(outcome: Either[String, Pass]): String =
     |     outcome match {
     |       case Right(pass) => s"Pass with score ${pass.score}"
     |     }
On line 2: warning: match may not be exhaustive.
       It would fail on the following input: Left(_)
def toMessage(outcome: Either[String,Pass]): String
// Left(_) indicates a Left instance containing any value
```

> **Quick Check 38.2** Implement a method called sqrtOrZero that takes an integer. It uses the function sqrt that you implemented in Quick Check 38.1 to compute the square root of the number. Use pattern matching to return zero when the operation is not supported.
>
> ```
> def sqrtOrZero(n: Int): Double
> ```

38.4 The map and flatMap operations

The class Either has an implementation for the map and flatMap functions (you'll learn how to use them in the following subsections). Starting from Scala 2.13, it also has a flatten method, but we won't discuss it because it's rarely used.

38.4.1 The map function

Let's consider your program to mark exams and imagine you'd like to provide an alternative score visualization. Rather than displaying the score itself, you'd like to convert it to a percentage. For example, rather than having a score of 60 with no indication about the maximum possible achievable mark, you want to represent 0.60 to indicate that 60% of it was correct. Instead of using a pattern-matching expression, you can use the map function.

Listing 38.4 Transforming a pass into a percentage

```scala
case class Pass(score: Int) {
  require(score >= 60 && score <= 100,
          "Invalid pass: score must be between 60 and 100")

  def toPercentage: Double = score / 100.0
}

def toPercentage(outcome: Either[String, Pass]): Either[String, Double] =
  outcome.right.map(_.toPercentage)
```

It accesses the value wrapped into the Right instance, if any. You can omit the function right if using Scala 2.12 or higher

You can use the map function to transform the value wrapped into a Left or Right instance of Either. The compiler needs to know if you'd like to manipulate the left or the right side of Either. The methods left and right allow you to specify which side to consider. The function map is a higher order function on Either[A, B] that takes a parameter f. When applied on its left projection (i.e., when you want to manipulate its left side), it takes a parameter f of type A => C to produce a value of type Either[C, B]. When working on its right projection (i.e., when you'd like to transform its right side), it takes a parameter f of type B => C to produce a value of type Either[A, C]. It behaves as follows:

- If your instance matches the selected side, it applies the function f to its value.
- If not, it returns the instance without performing any transformation.

A few examples on map on an instance of Either are following:

```scala
scala> val e: Either[String, Int] = Right(42)
val e: Either[String,Int] = Right(42)

scala> e.left.map(_.size)
val res0: scala.util.Either[Int,Int] = Right(42)
```

```
// Its left side has now type Int rather than String
// but your instance has not been modified

scala> e.right.map(_ * 2.0)
val res1: scala.util.Either[String,Double] = Right(84.0)
// Your instance is a right, so it transforms it into a Double
// by multiplying it by 2.0
```

When developers use the type Either for validation purposes, they usually assume that
its right side represents the happy case, the left for the rejection case. Starting from Scala
2.12, the class Either is *right-biased*: when making no selection, the compiler will assume
you want to manipulate its right side. You can omit the invocation to the right method
for Scala 2.12+:

```
scala> e.map(_ * 2.0)
val res2: scala.util.Either[String,Double] = Right(84.0)
// No need to invoke right as Either is right-biased
```

> **Quick Check 38.3** Implement a function called truncate that takes a parameter of
> type Either[Double, String] and truncates its text to its first 24 characters, if any.
> Use the map method on Either.
>
> ```
> def truncate(e: Either[Double, String]): Either[Double, String]
> ```

38.4.2 The flatMap function

Imagine that a student has received two exam marks and you'd like to combine them;
you should return their average score if they both pass, a fail otherwise.

Listing 38.5 Combining exam outcomes

```
def combine(outcomeA: Either[String, Pass],
            outcomeB: Either[String, Pass]): Either[String, Pass] = {
  outcomeA.flatMap { passA =>
    outcomeB.map { passB =>
      val averageScore = (passA.score + passB.score) / 2
      Pass(averageScore)
    }
  }
}
```

You can avoid calling the
right method if you are
using Scala 2.12+.

When working with an instance of Either[A, B], the flatMap function with a parameter f will have a different signature depending on which side of either you select to transform using the methods left and right. When applied on its left side, it takes a parameter f of type A => Either[C, D] and returns a value of type Either[C, BD]; the compiler infers BD as the type of the common superclass between B and D. When transforming its right projection, it takes a parameter f of type B => Either[C, D] and produces a value of type Either[AC, D]; the compiler infers AC as the type of the common superclass between A and C. It behaves as follows:

- If your instance matches the selected side, it applies the function f to its content to produce a new Either value.
- If not, no transformation happens.

A few examples on how to use flatMap on an instance of Either are the following:

```scala
scala> val e: Either[String, Int] = Right(25)
val e: Either[String,Int] = Right(25)

scala> e.flatMap { n =>
     |    if (n < 0) Left(s"Found Negative number $n")
     |    else Right(Math.sqrt(n))
     | }
val res0: scala.util.Either[String,Double] = Right(5.0)
// The compiler infers the type String for its left side

scala> e.flatMap { n =>
     |    if(n < 0) Left(-1)
     |    else Right(Math.sqrt(n))
     | }
val res1: scala.util.Either[Any,Double] = Right(5.0)
// The left side has type Any because it is
// the common superclass between String and Int

scala> Left("").left.flatMap { text =>
     | if (text.isEmpty) Right(42.0)
     | else Left(text)
     | }
val res2: scala.util.Either[String,Double] = Right(42.0)
```

Table 38.1 shows a summary of the functions map and flatMap on an instance of Either.

Quick Check 38.4 Consider the following snippet of code:

```
def validation(a: Either[String, Int],
               b: Either[String, Int]): Either[String, Int] =
  a.flatMap { aa =>
    b.map(bb => aa + bb)
  }
```

What value does the following function call return? Why? Use the REPL to validate your hypothesis.

```
validation(Left("first failure"), Left("second failure"))
```

Table 38.1 Recap of the map and flatMap operations on an instance of Either [A, B]. Where necessary, the method signature has been simplified to hide nonrelevant implementation details.

	Acts on	Signature	Usage
map	Either[A,B] .left	map(f: A => C): Either[C, B]	It applies a transformation f to the value of its left projection.
	Either[A,B] .right (default from Scala 2.12+)	map(f: B => C): Either[A, C]	It applies a transformation f to the value of its right projection.
flatMap	Either[A,B] .left	flatMap(f: A => Either[C,D]): Either[C, BD]	It produces a new Either instance by applying the function f to the value of its left projection. BD is the type of superclass of both B and D.
	Either[A,B] .right (default from Scala 2.12+)	flatMap(f: B => Either[C,D]): Either[AC, D]	It produces a new Either instance by applying the parameter f to the value of its right projection. AC is the type of the superclass of both A and C.

 ## 38.5 For-comprehension

Let's consider your implementation in listing 38.5 to combine the outcome of two exams. You could refactor it using for-comprehension.

Listing 38.6 **Combining exam outcomes using for-comprehension**

```scala
def combine(outcomeA: Either[String, Pass],
          outcomeB: Either[String, Pass]): Either[String, Pass] =
  for {
    passA <- outcomeA
    passB <- outcomeB
  } yield {
    val averageScore = (passA.score + passB.score) / 2
    Pass(averageScore)
  }
```

In Scala, you can use for-comprehension instead of using the map and flatMap functions on an instance of Either. For example, these expressions are equivalent:

```scala
scala> val value: Either[Int, String] = Left(1234)
val value: Either[Int,String] = Left(1234)

scala> value.left.map(v => v + 1)
val res0: scala.util.Either[Int,String] = Left(1235)

scala> for {
     |    v <- value.left
     | } yield v + 1
val res1: scala.util.Either[Int,String] = Left(1235)
```

> **Quick Check 38.5**   Reimplement the following snippet of code using for-comprehension:
>
> ```scala
> def validation(a: Either[String, Int],
>              b: Either[String, Int]): Either[String, Int] =
>   a.flatMap { aa =>
>     b.map(bb => aa + bb)
>   }
> ```

Summary

In this lesson, my objective was to teach you about the class Either.

- You learned that it has two possible implementations, called left and right, and how to instance them.
- You saw how to use pattern matching on it.

- You mastered how to manipulate its left and right projections using the map and flatMap functions.
- You discovered how to use for-comprehension to combine Either values.

Let's see if you got this!

> **TRY THIS**   In Quick Check 38.4, you saw that the given implementation of the function validation doesn't behave as expected when you need to accumulate errors. Change its return type to Either[List[String], Int] and its implementation to address this issue. HINT: Use pattern matching.

```
def validation(a: Either[String, Int],
               b: Either[String, Int]): Either[List[String], Int]
```

 Answers to quick checks

> **Quick Check 38.1**   A possible implementation for the function sqrt is the following:
>
> ```
> def sqrt(n: Int): Either[String, Double] =
>   if (n < 0) Left("Operation not supported for negative numbers")
>   else Right(Math.sqrt(n))
> ```

> **Quick Check 38.2**   You can implement the function sqrtOrZero using pattern matching as follows:
>
> ```
> def sqrtOrZero(n: Int): Double =
>   sqrt(n) match {
>     case Left(_) => 0
>     case Right(d) => d
>   }
> ```

> **Quick Check 38.3**   If your version of Scala is 2.12+, you can implement the function truncate as follows:
>
> ```
> def truncate(e: Either[Double, String]): Either[Double, String] =
>   e.map(_.take(24))
> ```
>
> If you are using an older version, you need to explicitly indicate that you'd like to transform its right side:
>
> ```
> def truncate(e: Either[Double, String]): Either[Double, String] =
>   e.right.map(_.take(24))
> ```

Quick Check 38.4 The function validation returns Left("first failure") because the flatMap operation doesn't evaluate its parameter if it finds an instance of Left:

```scala
scala> validation(Left("first failure"), Left("second failure"))
val res0: Either[String,Int] = Left(first failure)
```

The type Either does not work well when error accumulation is needed. Consider using cats.data.Validated from the typelevel cats project instead. Although this is not part of the standard library, it is relatively popular because it introduces more advanced functional programming techniques, such as applicatives, a topic we'll unfortunately not cover in this book.

Quick Check 38.5 You can reimplement the snippet of code using for-comprehension as follows:

```scala
def validation(a: Either[String, Int],
               b: Either[String, Int]): Either[String, Int] =
  for {
    aa <- a
    bb <- b
  } yield aa + bb
```

WORKING WITH EITHER

After reading this lesson, you will be able to

- Retrieve a value wrapped in the left or right side for Either
- Check if an instance is its left or right projection
- Inquire if its value respects a given predicate

In the previous lesson, you learned the structure of Either and its basic operations. In this lesson, you'll learn about other useful methods the class Either has to offer. They are very similar to the one you saw for Option. They do not share an interface, but this is a happy consequence of the consistent design and style of the Scala collections. You'll discover how to retrieve a value defined for its left or right side. You'll also inquire about its properties to check if a given instance is of type Left or Right and if it contains a value with specific features. You will use these operations to determine if your library has accepted a book-loaning request in the capstone.

> **Consider this**
> Imagine you need to validate a text representing an email address. If invalid, you should replace it with the string "Unknown." How would you implement it using Either?

39.1 Retrieving an Either value

In the previous lesson, you implemented a program to mark exams that produce a value of type Either[String, Pass] in which its left side represents a failure with a message for the student and its right side a pass with the obtained score.

Listing 39.1 Marking exams strategy

```
case class Pass(score: Int) {
  require(score >= 60 && score <= 100,
          "Invalid pass: score must be between 60 and 100")
}

def mark(score: Int, msg: Option[String] = None): Either[String, Pass] =
  if (score >= 60) Right(Pass(score))
  else Left(msg.getOrElse("Score below 60"))
```

Imagine you'd like to produce a message to anticipate the overall outcome of an exam. Rather than using pattern matching, you can use the getOrElse method on Either.

Listing 39.2 Generating a preview message

```
def getPreviewMessage(outcome: Either[String, Pass]): String =
  outcome.left.getOrElse("You passed the exam, well done!")
```

> It retrieves the value if outcome is left; otherwise, it returns the given default value.

When retrieving a value of an Either, you need to indicate which side you'd like to consider. You can use the left and right functions to do so. Then, you can invoke the getOrElse method to retrieve its value or generate an alternative one. Your program evaluates the default only if needed so that it can contain side effects.

```
scala> Right(42).getOrElse(0)
val res0: Int = 42
// You can omit the call to the right function because
// Either is right from Scala 2.12+

scala> Left("hello").left.getOrElse("scala")
val res1: String = hello

scala> Right(42).left.getOrElse("scala")
val res2: String = scala
```

```
scala> Right(42).getOrElse { println("generating default..."); 0 }
val res3: Int = 42
// It doesn't evaluate the default expression

scala> Left("hello").getOrElse { println("generating default..."); 0 }
generating default...
val res4: Int = 0
// It executes the default expression
```

Table 39.1 provides a recap on the getOrElse function to retrieve a left or right value of an Either instance.

Table 39.1 Recap of the map and flatMap operations on an instance of Either[A, B]. The expressions => A and => B indicate that your program will evaluate their values only when needed, which you can also refer to as *lazy evaluation*.

	Acts on	**Signature**	**Usage**
getOrElse	Either[A,B] .left	getOrElse(default: => A): A	It returns the value of its left projection if present. It evaluates default to produce a value A otherwise.
	Either[A,B] .right (default from Scala 2.12+)	getOrElse(default: => B): B	It retrieves the value of its right projection. If missing, it executes default to create a value of type B.

> **Quick Check 39.1** Implement a function called getOrZero that takes a value of type Either[String, Double] as its parameter. It returns the value wrapped in its right projection or zero.
>
> ```
> def getOrZero(value: Either[String, Double]): Double
> ```

 ## 39.2 Properties of an Either value

Imagine that you need to add extra functionalities to your program to mark exams. In particular, you need to

- determine if a given outcome is a pass and
- check if a mark is a distinction, which is a pass with a score of 80 or higher.

Listing 39.3 Checks on the outcome of an exam

```
def isPass(outcome: Either[String, Pass]): Boolean =
  outcome.isRight          ←———————   It returns true if an instance is a
                                       right projection, false otherwise.

def isDistinction(outcome: Either[String, Pass]): Boolean =
  outcome.exists(pass => pass.score >= 80)      ←
           It returns true is it is a right projection containing a
                value that respects the given predicate.
```

When inquiring on the properties on Either, you can use the following methods:

- isLeft—The function isLeft returns true if the instance is of type Left, false otherwise.

  ```
  scala> Right(42).isLeft
  val res0: Boolean = false

  scala> Left("hello").isLeft
  val res1: Boolean = true
  ```

- isRight—The method isRight is the complementary of isLeft. It returns true for an instance that is a right projection, false otherwise.

  ```
  scala> Right(42).isRight
  val res0: Boolean = true

  scala> Left("hello").isRight
  val res1: Boolean = false
  ```

- exists—For an instance of Either[A, B], the method exists takes one parameter. It takes a predicate function of type A => Boolean for its left projection, or one of type B => Boolean for its right one. It returns true if the instance matches the selected projection, and its value respects the given predicate, false otherwise.

  ```
  scala> val e: Either[String, Int] = Left("hello")
  val e: Either[String,Int] = Left(hello)

  scala> e.exists(_ > 0)
  val res0: Boolean = false
  // Omitting the function call to right because
  // Either is right-biased

  scala> e.left.exists(_.startsWith("scala"))
  val res1: Boolean = false
  ```

```
scala> e.left.exists(_.size > 3)
val res2: Boolean = true
```

Table 39.2 summarizes the methods to analyze the properties of an Either.

Table 39.2 Summary of the function to inquire about the properties of an instance of Either [A, B]

	Acts on	Signature	Usage
isLeft	Either[A,B]	isLeft: Boolean	It returns true if the instance is a left projection, false otherwise.
isRight	Either[A,B]	isRight: Boolean	It returns true if the instance is right, false otherwise.
exists	Either[A,B] .left	exists(p: A => Boolean): Boolean	It returns true if the instance is a left projection and its value respects the given predicate p, false otherwise.
	Either[A,B] .right (default from Scala 2.12+)	exists(p: B => Boolean): Boolean	It returns true if the instance is right, and if it contains an element that asserts the predicate p, false otherwise.

> **Quick Check 39.2** Implement a function called isPositive that takes a value of type Either[String, Double] and returns true if it contains a double bigger than zero, false otherwise.
>
> ```
> def isPositive(value: Either[String, Double]): Boolean
> ```

 Summary

In this lesson, my objective was to teach you about the operations you can perform on an instance of Either.

- You saw how to retrieve the value in one of its projections with a default for it.
- You learned how to discover if an instance is a left or right side for an Either.
- You saw how to inquire about the properties of the value wrapped in a projection.

Let's see if you got this!

> **TRY THIS**   Implement a function that takes either a string or an integer and returns true if the given text is "Scala," false otherwise.

 ## Answers to quick checks

Quick Check 39.1   You could implement the function getOrZero as follows:

```
def getOrZero(value: Either[String, Double]): Double =
  value.getOrElse(0)
```

Quick Check 39.2   A possible implementation for the function isPositive is the following:

```
def isPositive(value: Either[String, Double]): Boolean =
  value.exists(_ > 0)
```

If your Scala version is older than 2.12, you need to explicitly indicate to the compiler that you'd like to consider its right projection:

```
def isPositive(value: Either[String, Double]): Boolean =
  value.right.exists(_ > 0)
```

ERROR HANDLING WITH TRY

After reading this lesson, you will be able to

- Represent a computation that can fail using Try
- Decompose it using pattern matching
- Manipulate its value using the map, flatten, and flatMap operations
- Chain several Try instances using for-comprehension
- Check if a computation has failed and retrieve its value

In the previous lessons, you mastered the type Either. In this lesson, you'll learn about the class Try to represent a computation that can fail. Throwing exceptions is a risky and unpredictable practice. Knowing which exceptions a method may throw is challenging, if not impossible, as they are often not annotated and are highly dependent on the specifics of their implementation. The class Try allows you to control a computation that may throw exceptions, and it forces you to provide instruction for both the success and failure cases at compile time. Whenever possible, you should use Try instead of a try-catch expression. You'll find several similarities with the type Either; you can see Try[T] as an alternative implementation for Either[Throwable, T]. You'll learn about the purpose and structure of the type Try, and you'll use pattern matching to decompose its possible implementations. You'll transform and manipulate its value using its map, flatten, and flatMap methods. You'll combine multiple operations that can fail into one. You'll also inquire about the success of some computation and retrieve its value. In the capstone, you will use the type Try to handle possible failures when parsing data from a CSV to create a book collection for your library.

> **Consider this**
> Imagine you are developing software to check if a given postcode is correct. It relies on a third party that it invokes via a public HTTP API. What happens if your program can no longer connect to it? How would you ensure that it can survive this unforeseen outage?

 ## 40.1 Creating a Try

Imagine you are developing software to register students for exam sessions. You need to ensure students register only for exam sessions of topics they selected.

Listing 40.1 Registering a student for an exam session

```scala
import java.time.LocalDate                          Importing Try and its
import scala.util.{Failure, Success, Try}   ←────── implementations into
                                                     the current scope

case class Student(id: Int, name: String, topics: Set[String])
case class ExamSession(title: String,
                       localDate: LocalDate,
                       topic: String)
                                              LocalDate.now()
                                              returns today's
case class Registration(studentId: Int,            date.
                        examSession: ExamSession,
                        localDate: LocalDate = LocalDate.now())

def register(student: Student,
             examSession: ExamSession): Try[Registration] = {
  if (student.topics.contains(examSession.topic))
    Success(Registration(student.id, examSession))   ←──  Creating the
  else                                                     success instance if
    Failure(new IllegalStateException(                     the condition is true
      s"Student ${student.id} is missing topic ${examSession.topic}"))
}
   Creating the failure instance
   if the condition is false
```

In Scala, you can use the class Try to represent a computation that can fail. It lives in the package scala.util and has two possible implementations to define the success and failure cases.

Listing 40.2 **The structure of Try**

```
package scala.util

sealed abstract class Try[T]

case class Success[T](t: T) extends Try[T]

case class Failure[T](throwable: Throwable) extends Try[T]
```

The type Try is not available in your scope by default, so you need to add the instruction import scala.util.Try before you can use it. It is abstract, so you cannot initialize it directly. You should use one of its two implementations: scala.util.Success or scala.util.Failure. When creating an instance of failure, you need to provide a throwable. The class java.lang.Throwable is a Java type representing everything your system can throw: Exception is a subclass of Throwable. A few examples of how to create instances of Try are the following:

```
scala> import scala.util._
import scala.util._
// Adding Try, Success, Failure to your scope

scala> val a: Try[Int] = Success(1)
val a: scala.util.Try[Int] = Success(1)

scala> val b: Try[Int] = Success("scala")
       error: type mismatch;
        found   : String("scala")
        required: Int
// Success must contain an integer

scala> val b: Try[Int] = Failure(new Exception("error!"))
val b: scala.util.Try[Int] = Failure(java.lang.Exception: error!)

scala> val b: Try[Int] = Failure("error!")
       error: type mismatch;
        found   : String("error!")
        required: Throwable
// String does not extend Throwable
```

Figure 40.1 shows a visual summary of the structure of Try.

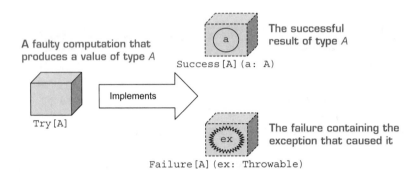

A faulty computation that produces a value of type A

Try[A]

Implements

The successful result of type A

Success[A](a: A)

The failure containing the exception that caused it

Failure[A](ex: Throwable)

Figure 40.1   Use the class Try[A] to represent a computation that can fail in producing a value of type A. It has only two possible implementations: Success and Failure. Success[A] represents a completed operation containing the created instance of type A, while Failure[A] represents a faulty execution containing the exception that caused it.

When initializing an instance of Try, you can also use its apply method.

Listing 40.3   The method Try.apply

```scala
package scala.util

import scala.util.control.NonFatal

object Try {

  def apply[T](r: => T): Try[T] =
    try Success(r) catch {
      case NonFatal(e) => Failure(e)
    }
}
```

The parameter r is not evaluated until needed.

NonFatal matches throwable instances that are recoverable

Its apply method takes one parameter returning a value of type T. The symbol => T indicates to delay its evaluation until its invocation. It executes the value r inside a try-catch expression to handle recoverable exceptions. NonFatal matches only Throwable instances that Scala considers recoverable. OutOfMemoryError, ThreadDeath, and InterruptedException are some of the ones it marks as fatal. You can rewrite the function in listing 40.1 using the function Try.apply.

```
def register(student: Student,
            examSession: ExamSession): Try[Registration] =
  Try {
    if (student.topics.contains(examSession.topic))
      Registration(student.id, examSession)
    else
      throw new IllegalStateException(
        s"Student ${student.id} is missing topic ${examSession.topic}")
  }
```

Expression equivalent to Try.apply

Creating a Try instance by initializing its implementations or using the Try.apply method is equivalent and up to your preference. A few more examples of how to use the Try.apply function are the following:

```
scala> import scala.util.Try
import scala.util.Try
// Adding the type Try into your scope

scala> val b: Try[Int] = Try(10/2)
val b: scala.util.Try[Int] = Success(5)
// equivalent to Try.apply(10/2)

scala> val b: Try[Int] = Try(10/0)
val b: scala.util.Try[Int] = Failure(java.lang.ArithmeticException: /
        by zero)
// The expression 10/0 throws an ArithmeticException instance
```

Quick Check 40.1 Implement a function called toTry that converts an instance of Either[Throwable, T] into one of type Try[T].

```
def toTry[T](either: Either[Throwable, T]): Try[T]
```

40.2 Pattern matching on Try

Let's consider your program to register a student for an exam session. After you try to produce a registration, you now need to analyze its result to produce a message to display to the user.

Listing 40.5 Producing a message for a possibly faulty registration

```scala
def toPrettyMsg(registration: Try[Registration]): String =
  registration match {
    case Success(reg) =>
      s"Student registered for exam session ${reg.examSession.title}"
    case Failure(ex) =>
      s"Registration failed: ${ex.getMessage}"
  }
```

It matches a successful registration.

It matches a failed computation.

The implementation of Try uses the keyword *sealed*. You need to provide cases for both Success and Failure when defining pattern matching to prevent the compiler from producing a warning.

```scala
scala> import scala.util._
import scala.util._

scala> Try(1) match {
     |    case Success(n) => n
     | }
warning: match may not be exhaustive.
It would fail on the following input: Failure(_)
val res0: Int = 1
```

> **Quick Check 40.2** Implement a function called toEither that converts an instance of type Try[T] into one of type Either[Throwable, T].
>
> ```scala
> def toEither[T](tryT: Try[T]): Either[Throwable, T]
> ```

40.3 The map, flatten, and flatMap operations

The class Try has an implementation for the methods map, flatten, and flatMap. They behave similarly to those for Option. Let's see them in action in the following subsections.

40.3.1 The map function

Suppose you now need to extract the date of an exam registration. You can achieve this using the function map.

> **Listing 40.6 Getting the date of an exam registration**

```
def getRegistrationDate(
      registration: Try[Registration]): Try[LocalDate] =
  registration.map(_.localDate)
```

You can use the function map to transform the value that is the result of a successful computation. If your instance is of type Failure, nothing happens:

```
scala> import scala.util._
import scala.util._

scala> Try(5).map(_ + 1.23)
val res0: scala.util.Try[Double] = Success(6.23)

scala> Try(5/0).map(_ + 1.23)
val res1: scala.util.Try[Double] =
          Failure(java.lang.ArithmeticException: / by zero)
```

> **Quick Check 40.3** Implement a function to transform an instance of Try[Double] into one of Try[Float] using the map method.
>
> ```
> def toFloat(d: Try[Double]): Try[Float]
> ```

40.3.2 The flatten function

Suppose that your program should allow students to register for the next exam session available for a given topic. Imagine that your code has a function called getNextExamSession that tries to find the next exam session; it will return a failure if it can't select one.

```
def getNextExamSession(topic: String): Try[ExamSession]
```

You could compose the getNextExamSession with the function register you implemented in listing 40.1 by chaining the two values using the map method:

```
def registerForNextExamSession(student: Student,
                               topic: String): Try[Try[Registration]] =
  getNextExamSession(topic).map { examSession =>
    register(student, examSession)
  }
```

This function produces a value of type Try[Try[Registration]]. A failure in the outer Try indicates an issue in the exam session selection, while one in the inner instance suggests a problem with the registration process. This distinction may not be informative to the user, and you may want to unify all the failures independently by what caused them.

Listing 40.7 Registering a student for the next exam session

```
import scala.util.Try

def registerForNextExamSession(student: Student,
                               topic: String): Try[Registration] =
  getNextExamSession(topic).map { examSession =>
    register(student, examSession)
  }.flatten
```

You can use the method flatten to merge two nested Try instances into one: it acts on an instance of Try[Try[T]] to produce a value of type Try[T]:

```
scala> import scala.util._
import scala.util._

scala> Try(Try(1)).flatten
val res0: scala.util.Try[Int] = Success(1)

scala> Try(Try(1/0)).flatten
val res1: scala.util.Try[Int] = Failure(java.lang.ArithmeticException:
          / by zero)

scala> Try(1).flatten
error: Cannot prove that Int <:< scala.util.Try[U].
// You can invoke the function flatten only on nested structures
```

> **Quick Check 40.4** Implement a function called superFlatten that takes an instance of Try[Try[Try[T]]] and returns one of type Try[T].
>
> ```
> def superFlatten[T](tryT: Try[Try[Try[T]]]): Try[T]
> ```

40.3.3 The flatMap function

Let's consider the function registerForNextExamSession you implemented in listing 40.7. You can also rewrite it using the flatMap function.

Listing 40.8 Registering for next exam session using flatMap

```
import scala.util.Try

def registerForNextExamSession(student: Student,
                               topic: String): Try[Registration] =
  getNextExamSession(topic).flatMap { examSession =>
    register(student, examSession)
  }
```

When performing a map operation followed by a flatten one, you should combine them and invoke the flatMap function instead. A few more examples of how to use it are the following:

```
scala> import scala.util._
import scala.util._

scala> Try(1).flatMap(n => Try(2/n))
val res0: scala.util.Try[Int] = Success(2)

scala> Try(0).flatMap(n => Try(2/n))
val res1: scala.util.Try[Int] = Failure(java.lang.ArithmeticException:
        / by zero)
```

Table 40.1 shows a summary of the map, flatten, and flatMap functions acting on an instance of type Try.

Table 40.1 Technical recap of the three fundamental operations on Try. The function `map` applies a given function to the successful result of a computation, while the method `flatten` creates a new instance of Try by merging two nested structures. The `flatMap` operation combines the `map` and `flatten` ones to chain values together.

	Acts on	Signature	Usage
map	Try[A]	map(f: A => B): Try[B]	It applies a function to the successful result of the computation, if any.
flatten	Try[Try[A]]	flatten: Try[A]	It merges two nested Try instances into one.
flatMap	Try[A]	flatMap(f: A => Try[B]): Try[B]	The combination of map followed by flatten. It chains Try instances together.

Quick Check 40.5 Imagine you implemented a function to find a student by an ID:

```
import scala.util._

case class Student(id: Int, name: String, topics: Set[String])
def findStudent(id: Int): Try[Student] = ???
```

Implement another function with the same name that takes a string as its parameter and returns an instance of Try[Student] by reusing the existing findStudent(id: Int) function.

```
def findStudent(id: String): Try[Student]
```

HINT: You can parse a string instance into an integer using the toInt function, which throws an exception if this is not possible.

40.4 For-comprehension

Let's look at the function you implemented in listing 40.8 to register a student for the next exam session available. You could rewrite it using `for-comprehension`.

Listing 40.9 Registering for the next exam session using for-comprehension

```
import scala.util.Try

def registerForNextExamSession(student: Student,
                               topic: String): Try[Registration] =
```

It extracts
the found
exam
session,
if any.

```
for {
  examSession <- getNextExamSession(topic)
  registration <- register(student, examSession)
} yield registration
```

It binds the suc-
cessful registration
to the registration
variable, if any.

You can use for-comprehension to express a chain of flatMap and map operations to improve their readability. For example, you can rewrite the expression Try(1).flatMap(n => Try(2/n)) using for-comprehension:

```
for {
  n <- Try(1)
  res <- Try(2/n)
} yield res
```

> **Quick Check 40.6** Rewrite the function findStudent(id: String) that you implemented in Quick Check 40.5 using for-comprehension.

 ## 40.5 Other operations on Try

Suppose that your program has logic to select the next available exam session for a given topic and you'd like to perform the following operations on it:

- Check if it was able to find an exam session.
- Retrieve the selected one or provide an alternative to the student.

Listing 40.10 Checking if registration is successful

```
import java.time.LocalDate
import scala.util.Try

def exists(nextSession: Try[ExamSession]): Boolean =
  nextSession.isSuccess

private val defaultExamSession: ExamSession = ???
def getExamSession(nextSession: Try[ExamSession]): ExamSession =
  nextSession.getOrElse(defaultExamSession)
```

The class Try offers a few helper functions you can use as alternatives to pattern matching:

- isSuccess—The function isSuccess returns true if the instance is of type Success.

    ```
    scala> Try(5/2).isSuccess
    val res0: Boolean = true
    ```

- isFailure—The method isFailure is complementary to isSuccess; it returns true if the instance is of type Failure.

  ```scala
  scala> Try(5/2).isFailure
  val res0: Boolean = false
  ```

- getOrElse—For an instance of Try[T], the function getOrElse takes an expression that produces a value of type T as its parameter. It returns its value if your instance is of type Success. In case of failure, it evaluates the given parameter to produce an alternative value to return only if needed to handle side effects correctly.

  ```scala
  scala> Try(5/2).getOrElse { println("Side Effect!");  42 }
  val res0: Int = 2

  scala> Try(5/0).getOrElse { println("Side Effect!");  42 }
  Side Effect!
  val res1: Int = 42
  ```

> **Quick Check 40.7** The class String offers a method called toBoolean to convert text into a Boolean value, which is unsafe because it throws an exception for any string that does not match true or false. Implement a function called toSafeBoolean by reusing toBoolean and returning false rather than throwing an exception.
>
> ```scala
> def toSafeBoolean(text: String): Boolean
> ```

 Summary

In this lesson, my objective was to teach you about the type Try.

- You learned how to create a Try instance by initializing one of its implementations or by using its apply method.
- You saw how to manipulate and chain its values using map, flatten, flatMap, and for-comprehension.
- You discovered how to check if a Try instance is successful and how to retrieve its value.

Let's see if you got this!

TRY THIS   Imagine you are developing software to read and manipulate data from a file. Implement a function to parse a string into an instance of Person:

```scala
case class Person(age: Int, name: String)
```

For example, the text "35, Jane Doe" should result in a Person instance equal to Person(35, "Jane Doe"). Make sure not to throw exceptions if your function cannot parse the given text by returning an informative failure without throwing exceptions. HINT: You can use the method split to tokenize a string.

```scala
scala> "a-b-c".split("-").toList
val res0: List[String] = List(a, b, c)

scala> "a-b-c".split("-", 2).toList
val res1: List[String] = List(a, b-c)
// limiting to up to two tokens
```

 # Answers to quick checks

Quick Check 40.1 A possible implementation for the function toTry is the following:

```scala
import scala.util._

def toTry[T](either: Either[Throwable, T]): Try[T] =
  either match {
    case Left(ex) => Failure(ex)
    case Right(t) => Success(t)
  }
```

Quick Check 40.2 You can implement the method toEither as the following:

```scala
import scala.util._

def toEither[T](tryT: Try[T]): Either[Throwable, T] =
  tryT match {
    case Success(t) => Right(t)
    case Failure(ex) => Left(ex)
  }
```

Quick Check 40.3 A possible implementation for the function toFloat is the following:

```scala
import scala.util.Try

def toFloat(d: Try[Double]): Try[Float] = d.map(_.toFloat)
```

Quick Check 40.4 You can implement the function superFlatten by invoking the method flatten twice:

```scala
import scala.util._

def superFlatten[T](tryT: Try[Try[Try[T]]]): Try[T] =
  tryT.flatten.flatten
```

Quick Check 40.5 A possible implementation for the function findStudent is the following:

```scala
def findStudent(id: String): Try[Student] =
  Try(id.toInt).flatMap(findStudent)
```

Quick Check 40.6 Your function findStudent should look similar to the following:

```scala
def findStudent(id: String): Try[Student] =
  for {
    n <- Try(id.toInt)
    student <- findStudent(n)
  } yield student
```

Quick Check 40.7 A possible implementation for the function toSafeBoolean is the following:

```scala
import scala.util.Try

def toSafeBoolean(text: String): Boolean =
  Try(text.toBoolean).getOrElse(false)
```

THE LIBRARY APPLICATION

In this capstone, you will

- Define an ordered sequence of items using Set
- Add and remove elements to it to track book loans
- Create book instances from a parsed CSV file using Map
- Handle parsing failures using Try
- Validate book loans or returns by providing expressive error messages using Either

In this capstone, you'll create an application to keep track of books loaned in a library. Each book has a unique ID and can be checked out by only one user at a time but returned by anyone. Each user can take up to 5 books. You need to write the code to read and parse the available books from a CSV file. In particular, you'll use a publicly accessible data set called "goodbooks-10k" by Zajac Zygmunt. You can find its latest version as well as a detailed description of its content on its website:

> The data set contains 6 million ratings for 10,000 popular books (with most ratings). There are also the following:
>
> - Books marked by users to read
> - Book metadata (author, year, etc.)
> - Tags/shelves/genres
>
> From http://fastml.com/goodbooks-10k

For this capstone, you'll focus on the book metadata only in the file books.csv. The file provides lots of information for each record. You'll need only its title, authors, image URL, and GoodReads ID. Table 41.1 summarizes their features. GoodReads is an online platform for book recommendations (http://goodreads.com). For simplicity, let's assume the library has only one copy of each book so that you can use the GoodReads ID as a unique identifier for each of its physical copies.

Table 41.1 Summary of the book features you'll consider from the goodbooks-10k data set by Zajac Zygmunt. (For a full list of the analyzed characteristics, go to http://fastml .com/goodbooks-10k or the header of file books.csv.)

Feature	Description	Format	Nullable
goodreads_book_id	The unique ID for the book, taken from the GoodReads online platform	Long	No
title	Its English title	String	No
authors	The comma-separated list of its authors	String	No
image_url	A link to the image of its cover	String	Yes

41.1 Download the base project

Let's use git to download the data set with a baseline sbt project containing the needed external dependencies and some ready-to-implement classes to help you get started. Navigate to an empty folder of your choice and review the remote branch with the code:

```
$ git init
$ git remote add get-prog-with-scala https://github.com/DanielaSfregola/
          get-programming-with-scala.git
$ git fetch get-prog-with-scala
$ git checkout -b my_lesson41 get-prog-with-scala/baseline_unit6_lesson41
```

The files project/build.properties and build.sbt provide information on the sbt and Scala versions to use and which external dependencies to use. The src/main/resources/books.csv is the resource containing the data set you'll parse to create the library's book collection. Finally, the src/scala folder contains some base classes to implement:

- org.example.books.entities.Book provides the structure of a book.

    ```
    case class Book(id: Long,
                    title: String,
                    authors: List[String],
                    imageUrl: Option[URL])
    ```

    You will implement a function in its companion object called parse that tries to create a Book instance movie from a dictionary containing fields and values.

- `org.example.books.entities.User` has an ID and a full name to represent a user reserving a book from the library.

  ```
  case class User(id: Long, fullName: String)
  ```

- `org.example.books.entities.BookLoan` keeps track of which user has checked out a given book.

  ```
  case class BookLoan(book: Book, user: User)
  ```

- `org.example.books.BookParser` uses the scala-csv external dependency to read a CSV file and produce an instance of type `List[Map[String, String]]` to represent the fields and values of each of its lines. You'll parse each line to create a `Book` instance tentatively.

- `org.example.books.BookService` contains the function signatures representing the business functionalities your library must offer: you can search a book, request a book loan, and return a book. You'll implement them as part of this lesson.

Execute the command `sbt compile` to download all the external dependencies and compile the existing code. You are now ready to start coding!

 ## 41.2 Parsing a book entity

Let's begin by implementing a function that tentatively converts a dictionary of headers and values into a book presentation:

```
object Book {
  def parse(row: Map[String, String]): Try[Book] =???
}
```

For each component of our book representation, you'll need to retrieve the value matching the correct headers and convert it into the expected type. The possible failures are that a header may be missing or that your program cannot convert it into the expected type. These failures apply to potentially any parsing scenario, so let's abstract them using higher-order functions.

Listing 41.1 Handling parsing failures

```scala
// file src/main/scala/org/example/books/entities/Book.scala

// […]

object Book {

  // […]

  private def parseAs[T](row: Map[String, String],
                    key: String, parser: String => T): Try[T] =
    for {
      value <- getValue(row, key)
      t <- Try(parser(value))
    } yield t

  private def getValue(row: Map[String, String],
                    key: String): Try[String] =
    row.get(key) match {
      case Some(value) => Success(value)
      case None => Failure(new IllegalArgumentException(
        s"Couldn't find column $key in row - row was $row"))
    }
}
```

It combines all the parsing failures.

Evaluating the parser function inside a Try as it may fail

It retrieves a value associated with a key, or it fails with a meaningful message.

The function get reminds you to handle the case of missing value by returning an optional value.

You can now define functions to parse a value associated with a header into the types you need and combine them to create a Book instance.

Listing 41.2 Parsing a Book instance from a dictionary

```scala
// file src/main/scala/org/example/books/entities/Book.scala

package org.example.books.entities

import scala.util.{Failure, Success, Try}
import java.net.URL

case class Book(id: Long,
                title: String,
                authors: List[String],
                imageUrl: Option[URL]) {
```

```
    def toPrettyString: String =
      s"[$id] $title ${authors.mkString("{", ", ", "}")}"
}

object Book {

    def parse(row: Map[String, String]): Try[Book] =
      for {
        id <- parseLong(row, "goodreads_book_id")
        title <- parseString(row, "title")
        authors <- parseStrings(row, "authors")
      } yield {
        // optional fields
        val imageUrl = parseURL(row, "image_url").toOption

        Book(id, title, authors, imageUrl)
      }

    private def parseLong(row: Map[String, String],
                          key: String): Try[Long] =
      parseAs(row, key, _.toLong)

    private def parseString(row: Map[String, String],
                            key: String): Try[String] =
      parseAs(row, key, x => x)

    private def parseStrings(row: Map[String, String],
                             key: String): Try[List[String]] =
      parseAs(row, key, _.split(",").map(_.trim).toList)

    private def parseURL(row: Map[String, String],
                         key: String): Try[URL] =
      parseAs(row, key, s => new URL(s))

    // […]
}
```

It combines all the parsers to create a book.

It returns None if parsing an image URL was not possible. It is an optional field, so you can still create a book instance if not available.

You already have an instance of type String, so you return it as is.

It applies a map operation over an array and converts it into a list.

You can now apply your Book.parse function to each line of the read CSV file and move those unsuccessful into the BookParser class.

Listing 41.3 Parsing each line of the CSV file

```scala
// file src/main/scala/org/example/books/BookParser.scala

package org.example.books

import org.example.books.entities.Book
import com.github.tototoshi.csv._
import org.slf4j.{Logger, LoggerFactory}

import scala.io.Source
import scala.util.{Failure, Success, Try}

class BookParser(filePath: String) {

  private val logger: Logger = LoggerFactory.getLogger(this.getClass)

  val books: List[Book] = {
    loadCSVFile(filePath).flatMap { rowData =>
      Book.parse(rowData) match {
        case Success(book) => Some(book)
        case Failure(ex) =>
          logger.warn("Skipping book: Unable to parse row because " +
                      s"of ${ex.getMessage} - row was $rowData")
          None
      }
    }
  }

  private def loadCSVFile(path: String): List[Map[String, String]] = {
    logger.info(s"Processing file $path...")
    val file = Source.fromResource(
      path, classOf[BookParser].getClassLoader)
    val reader = CSVReader.open(file)
    val data = reader.allWithHeaders()
    logger.info(s"Completed processing of file $path! " +
                s"${data.size} records loaded")
    data
  }
}
```

It transforms each dictionary with fields and values of a line of the CSV file.

It logs a warning when a CSV record finds an unparsable record.

It uses the external dependency scala-csv to read the CSV file into a list of dictionaries.

41.3 The business logic layer

After implementing the logic to parse the books from a file, let's see how to implement your library's business functionalities: search for, reserve, and return a book. The base structure of BookService has given you a possible signature for these functions.

Listing 41.4 The base structure of BookService

```scala
// file src/main/scala/org/example/books/BookService.scala

package org.example.books

import org.example.books.entities._
import org.slf4j.{Logger, LoggerFactory}

class BookService(bookCatalogPath: String) {
  private val logger: Logger = LoggerFactory.getLogger(this.getClass)

  private val books: List[Book] =          It loads the books for
    new BookParser(bookCatalogPath).books   the book parser.

  private var bookLoans: Set[BookLoan] = ???   It tracks book loans
                                               with a private mutable
                                               assignment.
  def search(title: Option[String] = None,
             author: Option[String] = None): List[Book] = ???

  def reserveBook(bookId: Long,
                  user: User): Either[String, BookLoan] = ???

  def returnBook(bookId: Long): Either[String, BookLoan] = ???

}
```

41.3.1 Performing a book search

Let's implement the search by filtering the books based on their title or any of the authors.

Listing 41.5 Searching for a book by title or author

```scala
// file src/main/scala/org/example/books/BookService.scala

package org.example.books

import org.example.books.entities._
import org.slf4j.{Logger, LoggerFactory}

class BookService(bookCatalogPath: String) {
  private val logger: Logger = LoggerFactory.getLogger(this.getClass)

  private val books: List[Book] =
    new BookParser(bookCatalogPath).books

  // [...]

  def search(title: Option[String] = None,
             author: Option[String] = None): List[Book] =
    books.filter { book =>
      title.forall(t => containsCaseInsensitive(book.title, t)) &&
      author.forall(a => book.authors.exists(
        containsCaseInsensitive(_, a)))
    }

  private def containsCaseInsensitive(text: String,
                                      substring: String): Boolean =
    text.toLowerCase.contains(substring.toLowerCase)

  // [...]
}
```

Helper function to make the search case insensitive

The function `forall` is a function defined in the `Option` class that returns `true` if it contains a value that respects the given predicate or is empty. It is equivalent to performing a `map` operation following by a `getOrElse(true)` invocation:

```scala
title.forall(t => book.title.contains(t))
// ...is equivalent to...
title.map(t => book.title.contains(t)).getOrElse(true)
```

41.3.2 Reserving a book

Let's implement the functionality for a user to reserve a book. It has the following business requirements:

- A user cannot reserve more than 5 books at the same time.
- The requested book must exist.
- It must be available; in other words, no other user has it currently.

You can implement a function representing each check and then chain them together with for-comprehension.

Listing 41.6 Reserving a book

```scala
// file src/main/scala/org/example/books/BookService.scala

package org.example.books

import org.example.books.entities._
import org.slf4j.{Logger, LoggerFactory}

class BookService(bookCatalogPath: String) {
  private val logger: Logger = LoggerFactory.getLogger(this.getClass)

  private val books: List[Book] = new BookParser(bookCatalogPath).books

  private var bookLoans: Set[BookLoan] = Set.empty      // Assuming that there are no book loans initially

  // [...]

    def reserveBook(bookId: Long,
                                user: User): Either[String, BookLoan] = {
    val res = for {
      _ <- checkReserveLimits(user)
      book <- checkBookExists(bookId)
      _ <- checkBookIsAvailable(book)
    } yield registerBookLoan(book, user)
    logger.info(s"Book $bookId - User ${user.id} - " +
            s"Reserve request: ${outcomeMsg(res)}")    // It logs the request and its outcome as info level.
    res
  }
```

```
private def outcomeMsg[T](res: Either[String, T]): String =
  res.left.getOrElse("OK")
```

It checks if the user is within
the maximum loan limit.

```
private val loanLimit = 5
private def checkReserveLimits(user: User): Either[String, User] =
  if (bookLoans.count(_.user == user) < loanLimit) Right(user)
  else Left(
    s"You cannot loan more than $loanLimit books at the same time")
```

```
private def checkBookExists(bookId: Long): Either[String, Book] =
  books.find(_.id == bookId) match {
    case Some(book) => Right(book)
    case None => Left(s"Book with id $bookId not found")
  }
```

It checks if
the book
exists.

```
private def checkBookIsAvailable(book: Book): Either[String, Book] =
  findBookLoan(book) match {
    case Some(_) => Left(s"Another user has book ${book.id}")
    case None => Right(book)
  }
```

It checks if
the book is
available
for loan.

```
private def findBookLoan(book: Book): Option[BookLoan] =
  bookLoans.find(_.book == book)
```

```
private def registerBookLoan(book: Book, user: User): BookLoan = {
  val bookLoan = BookLoan(book, user)
  updateBookLoans(loans => loans + bookLoan)
  bookLoan
}
```

It registers
the book
loan.

```
// [...]
```

```
private def updateBookLoans(
    f: Set[BookLoan] => Set[BookLoan]): Unit =
  synchronized { bookLoans = f(bookLoans) }
}
```

The method synchronized ensures that
no simultaneous updates can happen
for the mutable assignment bookLoans,
causing data inconsistencies.

The function synchronized mimics the behavior of the Java qualifier synchronized: it prevents the execution of a block of code more than ones simultaneously. Imagine a scenario in which two requests invoke the function updateBookLoans at the same time. They both read the current assignment for bookLoans; suppose this is the empty set. They both produce a new instance for bookLoans. Let's imagine these are Set(bookLoanA) and Set(bookLoanB), respectively. The requests will override each other's assignments: if the first one goes after the second one, bookLoans will contain bookLoanA but not bookLoanB, and vice versa. The method synchronized ensures that one request can read, modify, and reassign the mutable assignment bookLoans at any time, which prevents the described data inconsistency.

41.3.3 Returning a book

Finally, let's define the logic to return a book. You'll need to check the following:

- The book must exist.
- It must be out for a loan.

Its implementation reuses some of the checks you are already implemented for reserving a book.

Listing 41.7 Returning a book

```scala
// file src/main/scala/org/example/books/BookService.scala

package org.example.books

import org.example.books.entities._
import org.slf4j.{Logger, LoggerFactory}

class BookService(bookCatalogPath: String) {
  private val logger: Logger = LoggerFactory.getLogger(this.getClass)

  private val books: List[Book] =
    new BookParser(bookCatalogPath).books

  private var bookLoans: Set[BookLoan] = Set.empty

  // [...]

  def returnBook(bookId: Long): Either[String, BookLoan] = {
    val res = for {
      book <- checkBookExists(bookId)
      user <- checkBookIsTaken(book)
    } yield unregisterBookLoan(book, user)
    logger.info(s"Book $bookId - Return request: ${outcomeMsg(res)}")
```

It logs the request and its outcome as info level.

```
    res
  }
  // [...]
```

> It implements a new function rather than reusing the existing one called checkBookIsAvailable to have a meaningful validation message.

```
  private def checkBookIsTaken(book: Book): Either[String, User] =
    findBookLoan(book) match {
      case Some(BookLoan(_, user)) => Right(user)
      case None => Left(
        s"Book ${book.id} does not result out on loan")
    }

  private def unregisterBookLoan(book: Book, user: User): BookLoan = {
    val bookLoan = BookLoan(book, user)
    updateBookLoans(loans => loans - bookLoan)
    bookLoan
  }

  // [...]
}
```

You have now completed your library's implementation. Let's see it in action in a simple scenario.

41.4 Let's give it a try!

Let's investigate a simple scenario to demonstrate how to use your library program by using the sbt interactive console. Navigate to the root directory of your project and execute the sbt console command to compile and load your code in memory:

```
$ sbt console
[...]

scala>
```

Let's initialize your library and search for books with titles containing the words "Harry Potter":

```
scala> import org.example.books.BookService
import org.example.books.BookService

scala> val library = new BookService("books.csv")
12:19:34.671 [run-main-0] INFO org.example.books.BookParser -
        Processing file books.csv...
```

```
12:19:35.475 [run-main-0] INFO org.example.books.BookParser -
         Completed processing of file books.csv! 10000 records loaded
val library: org.example.books.BookService =
         org.example.books.BookService@155bee8d

scala> val books = library.search(title = Some("Harry Potter"))
val books: List[org.example.books.entities.Book] = List(Book(3,Harry
         Potter and the Sorcerer's Stone (Harry Potter, #1),List(J.K.
         Rowling...

scala> books.size
val res0: Int = 22
```

Your search returned 22 books. Let's focus on the first two and create two users:

```
scala> val bookA = books(0)
val bookA: org.example.books.entities.Book = Book(3,Harry Potter and
         the Sorcerer's Stone (Harry Potter, #1),List(J.K. Rowling,
         Mary GrandPré),Some(https://images.gr-
         assets.com/books/1474154022m/3.jpg))
// You can safely use the method apply here because
// you have verified that the collection books has 22 items

scala> val bookB = books(1)
val bookB: org.example.books.entities.Book = Book(5,Harry Potter and
         the Prisoner of Azkaban (Harry Potter, #3),List(J.K.
         Rowling, Mary GrandPré, Rufus Beck),Some(https://images.gr-
         assets.com/books/1499277281m/5.jpg))
// You can safely use apply here because you know that
// books has 22 items

scala> import org.example.books.entities.User
import org.example.books.entities.User

scala> val alice = User(1, "Alice Abbott")
val alice: org.example.books.entities.User = User(1,Alice Abbott)

scala> val bob = User(2, "Bob Brown")
val bob: org.example.books.entities.User = User(2,Bob Brown)
```

Alice takes the first two books:

```
scala> library.reserveBook(bookA.id, alice)
12:50:58.412 [run-main-0] INFO org.example.books.BookService - Book 3
         - User 1 - Reserve request: OK
[…]
```

```
scala> library.reserveBook(bookB.id, alice)
12:51:10.465 [run-main-0] INFO org.example.books.BookService - Book 5
          - User 1 - Reserve request: OK
[…]
```

Then, Bob tries to reserve a book that Alice has and a book that does not exist:

```
scala> library.reserveBook(bookA.id, bob)
12:53:53.131 [run-main-0] INFO org.example.books.BookService - Book 3
          - User 2 - Reserve request: Another user has book 3
[…]
```

```
scala> library.reserveBook(-1, bob)
12:55:55.292 [run-main-0] INFO org.example.books.BookService - Book -1
          - User 2 - Reserve request: Book with id -1 not found
[…]
```

After Alice returns the book, Bob should be able to reserve it:

```
scala> library.returnBook(bookA.id)
12:58:21.783 [run-main-0] INFO org.example.books.BookService - Book 3
          - Return request: OK
[…]
```

```
scala> library.reserveBook(bookA.id, bob)
12:58:28.352 [run-main-0] INFO org.example.books.BookService - Book 3
          - User 2 - Reserve request: OK
[…]
```

Try to write a new example scenario by searching for your favorite book, reserving it, and returning it. Can you spot any bugs or disadvantages of your implementation?

 ## 41.5 Possible improvements to our solution

Congratulations on completing the implementation! Although it respects the requirements, it has a few aspects you could improve. Let's see what these are and what techniques will help you overcome them.

LACK OF PERSISTENT STORAGE   All your book loans are in memory; as soon as your application shuts down, it will lose them. You should consider storing them in a more permanent storage solution that you can persist and share between multiple applications. In the next unit, you'll learn how to connect to a PostgreSQL database using a library called Quill.

APPLICATION LOAD TIME Your application parses and reads a file to populate its collection of books on startup; until this operation is complete, its users cannot perform any action with it. In this capstone, you parsed 10,000 records in seconds, but this could take a lot longer if using a much bigger file or multiple ones. Ideally, you'd want your software to be ready to use as soon as possible and be able to perform expensive operations in the background. In the next unit, you'll learn about the type Future to handle asynchronous computations.

VARS ARE DANGEROUS You should avoid using vars as they make your code more complex and potentially unsafe. You had to use the synchronized method to ensure your program doesn't lose data when multiple requests try to update a mutable assignment simultaneously. Unfortunately, the use of synchronized is not enough to guarantee your program will always perform as expected. One of the business requirements demands a book to be loaned to one user at a time. Imagine two users request to borrow the same book simultaneously. Both of them pass the checks: both users are within their loan limits, the book exists, and nobody has completed a request for it yet. They then both register a book loan. You now have the same book reserved by two users—which the business requirements explicitly forbid. Concurrency is hard, and mutability makes it even more challenging. Storing your book loans in a database can help mitigate this problem, as you can express at the database table level that the combination of user and book must be unique.

 ## Summary

In this capstone, you created an application to search, reserve, and return books.

- You implemented the logic to parse a book record from a file using the classes Try and Map.
- You represented its unordered book loans using the Set collection.
- You created a function to search a book by its title or author.
- You used the type Either to provide meaning validation messages when rejecting reserve and return book requests.

Concurrency

In Unit 6, you learned how to use different collections and handle errors in a more functional style. In this unit, you'll discover how to retrieve and store data in a database asynchronously. In the capstone, you'll implement the data access layer of an application to create and answer quizzes. In particular, you'll learn about the following subjects:

- Lesson 42 introduces you to implicit, a feature in the language that allows the compiler to enrich and expand your code at compile time. You'll also learn about the type class pattern to define more powerful abstractions.

- Lesson 43 gives you an overview of synchronous versus asynchronous computations and how they can impact your application's runtime performance. You'll learn how to represent asynchronous computations using the type Future.

- Lesson 44 shows you how to apply the map, flatten, and flatMap operations on a Future instance to manipulate and transform its value.

- Lesson 45 teaches you how to efficiently coordinate multiple asynchronous computations by running them in sequence or parallel.

- Lesson 46 introduces you to Quill, a popular library that provides a domain-specific language (DSL) to generate and run database queries. You'll use one of its asynchronous modules to connect to a `PostgreSQL` instance and execute queries on it.

- Finally, you'll implement the data access layer of a quiz application in lesson 47. You'll connect to its database and define the queries to run to store and retrieve categories and questions assigned to them.

After learning about asynchronous computations, you'll learn about JSON serialization and deserialization in unit 8.

IMPLICIT AND TYPE CLASSES

After reading this lesson, you will be able to

- Define a function that takes implicit parameters using the keyword using
- Mark values as given
- Use the type class pattern to express ad hoc polymorphism

In the previous unit, you learned about collections and error handling. In this lesson, you'll discover a feature of the Scala language called *implicit*. It is one of its most controversial traits. On one hand, it allows you to write less code and express extremely powerful abstractions. On the other hand, it can make your program more difficult to understand, and it increases its compilation time if misused. In this lesson, rather than introducing you to all the uses implicits have, you'll focus on its primary usage. Implicits also have a slightly different syntax between Scala 2 and Scala 3, but their core principles remain the same. You'll define a function that takes implicit parameters and mark a value as implicit in Scala 2 or as using in Scala 3. You'll learn how the compiler searches for a match for an implicit parameter, which is a process called *implicit resolution*. You'll also see how to express ad hoc polymorphism using a pattern called *type class* using the keywords *implicit* in Scala 2 and *given . . . with* in Scala 3. In the capstone, you will use implicits to define the number of threads to use when reading and writing the questions and answers to the database for your quiz application.

Consider this

Suppose you are developing an application to manage a bank account. Only bank employees with a manager role can perform critical operations, such as money withdrawals over a certain amount. How would you structure your code to ensure that this business requirement is respected?

42.1 Implicit parameters and values

Imagine you are developing an application to place orders to deliver for a store and that you have written the following group of functions to validate and place an order.

Listing 42.1 Placing an order

```scala
case class User(id: Int)
case class UserContext(id: Int,
                       details: PersonalDetails,
                       account: Account)
case class ProductSelection(productIds: List[Int])

def purchase(userId: Int,
             selection: ProductSelection): Either[String, Int] = {
  val userContext = getUserContext(userId)
  for {
    _ <- validateAddressWithinDistance(userContext)
    _ <- validateSelection(selection, userContext)
    _ <- validateBalance(selection, userContext)
  } yield placeOrder(selection, userContext)
}

private def getUserContext(userId: Int): UserContext = ???

private def validateBalance(
      selection: ProductSelection,
      userContext: UserContext): Either[String, Double] = ???

private def validateAddressWithinDistance(
      userContext: UserContext): Either[String, UserContext] = ???
```

It checks the user balance is enough to buy the selected product.

It retrieves all the user information.

It ensures the user address is within a certain distance.

```
private def validateSelection(
        selection: ProductSelection,
        userContext: UserContext): Either[String, ProductSelection] = ???

private def placeOrder(
        selection: ProductSelection,
        userContext: UserContext): Int = ???
```

It verifies that
the selected
products are available
and age-appropriate
for the user.

It returns the ID
of the placed
order.

In Scala, functions can have function parameters split into different groups. You decide
to change your code so that the user context is on a different parameter group than the
product selection where applicable.

Listing 42.2 Placing an order using due groups of parameters

```
case class User(id: Int)
case class UserContext(id: Int,
                       details: PersonalDetails,
                       account: Account)
case class ProductSelection(productIds: List[Int])

def purchase(userId: Int,
             selection: ProductSelection): Either[String, Int] = {
  val userContext = getUserContext(userId)
  for {
    _ <- validateAddressWithinDistance(userContext)
    _ <- validateSelection(selection)(userContext)
    _ <- validateBalance(selection)(userContext)
  } yield placeOrder(selection)(userContext)
}

private def getUserContext(userId: Int): UserContext = ???

private def validateBalance(selection: ProductSelection)
    (userContext: UserContext): Either[String, Double] = ???

private def validateAddressWithinDistance
    (userContext: UserContext): Either[String, UserContext] = ???

private def validateSelection(selection: ProductSelection)
    (userContext: UserContext): Either[String, ProductSelection] = ???
```

```
private def placeOrder(selection: ProductSelection)
    (userContext: UserContext): Int = ???
```

All the functions you specified rely on the presence of an instance of UserContext to provide information about the user placing the order. You could avoid this visual repetition when calling each function by declaring it an implicit parameter.

Listing 42.3 Placing an order using implicit

```
case class User(id: Int)
case class UserContext(id: Int,
                       details: PersonalDetails,
                       account: Account)
case class ProductSelection(productIds: List[Int])          Declaring a
                                                            value as
                                                            implicit in
def purchase(userId: Int, selection: ProductSelection):      Scala 2
Either[String, Int] = {
    // In Scala 2: implicit val userContext = getUserContext(userId)
    given userContext: UserContext = getUserContext(userId)
    for {                                                    Declaring a
                                                             value as implicit
        _ <- validateAddressWithinDistance                   in Scala 3
        _ <- validateSelection(selection)
        _ <- validateBalance(selection)                  Invoking the function
    } yield placeOrder(selection)                        without explicitly providing
}                                                        a user context parameter

private def getUserContext(userId: Int): UserContext = ???

private def validateBalance(selection: ProductSelection)
    (using userContext: UserContext): Either[String, Double] = ???

private def validateAddressWithinDistance
    (using userContext: UserContext): Either[String, UserContext] = ???

private def validateSelection(selection: ProductSelection)
                        (using userContext: UserContext):
                            Either[String, ProductSelection] = ???

private def placeOrder(selection: ProductSelection)
                        (using userContext: UserContext): Int = ???
```

Declaring a function parameter as implicit
in Scala 3. In Scala 2; use the keyword
implicit instead of the keyword using.

When defining a function, you can declare its last groups of parameters as implicit using the keyword *using* in Scala 3 or *implicit* in Scala 2. You can either specify or omit its implicit parameters. If missing, the compiler will try to fill the gaps for you and find a suitable match at compile time to pass to your function. It will search the elements marked as given or implicit if using Scala 2, within your function's scope. If it finds no unique and unambiguous match, the compiler will fail with a compilation error.

Let's see a simple example in action:

```
// In Scala 2: def welcome(name: String)(implicit msg: String): Unit
scala> def welcome(name: String)(using msg: String): Unit =
     |    println(s"$msg, $name!")
def welcome: (name: String)(using msg: String)Unit
// the function welcome requires an implicit parameter of type String

// In Scala 2: welcome("Jane")("Hello")
scala> welcome("Jane")(using "Hello")
Hello, Jane!
// You need to provide the keyword using when passing
// an implicit parameter explicitly in Scala 3.
// You do not need to pass any keyword in Scala 2.

scala> welcome("Jane")
error: no implicit argument of type String was found for parameter msg
           of method welcome
// You didn't provide a value for msg, so the compiler
// searches one to use and fails to find one
// (there are no implicit elements!)

scala> val hi = "Hi"
val hi: String = Hello

scala> welcome("Jane")
error: no implicit argument of type String was found for parameter msg
           of method welcome
// The compiler does not detect hi as a valid match
// because it is not marked as given (or implicit in Scala 2).

// In Scala 2: implicit val hi2 = "Hi"
scala> given hi2: String = "Hi"
lazy val hi2: String = Hi
```

```
scala> welcome("Jane")
Hi, Jane!
// The compiler passes the value hi2 implicitly

// In Scala 2: implicit val hola = "Hola"
scala> given hola: String = "Hola"
lazy val hola: String = Hola
scala> welcome("Jane")
error: ambiguous implicit arguments: both method hola and method hi
          match type String of parameter msg of method welcome

// The compiler finds two values of type String
// and it cannot pick one unambiguously.
```

Figures 42.1 and 42.2 summarize how to declare implicit parameters and values in Scala 2 and 3.

SCALA 2: IMPLICIT VALUE

The name of your
implicit value

An assignment for
your implicit value

```
implicit val name: type = expression
```

The type of your implicit value

SCALA 3: IMPLICIT VALUE

The name of your
implicit value

An assignment for
your implicit value

```
given name: type = expression
```

The type of your implicit value

Figure 42.1 Syntax summary of the implicit values
in Scala 2 and Scala 3

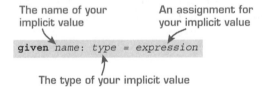

Quick Check 42.1 Consider the following snippet of code. Does it compile? If not, how would you fix it?

```
def plusOne(using n: Int): Int = n + 1
plusOne(using 3)
```

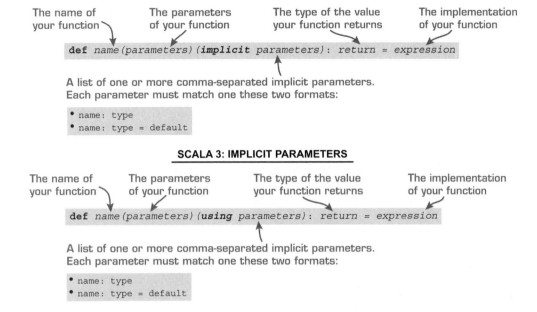

Figure 42.2 Syntax summary of how to define implicit parameters in Scala 2 and Scala 3

42.2 Implicit resolution

When invoking a function, you can omit its implicit parameters. The compiler will search for suitable matches to automatically pass for you at compile time; this process is called *implicit resolution*. Let's outline how it performs its search.

First, the compiler looks at the *current scope*:

- Your function's local scope (i.e., the portion of code accessible without imports)

```
// In Scala 2: def pow(exp: Int)(implicit base: Int): Double = …
def pow(exp: Int)(using base: Int): Double = Math.pow(base, exp)

// In Scala 2: implicit val a: Int = …
given b: Int = 2 // implicit found in the local scope

pow(5)
```

- The code you imported:

```
// In Scala 2: def pow(exp: Int)(implicit base: Int): Double = …
def pow(exp: Int)(using base: Int): Double = Math.pow(base, exp)

object Base {

    // In Scala 2: implicit val b: Int = 2
    given b: Int = 2
}

// In Scala 2: import Base._
import Base.given // importing all the implicit instances in Base

// implicit found in the imported code
pow(5)
```

  If it finds no match, it searches the associated types.

- The companion object of the type marked given (or implicit in Scala 2):

```
trait Name[A] {
  def name(): String
}

object Name {

    // implicit selected
    // In Scala 2: implicit val intName: Name[Int] =
    //      new Name[Int] { … }
    given intName: Name[Int] with {
        def name() = "integer"
    }

}

// In Scala 2: def describe[T](implicit t: Name[T]): String = …
def describe[T](using t: Name[T]): String = t.name()

describe[Int]
```

  The compiler cannot find an implicit instance of Name[Int] into the current scope. It then looks at the companion object Name and selects the value intName.

- The companion object of any type parameter of the type marked given, or implicit in Scala 2:

```
trait Name[A] {
    def name(): String
}

class Test()
object Test {

    // implicit selected
    // In Scala 2: implicit val name: Name[Test] =
    //      new Name[Test] { … }
    given name: Name[Test] with {
        override def name(): String = "my-test"
    }
}

// In Scala 2: def describe[T](implicit t: Name[T]): String = …
def describe[T](using t: Name[T]): String = t.name()

describe[Test]
```

The compiler fails to find any implicit value in the current scope. Then, it finds a valid match of type Name[Test] in the companion object of the class Test.

Figure 42.3 provides a summary of how the compiler searches implicit matches to use in your code.

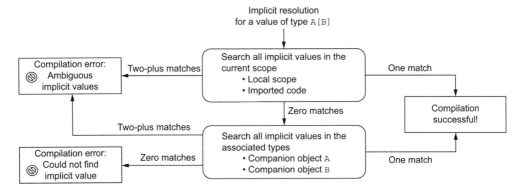

Figure 42.3 The implicit resolution algorithm that the compiler uses to find an implicit match of type A[B]. First, it looks at the current scope. Then it searches into the companion objects of the associated types *A* and *B*. If it finds one match, it uses the code element as a parameter. Otherwise, the compiler errors with either an implicit not found or an ambiguous implicit values error.

Quick Check 42.2 Consider the following snippet of code. Does it compile? If not, how would you fix it?

```scala
class A {
  def test(using n: Int): String = n.toString
}

object A {
  given n: Int = 2
}

(new A()).test
```

42.3 Type classes

Let's consider your application to deliver store orders again. Imagine you have a requirement to consistently sort your orders across all your program's functionalities by their ID in reverse order.

Listing 42.4 Sorting by ID in reverse order

```scala
case class Order(id: Int)

object Order {
  // In Scala 2:
  // implicit val ordering: Ordering[Order] =
  //        new Ordering[Order] { ... }
  given ordering: Ordering[Order] with {
    override def compare(x: Order, y: Order): Int =
      - x.id.compare(y.id)
  }
}
```

Ordering is the interface Scala requires you to implement to define sorting rules.

The minus symbol expresses the inverse order.

After providing a default implicit implementation for Ordering[Order], you can use it in your code. For example, you learned that the List collection has a few methods, such as sorted, min, max, that use it to define how to compare instances of the same type. Another example you encountered is the trait Numeric[T], which is used by its method sum.

Scala offers *ad hoc polymorphism*. Polymorphism is the concept of having an interface that defines the form of many types. It is ad hoc because you can override the behavior by providing an implicit in your current scope rather than using the one you defined in the associated types. This behavior is possible because the compiler only searches the associated types if it finds no matches in the current scope. This pattern is called *type class*, and it is popular when coding in a functional programming style.

Suppose you need to ensure that any information your program displays to a user must be human readable. The function toString is not fit for this purpose:

```scala
scala> class A; (new A()).toString
class A
val res0: String = A@55b7f0d
// Incomprehensible for a human!

scala> List(1, 2, 3).toString
val res1: String = List(1, 2, 3)
// Humans may find "1, 2, 3" simpler to read
```

Let's define a trait with a method show to produce a human-readable text from a given instance and provide a few default implementations for some of the basic types.

Listing 42.5　The trait Show

```scala
trait Show[T] {

  def show(t: T): String
}

object Show {

  // In Scala 2:
  // implicit val stringShow: Show[String] = new Show[String] { … }
  given stringShow as Show[String] with {
    override def show(s: String): String = s
  }

  // In Scala 2:
  // implicit val intShow: Show[Int] = new Show[Int] { … }
  given intShow: Show[Int] with {
    override def show(i: Int): String = i.toString
  }

  // In Scala 2:
  // implicit def listShow[T]: Show[List[T]] = new Show[List[T]] { … }
  given listShow[T]: Show[List[T]] with {
```

```
    override def show(l: List[T]): String = l.mkString(", ")
  }
}
```

You can now define a function prettyPrintln and invoke it every time you need to display data to the user:

```
// In Scala 2: def prettyPrintln[T](t: T)(implicit s: Show[T]): Unit = …
def prettyPrintln[T](t: T)(using s: Show[T]): Unit =
  println(s.show(t))

prettyPrintln(1) // prints "1"
prettyPrintln("hello") // prints "hello"
prettyPrintln(List(1, 2, 3)) // prints "1, 2, 3"
```

The trait Show is part of an external typelevel library called cats. It offers a collection of useful type classes (full list available at https://typelevel.org/cats).

Quick Check 42.3   Consider the following class Person:

```
case class Person(name: String, age: Int)
```

Define a default implementation for Show[Person] so that your function pretty-Println can print the person's name followed by their age. For example, the expression prettyPrintln(Person("Jon Doe", 25)) should print "Jon Doe (25)" to the console.

 Summary

In this lesson, my objective was to teach you the basics of implicits.

- You saw how to define implicit parameters and values.
- You discovered the implicit resolution algorithm the compiler uses to find a valid implicit match.
- You learned how to use the type class pattern to express ad hoc polymorphism.

Let's see if you got this!

TRY THIS   Suppose your program needs to perform monetary calculations. Your money representation looks like the following:

```
import java.util.Currency
case class Money(amount: Double, currency: Currency)
```

Define an instance of Numeric[Money] so that Scala can recognize it as a numeric value and perform calculations, such as finding the sum of two Money instances. Forbid operations between monetary amounts that have different currencies.

 # Answers to quick checks

Quick Check 42.1 The code compiles, and it returns 4. The compiler doesn't search for an implicit parameter because you provided a value for it explicitly.

Quick Check 42.2 The compiler fails in finding an implicit value for the parameter n:

```
error: no implicit argument of type Int was found for parameter n
       of method test in class A
  |
  |The following import might fix the problem:
  |
  |  import A.n
```

First, it searches in the current scope; this is the code accessible from (new A()).test and from def test(using n: Int): String. It fails to find a good match, so it looks at the companion object of Int, which has no accessible implicit value of type Int. The compiler stops the implicit resolution and fails the compilation. You need to include the implicit value A.n into the current scope using an import to fix the compilation error:

```
// In Scala 2: import A._
import A.given
(new A()).test
```

Alternatively, you can also do the following:

```
class A {
   // In Scala 2: import A._
   import A.given

   // In Scala 2: def test(implicit n: Int): String = …
   def test(using n: Int): String = n.toString
}
```

Quick Check 42.3 Your implementation of Show[Person] should live in the companion object of Person, and it should look similar to the following:

```scala
object Person {

  // In Scala 2: implicit val show: Show[Person] =
  //           new Show[Person] { … }
  given show: Show[Person] with {
    override def show(p: Person): String =
      s"${p.name} (${p.age})"
  }

}
```

FUTURE

After reading this lesson, you will be able to

- Represent an asynchronous computation using Future
- Process its result on completion

In the previous lesson, have learned about implicit parameters and values; you'll now see them in action when defining an instance of type Future. You'll discover the difference between synchronous and asynchronous computations and how they can affect your program's performance. You'll see how you can use the type Future to define asynchronous computations that can fail. An operation is asynchronous if your program can continue to run without waiting for its outcome. You'll also process its result once completed. In the capstone, you'll use the type Future to read and write data to a database asynchronously for your quiz application.

> **Consider this**
> Imagine you are developing an application to book tickets for events. It needs to accept and process as many booking requests as possible at the same time. How would you structure your application so that it can maximize its available resources?

43.1 Why Future?

Latency is the time spent between requesting an operation and getting a response back. Brendan Gregg discusses how system operations can differ in duration in his book *Systems Performance: Enterprise and the Cloud* (Prentice Hall, 2014). For example, a 3.3 GHz processor can execute on average one CPU cycle in 0.3 nanoseconds (ns) and a rotational hard disk I/O operation in up to 10 milliseconds (ms). As humans, we struggle to grasp how different these numbers are, so Gregg decided to scale these and other system events to a more understandable scale; you can see them in table 43.1. If you scale one CPU cycle up to 1 second, a single I/O operation can last up to 12 months!

Table 43.1 Example time scale of system latencies, taken from Brendan Gregg's *Systems Performance: Enterprise and the Cloud* (Prentice Hall, 2014, p. 20)

Event	Latency	Scaled
One CPU cycle	0.3 ns	1 s
Level 1 cache access	0.9 ns	3 s
Level 2 cache access	2.8 ns	9 s
Level 3 cache access	12.9 ns	43 s
Main memory access (DRAM, from CPU)	120 ns	6 min
Solid-state disk I/O (flash memory)	50–150 μs	2-6 days
Rotational disk I/O	1–10 ms	1–12 months
Internet: San Francisco to New York	40 ms	4 years
Internet: San Francisco to United Kingdom	81 ms	8 years
Internet: San Francisco to Australia	183 ms	19 years
TCP packet retransmit	1–3 s	105–317 years
OS virtualization system reboot	4 s	423 years
SCSI command time-out	30 s	3 millennia
Hardware (HW) virtualization system reboot	40 s	4 millennia
Physical system reboot	5 m	32 millennia

Programs traditionally perform operations synchronously: they wait for an instruction to finish before starting with the next one. This approach is a popular strategy, but it has a considerable performance cost when dealing with procedures with significant latency.

Another option is to perform operations asynchronously: starting the next instruction without waiting for the current one to be complete. This approach can make your program do more with its resources as it will not spend as much time waiting for operations to complete, but its execution flow will be more difficult to predict. Your CPU can split a program into smaller independent sequences of instructions called *threads of executions*, or just threads. A multithreaded platform, such as the JVM, allows your program to run more than one thread simultaneously, making asynchronous computations possible.

The type Future allows you to define an operation to execute asynchronously: the JVM delegates its execution to another thread, it moves on to other instructions, and it returns to it when notified of its completion.

 ## 43.2 Creating an instance of Future

Imagine you are developing a program to handle orders for a store. You need to confirm a product's availability with its warehouse via an HTTP API, a known bottleneck of your application. You can perform it asynchronously using Future to improve its overall performance.

Listing 43.1 Checking product availability

Importing the class Future

Adding the implicit global execution context to your scope. It contains information about the resources available to your program.

```scala
import scala.concurrent.Future
import scala.concurrent.ExecutionContext.Implicits.global

def isProductAvailable(productId: Int,
                       quantity: Double): Future[Boolean] = Future {
  requestAvailability(productId, quantity)
}

private def requestAvailability(productId: Int,
                                quantity: Double): Boolean = ???
```

Calling the function Future.apply

In Scala, the class Future allows you to specify an operation to execute asynchronously: a separate thread eventually completes its execution while your program's current thread processes other instructions. The method Future.apply allows you to create an instance of Future.

Listing 43.2 **The method Future.apply**

```scala
package scala.concurrent

object Future {

  def apply[T](r: => T)
              (using ec: ExecutionContext): Future[T] = {
    ???
  }
}
```

The parameter is not evaluated until needed.

The ExecutionContext defines the available set of threads to use.

Implementation omitted as nontrivial

First, include the companion object Future in your scope by adding import scala.concurrent .Future. Then, invoke its method Future.apply by providing the instructions to execute asynchronously and with an execution context. Figure 43.1 compares the signature of Try.apply with Future.apply. The two methods look very similar. However, Future.apply requires an extra implicit parameter of type ExecutionContext, which provides information that makes the asynchronous computation possible.

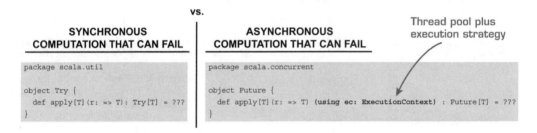

vs.

SYNCHRONOUS COMPUTATION THAT CAN FAIL

```scala
package scala.util

object Try {
  def apply[T](r: => T): Try[T] = ???
}
```

ASYNCHRONOUS COMPUTATION THAT CAN FAIL

Thread pool plus execution strategy

```scala
package scala.concurrent

object Future {
  def apply[T](r: => T) (using ec: ExecutionContext) : Future[T] = ???
}
```

Figure 43.1 A comparison between the apply method for Try and Future. The first represents synchronous computations that can fail, the second asynchronous ones. They both delay the execution of an expression. However, the Future one requires an instance of ExecutionContext, which contains information about the resources and execution strategy.

The ExecutionContext class gives your Future instance a thread pool to use and an execution strategy to follow. Scala offers a default implementation for it called Execution-Context.global, which is designed to work in the majority of the cases. You can define a custom execution context, but it goes beyond this book's scope. This is nontrivial and can cause significant performance degradation to your application if not done carefully. You can include ExecutionContext.global as implicit in your scope by adding the following instruction:

```scala
import scala.concurrent.ExecutionContext.Implicits.global
```

This expression is equivalent to defining the following implicit value:

```
import scala.concurrent.ExecutionContext
using val ec = ExecutionContext.global
```

ExecutionContext as an implicit parameter rather than an import
When developing a large application, you should prefer passing your Execution-Context as an implicit parameter to your classes and functions rather than directly using the global execution context. You could then select which execution context to use in one place of your codebase, usually its entry point. This approach gives you more control over which execution context your program uses and is easier to customize if needed.

Let's see a few more examples of how you can use the method Future.apply:

```
scala> import scala.concurrent.Future
import scala.concurrent.Future

scala> Future(10/2)
error: Cannot find an implicit ExecutionContext. You might pass
an (using ec: ExecutionContext) parameter to your method
or import scala.concurrent.ExecutionContext.Implicits.global.
        Future(10/2)
              ^
// You need to provide an ExecutionContext to Future.apply!

scala> import scala.concurrent.ExecutionContext.Implicits.global
import scala.concurrent.ExecutionContext.Implicits.global

scala> Future(10/2)
val res0: scala.concurrent.Future[Int] = Future(Success(5))
// Its execution has completed with success
// before the REPL displays its content

scala> val tenOverZero = Future(10/0)
val tenOverZero: scala.concurrent.Future[Int] = Future(<not
            completed>)
// This time, its execution has not completed yet

scala> tenOverZero
val tenOverZero: scala.concurrent.Future[Int] =
            Future(Failure(java.lang.ArithmeticException: / by zero))
```

```
// Checking its content again after some time,
// it has completed with a failure

scala> val foo = {
     |   println("Hello")
     |   Future(println("World"))
     |   println("!")
     | }
Hello
!
World
val foo: Unit = ()
// Your program does not wait for the Future instance to complete
// and it moves on to print the text "!"
```

Quick Check 43.1 Consider the following function. Does it compile? What output does it produce when invoked?

```
import scala.concurrent.Future
import scala.concurrent.ExecutionContext.Implicits.global

def test(): Unit = {
  Future(('a' to 'c').map(print))
  (0 to 2).map(print)
}
```

 ## 43.3 Processing Future on completion

Consider your program to place orders in a store. Suppose that the third-party API can provide information on the quantity available for a certain product. You want to keep track of it to help the store decide on the items to restock.

Listing 43.3 Tracking the availability of a product

```
import scala.concurrent.Future
import scala.util.{Failure, Success}
import scala.concurrent.ExecutionContext.Implicits.global

case class Availability(id: Int, quantity: Double)
```

```
def trackAvailability(availability: Future[Availability]): Unit =
  availability.onComplete {
    case Success(p) if p.quantity <= 0 =>
      println(s"Product ${p.id} is not available")
    case Success(p) =>
      println(s"Product ${p.id} has available quantity ${p.quantity}")
    case Failure(ex) =>
      println(s"Couldn't get the availability " +
              s"because of ${ex.getMessage}")
  }
```

It processes the result of a completed future as an instance of Try.

You can use pattern matching on many of the types you have encountered; unfortunately, Future is not one of them. A pattern-matching operation is synchronous as it requires the value wrapped inside your type to be available. For an instance of Future[T], the method onComplete allows you to execute a function once completed:

```
def onComplete[U](f: Try[T] => U)
              (using executor: ExecutionContext): Unit
```

The function onComplete returns a value of type Unit. Any result that your callback function f produces will be lost. If you need to retain its result, you should consider using its method map instead. You'll learn more about this in the next lesson. A few more examples of how to use the method onComplete are the following:

```
scala> Future(10/2).onComplete { value =>
     |     if (value.isFailure) println("bad!")
     |     else println("good!")
     | }
good!
// It prints "good!" to the console

scala> Future(10/2).onComplete { value =>
     |     if (value.isFailure) "bad!"
     |     else "good!"
     | }
// It produces no value because it discards the string value
```

> **Quick Check 43.2** Consider the following function. Does it compile? What output does it produce when invoked?
>
> ```
> import scala.concurrent.ExecutionContext.Implicits.global
> import scala.concurrent.Future
>
> def isSuccess[T](f: Future[T]): Unit = f.onComplete(_.isSuccess)
> ```

 **Summary**

In this lesson, my objective was to introduce you to asynchronous computation using the type Future.

- You learned that an asynchronous computation allows your program to execute other instructions without waiting for it to complete first.
- You saw how to create an instance of type Future using the global execution context.
- You discovered how to use the method onComplete to process a value provided by an asynchronous computation.

Let's see if you got this!

> **TRY THIS**   The following snippet of code prints all the files in the current directory to the terminal. Change its code to execute it asynchronously.

```
import java.io.File
new File(".").listFiles().foreach(println)
```

 Answers to quick checks

> **Quick Check 43.1**   The function test compiles: an instance of ExecutionContext .global is available through the import of scala.concurrent.ExecutionContext .Implicits.global. Its output is non-deterministic: it changes based on when how the executor schedules its threads.
>
> ```
> scala> import scala.concurrent.Future
>      | import scala.concurrent.ExecutionContext.Implicits.global
>      |
>      | def test(): Unit = {
>      |   Future(('a' to 'c').map(print))
>      |   (0 to 2).map(print)
>      | }
>      |
> import scala.concurrent.Future
> import scala.concurrent.ExecutionContext.Implicits.global
> def test: ()Unit
>
> scala> test()
> abc012
> scala> test()
> ```

```
0abc12
scala> test()
012abc
```

Quick Check 43.2 The function isSuccess compiles, but it returns no value. When your Future instance completes, the callback produces a Boolean value that the method onComplete then discards.

```
scala> import scala.concurrent.ExecutionContext.Implicits.global
     | import scala.concurrent.Future
     |
     | def isSuccess[T](f: Future[T]): Unit =
           f.onComplete(_.isSuccess)
import scala.concurrent.ExecutionContext.Implicits.global
import scala.concurrent.Future
def isSuccess: [T](f: scala.concurrent.Future[T])Unit

scala> isSuccess(Future("hello"))

scala> isSuccess(Future(throw new Exception("BOOM!")))
```

WORKING WITH FUTURE: MAP AND FLATMAP

After reading this lesson, you will be able to

- Manipulate the result of an asynchronous computation using the map operation
- Merge two nested asynchronous computations using the flatten method
- Combine multiple asynchronous operations using the flatMap function

In the previous lesson, you learned the basics of expressing asynchronous computations using the type Future. In this lesson, you'll learn how to use the methods map, flatten, and flatMap for an instance of Future. You'll notice that they share many commonalities with the map, flatten, and flatMap methods you have mastered for other types. The map function allows you to transform the value that an asynchronous computation produces. The flatten method merges two nested instances of Future into one. The flatMap operation is the composition of the methods map and flatten, and it allows you to chain multiple asynchronous instances. In the capstone, you'll need to coordinate several asynchronous calls to read or write questions to a database for your quiz application.

Consider this

Imagine that your application to book tickets for events performs an asynchronous computation to produce a registration receipt. After its completion, you'd like to show the user a message to confirm its registration number and provide more details about the event. How would you achieve this?

 ## 44.1 The map, flatten, and flatMap operations

The type Future has an implementation for the map, flatten, and flatMap methods. You'll see them in action in the following subsections. You will notice that they have many similarities with those you are already encountered, such as Option, List, and Try.

44.1.1 The map function

Let's consider again your program to place orders in a store. Suppose that after checking for a product's availability, you'd like to either place an order or reject the request.

Listing 44.1 Placing an order if the product is available

```scala
import scala.concurrent.Future
import scala.concurrent.ExecutionContext

case class Availability(id: Int, quantity: Double)
case class Order(id: Int,
                 customerId: Int,
                 productId: Int,
                 quantity: Double)

private def getAvailability(productId: Int)
             (using ec: ExecutionContext): Future[Availability] = ???

private def createOrder(customerId: Int,
                        productId: Int,
                        quantity: Double): Order = ???

def placeOrder(customerId: Int,
               productId: Int,
               quantity: Double)
  (using ec: ExecutionContext): Future[Order] = {
  getAvailability(productId).map { availability =>
```

It accesses the value wrapped into a Future instance, and it applies a function to it.

```
    if (quantity <= availability.quantity)
      createOrder(customerId = customerId,
              productId = productId,
              quantity)
    else throw new IllegalStateException(
      s"Product $productId unavailable: " +
      s"requested $quantity, available ${availability.quantity}")
  }
}
```

Future catches
any exception;
you can throw
them knowing
that Future will
contain them.

When working with an asynchronous computation, you can use its method map to transform its produced result. For an instance of Future[T], the function map takes one parameter f of type T => S and an implicit execution context to produce an instance of type Future[S]. It has the following signature:

```
def map[S](f: T => S)(using ec: ExecutionContext): Future[S]
```

If your Future[T] instance has completed successfully, it will apply the parameter f to its result to produce a value of type Future[S]. Nothing happens if your Future[T] instance has completed with a failure. A few examples of how to use it are the following:

```
scala> import scala.concurrent.Future
import scala.concurrent.Future

scala> import scala.concurrent.ExecutionContext.Implicits.global
import scala.concurrent.ExecutionContext.Implicits.global

scala> Future(12/2).map(_ * 3)
val res0: scala.concurrent.Future[Int] = Future(Success(18))

scala> Future(12/0).map(_ * 3)
val res1: scala.concurrent.Future[Int] =
        Future(Failure(java.lang.ArithmeticException: / by zero))

scala> Future(12/2).map { n =>
     |   if (n > 10) n
     |   else throw new Exception(s"Too small: $n")
     | }
val res2: scala.concurrent.Future[Int] = Future(Failure(
java.lang.Exception: Too small: 6))
```

> **Quick Check 44.1** Define a function called toInt to parse a value of type Future[String] into one of Future[Int]. Provide an execution context as an implicit parameter rather than importing one directly.

44.1.2 The flatten function

Consider the function you wrote in listing 44.1 to check the availability for a product and create an order. Its function createOrder returns a value of type Order. Imagine the function createOrder now needs to write to a database asynchronously and that you need to change its return type from Order to Future[Order]. This causes its function placeOrder to return a value of type Future[Future[Order]].

Listing 44.2 Placing an order by writing to a database

```scala
private def getAvailability(productId: Int)
            (using ec: ExecutionContext): Future[Availability] = ???

private def createOrder(customerId: Int,
                productId: Int,
                quantity: Double)
            (using ec: ExecutionContext): Future[Order] = ???

def placeOrder(customerId: Int,
            productId: Int,
            quantity: Double)
            (using ec: ExecutionContext): Future[Future[Order]] = {
  getAvailability(productId).map { availability =>
    if (quantity <= availability.quantity)
      createOrder(customerId = customerId, productId = productId,
          quantity)
    else throw new IllegalStateException(
      s"Product $productId unavailable: " +
      s"requested $quantity, available ${availability.quantity}")
  }
}
```

The type Future[Future[Order]] represents two nested asynchronous computations that will eventually either return an instance of type Order or fail. The function flatten can simplify this expression by considering the two nested operations as one; it will now produce a value of type Future[Order] instead.

Listing 44.3 Placing an order by writing to a database using flatten

```scala
private def getAvailability(productId: Int)
            (using ec: ExecutionContext): Future[Availability] = ???
```

```
private def createOrder(customerId: Int,
                        productId: Int,
                        quantity: Double)
                       (using ec: ExecutionContext): Future[Order] = ???

def placeOrder(customerId: Int,
               productId: Int,
               quantity: Double)
              (using ec: ExecutionContext): Future[Order] = {
  getAvailability(productId).map { availability =>
    if (quantity <= availability.quantity)
      createOrder(customerId = customerId,
                  productId = productId,
                  quantity)
    else throw new IllegalStateException(
      s"Product $productId unavailable: " +
      s"requested $quantity, available ${availability.quantity}")
  }.flatten
}
```

The method flatten on Future allows you to transform an instance of Future[Future[T]]
into one of type Future[T]. A few examples are following:

```
scala> import scala.concurrent.Future
import scala.concurrent.Future

scala> import scala.concurrent.ExecutionContext.Implicits.global
import scala.concurrent.ExecutionContext.Implicits.global

scala> val twelveOverZero = Future(Future(12/0)).flatten
val twelveOverZero: scala.concurrent.Future[Int] = Future(<not
        completed>)

scala> twelveOverZero
val twelveOverZero: scala.concurrent.Future[Int] =
        Future(Failure(java.lang.ArithmeticException: / by zero))

scala> Future(Future(12/2)).flatten
val res0: scala.concurrent.Future[Int] = Future(Success(6))

scala> Future(5).flatten
error: Cannot prove that Int <:< scala.concurrent.Future[S].
// You can only invoke the method flatten on nested structures
```

> **Quick Check 44.2**   Consider the following snippet of code:
>
> ```scala
> import scala.concurrent.{ExecutionContext, Future}
>
> case class Account(id: String)
> case class User(name: String)
>
> def getAccount(orderId: Int)
>              (using ec: ExecutionContext): Future[Account] = ???
>
> def getUser(accountId: String)
>            (using ec: ExecutionContext): Future[User] = ???
> ```
>
> Use the functions getAccount and getUser to create a new function that will return
> the user associated with a given order ID. This function should have the following
> signature:
>
> ```scala
> def getUser(orderId: Int)
>            (using ec: ExecutionContext): Future[User]
> ```

44.1.3 The flatMap function

Consider the snippet of code you wrote in listing 44.3. There is a more elegant way of
achieving the same result.

Listing 44.4 Placing an order by writing to a database using flatMap

```scala
private def getAvailability(productId: Int)
               (using ec: ExecutionContext): Future[Availability] = ???

private def createOrder(customerId: Int,
                        productId: Int,
                        quantity: Double)
                       (using ec: ExecutionContext): Future[Order] = ???

def placeOrder(customerId: Int,
               productId: Int,
               quantity: Double)
              (using ec: ExecutionContext): Future[Order] = {
  getAvailability(productId).flatMap { availability =>
    if (quantity <= availability.quantity)
      createOrder(customerId = customerId,
                  productId = productId,
```

```
                          quantity)
        else throw new IllegalStateException(
          s"Product $productId unavailable: " +
          s"requested $quantity, available ${availability.quantity}")
    }
  }
```

The method flatMap is the combination of the map and flatten operations. For an instance of Future[T], the function flatMap takes one parameter f of type T => Future[S] and an implicit execution context to produce an instance of type Future[S]. It has the following signature:

```
def flatMap[S](f: T => Future[S])
              (using ec: ExecutionContext): Future[S]
```

If your instance of Future[T] has completed successfully, it will apply the parameter f to produce a value of type Future[S]. Nothing happens if your instance has completed with a failure. A few examples of how to use it are the following:

```
scala> import scala.concurrent.Future
import scala.concurrent.Future

scala> import scala.concurrent.ExecutionContext.Implicits.global
import scala.concurrent.ExecutionContext.Implicits.global

scala> val twelveOverTwo = Future(12/2).flatMap(n => Future(n.toString))
val twelveOverTwo: scala.concurrent.Future[String] = Future(<not
          completed>)
// twelveOverTwo has not completed yet - let give it another try

scala> twelveOverTwo
val twelveOverTwo: scala.concurrent.Future[String] = Future(Success(6))
// twelveOverTwo has now completed successfully

scala> Future(12/0).flatMap(n => Future(n.toString))
val res0: scala.concurrent.Future[String] =
          Future(Failure(java.lang.ArithmeticException: / by zero))
```

The flatMap method allows you to express an execution dependency: asynchronous computations. For example, the placeOrder function you implemented in listing 44.4 defines that the product availability check must complete successfully before creating an order. You will learn more about this in the next lesson where you will master how to use for-comprehension on instances of type Future.

> **Quick Check 44.3** In Quick Check 44.2, you implemented a function getUser(orderId: Int) using the function flatten. Refactor it to use the flatMap method instead.

Table 44.1 summarizes the signature and usage of the methods map, flatten, and flatMap acting on Future.

Table 44.1 Technical recap of the three fundamental operations on the type Future. The function map transforms the result of an asynchronous computation while flatten merges two executions. The flatMap function combines the map and flatten operations to define an execution order between values.

	Acts on	Signature	Usage
map	Future[T]	map(f: T => S)(using ec:ExecutionContext): Future[S]	It applies a function to the value the future produced.
flatten	Future[Future[T]]	flatten: Future[T]	It merges two nested futures into one.
flatMap	Future[T]	flatMap(f: T => S)(using ec:ExecutionContext): Future[S]	The combination of map followed by flatten chains futures together.

Summary

In this lesson, my objective was to teach you the fundamental operations you can perform on an instance of type Future.

- You saw how to use the function map to transform the value your asynchronous computation produces.
- You learned how to merge two nested instances of Future into one using the flatten operation.
- You discovered how the flatMap method allows you to express an execution dependency between two asynchronous computations.

Let's see if you got this!

> **TRY THIS** Consider the following snippet of code that defines a function to list the content in a given directory:
>
> ```
> import java.io.File
> import scala.concurrent.{ExecutionContext, Future}
> ```

```scala
def contentInDir(path: String)
                (using ec: ExecutionContext): Future[List[String]] =
  Future {
    val file = new File(path)
    if (file.isDirectory)
      // unfortunately, listFiles returns null
      // if invoked on a file that is not directory
      file.listFiles().toList.map(_.getAbsolutePath)
    else List.empty
  }
```

Define a new function that invokes the function contentInDir to count the number of items in a directory.

 # Answers to quick checks

> **Quick Check 44.1** Your function toInt should have a signature and implementation similar to the following:
>
> ```scala
> import scala.concurrent.{ExecutionContext, Future}
>
> def toInt(f: Future[String])
>          (using ec: ExecutionContext): Future[Int] =
>   f.map(_.toInt)
> ```

> **Quick Check 44.2** A possible implementation for the function getUser(orderId: Int) is the following:
>
> ```scala
> def getUser(orderId: Int)
>            (using ec: ExecutionContext): Future[User] =
>   getAccount(orderId).map(account => getUser(account.id)).flatten
> ```

> **Quick Check 44.3** You should refactor your function getUser(orderId: Int) as follows:
>
> ```scala
> def getUser(orderId: Int)
>            (using ec: ExecutionContext): Future[User] =
>   getAccount(orderId).flatMap(account => getUser(account.id))
> ```

WORKING WITH FUTURE: FOR-COMPREHENSION AND OTHER OPERATIONS

After reading this lesson, you will be able to

- Define a chain of asynchronous operations using for-comprehension
- Select the first Future instance to complete, either successfully or not
- Find the fastest asynchronous operation to produce a value with specific properties
- Run independent Future instances in parallel and collect their results in a sequence

You discovered how you can use the map, flatten, and flatMap operations to manipulate the value that asynchronous computations produce. In this lesson, you'll learn how to coordinate multiple Future instances using for-comprehension. In particular, you'll see how to provide requirements on when each asynchronous computation should start. You'll discover how to select the first Future instance to complete among many and find the one that successfully produces a value with given features. You'll also see how to combine the results of several asynchronous independent computations running in parallel into one sequence. In the capstone, you'll use for-comprehension to define asynchronous computations to execute in a given order for your quiz program.

Consider this

Suppose you are developing a program that depends on a third-party API, which has servers deployed in several regions, such as London, Virginia (United States), and Hong Kong. The servers vary in performance during the day based on their requests volume. You'd like to send the same call to all its servers and get a response from any of them. How would you implement this?

 ## 45.1 For-comprehension

Let's consider your program to order items in a store and imagine that you now need to retrieve the full details of an existing order. You already have code to retrieve information of an entity based on its ID.

Listing 45.1 Retrieving an order, user, and product by ID

```scala
import scala.concurrent.{ExecutionContext, Future}

case class Order(id: Int,
                 userId: Int,
                 productId: Int,
                 quantity: Double)

case class Product(id: Int, description: Int, price: Double)

case class User(id: Int, fullname: String, email: String)

def getOrder(id: Int)(using ec: ExecutionContext): Future[Order] = ???

def getUser(id: Int)(using ec: ExecutionContext): Future[User] = ???

def getProduct(id: Int)
              (using ec: ExecutionContext): Future[Product] = ???
```

You can combine these functions using `map` and `flatMap` to retrieve the full details of an order.

Listing 45.2 Retrieving the order details by an order ID using map and flatMap

```scala
case class OrderDetails(order: Order, user: User, product: Product)

def getOrderDetails(orderId: Int)
                   (using ec: ExecutionContext): Future[OrderDetails] =
```

```
getOrder(orderId).flatMap { order =>
  getUser(order.userId).flatMap { user =>
    getProduct(order.productId).map { product =>
      OrderDetails(order, user, product)
    }
  }
}
```

Extracting
an order

Extracting
its user

Extracting
its product

Combining the three
entities to create an
OrderDetails instance

You can refactor its implementation in a more elegant and readable style using for-comprehension.

Listing 45.3 Retrieving the order details by an order ID using for-comprehension

```
case class OrderDetails(order: Order, user: User, product: Product)

def getOrderDetails(orderId: Int)
                    (using ec: ExecutionContext): Future[OrderDetails] =
  for {
    order <- getOrder(orderId)
    user <- getUser(order.userId)
    product <- getProduct(order.productId)
  } yield OrderDetails(order, user, product)
```

Extracting
an order

Extracting
its user

Extracting
its product

Combining the three entities to
create an OrderDetails instance

In Scala, for-comprehension allows you to express the combination of the map and flatMap operations in a more elegant and readable way. The following expressions are equivalent:

```
scala> import scala.concurrent.Future
import scala.concurrent.Future

scala> import scala.concurrent.ExecutionContext.Implicits.global
import scala.concurrent.ExecutionContext.Implicits.global

scala> Future(12/2).flatMap(n => Future(n.toString))
val res0: scala.concurrent.Future[String] = Future(Success(6))

scala> for {
     |   n <- Future(12/2)
     |   res <- Future(n.toString)
     | } yield res
val res1: scala.concurrent.Future[String] = Future(Success(6))
```

Quick Check 45.1 Consider the following snippet of code. Refactor the function getUserId to use for-comprehension.

```scala
import scala.concurrent.{ExecutionContext, Future}

case class Order(id: Int,
                 userId: Int,
                 productId: Int,
                 quantity: Double)

def getOrder(id: Int)
            (using ec: ExecutionContext): Future[Order] = ???

def getUserId(orderId: Int)
             (using ec: ExecutionContext): Future[Int] =
   getOrder(orderId).map(_.userId)
```

Let's look again at the code you wrote in listing 45.3, in which you chained three asynchronous computations. First, the operation to get the order by ID will run. Once it completes, the operation to retrieve the user will commence. Finally, the third operation to recover the product starts after the user entity is received. If any fail, the entire chain will result in a failed asynchronous computation. Running all of them in sequence may seem the most efficient option. However, it is not because the functions getUser and getProduct are independent; you could execute them in parallel after retrieving the order.

Listing 45.4 Retrieving order details more efficiently

```scala
def getOrderDetails(orderId: Int)
                   (using ec: ExecutionContext): Future[OrderDetails] =
   for {
     order <- getOrder(orderId)
     futureUser = getUser(order.userId)
     futureProduct = getProduct(order.productId)
     user <- futureUser
     product <- futureProduct
   } yield OrderDetails(order, user, product)
```

Scheduling the operation to start. You can omit the keyword val here because inside is a for-comprehension construct.

Extracting the result of the computation once completed successfully

The following listing shows an alternate option.

Listing 45.5 Another way of retrieving order details more efficiently

```
def getOrderDetails(orderId: Int)
                    (using ec: ExecutionContext): Future[OrderDetails] =
  getOrder(orderId).flatMap { order =>
    val futureUser = getUser(order.userId)
    val futureProduct = getProduct(order.productId)
    for {
      user <- futureUser
      product <- futureProduct
    } yield OrderDetails(order, user, product)
  }
```

Scheduling the operation to start

Extracting the result of the computation once completed successfully

Using flatMap to attach an asynchronous callback to getOrder

Thanks to this minor change, your program retrieves the order details more efficiently: it fetches the user and product data in parallel instead of waiting for the user entity before requesting the product entity.

Quick Check 45.2 Consider the following snippet of code. Improve the execution time of the function myOp by running asynchronous operations in parallel where possible.

```
import scala.concurrent.{ExecutionContext, Future}

def opA(a: String)(using ec: ExecutionContext): Future[Long] = ???
def opB(b: Int)(using ec: ExecutionContext): Future[Long] = ???
def opC(c: Long)(using ec: ExecutionContext): Future[Long] = ???

def myOp(text: String)
        (using ec: ExecutionContext): Future[Long] =
  for {
    a <- opA(text)
    b <- opB(text.length)
    c <- opC(a - b)
  } yield a * b * c
```

45.2 Retrieving the first Future to complete

Consider your program to place an order and imagine your store now has multiple warehouses that can supply a product. When checking the availability of a product, you'd like to do so for all warehouses and choose the first one that successfully replied with enough available stock.

Listing 45.6 Getting the availability of a product from multiple warehouses

```scala
import scala.concurrent.{ExecutionContext, Future}

sealed trait Warehouse
case object London extends Warehouse
case object Brighton extends Warehouse
case object Leeds extends Warehouse

object Warehouse {
  val all: List[Warehouse] = List(London, Brighton, Leeds)
}

case class Availability(productId: Int,
                        quantity: Double,
                        location: Warehouse)

def checkAvailability(productId: Int, warehouse: Warehouse)
    (using ec: ExecutionContext): Future[Availability] = ???

def getAvailability(productId: Int, quantity: Double)
    (using ec: ExecutionContext): Future[Option[Availability]] =
  Future.find(
    Warehouse.all.map(checkAvailability(productId, _))
  )(availability => availability.quantity >= quantity)
```

It returns the first asynchronous computation to produce a value with given features, if any.

A sequence of asynchronous operations run in parallel.

This is the predicate to select a successfully-produced result.

When working with several asynchronous computations that run independently and in parallel, Scala offers you several methods to help coordinate them. The most common are the following:

- firstCompletedOf—The function Future.firstCompletedOf[T] has one parameter of
  type Iterable[Future[T]], and it returns a value of type Future[T] that contains the
  first instance in the sequence to complete, either successfully or unsuccessfully.

```scala
scala> import scala.concurrent.Future
import scala.concurrent.Future

scala> import scala.concurrent.ExecutionContext.Implicits.global
import scala.concurrent.ExecutionContext.Implicits.global

scala> def futureA = Future { Thread.sleep(42); 42 }
def futureA: scala.concurrent.Future[Int]

scala> def futureB = Future(123/0)
def futureB: scala.concurrent.Future[Int]

scala> Future.firstCompletedOf(Seq(futureA, futureB))
val res0: scala.concurrent.Future[Int] =
    Future(Failure(java.lang.ArithmeticException: / by zero))
```

- find—The method Future.find[T] takes a sequence of asynchronous computations returning a value of type T and a predicate T => Boolean. It returns a new
  instance of type Future[T] containing the first value produced that respects the
  given requirement, if any.

```scala
scala> import scala.concurrent.Future
import scala.concurrent.Future

scala> import scala.concurrent.ExecutionContext.Implicits.global
import scala.concurrent.ExecutionContext.Implicits.global

scala> def futureA = Future { Thread.sleep(42); 42 }
def futureA: scala.concurrent.Future[Int]

scala> def futureB = Future(123/0)
def futureB: scala.concurrent.Future[Int]

scala> val seqAB = Future.find(Seq(futureA, futureB))(_ > 10)
val seqAB: scala.concurrent.Future[Option[Int]] = Future(<not
    completed>)

scala> seqAB
val seqAB: scala.concurrent.Future[Option[Int]] =
    Future(Success(Some(42)))
```

```
scala> Future.find(Seq(futureA, futureB))(_ > 100)
val res0: scala.concurrent.Future[Option[Int]] =
    Future(Success(None))
// No Future instance in the sequence
// produces a value bigger than 100!
```

- sequence—The function Future.sequence[T] takes a sequence of asynchronous computations producing a value T and returns a new asynchronous computation containing all the results in a sequence in the same order. If any of them fail, it completes the new asynchronous computation as a failure.

```
scala> import scala.concurrent.Future
import scala.concurrent.Future

scala> import scala.concurrent.ExecutionContext.Implicits.global
import scala.concurrent.ExecutionContext.Implicits.global

scala> def futureA = Future { Thread.sleep(42); 42 }
def futureA: scala.concurrent.Future[Int]

scala> def futureB = Future(123/0)
def futureB: scala.concurrent.Future[Int]

scala> def futureC = Future(123)
def futureC: scala.concurrent.Future[Int]

scala> Future.sequence(Seq(futureA, futureB, futureC))
val res0: scala.concurrent.Future[Seq[Int]] =
    Future(Failure(java.lang.ArithmeticException: / by zero))

scala> val seqAC = Future.sequence(Seq(futureA, futureC))
val seqAC: scala.concurrent.Future[Seq[Int]] = Future(<not
    completed>)

scala> seqAC
val seqAC: scala.concurrent.Future[Seq[Int]] =
    Future(Success(List(42, 123)))
```

Table 45.1 for shows summary of the functions you can use to coordinate a sequence of independent asynchronous computations.

Table 45.1 Summary of some of the operations you can use to combine a list of Future instances. The method firstCompletedOf returns the first instance of Future to complete, either successfully or unsuccessfully. The function find returns the first result of an asynchronous computation that respects a given predicate. The method sequence collects all the values that Future instances run in parallel produce.

	Acts on	Signature	Usage

firstCompletedOf	Future	firstCompletedOf[T](
		  in: Iterable[Future[T]])(
		  using ec: ExecutionContext):
		                    Future[T]
			It returns the first Future to complete, either successfully or unsuccessfully.

find	Future	find[T](
		  in: Iterable[Future[T]])(
		  p: T => Boolean)(
		  using ec: ExecutionContext):
		                    Future[Option[T]]
			It returns the first Future to successfully produce a value respecting the given predicate, if any.

sequence	Future	sequence[T](
		  in: Iterable[Future[T]])(
		  using ec: ExecutionContext):
		                    Future[Iterable[T]]
			It combines all the values produced in a sequence into a new Future instance. If any of them fail, it returns a failed Future instance.

Quick Check 45.3 Define a function called firstSuccessful that takes a list of Future instances and returns the first future instance to complete successfully, if any.

```
import scala.concurrent.{ExecutionContext, Future}

def firstSuccessful[T](in: List[Future[T]])
    (using ec: ExecutionContext): Future[Option[T]]
```

Blocking on Future

When coding using asynchronous computation, you should never block a thread waiting for a Future to complete. However, there are cases where this is needed, particularly when writing tests.

For example, you may want to write a test in which you assert that a certain asynchronous computation should complete, either with a failure or a success, within some time. You can achieve this by using the function Await .ready, which takes a future instance and a duration and either returns the

(continued)
completed Future instance once it completes or throws an exception when the time has run out.

```
def myFuture: Future[Int] = Future{Thread.sleep(10 /*ms*/); 42 }
```

```
import scala.concurrent.Await
import scala.concurrent.duration._
Await.ready(myFuture, atMost = 5 milliseconds)
```

You may also want to assert that your Future instance can successfully produce a value within a given time. The method Await.result takes a Future instance and a duration and either returns the produced value produced or throws an exception on failure or on timeout.

```
import scala.concurrent.Await
import scala.concurrent.duration._
val n: Int = Await.result(myFuture, atMost = 2 seconds)
```

 Summary

In this lesson, my objective was to teach about some of the operations you can perform on asynchronous computations.

- You learned how to combine asynchronous computation in a sequence using for-comprehension.
- You discovered how to select the first asynchronous computation to complete using the Future.firstCompletedOf method.
- You mastered how to produce a value that respects given properties thanks to the function Future.find.
- You saw how to execute independent asynchronous computations in parallel and collect their results into a sequence using Future.sequence.

Let's see if you got this!

TRY THIS Let's consider the function contentInDir you saw in lesson 44's "Try This" section to list the content of a given directory:

```
import java.io.File
import scala.concurrent.{ExecutionContext, Future}
```

```
def contentInDir(path: String)
                (using ec: ExecutionContext): Future[List[String]] =
  Future {
    val file = new File(path)
    if (file.isDirectory)
      file.listFiles().toList.map(_.getAbsolutePath)
    else List.empty
  }
```

Write a function to asynchronously list the content of a directory and all its subdirectories. Visit each subdirectory independently to improve its runtime performance.

```
def allContentInDir(path: String)
    (using ec: ExecutionContext): Future[List[String]]
```

Answers to quick checks

Quick Check 45.1 You should reimplement your getUserId function as follows:

```
def getUserId(orderId: Int)
            (using ec: ExecutionContext): Future[Int] =
  for {
    order <- getOrder(orderId)
  } yield order.userId
```

Quick Check 45.2 You can improve the execution time of myOp by scheduling the functions opA and opB in parallel because they are independent. Your solution should look similar to the following:

```
def myOp(text: String)
        (using ec: ExecutionContext): Future[Long] = {
  val futureOpA = opA(text)
  val futureOpB = opB(text.length)
  for {
    a <- futureOpA
    b <- futureOpB
    c <- opC(a - b)
  } yield a * b * c
}
```

Quick Check 45.3 A possible implementation for the function firstSuccessful is the following:

```
def firstSuccessful[T](in: List[Future[T]])
    (using ec: ExecutionContext): Future[Option[T]] =
  Future.find(in)(_ => true)
```

DATABASE QUERIES WITH QUILL

After reading this lesson, you will be able to

- Connect to a database and execute SQL queries asynchronously using the Quill library
- Match database tables to case classes
- Write code to generate and run queries to select, insert, update, and delete records

Now that you've learned about the type Future, you'll discover how to connect and asynchronously perform queries to a database using a popular library called Quill. In particular, you'll see how to start a test PostgreSQL database instance and connect to it. You'll see how to execute SQL queries. You'll master how to define case classes that correspond to their tables and write code that generates SQL queries to retrieve, insert, update, and delete their records. In the capstone, you'll use a database to store the questions and user information for a quiz application.

> **Consider this**
>
> Suppose you are developing software to manage orders and bookings in a restaurant that uses a database to read and write data. How would you connect to it and retrieve and save records?

This lesson uses Scala 2
The code examples in this lesson use Scala 2 because, at the time of this publication, the library Quill doesn't support Scala 3 yet. An experimental Quill version for Scala 3 is currently under development, and it will be released once feature-complete and stable.

 ## 46.1 Project setup

Rather than creating an sbt project from scratch, let's download a base project as your starting point.

46.1.1 Download the base project

First, you need to create an sbt project and download its external dependencies. Navigate to an empty folder and use the `git` command to download the base project for this lesson:

```
$ git init
$ git remote add get-prog-with-scala https://github.com/
          DanielaSfregola/get-programming-with-scala.git
$ git fetch get-prog-with-scala
$ git checkout -b my_lesson46 get-prog-with-scala/baseline_unit7_lesson46
```

In this lesson, you'll also use a library called testcontainers, which uses Docker to initialize a temporary PostgreSQL database instance for your application. Make sure that your machine has Docker installed by running the following command:

```
$ docker --version
Docker version 20.10.0, build 7287ab3
```

If you need to install Docker, please refer to the instructions in section 2.4.2.

After running these commands, your directory should contain a base sbt project including the following files:

- project/build.properties has the sbt version of your project.
- build.sbt defines your Scala version and the dependencies you are going to use.

Listing 46.1 The build.sbt file

```
//build.sbt file

name := "get-programming-with-scala-lesson46"
```

```
version := "0.1"

scalaVersion := "2.13.6"

libraryDependencies ++= List(
  "io.getquill" %% "quill-jasync-postgres" % "3.7.2",
  "org.testcontainers" % "postgresql" % "1.15.3",
  "org.postgresql" % "postgresql" % "42.2.22",
  "ch.qos.logback"  %  "logback-classic" % "1.2.3"
)
```

Quill allows you to connect and query a database from a Scala codebase.

Java library to spin database instances up for test purposes

The PostgreSQL driver

Logback manages the logs of your application.

- src/main/resource/logback.xml specifies the logging format to use in your application.
- src/main/resource/init.sql is an SQL script to create the tables of your database and insert a few records.
- src/main/scala/org/example/registrations/PostgreSQL.scala defines a class to start a test PostgreSQL database instance.

Execute the command sbt compile to download all the external dependencies and compile the existing code.

46.1.2 Starting the PostgreSQL server

When developing a real-world application, you should rely on a database that is the appropriate size, is secure, and is periodically backed up (explaining how to do this is beyond this book's scope). You are going to run a small temporary PostgreSQL database using the org.testcontainers library. The PostgreSQL class allows you to configure, start, and stop a base Docker container containing a PostgreSQL database.

Listing 46.2 The PostgreSQL class

```
package org.example.registrations

import java.net.URL

import com.typesafe.config._
import org.testcontainers.containers.PostgreSQLContainer
import org.slf4j.LoggerFactory

class PostgreSQL(initScript: String) {
```

```
private val logger = LoggerFactory.getLogger(this.getClass)

private val container: PostgreSQLContainer[_] = {
  val psql: PostgreSQLContainer[_] =
    new PostgreSQLContainer("postgres")
        .withInitScript(initScript)
  logger.info(s"Starting container...")
  psql.start()
  psql
}

def stop() = {
  logger.info("Stopping container...")
  container.stop()
}

val config: Config = {
  val components = List(
    container.getJdbcUrl,
    s"user=${container.getUsername}",
    s"password=${container.getPassword}"
  )
  ConfigFactory.empty().withValue(
    "url", ConfigValueFactory.fromAnyRef(components.mkString("&"))
  )
}

}
```

A reference to the PostgreSQL server inside the Docker container

It initializes the database with a given script.

It starts the PostgreSQL server.

It stops the PostgresSQL server.

Details on how to connect to the PostgreSQL server

The library org.testcontainers is a popular Java library for throwaway, lightweight instances of common databases for test purposes. Some of the supported databases are MySQL, Cassandra, PostgreSQL, Kafka, and Neo4j; the website testcontainers.org lists all the modules offered.

In this lesson, you'll write queries to read and write data about customers of a store. The init.sql file defines a table to represent a user, and it inserts some sample records into it.

Listing 46.3 The init.sql script

```
// src/main/resource/init.sql file

CREATE TABLE IF NOT EXISTS customer (
    id INTEGER,
```

```
    name VARCHAR(45) NOT NULL,
    PRIMARY KEY (id)
);

INSERT INTO customer (id, name)
VALUES
    (1, 'Alice Abbott'),
    (2, 'Bob Brown'),
    (3, 'Charlie Clarke');
```

Let's try to start and stop your PostgresSQL server. Your machine will download everything needed the first time. Execute the command sbt console from your sbt project's root directory to try your code interactively:

```
$ sbt console
 [...]

scala>
```

You can initialize and start your PostgreSQL server as follows:

```
scala> import org.example.registrations._
import org.example.registrations._

scala> val psqlServer = new PostgreSQL("init.sql")
Starting container...
...
Container postgres:9.6.12 started in PT8.103S
Executing database script from init.sql
Executed database script from init.sql in 150 ms.
HikariPool-1 - Starting...
HikariPool-1 - Start completed.
val psqlServer: org.example.registrations.PostgreSQL =
            org.example.registrations.PostgreSQL@212bd091

scala>
```

Invoking the stop function will destroy the container:

```
scala> psqlServer.stop
Stopping container...
```

The setup is now complete, and you are ready to connect to your database and run queries on it.

46.2 Connecting to the PostgreSQL server

When connecting to a database, you need to provide information about its type, driver, and location.

Listing 46.4 Defining a database context

```scala
// file src/main/scala/org/example/registrations/TestDatabase.scala

package org.example.registrations

import io.getquill.{PostgresJAsyncContext, SnakeCase}

object TestDatabase {

  private val psqlServer = new PostgreSQL("init.sql")
  val ctx = new PostgresJAsyncContext(SnakeCase, psqlServer.config)

  def stop(): Unit = psqlServer.stop()
}
```

It starts the PostgreSQL test server.

It defines how to connect to it.

It stops the PostgreSQL test server.

When using Quill, you need to initialize a context with information about your database and its connection details. First, you need to pick a general naming convention; use UpperCase, LowerCase, SnakeCase, or CamelCase. If this is not consistent, you can still provide custom settings when matching tables with your Scala code. You then need to give its location and driver by supplying a Config instance or a configuration file to parse. This is usually called application.properties and lives in your resources directory. The Quill library offers you several modules to support various types of databases. (See the website https://getquill.io for more information on defining a database context and the full list of supported databases.)

Listing 46.5 Example of context creation from for a MySql database

```scala
// In your build.sbt, add the Quill module and
// the driver for your database

libraryDependencies ++= List(
  "mysql" % "mysql-connector-java" % "8.0.15",
```

```
    "io.getquill" %% "quill-jdbc" % "3.7.2"
)
```

```
// file src/main/resource/application.properties

mydb {
  dataSourceClassName=com.mysql.cj.jdbc.MysqlDataSource
  dataSource.url=jdbc:mysql://host/database
  dataSource.user=root
  dataSource.password=root
  dataSource.cachePrepStmts=true
  dataSource.prepStmtCacheSize=250
  dataSource.prepStmtCacheSqlLimit=2048
  connectionTimeout=30000
}
```

```
// In your Scala file, define a quill context

import io.getquill._
val ctx = new MysqlJdbcContext(CamelCase, "mydb")
```

> **Quick Check 46.1** Define a Quill context to connect to a PostgreSQL database by parsing a configuration file and using a CamelCase naming convention. Your application.properties contains the following data:
>
> ```
> db.url=postgresql://host:5432/database?user=root&password=root
> app {
>     name=my_application
>     owner=my_team
>     port=8080
> }
> ```

 ## 46.3 Executing queries

Imagine that you'd like to run a simple query to ensure you can connect to your database.

Listing 46.6 Testing a database connection

```
// file src/main/scala/org/example/registrations/Queries.scala

package org.example.registrations

import io.getquill.{PostgresJAsyncContext, SnakeCase}
import scala.concurrent.{ExecutionContext, Future}

class Queries(ctx: PostgresJAsyncContext[SnakeCase.type]) {
  import ctx._

  def testConnection()
      (implicit ec: ExecutionContext): Future[Boolean] = {
    val q = quote { infix"SELECT 1".as[Int] }
    val result: Future[Int] = run(q)
    result.map(_ == 1)
  }

}
```

The Quill context provides information on your database. SnakeCase.type returns the type of the object SnakeCase.

It enables Quill's DSL.

The query returns a Future, so you need an execution context.

It defines a SQL query that returns an integer.

It checks that the result matches expectations.

It runs the defined query asynchronously. Quill uses an implicit conversion to transform its instance of type ctx.Result that produces a Future one.

You can now check if you can connect to your database as follows:

```
scala> import org.example.registrations._
import org.example.registrations._

scala> import scala.concurrent.ExecutionContext.Implicits.global
import scala.concurrent.ExecutionContext.Implicits.global

scala> val queries = new Queries(TestDatabase.ctx)
val queries: org.example.registrations.Queries =
        org.example.registrations.Queries@7107c07d

scala> queries.testConnection()
val res0: scala.concurrent.Future[Boolean] = Future(<not completed>)

scala> res0
val res1: scala.concurrent.Future[Boolean] = Future(Success(true))
```

When connecting to a database, you need to provide a Quill context. The class Queries requires one for a PostgreSQL database with a SnakeCase naming convention. The compiler will use this information to ensure your queries are syntactically correct. You need to include the instruction import ctx._ to enable a DSL that Quill offers to define SQL queries, such as the functions quote and run. The prefix infix indicates that the string should be a parsable SQL instruction, while the method as defines the expected type of each record of the query. Finally, you invoke the function run on your context to execute the query asynchronously.

Quick Check 46.2 The following snippet of code defines a SQL query to retrieve all the customers' names in the database. What happens when you execute it? Use the Scala REPL within your sbt console to validate your hypothesis.

```
import org.example.registrations._
import TestDatabase.ctx._
import io.getquill.Query

import scala.concurrent.Future
import scala.concurrent.ExecutionContext.Implicits.global


val customers: Future[Seq[String]] = run(quote {
  infix"SELECT name FROM customers".as[Query[String]]
})
```

 46.4 Running generated queries

Imagine you want to manipulate the customer data stored in the database. In particular, you'd like to do the following:

- Retrieve all customers.
- Get the customer name by its ID.
- Insert a new customer.
- Update the name of a customer by ID.
- Delete a customer by ID.

Listing 46.7 Generated queries for customers

```
// file src/main/scala/org/example/registrations/CustomerQueries.scala

package org.example.registrations
```

```scala
import io.getquill.{PostgresJAsyncContext, SnakeCase}
import scala.concurrent.{ExecutionContext, Future}
```

The case class to represent a customer

```scala
case class Customer(id: Int, name: String)

class CustomerQueries(ctx: PostgresJAsyncContext[SnakeCase.type]) {
  import ctx._
```

query[Customer] matches your case class to a table with name customer and two columns, id and name.

```scala
  private val customers = quote { query[Customer] }

  def all()(implicit ec: ExecutionContext): Future[Seq[Customer]] = {
    // Generated SQL: SELECT x.id, x.name FROM customer x
    run(customers)
  }
```

The type Seq is an interface that indicates a list-like structure. List is its default implementation.

```scala
  def nameById(id: Int)
            (implicit ec: ExecutionContext): Future[Seq[String]] = {
    // Generated SQL: SELECT x1.name FROM customer x1 WHERE x1.id = ?
    val q = quote {
      customers.filter(_.id == lift(id))
               .map(_.name)
    }
    run(q)
  }
```

filter allows you to select only records that respect a given predicate. The function lift indicates that the value is not static; your program will provide it at runtime.

map selects only specific columns in your query.

```scala
  def save(customer: Customer)
         (implicit ec: ExecutionContext): Future[String] = {
    // Generated SQL:
    // INSERT INTO customer (id,name) VALUES (?, ?) RETURNING name
    val q = quote {
      customers.insert(lift(customer))
               .returning(_.name)
    }
    run(q)
  }
```

insert allows you to save new records in your database.

returning defines what information to return after an operation.

```scala
  def updateNameById(id: Int, nameToUpdate: String)
                    (implicit ec: ExecutionContext): Future[Long] = {
    // Generated SQL: UPDATE customer SET name = ? WHERE id = ?
    val q = quote {
      customers.filter(_.id == lift(id))
               .update(_.name -> lift(nameToUpdate))
```

update changes the value of the given fields.

```
    }
    run(q)
  }

  def deleteById(id: Int)
                (implicit ec: ExecutionContext): Future[Long] = {
    // Generated SQL: DELETE FROM customer WHERE id = ?
    val q = quote {
      customers.filter(_.id == lift(id)).delete
    }
    run(q)
  }

}
```

delete removes all the selected records.

Writing queries by hand can have disadvantages: different types of databases use different SQL dialects. Ensuring that they match your program's expectations can be challenging to maintain. Quill offers you a DSL to generate queries at compile time and help you mitigate these issues.

In the example in listing 46.7, your Quill context uses a SnakeCase naming convention. The library uses this information to match the database tables with your case classes. For example, the expression query[Customer] indicates that it should match the table customer containing two columns, id and name, to your case class Customer. You can also provide custom matching using the function querySchema. For example, consider the following instruction:

```
quote { querySchema[Customer]("customers_table",
                              _.id -> "customer_id",
                              _.name -> "name_column") }
```

This defines a match between your case class Customer and a table with the name customers_table and the columns customer_id and name_column.

Quill generates queries at compile time. You will see how it translates them into SQL statements in the console when you compile. The function lift indicates which values in your queries are dynamic and need adjusting during execution. Dynamic values are values your program cannot provide at compile time, but they depend on its runtime execution. Generated queries mark them with a "?" symbol until their value is known.

You can now connect to the database and manipulate your customer data:

```
scala> import org.example.registrations._
import org.example.registrations._
```

```
scala> import scala.concurrent.ExecutionContext.Implicits.global
import scala.concurrent.ExecutionContext.Implicits.global

scala> val customers = new CustomerQueries(TestDatabase.ctx)
val customers: org.example.registrations.CustomerQueries =
        org.example.registrations.CustomerQueries@2dd8d946

scala> customers.all()
val res0: scala.concurrent.Future[Seq[org.example.registrations
        .Customer]] = Future(Success(List(Customer(1,Alice Abbott),
        Customer(2,Bob Brown), Customer(3,Charlie Clarke))))

scala> customers.save(Customer(4, "Martin"))
val res1: scala.concurrent.Future[String] = Future(Success(Martin))

scala> customers.updateNameById(4, "Jane")
val res2: scala.concurrent.Future[Long] = Future(Success(1))

scala> customers.nameById(4)
val res3: scala.concurrent.Future[Seq[String]]=
        Future(Success(List(Jane)))

scala> customers.deleteById(4)
val res4: scala.concurrent.Future[Long] = Future(Success(1))

scala> customers.all()
val res5: scala.concurrent.Future[Seq[org.example.registrations
        .Customer]] = Future(Success(List(Customer(1,Alice Abbott),
        Customer(2,Bob Brown), Customer(3,Charlie Clarke))))
```

> **Quick Check 46.3** Add the function customersByName to your class CustomerQueries to generate and run a query to retrieve customers with a given name.
>
> ```
> def customersByName(name: String)
>     (implicit ec: ExecutionContext): Future[Seq[Customer]]
> ```

Summary

In this lesson, my objective was to teach you how to query a database using the library Quill.

- You learned how to connect a database and run queries asynchronously on Quill.
- You saw how to match the results from your queries to your case classes.
- You discovered how to generate SQL queries to select, insert, update, and delete records using Quill's DSL.

Let's see if you got this!

> **TRY THIS** The init.sql file you downloaded for this lesson also creates another table called product with the following structure:
>
> ```
> CREATE TABLE IF NOT EXISTS product (
>     id INTEGER,
>     title VARCHAR(45) NOT NULL,
>     creation_date DATE NOT NULL,
>     PRIMARY KEY (id)
> );
> ```
>
> Define functions to perform the following operations:
>
> - Create a product.
> - Select all of those with a given title.
> - Change the title of a specific product.
> - Delete a product by ID.

Answers to quick checks

> **Quick Check 46.1** You can define a Quill context for your database as the following:
>
> ```
> import io.getquill._
> new PostgresJAsyncContext(CamelCase, "db")
> ```

Quick Check 46.2 The code compiles, but it fails at runtime because the table's name is incorrect: the correct table name is *customer*, not *customers*.

```
scala> import org.example.registrations._
     | import TestDatabase.ctx._
     | import io.getquill.Query._
     |
     | import scala.concurrent.Future
     | import scala.concurrent.ExecutionContext.Implicits.global
     |
     | val customers: Future[Seq[String]] = run(quote {
     |   infix"SELECT name FROM customers".as[Query[String]]
     | })
     |
val customers: Future[Seq[String]] = run(quote {
                                          ^
<pastie>:7: SELECT x.* FROM (SELECT name FROM customers) AS x
import org.example.registrations._
import TestDatabase.ctx._
import scala.concurrent.Future
import scala.concurrent.ExecutionContext.Implicits.global
val customers: scala.concurrent.Future[Seq[String]] = Future(<not
        completed>)
Error with message -> ErrorMessage(fields=HashMap(Position -> 35,
        Line -> 1160, V -> ERROR, Message -> relation "custom-
        ers" does not exist, Severity -> ERROR, File ->
        parse_relation.c, SQLSTATE -> 42P01, Routine ->
        parserOpenTable))
```

If you correct your query, you code will return the name of the three customers in your database:

```
scala> val customers: Future[Seq[String]] = run(quote{
     | infix"SELECT name FROM customer".as[Query[String]] } )
                                          ^
        SELECT x.* FROM (SELECT name FROM customer) AS x
val res0: Future[Seq[String]] =
Future(Success(List(Alice Abbott, Bob Brown, Charlie Clarke)))
```

Note that this snippet uses *as[Query[String]]* instead of *as[String]* because the defined query can return zero or more records rather than one.

Quick Check 46.3 A possible implementation for the function customersByName is the following:

```
def customersByName(name: String)
    (implicit ec: ExecutionContext): Future[Seq[Customer]] = {
    val q = quote { customers.filter(_.name == lift(name)) }
    run(q)
}
```

THE QUIZ APPLICATION: PART 1

In this capstone, you will

- Read and write the quiz data from a PostgreSQL database asynchronously
- Define SQL queries to create, retrieve, update, and delete records
- Chain multiple asynchronous computations to safely store a question and its answers

In this capstone, you'll define an application's data access layer to create and answer quizzes. You'll implement its business logic and HTTP API at the end of the next unit. Your quiz application has the following requirements:

- It should read and write categories and a set of questions and answers assigned to them.
- Its users should pick a category, answer randomly selected questions about it, and receive a final score based on their performance.

Your application has access to a PostgreSQL database containing three tables called category, question, and answers. Figure 47.1 shows their table structure.

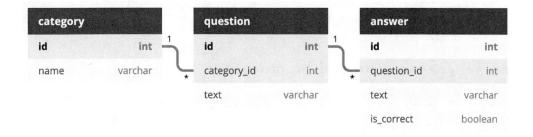

Figure 47.1 Visualization of your database schema. Primary keys are in bold, while foreign keys are linked to their reference. The entity-relationship diagram has been drawn using dbdiagram.io.

This lesson uses Scala 2

The code examples in this lesson use Scala 2 because, at the time of this publication, the library Quill doesn't support Scala 3 yet. An experimental Quill version for Scala 3 is currently under development, and it will be released once feature-complete and stable.

 47.1 Download the base project

First, let's speed things up by downloading a base project for you to use. In an empty directory of your choice, run the following `git` commands to download the remote branch:

```
$ git init
$ git remote add get-prog-with-scala https://github.com/
        DanielaSfregola/get-programming-with-scala.git
$ git fetch get-prog-with-scala
$ git checkout -b my_lesson47 get-prog-with-scala/baseline_unit7_
        lesson47
```

You will notice lots of similarities with the baseline project you used in the previous lesson. It contains the following files:

- The file project/build.properties defines the sbt version.
- build.sbt defines the Scala version and the external dependencies for your project (see listing 47.1).

Listing 47.1 The build.sbt file

```
// file build.sbt

name := "get-programming-with-scala-lesson47"

version := "0.1"

scalaVersion := "2.13.6"

libraryDependencies ++= Seq(
  "io.getquill" %% "quill-jasync-postgres" % "3.7.2",
  "org.testcontainers" % "postgresql" % "1.15.3",
  "org.postgresql" % "postgresql" % "42.2.22",
  "ch.qos.logback"  % "logback-classic" % "1.2.3"
)
```

- src/main/resources/logback.xml provides the logging format your application will use.
- The files PostgreSQL.scala and TestDatabase.scala in the directory src/main/scala/org/example/quiz have been copied from the previous lesson. They allow your application to start a small temporary instance of a PostgreSQL database initialized by loading an SQL script. In a real-world application, you should use a database that is permanent, monitored, and backed up regularly.
- src/main/resources/init.sql is the SQL script to create the tables in the temporary database.

Listing 47.2 The init.sql file

```
CREATE TABLE IF NOT EXISTS category (
  id SERIAL,
  name VARCHAR(45) NOT NULL UNIQUE,
  PRIMARY KEY (id)
);

CREATE TABLE IF NOT EXISTS question (
  id SERIAL,
  category_id INTEGER,
  text VARCHAR(45) NOT NULL,
  PRIMARY KEY (id),
  FOREIGN KEY (category_id) REFERENCES category(id) ON DELETE CASCADE
);
```

The database generates a value for it during the record insertion.

It deletes the record if deleting the reference.

```
CREATE TABLE IF NOT EXISTS answer (
    id SERIAL,                          ←── The database
    question_id INTEGER,                    generates a value
    text VARCHAR(45) NOT NULL,              for it during the
    is_correct BOOLEAN,                     record insertion.
    PRIMARY KEY (id),
    FOREIGN KEY (question_id) REFERENCES question(id) ON DELETE CASCADE  ←──
);
                                        It deletes the record if
                                        deleting the reference.
```

You can now launch sbt to download the external dependencies and compile the existing code using the command sbt compile. You are now ready to start developing your application!

 ## 47.2 Health check queries

In this capstone, your objective is to implement your application's data access layer, a set of classes that allow you to read and write data from a database. First, let's create a package to group these classes; let's call it dao. The term *dao* stands for "data access object" and indicates the abstraction between an application and its persistence layer in software design. Separating how your application exposes data to the public from how it stores them makes them easier to maintain and evolve.

You can now add the class GenericDao to perform a simple query to ensure your application can successfully connect to the database.

Listing 47.3 The class GenericDao

```scala
// file src/main/scala/org/example/quiz/dao/GenericDao.scala

package org.example.quiz.dao

import io.getquill.{PostgresJAsyncContext, SnakeCase}

import scala.concurrent.{ExecutionContext, Future}

class GenericDao(ctx: PostgresJAsyncContext[SnakeCase.type])
              (implicit ec: ExecutionContext) {       Importing the
    import ctx._                        ←──           Quill query DSL

    def testConnection(): Future[Boolean] = {   ←── Returning true if it returned
        val q = quote { infix"SELECT 1".as[Int] }    the expected value
```

```
      val result: Future[Int] = run(q)
      result.map(_ == 1)
    }
}
```

Your application will use the testConnection function to perform a health check on the connectivity to its database.

 ## 47.3 Category queries

Let's now define how to interact with the table category in your database. First, let's define a case class that matches its structure. This representation is specific to the database structure. Let's define a new package called dao.records.

Listing 47.4 The category Record

```
// file src/main/org/example/quiz/dao/records/Category.scala

package org.example.quiz.dao.records          The column is a serial pri-
                                              mary key, which means the
                                              database is responsible for
case class Category(id: Long = 0,    ◄─────   assigning a value for it.
                    name: String)
```

Your application can perform the following operations on the table category:

- Create a category.
- Retrieve all categories.
- Delete a category with a given ID.

The class CategoryDao.scala in the package dao defines how to execute them.

Listing 47.5 The CategoryDao class

```
// file src/main/org/example/quiz/dao/CategoryDao.scala

package org.example.quiz.dao

import io.getquill.{SnakeCase, PostgresJAsyncContext}
import org.example.quiz.dao.records.Category

import scala.concurrent.{ExecutionContext, Future}
```

```
class CategoryDao(ctx: PostgresJAsyncContext[SnakeCase.type])
                   (implicit ec: ExecutionContext) {
  import ctx._

  private val categories = quote { query[Category] }

  def save(category: Category): Future[Long] = {
    val q = quote {
      categories.insert(lift(category))
                 .returningGenerated(_.id)
    }
    run(q)
  }

  def all(): Future[Seq[Category]] = run(categories)

  def deleteById(id: Long): Future[Boolean] = {
    val q = quote { categories.filter(_.id == lift(id)).delete }
    run(q).map(_ > 0)
  }

}
```

It imports the Quill query DSL.

It picks a naming convention for the table.

It returns the ID the database has assigned to the category.

It uses returningGenerated rather than returning because ID is a value that the database generated.

It returns true if it deleted at least one record.

When deleting a category, the database will also delete its questions.

Thanks to the returningGenerated function, Quill excludes the value ID from the insertion query as the database selects its value.

Your application will use these operations to define quiz categories and display them to the user.

47.4 Question and answer queries

You now need to define a representation for the tables question and answer. Define two case classes in the package dao.records.

Listing 47.6 The question and answer records

```
// file src/main/scala/org/example/quiz/dao/records/
           QuestionAnswer.scala

package org.example.quiz.dao.records
```

```
case class Question(id: Long = 0,
                    text: String,
                    categoryId: Long)


case class Answer(id: Long = 0,
                  questionId: Long = 0,
                  text: String,
                  isCorrect: Boolean = false)
```

Your application will adjust its value as soon as the database assigns an ID to the new question record.

The column is a serial primary key, which means the database is responsible for assigning a value for it.

The records in the tables question and answer are strictly correlated: having a question without answers or answers without questions is not meaningful to your quiz application. To ensure they will be consistent, let's define a class called QuestionAnswerDao that acts on both the tables.

Your application can perform the following operations on the tables question and answer:

- Create a question together with its answers.
- Find all the questions and their answers assigned to an existing category.
- Delete a question and its answers by a given question ID.

Listing 47.7 The QuestionAnswerDao class

```
// file src/main/scala/org/example/quiz/dao/QuestionAnswerDao.scala

package org.example.quiz.dao

import io.getquill.{SnakeCase, PostgresJAsyncContext}
import org.example.quiz.dao.records.{Answer, Question}

import scala.concurrent.{ExecutionContext, Future}


class QuestionAnswerDao(ctx: PostgresJAsyncContext[SnakeCase.type])
                       (implicit ec: ExecutionContext) {

  import ctx._
```

It imports the Quill query DSL.

Both tables have a SnakeCase naming convention.

```
private val questions = quote { query[Question] }
private val answers = quote { query[Answer] }

def save(newQuestion: Question,
         newAnswers: Seq[Answer]): Future[(Long, Seq[Long])] = {
  val saveQuestion = quote {
    questions.insert(lift(newQuestion)).returningGenerated(_.id)
  }

  val saveAnswers = { questionId: Long =>
    val newAnswersWithQuestionId =
      newAnswers.map(_.copy(questionId = questionId))
    quote {
      liftQuery(newAnswersWithQuestionId).foreach { a =>
        answers.insert(a).returningGenerated(_.id)
      }
    }
  }

  transaction { implicit ec =>
    for {
      questionId <- run(saveQuestion)
      answerId <- run(saveAnswers(questionId))
    } yield questionId -> answerId
  }
}

def pickByCategoryId(
  categoryId: Long,
  n: Int): Future[Map[Question, Seq[Answer]]] = {
  val result: Future[Seq[(Question, Answer)]] = run {
    for {
      question <- questions.filter(_.categoryId == lift(categoryId))
                           .sortBy(_ => infix"random()").take(lift(n))
      answer <- answers.filter(_.questionId == question.id)
    } yield question -> answer
  }

  result.map { questionsAndAnswers =>
    val questions: Seq[Question] =
      questionsAndAnswers.map { case (q, _) => q }.distinct
    val answersByQuestionId: Map[Long, Seq[Answer]] =
      questionsAndAnswers.map {
```

It returns the IDs the database assigned to the question and answers.

The function liftQuery allows you to generate a query to perform a bulk insert.

It updates the answers with the generated question ID before inserting them.

It defines a transaction so that we can rollback all insertions in case of failure.

It returns the questions and their answers in a dictionary-like structure.

It sorts records randomly and selecting up to n.

It converts from a flat structure of type Future[Seq[(Question, Answer)]] to one of type Future[Map[Question, Seq[Answer]].

```
            case (_, a) => a
         }.groupBy(_.questionId)
      questions.map { question =>
        question -> answersByQuestionId.getOrElse(
          question.id, List.empty)
      }.toMap
    }
  }

  def deleteById(id: Long): Future[Boolean] = {
    val q = quote { questions.filter(_.id == lift(id) ).delete }
    run(q).map(_ > 0)
  }

  def getCorrectQuestionAnswers(
    questionIds: Seq[Long]): Future[Seq[(Long, Long)]] = {
    val q = quote {
      for {
        question <- questions.filter(q =>
            lift(questionIds).contains(q.id))
        correctAnswer <- answers.filter(a =>
            a.questionId == question.id && a.isCorrect)
      } yield question.id -> correctAnswer.id
    }
    run(q)
  }
}
```

It returns true if it deleted at least one record.

When deleting a question, the database deletes its answers.

It returns the correct answer IDs for the given question IDs.

The transaction function allows you to define a database transaction when running queries: it rolls back all the applied changes if any of them fail, maintaining the database data consistency. The transaction function is a higher order function that takes a function of type TransactionExecutionContext => Future[T] as its parameter. The class TransactionExecutionContext lives in the package io.getquill.context.async, and it is a custom implementation of the class scala.concurrent.ExecutionContext.

The implementation of the data access layer is now complete and ready to use.

 ## 47.5 Let's give it a try!

The implementation of your application is not complete yet. Let's use the sbt console to load the project inside the Scala REPL and see it in action. Navigate to the root directory of your project and run the command sbt console:

```
$ sbt console
...
[info] /Users/danielasfregola/Development/get-programming-with-
        scala/unit7/lesson47/src/main/scala/org/example/quiz/dao/
        CategoryDao.scala:22:8: SELECT x.id, x.name FROM category x
[info]      run(categories)
[info]          ^
...
[info] /Users/danielasfregola/Development/get-programming-with-
        scala/unit7/lesson47/src/main/scala/org/example/quiz/dao/
        QuestionAnswerDao.scala:64:8: DELETE FROM question WHERE
        id = ?
[info]      run(q).map(_ > 0)
[info]          ^
[info] Starting scala interpreter...

scala>
```

When compiling, Quill shows you the SQL queries it generated according to the naming convention you provided. First, let's start your temporary database instance and define the classes to run queries on it:

```
scala> import scala.concurrent.ExecutionContext.Implicits.global
     | import org.example.quiz._
     | import org.example.quiz.dao._
     | import org.example.quiz.dao.records._
     |
     | val genericDao = new GenericDao(TestDatabase.ctx)
     | val categoryDao = new CategoryDao(TestDatabase.ctx)
     | val qaDao = new QuestionAnswerDao(TestDatabase.ctx)
     |
Starting container...
Loaded org.testcontainers.dockerclient.UnixSocketClientProvider
        Strategy from ~/.testcontainers.properties, will try it
        first
Accessing docker with local Unix socket
...
Executing database script from init.sql
Executed database script from init.sql in 174 ms.
import scala.concurrent.ExecutionContext.Implicits.global
import org.example.quiz._
import org.example.quiz.dao._
import org.example.quiz.dao.records._
```

```
val genericDao: org.example.quiz.dao.GenericDao =
        org.example.quiz.dao.GenericDao@77531d42
val categoryDao: org.example.quiz.dao.CategoryDao =
        org.example.quiz.dao.CategoryDao@2ae37a6b
val qaDao: org.example.quiz.dao.QuestionAnswerDao =
        org.example.quiz.dao.QuestionAnswerDao@23787cc0
```

You can now check if you can connect to the database:

```
scala> genericDao.testConnection()
val res0: scala.concurrent.Future[Boolean] = Future(Success(true))
```

Let's try to create a category and then define two questions for it:

```
scala> import scala.concurrent.Future
import scala.concurrent.Future

scala> val questionA = { (categoryId: Long) =>
     |    val question = Question(categoryId = categoryId, text = "Is
     |    this a test?")
     |    val answers = List(Answer(text = "True", isCorrect = true),
     |        Answer(text = "False"))
     |   qaDao.save(question, answers)
     | }
     |
     | val questionB = { (categoryId: Long) =>
     |   val question = Question(categoryId = categoryId, text =
     |   "Another test?")
     |    val answers = List(Answer(text = "XXX"),
     |                    Answer(text = "YYY", isCorrect = true),
     |                    Answer(text = "ZZZ"))
     |   qaDao.save(question, answers)
     | }
     |
     |
     | for {
     |   categoryId <- categoryDao.save(Category(name = "Test"))
     |   _ <- Future.sequence(List(questionA(categoryId),
     |             questionB(categoryId)))
     | } yield categoryId
     |
val questionA: Long => scala.concurrent.Future[(Long, Seq[Long])] =
        $$Lambda$5405/1534932780@383f2392
```

```
val questionB: Long => scala.concurrent.Future[(Long, Seq[Long])] =
        $$Lambda$5406/1081244036@6435c63c
val res0: scala.concurrent.Future[Long] = Future(<not completed>)

scala> res0
val res1: scala.concurrent.Future[Long] = Future(Success(1))
```

You can now retrieve the created category, questions, and answers:

```
scala> categoryDao.all()
val res2: scala.concurrent.Future[Seq[org.example.quiz.dao.records
        .Category]] = Future(Success(List(Category(1,Test))))

scala> qaDao.pickByCategoryId(1, n = 5)
val res3: scala.concurrent.Future[Map[org.example.quiz.dao.records
        .Question,Seq[org.example.quiz.dao.records.Answer]]] =
        Future(Success(Map(Question(1,Is this a test?,1) ->
        List(Answer(1,1,True,true), Answer(3,1,False,false)),
        Question(2,Another test?,1) -> List(Answer(2,2,XXX,false),
        Answer(4,2,YYY,true), Answer(5,2,ZZZ,false)))))
```

Finally, let's ensure that your application can delete a category, together with its questions and answers:

```
scala> categoryDao.deleteById(1)
val res4: scala.concurrent.Future[Boolean] = Future(Success(true))

scala> qaDao.pickByCategoryId(1, n = 5)
val res5:
scala.concurrent.Future[Map[org.example.quiz.dao.records.Question,
        Seq[org.example.quiz.dao.records.Answer]]] =
        Future(Success(Map()))
```

The database automatically deletes any questions and answers that reference a deleted category ID because of the "DELETE ON CASCADE" selected strategy.

Summary

In this capstone, you implemented an application's data access layer to create and play quizzes.

- You implemented a query to check the connectivity to the database.
- You represented each table with a case class.
- You defined which operations your application can perform in each table.
- You used your code to read and write records in the database.

JSON (de)serialization

In unit 7, you mastered how to represent asynchronous computations in Scala. In this unit you'll discover how to serialize and deserialize data in JSON format and how to lazily represent side effects. In the capstone, you'll complete the implementation of your quiz application by defining its business logic and HTTP API. In particular, you'll learn about the following topics:

- Lesson 48 shows you how to use a popular library called circe to convert a class into a JSON string and vice versa by defining JSON encoders and decoders.
- Lesson 49 teaches you about lazy evaluation and how it differs from eager evaluation. You'll see how by-name parameters behave differently from by-value ones. You'll also discover how to lazily initialize a value using the *lazy* keyword.
- Lesson 50 introduces you to the type IO from the library cats-effect to lazily evaluate both synchronous and asynchronous side effects.
- Lesson 51 shows you how to apply the map and flatMap operations on an IO instance to manipulate and transform its value. You'll also learn how to coordinate multiple side effects by running them in sequence or parallel.

- Lesson 52 introduces you to the basics of writing tests using a library called ScalaTest for both synchronous and asynchronous code.
- Finally, you'll define an HTTP server with an API that exposes and accepts data in JSON format in lesson 53. You'll implement an app that picks 10 questions for a given category and calculate a score based on the received answers.

JSON (DE)SERIALIZATION WITH CIRCE

After reading this lesson, you will be able to

- Convert a data structure or Scala instance into JSON format
- Parse JSON data as Scala code

You learned about asynchronous computations in the previous unit. In this lesson, you are going to learn about working with JSON in Scala. Scala doesn't offer JSON support natively, so you'll use circe, a popular library to work with JSON in Scala. JSON stands for "JavaScript Object Notation" and is a commonly used lightweight format to exchange straightforward data for humans to read and for machines to parse. You'll see how to represent data in JSON format. You can refer to this process as serialization. You'll also discover the inverse operation of defining a Scala instance by parsing a JSON structure, called *deserialization*. Figure 48.1 provides a visual comparison between the processes of JSON serialization and deserialization.

In the capstone, your quiz application's HTTP API will send and receive data using the JSON format.

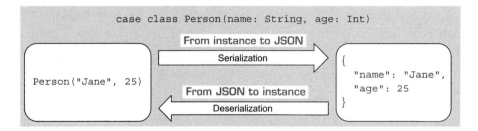

Figure 48.1   The process of serialization allows you to represent a Scala instance in JSON format. Its inverse is deserialization, which allows you to parse data in JSON format into a Scala instance.

Consider this

Imagine you are developing a weather application to analyze how the temperature changes over time. It uses a third-party's HTTP API to receive weather information daily on your areas of interest; it represents its data in JSON format. How would you parse it so that your application can process it?

 48.1 Project setup

Before you can learn how to work with JSON data, you need to include a JSON library as an external dependency in your project. First, create an empty sbt project and include the modules of the circe library you are going to use as external dependencies by adding the following to your build.sbt file.

Listing 48.1 Including the circe modules as external dependencies

```
// file build.sbt

// …

val CirceVersion = "0.14.1"

libraryDependencies ++= List(
  "io.circe" %% "circe-core" % CirceVersion,
  "io.circe" %% "circe-generic" % CirceVersion,
  "io.circe" %% "circe-parser" % CirceVersion
)
```

You can now launch sbt using the command sbt console to download the modules and load them into a Scala REPL session. You are now ready to discover how to use the circe library to serialize and deserialize data in JSON format.

 ## 48.2 JSON serialization: From instance to JSON

Imagine you are developing a program to keep track of a person's full name and age. Your program exposes this information via an HTTP API to retrieve the person's details with a given ID.

Listing 48.2 Converting person to JSON

```
import java.time.{LocalDate, Period}         Importing the
import io.circe._                            circe library

case class Person(fullName: String, dateOfBirth: LocalDate)

object Person {
                                             The trait Encoder
                                             defines how to convert
  given personEncoder: Encoder[Person] with {   an instance into a
    def apply(p: Person): Json = {           JSON object.
      val age = Period.between(
        p.dateOfBirth, LocalDate.now()
      ).getYears                             Computing the age
      Json.obj(                              based on today's
        "fullName" -> Json.fromString(p.fullName),  date and their date
        "age" -> Json.fromInt(age)           of birth
      )
    }
  }
}
```

Your encoder calculates it on the fly from the person's date of birth when converting an instance into JSON to ensure that the field age is always up to date. After defining an encoder, you can import the package io.circe.syntax._ and use its asJson function to perform the encoding. The method asJson has the following (simplified) signature:

```
def asJson[A](using encoder: Encoder[A]): Json
```

You can use it to convert a Person instance to JSON in the following way:

```
scala> import io.circe.syntax._
import io.circe.syntax._
// it includes several helper functions such as asJson

scala> val p = Person("John Doe", LocalDate.of(1987, 11, 22))
val p: Person = Person(John Doe,1987-11-22)

scala> val json = p.asJson
val json: io.circe.Json =
{
  "fullName" : "John Doe",
  "age" : 32
}
// it returns an instance of type io.circe.Json

scala> json.toString
val res0: String =
{
  "fullName" : "John Doe",
  "age" : 32
}
// it returns an instance of type String
```

The library circe uses the type class pattern to define a conversion to JSON for any instance. You can convert any type T to JSON that has an instance of Encoder[T]. It has a predefined set of encoders for basic types, ready for you to use:

```
scala> import io.circe.syntax._
import io.circe.syntax._

scala> List("Hello", "World").asJson
val res0: io.circe.Json =
[
  "Hello",
  "World"
]

scala> Map(1 -> "Scala").asJson
val res1: io.circe.Json =
{
  "1" : "Scala"
}
```

```
scala> import java.time.LocalDate
import java.time.LocalDate

scala> LocalDate.of(1985, 5, 12).asJson
val res2: io.circe.Json = "1985-05-12"
```

When using case classes, you can request to generate an encoder for them automatically.

Listing 48.3 Deriving an encoder for Person

```
import java.time.LocalDate

import io.circe._
import io.circe.generic.semiauto._
```
Importing the package that contains the encoder generation

```
case class Person(fullName: String, dateOfBirth: LocalDate)

object Person {

  given personEncoder: Encoder[Person] = deriveEncoder[Person]
}
```
Derivation of an encoder based on the structure of the case class

The generated encoder analyzes the structure of a case class to define a new encoder. For example, the derived instance for Encoder[Person] produces the following JSON representation; it does not contain the logic to compute the person's age, but it shows the date of birth:

```
scala> import io.circe.syntax._
import io.circe.syntax._

scala> val p = Person("John Doe", LocalDate.of(1987, 11, 22))
val p: Person = Person(John Doe,1987-11-22)

scala> p.asJson
val res0: io.circe.Json =
{
  "fullName" : "John Doe",
  "dateOfBirth" : "1987-11-22"
}
```

Quick Check 48.1 The library circe uses the ISO-8601 format to convert a local date to its text representation by default:

```scala
scala> import java.time.LocalDate
import java.time.LocalDate

scala> import io.circe.syntax._
import io.circe.syntax._

scala> LocalDate.of(1981,7, 25).asJson
val res0: io.circe.Json = "1981-07-25"
```

Define a new encoder for LocalDate to convert dates using the following date formatter instead:

```scala
import java.time.format.DateTimeFormatter
val formatter = DateTimeFormatter.ofPattern("MM/dd/yyyy")
```

HINT: You can use the function formatter.format(myDate) to convert an instance myDate of type LocalDate to String.

48.3 JSON deserialization: From JSON to instance

Let's consider your application to track people's names and ages, and imagine that it also offers an HTTP API to send new records using the following JSON structure:

```json
{  "fullName" : "John Doe",  "dateOfBirth" : "1987-11-22" }
```

Listing 48.4 Converting JSON to Person

```scala
import java.time.LocalDate         Importing the
import io.circe._                  circe library

case class Person(fullName: String, dateOfBirth: LocalDate)

object Person {                              The trait Decoder
                                             defines how to parse
                                             a JSON object into
  given personDecoder: Decoder[Person] with {   an instance.

    def apply(c: HCursor): Either[DecodingFailure, Person] =
      for {
                        The parsing that either results in a decoding
                            failure or returns a Person instance
```

```
        fullName <- c.downField("fullName").as[String]
        dateOfBirth <- c.downField("dateOfBirth").as[LocalDate]
      } yield Person(fullName, dateOfBirth)
    }
  }
```

Selecting a field with name dateOfBirth
and converting it to LocalDate

Finding a field with name fullName
and parsing it as String

The function downField selects a JSON component by a given name. Then the function
as[T] uses the decoder for T to parse and produce a value of its type. Once you have
defined a decoder, you can import the package io.circe.parser._ and use its decode
function to produce an instance representing the JSON structure. The function decode
has the following (simplified) signature:

```
def decode[A](input: String)(using decoder: Decoder[A]): Either[Error, A]
```

It returns a value of type Person if the parsing is successful. Otherwise, it returns an
error. A few examples of how to use the decode function are the following:

```
scala> import io.circe.parser._
import io.circe.parser._

scala> val goodData: String =
""" { "fullName": "John Doe", "dateOfBirth": "1987-11-22" } """

val goodData: String = " { "fullName": "John Doe", "dateOfBirth":
        "1987-11-22" } "
// Using triple quotes when defining a String allows you
// to automatically escape any special character, such as " or \

scala> decode[Person](goodData)
val res0: Either[io.circe.Error,Person] = Right(Person(John Doe,1987-
        11-22))
// The decoding was successful

scala> val badData: String = """ { "fullName": "John Doe" } """
val badData: String = " { "fullName": "John Doe" } "

scala> decode[Person](badData)
val res1: Either[io.circe.Error,Person] = Left(DecodingFailure(Attempt
        to decode value on failed cursor,
        List(DownField(dateOfBirth))))
// The decoding fails because the field dateOfBirth is missing
```

The library circe offers a set of predefined decoders for commonly used types:

```
scala> import io.circe.parser._
import io.circe.parser._

scala> decode[List[String]](""" ["Hello", "World"] """)
val res0: Either[io.circe.Error,List[String]] = Right(List(Hello, World))

scala> decode[Map[Int, String]](""" { "1": "Scala" } """)
val res1: Either[io.circe.Error,Map[Int,String]] = Right(Map(1 -> Scala))

scala> import java.time.LocalDate
import java.time.LocalDate

scala> decode[LocalDate]("1985-05-12")
val res2: Either[io.circe.Error,java.time.LocalDate] =
        Left(io.circe.ParsingFailure: expected whitespace or eof got
        '-05-12' (line 1, column 5))
// The text '1985-05-12' is not a valid JSON

scala> decode[LocalDate](""" "1985-05-12" """)
val res3: Either[io.circe.Error,java.time.LocalDate] = Right(1985-05-12)
// The text ' "1985-05-12" ' is a valid
// JSON representation for LocalDate
```

When using case classes, circe can automatically infer a decoder by analyzing their structure.

Listing 48.5 Deriving a decoder for Person

```
import java.time.LocalDate

import io.circe._
import io.circe.generic.semiauto._          ←  Importing the package
                                               that contains the
                                               decoder generation

case class Person(fullName: String, dateOfBirth: LocalDate)

object Person {

  given personDecoder: Decoder[Person] = deriveDecoder[Person]   ←
}
                                             Derivation decoder based on the
                                             structure of the case class
```

The decoder circe generated in listing 48.5 is equivalent to the one you implemented in listing 48.4.

> **Quick Check 48.2** The library circe uses the ISO-8601 format to decode a JSON string into a local date instance by default:
>
> ```scala
> scala> import java.time.LocalDate
> import java.time.LocalDate
>
> scala> import io.circe.parser._
> import io.circe.parser._
>
> scala> decode[LocalDate](""" "1981-07-25" """)
> val res0: Either[io.circe.Error,java.time.LocalDate] =
>           Right(1981-07-25)
> ```
>
> Define a new decoder for LocalDate to convert to dates using the following date formatter instead:
>
> ```scala
> import java.time.format.DateTimeFormatter
> val formatter = DateTimeFormatter.ofPattern("MM/dd/yyyy")
> ```
>
> HINT: You can use the method LocalDate.parse(myDate, formatter), which converts an instance myDate of type String to LocalDate.

Summary

In this lesson, my objective was to show you how to use the library circe to serialize and deserialize data into JSON format.

- You learned how to define an encoder to convert a Scala instance into a JSON structure.
- You discovered how to define a decoder to generate a Scala instance from a JSON representation.
- You saw how you can automatically derive encoders and decoders for case classes.

Let's see if you got this!

> **TRY THIS** Consider the following case class to represent a book:
>
> ```scala
> case class Book(title: String,
>                 authors: List[String],
>                 tags: Set[String])
> ```
>
> Serialize and deserialize its instances to JSON using the circe library.

Answers to quick checks

Quick Check 48.1   The new encoder for LocalDate should look similar to the following:

```scala
import java.time.LocalDate
import io.circe._

given dateEncoder: Encoder[LocalDate] with {
  def apply(date: LocalDate): Json =
    Json.fromString(formatter.format(date))
}
```

You can now import the new encoder in your local implicit scope and circe will use it when converting local dates:

```scala
scala> import io.circe.syntax._
import io.circe.syntax._

scala> LocalDate.of(1981,7,25).asJson
val res0: io.circe.Json = "25/07/1981"
```

Quick Check 48.2   A possible implementation for the local date decoder is as follows:

```scala
import java.time.LocalDate
import io.circe._

given dateDecoder: Decoder[LocalDate] with {
  override def apply(
    c: HCursor): Either[DecodingFailure, LocalDate] =
    c.as[String].map(text => LocalDate.parse(text, formatter))
}
```

After adding the decoder into your implicit scope, you can use it to convert to dates using the new format:

```scala
scala> import io.circe.parser._
import io.circe.parser._

scala> decode[LocalDate](""" "11/22/1987" """)
val res0: Either[io.circe.Error,java.time.LocalDate] =
        Right(1987-11-22)
```

LAZY EVALUATION

After reading this lesson, you'll be able to

- Implement functions that use by-name parameters
- Initialize a value lazily by using the keyword *lazy*

Now that you've mastered JSON serialization and deserialization, you'll learn about lazy evaluation. You already encountered examples of lazy evaluations when discussing Scala collections. For example, the function getOrElse(key: K, default: => V) acting on an instance of type Map[K,V] has two parameters: key, which is eagerly evaluated (or called by value), and default, which is lazily evaluated (or called by name). In this lesson, you'll see how to evaluate parameters by name (i.e., lazy evaluation), rather than by value (i.e., eager evaluation). You'll also learn how to initialize values lazily using the keyword *lazy*. This can be useful when its initialization is expensive either in terms of time or resources. In the capstone, you'll implement the logic and API layer of your quiz application using a type called IO, which allows you to represent computations lazily.

> **Consider this**
> Imagine you are developing a program that relies on a third-party HTTP API to validate postcodes. Unfortunately, network issues outside of your control can cause errors in your application, and you'd like to implement an automatic retry system for any of those problematic HTTP calls. How would you implement this?

 ## 49.1 By-name parameters

Suppose you are developing a game in which players roll one six-sided die to determine the outcome of actions they wish to perform. They succeed if they roll 4 or higher. Its implementation is the following:

```scala
import scala.util.Random

def rollDie(): Int = {
  // selecting random number between 1 inclusive and 7 exclusive
  val n = Random.nextInt(6) + 1
  println(s"Rolled $n...")
  if (n < 4) throw new IllegalStateException(s"Failure! Rolled $n")
  else n
}
```

On some occasions, players can reroll the die up to two more times.

Listing 49.1 Rerolling die: Eager evaluation

```scala
import scala.annotation.tailrec          ◄──  Using the @tailrec
import scala.util.Try                          annotation to ensure the
                                               function is tail recursive
@tailrec                              ◄────                                Evaluating
def retry[T](n: Int, operation: T): Try[T] = {           ◄────            operation
  val result = Try(operation)            ◄────                            by value
  if (result.isFailure && n > 0) retry(n -1, operation)
  else result                                      Wrapping any exception
}                                                  the function may throw
```

The annotation @tailrec ensures the recursive function is tail recursive, which means it is safe to use as the compiler can optimize it at compile time and not exhaust its function call stack. It will produce a compilation error if it detects your function is not tail recursive. Let's call the retry function to reroll the die and see if it behaves as expected:

```
scala> retry(n = 2, rollDie())
Rolled 4...
val res0: scala.util.Try[Int] = Success(4)
// Success! The first roll gave you a 4, so no re-roll is needed.

scala> retry(n = 2, rollDie())
Rolled 1...
java.lang.IllegalStateException: Failure! Rolled 1
  at .rollDie(<console>:16)
  ... 28 elided
// What? Something doesn't look right...
```

Something unexpected happens: your program doesn't reroll the die for numbers lower than 4, and the exception that rollDie throws leaks outside your function rather than is contained inside the Try class.

By default, Scala evaluates a function parameter by value (i.e., eager evaluation): it computes its value and then passes it to the function. However, there are cases where you may want to evaluate a parameter when the function invokes it, not before; you can refer to this as *parameter evaluated by name* (i.e., lazy evaluation). Use the symbol => to indicate that your program should evaluate a parameter by name. When declaring that your code should evaluate a parameter T by name, the compiler transforms it to a function parameter that takes no parameters, and it returns a value of type T (i.e., with shape () => T).

Listing 49.2 Rerolling die: Lazy evaluation

```
import scala.annotation.tailrec
import scala.util.Try

@tailrec
def retry[T](n: Int, operation: => T): Try[T] = {        ← Evaluating
  val result = Try(operation)                                operation
  if (result.isFailure && n > 0) retry(n -1, operation)      by name
  else result
}
```

The retry function now behaves as expected:

```
scala> retry(n = 2, rollDie())
Rolled 1...
```

```
Rolled 5...
val res0: scala.util.Try[Int] = Success(5)
// Success on the second try

scala> retry(n = 2, rollDie())
Rolled 6...
val res1: scala.util.Try[Int] = Success(6)
// Success on the first try

scala> retry(n = 2, rollDie())
Rolled 3...
Rolled 1...
Rolled 2...
val res2: scala.util.Try[Int] =
          Failure(java.lang.IllegalStateException: Failure! Rolled 2)
// A bit of bad luck: failure even after two re-rolls
```

Figure 49.1 shows the execution flow comparison between eager and lazy evaluations of parameters.

> **Quick Check 49.1** Consider the following functions. What is the behavior of their function calls? Use the REPL to validate your hypotheses.
>
> ```
> def fooByValue(n: Int): Int = n + n
> fooByValue { println("Scala"); 21 }
>
> def fooByName(n: => Int): Int = n + n
> fooByName { println("Scala"); 21 }
> ```

 ## 49.2 Lazy values

Imagine that the game you are developing gives players access to statistics about their past games. As your game becomes more and more popular, regular users start complaining about long loading times. After some investigation, you discover that the player statistics' initialization takes a long time.

VERSUS

EAGER EVALUATION PARAMETERS BY VALUE	LAZY EVALUATION PARAMETERS BY NAME

```scala
import scala.annotation.tailrec
import scala.util.Try

@tailrec
def retry[T](n: Int, operation: T):
Try[T] = {
  val result = Try(operation)
  if (result.isFailure && n > 0)
    retry(n -1, operation)
  else result
}
```

```scala
import scala.annotation.tailrec
import scala.util.Try

@tailrec
def retry[T](n: Int, operation: => T):
Try[T] = {
  val result = Try(operation)
  if (result.isFailure && n > 0)
    retry(n -1, operation)
  else result
}
```

```
1) retry(2, rollDie())

2) retry(2, <exception thrown>)   "Rolled 1..."

3) <exception thrown>
```

```
1) retry(2, rollDie())

2) { val result = Try(rollDie())
     if (result.isFailure && 2 > 0)
       retry(2 -1, rollDie())
     else result }

3) { val result = Failure(<exception thrown>)   "Rolled 1..."
     if (true && true)
       retry(2-1, rollDie())
     else result }

4) retry(1, rollDie())

5) { val result = Try(rollDie())
     if (result.isFailure && 1 > 0)
       retry(1, rollDie())
     else result }

6) { val result = Success(5)   "Rolled 5..."
     if (false && true)
       retry(1-1, rollDie())
     else result }

7) Success(5)
```

Figure 49.1 Execution flow comparison between eager and lazy evaluation. When passing the parameter by value (i.e., eagerly evaluating it), your program will first evaluate it, then use it in the function. When using a parameter by name (i.e., lazily evaluating it), your program will first pass it to the function, then evaluate it every time it is invoked.

Listing 49.3 Eagerly loading player stats

```scala
class Stats(playerId: Long) {
  /* some meaningful stats loaded here */

  // Sleeping here to simulate a slow operation
  Thread.sleep(10000) // 10 seconds
}
```

```scala
class Player(id: Long, name: String) {
  val stats: Stats = new Stats(id)
}
```

The initialization of each player now takes at least 10 seconds:

```scala
scala> import java.time._
     | val start = Instant.now()
     | val alice = new Player(1, "Alice")
     | val duration = Duration.between(start, Instant.now())
     | println(s"Took ${duration.getSeconds} seconds!")

Took 10 seconds!
val start: java.time.Instant = 2021-06-03T13:30:48.250Z
val alice: Player = Player@f53ebe2
val duration: java.time.Duration = PT10.01S
```

Scala eagerly evaluates values: your program initializes the field stats as part of the Player instance's initialization. A possible solution is to run stats as an asynchronous computation by wrapping it into a Future type. Another solution is to request the lazy evaluation for the field stats using the keyword *lazy*.

Listing 49.4 **Lazily loading player stats**

```scala
class Stats(playerId: Long) {
  /* some meaningful stats loaded here */

  // Sleeping here to simulate a slow operation
  Thread.sleep(10000) // 10 seconds
}



class Player(id: Long, name: String) {
  lazy val stats: Stats = new Stats(id)
}
```

It is evaluated the first time it is invoked, not during initialization.

Your program delays the evaluation of lazy values until their first invocation. The initialization of each player is no longer slow:

```scala
scala> import java.time._
     | val startA = Instant.now()
     | val alice = new Player(1, "Alice")
     | val durationA = Duration.between(startA, Instant.now())
     | println(s"Took ${durationA.getSeconds} seconds!")
```

```
Took 0 seconds!
import java.time._
val startA: java.time.Instant = 2021-06-03T13:32:10.343Z
val alice: Player = Player@3cfc3dd0
val durationA: java.time.Duration = PT0.001S
```

Loading the player statistics still takes 10 seconds, but your program does this the first time it invokes that field:

```
scala> import java.time._
     | val startB = Instant.now()
     | alice.stats
     | val durationB = Duration.between(startB, Instant.now())
     | println(s"Took ${durationB.getSeconds} seconds!")

Took 10 seconds!
import java.time._
val startB: java.time.Instant = 2021-06-03T13:32:56.068Z
val durationB: java.time.Duration = PT10.005S
```

Figure 49.2 provides a syntax diagram of how to declare lazy values.

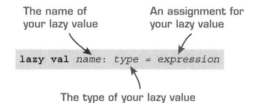

The name of   An assignment for
your lazy value   your lazy value

`lazy val` *name*: *type* = *expression*

The type of your lazy value

Figure 49.2 Syntax diagram of lazy values in Scala. Your program delays the initialization of a lazy value until its first invocation.

Quick Check 49.2 Consider the following snippet of code. What does it return? Why? What would happen if a wasn't lazy? Use the REPL to validate your hypothesis. Note: Make sure to evaluate all the instructions at the same time by copying and pasting the whole snippet of code in the REPL.

```
lazy val a = b
val b = "hello"
a.length
```

Summary

In this lesson, my objective was to compare eager and lazy evaluation in Scala.

- You learned how to pass parameters to function by value rather than by name.
- You saw how to delay the initialization of a value to its first invocation using the keyword *lazy*.

Let's see if you got this!

> **TRY THIS** In this lesson, you saw how to measure duration in seconds of two specific operations: initializing a player and retrieving its game statistics. Reuse the same logic to define a function, called `timed`, to measure the execution time in seconds of any operation.

Answers to quick checks

> **Quick Check 49.1** Both function calls return the value 42. However, the function fooByName prints the text "Scala" to the console twice, while fooByValue does it only once:
>
> ```scala
> scala> def fooByValue(n: Int): Int = n + n
> def fooByValue: (n: Int)Int
>
> scala> fooByValue { println("Scala"); 21 }
> Scala
> val res0: Int = 42
>
> scala> def fooByName(n: => Int): Int = n + n
> def fooByName: (n: => Int)Int
>
> scala> fooByName { println("Scala"); 21 }
> Scala
> Scala
> val res1: Int = 42
> ```

> **Quick Check 49.2** The snippet of code returns the number 5:
>
> ```scala
> scala> lazy val a = b
>      | val b = "hello"
>      | a.length
> ```

```
val a: String = <lazy>
val b: String = hello
val res0: Int = 5
```

The REPL initially does not assign a value to a, but it displays the message a: String = <lazy>. Then, it assigns b to the text "hello." It eventually initializes the value a when executing the instruction a.length, which returns the integer 5. If you do not mark the value a as lazy, the snippet of code throws a NullPointerException:

```
scala> val a = b
     | val b = "hello"
     | a.length
             ^
     warning: Reference to uninitialized value b
java.lang.NullPointerException: Cannot invoke "String.length()"
        because the return value of "a()" is null
   ... 32 elided
```

THE IO TYPE

After reading this lesson, you will be able to

- Represent synchronous and asynchronous side effects lazily
- Execute and process their result

Now that you've mastered the difference between eager and lazy evaluation, you are going to learn about cats.effect.IO. Impure functions produce side effects. The type IO, which is part of the cats-effect library, allows you to represent synchronous and asynchronous side effects lazily. You'll be able to separate the definition of what to execute from its actual execution, making it easier to maintain and test. You can consider the type IO as the lazy alternative to the eagerly evaluated Future. After discussing why lazily evaluating side effects can be advantageous, you'll see how to represent and execute side effects that are either synchronous or asynchronous. In the capstone, you'll use the type IO to define side effects in your quiz application.

> **Consider this**
> Imagine you are developing an application that accesses the list of transactions of a bank account. You need to log the date, the name of the user executing the operation, and the account number for security reasons. You'd like to write tests to ensure this happens as expected. How would you implement this?

50.1 Why IO?

In the previous unit, you learned that the type Future can improve your application's scalability and runtime performance by running expensive computations in the background. With time and experience, you will notice some of its stylistic disadvantages.

Most of your functions will return a value of type Future for good reason. You do not want to block your program waiting for the result of your asynchronous computation unless strictly necessary to gain the maximum performance benefit; functions that invoke functions returning Future values often return Future instances themselves. Most of them will also have an implicit ExecutionContext parameter. Your program eagerly evaluates Future value (i.e., it starts their execution as soon as it initializes them), so it must know how to run them, such as how many threads and retry policies to use.

Futures can also be challenging to understand.

Listing 50.1 Future is not referentially transparent

```scala
import scala.concurrent.{ExecutionContext, Future}

def fooA(using ec: ExecutionContext): Future[Int] = {
  def future = Future { println("Scala"); 5 }        ←  future is a function:
  for {                                                  you re-initialize it at
    a <- future                                          every invocation.
    b <- future
  } yield a + b
}

def fooB(using ec: ExecutionContext): Future[Int] = {
  val future = Future { println("Scala"); 5 }        ←  future is a value:
  for {                                                  you initialize it
    a <- future                                          only once.
    b <- future
  } yield a + b
}
```

The two functions are almost identical: future is a function in fooA, while it is a value in fooB. This minor detail drastically changes the two functions' behavior: fooA prints the text "Scala" twice, while fooB does it only once.

```scala
scala> fooA
Scala
```

```
Scala
val res0: scala.concurrent.Future[Int] = Future(<not completed>)

scala> fooB
Scala
val res1: scala.concurrent.Future[Int] = Future(<not completed>)
```

The type Future is not referentially transparent: you cannot replace its invocation with its returned value and be confident you will obtain the same result.

The type IO provides a solution to these problems by providing an alternative way to represent side effects lazily rather than eagerly. You evaluate its instances on demand rather than at initialization. You'll create a description of your computation (i.e., *what* to do), and then execute it by invoking a function in which you provide information on what resources to use (i.e., *how* to do it). The type IO is also referentially transparent, thanks to its clear separation between description and execution.

Listing 50.2 IO is referentially transparent

```
import cats.effect.IO

def fooA: IO[Int] = {                            io is a
  def io = IO { println("Scala"); 5 }    ←       function.
  for {
    a <- io
    b <- io
  } yield a + b
}

def fooB: IO[Int] = {                            io is a
  val io = IO { println("Scala"); 5 }    ←       value.
  for {
    a <- io
    b <- io
  } yield a + b
}
```

One is declaring io as a function, the other as a value, but this does not affect their behavior because the type IO is referentially transparent:

```
scala> val resultA = fooA
val resultA: cats.effect.IO[Int] = IO$976545953
// This is just the description of the task
```

```
scala> resultA.unsafeRunSync()
Scala
Scala
val res0: Int = 10
// Actually running the task

scala> val resultB = fooB
val resultB: cats.effect.IO[Int] = IO$976545953
scala> resultB.unsafeRunSync()
Scala
Scala
val res1: Int = 10
// fooA and fooB are equivalent!
```

The type IO is extremely powerful, and it has several other advantages. For example, the type IO is cancellable while Future is not. In this book, you'll learn only the basics about the IO type. (See https://typelevel.org/cats-effect to learn more about what you can achieve with it.)

 ## 50.2 Project setup

The type IO is not a standard type of the Scala language: you need to add the cats-effect library as your dependency before using it. Let's create an empty sbt project by defining the project/build.properties and build.sbt files.

Listing 50.3 An empty sbt project

```
// file project/build.properties

sbt.version = 1.5.2



// file build.sbt

name := "get-programming-wil-scala-lesson50"

version := "0.1"

scalaVersion := "3.0.0"
```

You can add the cats-effect library by adding the following configuration to your build.sbt file.

Listing 50.4 Adding cats-effect as an external dependency

```
// file build.sbt

libraryDependencies += "org.typelevel" %% "cats-effect" % "2.5.1"
```

Run the command sbt console in your project's root directory to launch sbt, download all its external dependencies, and load them into a Scala REPL session.

 ## 50.3 Synchronous side effect

Let's consider the function you wrote to roll one six-sided die for your game application in the previous lesson:

```
import scala.util.Random

def rollDie(): Int = {
    val n = Random.nextInt(6) + 1
    println(s"Rolled $n...")
    if (n < 4) throw new IllegalStateException(s"Failure! Rolled $n")
    else n
}
```

The function rollDie is impure because it has several side effects: it selects a random number, it prints a message to the console, and it throws an exception when the rolled number is not high enough.

Listing 50.5 Describing how to roll a die using IO.apply

```
import cats.effect.IO          ←——  Adding the type IO
import scala.util.Random             to the scope

def rollDie(): IO[Int] = IO {   ←——  Invoking the method IO.apply to
    val n = Random.nextInt(6) + 1     represent the synchronous side effect;
    println(s"Rolled $n...")          you can omit the apply function name.
    if (n < 4) throw new IllegalStateException(s"Failure! Rolled $n")
    else n
}
```

When calling the rollDie method, you will describe the side effect without evaluating it. When ready to do so, you can call its unsafeRunSync method:

```
scala> val myRoll = rollDie()
val myRoll: cats.effect.IO[Int] = IO$81277280
// The representation of the side effect

scala> myRoll.unsafeRunSync()
Rolled 4...
val res0: Int = 4
// Rolling the die: the execution returns a 4

scala> myRoll.unsafeRunSync()
Rolled 2...
java.lang.IllegalStateException: Failure! Rolled 2
  at .$anonfun$rollDie$1(<pastie>:7)
// Another roll: the execution throws an exception
```

When working with side effects, you can use the type IO to represent them by separating their description from their execution. The function IO.apply allows you to define a synchronous side effect. You can then use the method unsafeRunSync to run it synchronously.

Listing 50.6 IO.apply and unsafeRunSync

```
package cats.effect

class IO[A] {
  def unsafeRunSync(): A = ???
}

object IO {
  def apply[A](body: => A): IO[A] = ???
}
```

All the methods that evaluate a side effect use the word *unsafe*. This reminds you that they are impure functions that produce side effects. Be mindful when invoking them: calling them one or multiple times will change your program's behavior. Table 50.1 provides a summary of the methods you can use when representing synchronous side effects lazily.

Table 50.1 Summary of the main methods to use the type IO when coding with synchronous side effects. The function `apply` initializes a synchronous side effect without executing it. The method `unsafeRunSync` then allows you to evaluate it and produce a value as its result.

	Acts on	**Signature**	**Usage**
apply	IO	apply[A](body: => A): IO[A]	It describes a synchronous side effect lazily.
unsafeRunSync	IO[A]	unsafeRunSync(): A	It executes a side effect synchronously, and it returns its value.

Quick Check 50.1 The function `scala.io.StdIn.readLine()` allows you to read text from the terminal. Implement a function called `read` to describe this side effect using the type IO. Use the Scala REPL to execute it and type your name.

 ## 50.4 Asynchronous side effect

Let's consider your game application again and its functionality of loading statics of the player's previous games. Imagine you have the following function to compute the player's statistics:

```scala
class Stats(playerId: Long) {
  /* some meaningful stats loaded here */
  println(s"Loading statistics for player $playerId...")

  // Sleeping here to simulate a slow operation
  Thread.sleep(10000) // 10 seconds
}

object Stats {

  def load(playerId: Long): Stats = new Stats(playerId)

}
```

This operation is a side effect because its outcome depends on its historical data. It is also known to be slow at times, so you'd like to make it asynchronous.

Listing 50.7 Describing how to load the player's statistics

```
import cats.effect.IO                          ←──────  Adding the type
                                                         IO to the scope
class Stats(val playerId: Long) {
  /* some meaningful stats loaded here */
  println(s"Loading statistics for player $playerId...")

  // Sleeping here to simulate a slow operation
  Thread.sleep(10000) // 10 seconds
}
                                                  Calling the function
                                                  IO.async to represent the
object Stats {                                    asynchronous side effect

  def load(playerId: Long): IO[Stats] = IO.async { callback =>
    val either: Either[Throwable, Stats] = Right(new Stats(playerId))
    callback(either)
  }

}
```

Invoking the function Stats.load will give you a description of the side effect. You need to invoke one of the available functions to execute it. For example, you could use its method unsafeRunAsync:

```
scala> val myStats = Stats.load(1)
val myStats: cats.effect.IO[Stats] = IO$287324394

scala> myStats.unsafeRunAsync {
     |    case Left(ex) => println(s"Error: $ex")
     |    case Right(_) => println(s"Success!")
     | }
Loading statistics for player 1...
Success!
```

You can also use its function unsafeRunAsyncAndForget not to process its result further:

```
scala> myStats.unsafeRunAsyncAndForget()
Loading statistics for player 1...
```

You typically use this operation when computing side effects in the background that you are not interested in processing further, for example when saving data into a database.

You can use the function IO.async to describe a side effect your program should execute asynchronously. You can then invoke one of its methods, unsafeRunAsync or unsafeRun-AsyncAndForget, to evaluate it.

Listing 50.8 IO.async and its unsafe functions

```
package cats.effect

class IO[A] {

  def unsafeRunAsync(cb: Either[Throwable, A] => Unit): Unit = ???

  def unsafeRunAsyncAndForget(): Unit = ???

}

object IO {
  def async[A](k: (Either[Throwable, A] => Unit) => Unit): IO[A] = ???
}
```

Their signatures are relatively complex and will be confusing at first. Let's try to clarify their meaning.

When invoking the method IO.async, you need to implement a function that receives a callback as its parameter. Define the operation to run asynchronously by producing a value of type Either, and finally feed it back to the callback.

```
val myIO = IO.async { callback =>
  // result is an instance of type Either!
  val result: Either[Throwable, A] = ??? // your operation here
  callback(result)
}
```

When evaluating the side effect, you will receive the result that the last callback produced. The function unsafeRunAsync allows you process it on completion of its execution:

```
myIO.unsafeRunAsync {
  case Left(ex) => // do something with the error
  case Right(value) => // do something with the value
}
```

You can use its method unsafeRunAsyncAndForget if you do not wish to process its result:

```
myIO.unsafeRunAsyncAndForget()
```

Both functions unsafeRunAsync and unsafeRunAsyncAndForget return Unit; their behavior is comparable to Future.onComplete. Table 50.2 recaps the methods you have seen to describe and evaluate asynchronous side effects lazily.

Table 50.2 Recap of the functions you can use to represent and evaluate asynchronous side effects using the type IO

	Acts on	Signature	Usage

async	IO	async[A](
		  k: (Either[Throwable, A]
		  => Unit) => Unit): IO[A]
			It describes an asynchronous side effect lazily.

unsafeRunAsync	IO[A]	unsafeRunAsync[A](
		  cb: Either[Throwable, A]
		  => Unit): Unit
			It evaluates a side effect asynchronously and uses a given callback to process its result before discarding its value.

unsafeRunAsync AndForget	IO[A]	unsafeRunAsyncAndForget(): Unit	It runs a side effect asynchronously and discards its value.

You can also use unsafeRunSync to execute an asynchronous side effect: this will run synchronously and give you a value in return. This approach can be useful when running tests but extremely inefficient in your production code because it impacts your application's runtime performance.

> **Quick Check 50.2** Implement a function convertToIO to convert a Future instance into one of type IO using the IO.async function.
>
> ```
> import cats.effect.IO
> import scala.concurrent.{ExecutionContext, Future}
>
> def convertToIO[T](future: => Future[T])
>                   (using ec: ExecutionContext): IO[T]
> ```

 **Summary**

In this lesson, my objective was to introduce you to the type IO from the cats-effect library.

- You learned that representing side effects with a lazy approach can make your code less prone to errors.

- You saw how to describe and execute synchronous impure computations using the methods IO.apply and unsafeRunSync.
- You discovered how to represent and run asynchronous side effects using IO.async, unsafeRunAsync, and unsafeRunAsyncAndForget.

Let's see if you got this!

> **TRY THIS** Consider the following snippet of code that prints the list of files in the current directory:
>
> ```
> import java.io.File
> new File(".").listFiles().foreach(println)
> ```
>
> In lesson 43, you used Future to execute this operation asynchronously; implement it using IO instead.

 ## Answers to quick checks

> **Quick Check 50.1** The implementation for your read function should look like the following:
>
> ```
> import cats.effect.IO
>
> def read: IO[String] = IO(scala.io.StdIn.readLine())
> ```
>
> You can execute it using its method unsafeRunSync:
>
> ```
> scala> read.unsafeRunSync()
> // the cursor waits for you to type,
> // and it returns it after you press the enter key.
> val res0: String = Daniela
> ```

> **Quick Check 50.2** A possible implementation for your function convertToIO is the following:
>
> ```
> import cats.effect.IO
>
> import scala.concurrent.{ExecutionContext, Future}
> import scala.util.{Failure, Success}
>
> def convertToIO[T](future: => Future[T])
>                   (using ec: ExecutionContext): IO[T] =
> ```

```
    IO.async { callback =>
        future.onComplete {
          case Success(t) => callback(Right(t))
          case Failure(ex) => callback(Left(ex))
        }
    }
```

Note that the function passes the parameter future by name as you need to ensure your program executes it after receiving the callback, not before.

WORKING WITH THE IO TYPE

After reading this lesson, you will be able to

- Manipulate values produced by side effects using the map and flatMap operations
- Compute multiple IO instances in sequence using for-comprehension
- Execute side effects in parallel to maximize the resource of your program

In the previous lesson, you learned the basics of the type IO. You'll now see how to compose smaller side effects to create programs you can lazily describe and run. You'll master how to use the map and flatMap operations to manipulate values that impure functions produce. You'll discover how to combine them in sequence using for-comprehension. Also, you'll see how to run them in parallel using the parSequence method. In the capstone, you'll combine multiple IO instances to define the operations of your quiz application.

> **Consider this**
> Imagine your program has two functions using IO to print a message to the console and read from it. How would you compose these functions to create a program that asks for the names of your users and greets them accordingly?

51.1 The map and flatMap operations

The IO type offers implementations for the map and flatMap methods. They are consistent with those for Future and the other types you have encountered thus far. Let's recap their usage in the following sections. You are going to code using the IO type. Do not forget to add cats-effect as an external dependency for your sbt project by adding the following instruction to your build.sbt file:

```
libraryDependencies += "org.typelevel" %% "cats-effect" % "2.5.1"
```

51.1.1 The map function

Suppose you are developing a game that rolls one six-sided die using the following function:

```
import scala.util.Random
import cats.effect.IO

def rollDie: IO[Int] = IO(Random.nextInt(6) + 1)
```

You'd like to define a new function that instead returns a message to inform the user about the rolled die.

Listing 51.1 The outcome of a rolled die

```
import scala.util.Random
import cats.effect.IO

def rollDie: IO[Int] = IO(Random.nextInt(6) + 1)

def rollOutcome: IO[String] = rollDie.map(n => s"Rolled $n!")
```

The method map for the type IO allows you to transform its value by applying a given function. For an instance of IO[A], the function map takes one parameter f of type A => B, and it produces a value of type IO[B]. It has the following signature:

```
def map[B](f: A => B): IO[B]
```

If your IO[A] produces a value of type A during its evaluation, it will apply the parameter f to it to produce a value of type IO[B]. Nothing happens if your instance of IO[A] errors during execution. A few examples of how to use it are the following:

```
scala> import cats.effect.IO
import cats.effect.IO
```

```
scala> val ioA = IO("Hello World!").map(_.length)
val ioA: cats.effect.IO[Int] = <function1>

scala> ioA.unsafeRunSync()
val res0: Int = 12

scala> val ioB = IO(5/0).map(_ + 1)
val ioB: cats.effect.IO[Int] = <function1>

scala> ioB.unsafeRunSync()
java.lang.ArithmeticException: / by zero
  at $anonfun$ioB$1(<console>:1)
  ... 1 elided
```

> **Quick Check 51.1** Define a function called parseToInt to parse a numeric text of type IO[String] and produce an instance of type IO[Int].
>
> ```
> import cats.effect.IO
>
> def parseToInt(text: IO[String]): IO[Int]
> ```

51.1.2 The flatMap function

Consider your game application again. You'd like to define a function to roll a die twice and sum the results.

Listing 51.2 Rolling a die twice using flatMap

```
import cats.effect.IO
import scala.util.Random

def rollDie: IO[Int] = IO(Random.nextInt(6) + 1)

def rollDieTwice: IO[Int] = rollDie.flatMap { n1 =>
  rollDie.map(n2 => n1 + n2)
}
```

The operation flatMap combines the map and flatten methods to chain instances in a sequence. For an instance of IO[A], the function flatMap takes one parameter f of type A => IO[B] and produces a value of type IO[B]. It has the following signature:

```
def flatMap[B](f: A => IO[B]): IO[B]
```

If your IO[A] produces a value of type A during its evaluation, it will apply the parameter f to it to produce a value of type IO[B]. Nothing happens if your instance of IO[A] errors during execution. A few examples of its usage are the following:

```scala
scala> import cats.effect.IO
import cats.effect.IO

scala> val ioA = IO("Hello World!").flatMap(n =>
          IO(println(n.length)))
val ioA: cats.effect.IO[Unit] = IO$1731931686

scala> ioA.unsafeRunSync()
12

scala> val ioB = IO(5/0).flatMap(n => IO(println(n + 1)))
val ioB: cats.effect.IO[Unit] = IO$1948471530

scala> ioB.unsafeRunSync()
java.lang.ArithmeticException: / by zero
  at $anonfun$ioB$1(<console>:1)
  ... 1 elided
```

Does the type IO have a flatten operation?

The class IO does not have an implementation of the flatten function, but you can easily add it by adding the following import to your code:

```
import cats.syntax.flatMap._
```

For example, you can do the following:

```
import cats.effect.IO
import cats.syntax.flatMap._

def rollDieTwice: IO[Int] = rollDie.map { n1 =>
  rollDie.map(n2 => n1 + n2)
}.flatten
```

There is no need to explicitly implement a function flatten because you can reimplement it using flatMap:

```
def myFlatten[T](nestedIo: IO[IO[T]]): IO[T] =
  nestedIo.flatMap(x => x)
```

This concept of defining flatten as a special case of flatMap is applicable to any type with such an operation, not just the class IO.

Table 51.1 provides a technical summary of the map and flatMap operation for the type IO.

Table 51.1 Summary of the main methods for the type IO when coding with synchronous side effects. The function apply initializes a synchronous side effect without executing it. The method unsafeRunSync will then allow you to evaluate it and produce a value as its result.

	Acts on	Signature	Usage
map	IO[A]	map[B](f: A => B): IO[B]	It applies a function to the value that the side effect produces.
flatMap	IO[A]	flatMap[B](f: A => IO[B]): IO[B]	It combines two side effects sequentially.

> **Quick Check 51.2** Consider the following function to print a message to the console:
>
> ```
> import cats.effect.IO
>
> def printToConsole(msg: String): IO[Unit] = IO(println(msg))
> ```
>
> Implement a function called printRollOutcome to print the outcome of a roll to the console by composing the printToConsole method with rollOutcome from listing 51.1.

 ## 51.2 For-comprehension

Consider the function you implemented in listing 51.2 to roll a die twice. Listing 51.3 shows you an alternative implementation for it using for-comprehension.

Listing 51.3 Rolling a die twice using for-comprehension

```
import cats.effect.IO
import scala.util.Random

def rollDie: IO[Int] = IO(Random.nextInt(6) + 1)

def rollDieTwice: IO[Int] =          Rolling the die the
  for {                              first time
    n1 <- rollDie
    n2 <- rollDie                    Rolling the die the
  } yield n1 + n2                     second time

                                     Combining the
                                     results
```

The type IO offers you implementations for the map and flatMap operations, so you can use for-comprehension as an alternative to express their combination in an ordered sequence. A few more examples are the following:

```scala
scala> import cats.effect.IO
import cats.effect.IO

scala> val myIo = for {
     |    _ <- IO(println("Hello"))
     |    _ <- IO(println("World!"))
     | } yield ()
val myIo: cats.effect.IO[Unit] = IO$23096066

scala> myIo.unsafeRunSync()
Hello
World!
// First we print "Hello", then "World!"
```

> **Quick Check 51.3** In Quick Check 51.2, you implemented a function called print-RollOutcome. Refactor it to use for-comprehension.

51.3 Parallel execution

Imagine that in the game you are developing players need to throw four different die types simultaneously.

Listing 51.4 Rolling several dice at the same time

Including the IO and
ContextShift classes

```scala
import cats.effect.{ContextShift, IO}
import cats.syntax.parallel._

import scala.util.Random

def rollDie(n: Int): IO[Int] = IO {
  println(s"Rolling $n-side die...")
  Random.nextInt(n) + 1
}
```

Adding the method
parSequence into
the scope

The rollDie function
can now handle
any-sided dice.

```
def rollDice(using cs: ContextShift[IO]): IO[List[Int]] = {
  List(rollDie(6), rollDie(8), rollDie(12), rollDie(20)).parSequence
}
```

The function parSequence
requires a ContextShift[IO]
implicit parameter.

The parSequence lazily
executes a sequence of IO
instances in parallel.

You can now define a ContextShift[IO] instance from your global execution context and execute the dice roll in parallel as the following:

```
scala> import scala.concurrent.ExecutionContext
import scala.concurrent.ExecutionContext

scala> given cs: ContextShift[IO]=
         IO.contextShift(ExecutionContext.global)
val cs: cats.effect.ContextShift[cats.effect.IO] =
         cats.effect.internals.IOContextShift@7766ce6b

scala> rollDice.unsafeRunSync()
Rolling 8-side die...
Rolling 6-side die...
Rolling 12-side die...
Rolling 20-side die...
val res0: List[Int] = List(5, 6, 9, 14)

scala> rollDice.unsafeRunSync()
Rolling 20-side die...
Rolling 6-side die...
Rolling 8-side die...
Rolling 12-side die...
val res1: List[Int] = List(3, 7, 11, 12)
```

The function parSequence allows you to execute a sequence of IO instances in parallel. For an instance of List[IO[A]], the method parSequence requires an implicit context shift, and it returns a value of type IO[List[A]]. It will run the IO instances in parallel and collect results in a list during its evaluation. You can see its behavior as analogous to Future.sequence. The class ContextShift[IO] is equivalent to ExecutionContext: it defines which resources are available to your program. You can define a context shift from an execution context instance by calling the IO.contextShift function:

```
import scala.concurrent.ExecutionContext
given cs: ContextShift[IO] = IO.contextShift(ExecutionContext.global)
```

A few more examples of how to use the parSequence methods are the following:

```scala
scala> import cats.effect.{ContextShift, IO}
     | import cats.syntax.parallel._
     | import scala.concurrent.ExecutionContext
     | given cs: ContextShift[IO] =
                        IO.contextShift(ExecutionContext.global)
import cats.effect.{ContextShift, IO}
import cats.syntax.parallel._
import scala.concurrent.ExecutionContext
val cs: cats.effect.ContextShift[cats.effect.IO] =
          cats.effect.internals.IOContextShift@460d3361

scala> val ios = List(
     | IO(println("Hello")), IO(println("World!"))).parSequence
val ios: cats.effect.IO[List[Unit]] = <function1>

scala> ios.unsafeRunSync()
World!
Hello
val res0: List[Unit] = List((), ())

scala> ios.unsafeRunSync()
Hello
World!
val res1: List[Unit] = List((), ())
```

Quick Check 51.4 Implement a function called selectionAverage to pick 100 random integers and compute their average:

```
import cats.effect.{ContextShift, IO}
def selectionAverage(using cs: ContextShift[IO]): IO[Double]
```

Use the given value randomNumber to pick one random number between 1 and 10 and perform the number selection in parallel.

```
import cats.effect.IO
import scala.util.Random

val randomNumber: IO[Int] = IO(Random.nextInt(10) + 1)
```

HINT: The expression (0 to 99).toList returns a sequence of size 100, with all the numbers from 0 to 99 inclusive.

 ## Summary

In this lesson, my objective was to teach you some of the operations you can perform on lazily evaluated side effects.

- You saw how to manipulate and transform values produced by side effects using the map and flatMap operations.
- You learned how to evaluate IO instances in an ordered sequence using for-comprehension.
- You discovered how to run several independent side effects in parallel using the parSequence function.

Let's see if you got this!

> **TRY THIS**   Using the type IO, define a small program that prints a message asking for the user's name, reads it from the console, and displays a personalized greeting message in return.

 ## Answers to quick checks

Quick Check 51.1   A possible implementation for your function parseToInt is the following:

```
import cats.effect.IO

def parseToInt(text: IO[String]): IO[Int] = text.map(_.toInt)
```

Quick Check 51.2   Your printRollOutcome function should look similar to the following:

```
import cats.effect.IO

def printRollOutcome: IO[Unit] =
    rollOutcome.flatMap(printToConsole)
```

Quick Check 51.3 You can refactor your printRollOutcome function as the following:

```scala
import cats.effect.IO

def printRollOutcome: IO[Unit] =
  for {
    n <- rollOutcome
    res <- printToConsole(n)
  } yield res
```

Quick Check 51.4 You should implement the function selectionAverage as follows:

```scala
import cats.effect.{ContextShift, IO}
import cats.syntax.parallel._

import scala.util.Random

val randomNumber: IO[Int] = IO(Random.nextInt(10) + 1)

def selectionAverage(using cs: ContextShift[IO]): IO[Double] =
  (0 to 49).toList.map(_ => randomNumber).parSequence.map {
        numbers =>
    1.0 * numbers.sum / numbers.size
  }
```

You need to provide a ContextShift[IO] instance to run it:

```scala
import scala.concurrent.ExecutionContext
given cs: ContextShift[IO] =
        IO.contextShift(ExecutionContext.global)

selectionAverage.unsafeRunSync()
// val res0: Double = 5.92
```

TESTING WITH SCALATEST

After reading this lesson, you'll be able to

- Write and run tests using ScalaTest
- Test synchronous and asynchronous code

You've been learning how to create a fully working Scala application that connects to a database, processes data asynchronously, and exposes an HTTP API. Your application must include tests to check that it behaves as expected, implements its business requirements correctly, and prevents the introduction of bugs with future code changes. This lesson completes the picture by introducing you to the basics of writing tests in Scala. You'll write tests using a popular library called ScalaTest, and you'll run them using sbt. After writing and running your first test, you'll learn how to test code that runs asynchronously. In the capstone, you'll write tests for your quiz application to check the correctness of its business logic.

> **Consider this**
>
> Suppose you wrote a weather forecast application that processes data using a third-party API. You have sample data and expected results to use during development. How would you write tests to check that your implementation behaves as expected and prevent new bugs with future code changes?

52.1 Project setup

The first step in writing tests in Scala is to pick a testing library to use. In this lesson, you'll use ScalaTest, which is among the most popular. Define an empty sbt project and specify it as one of your library dependencies in your build.sbt file by adding a configuration.

Listing 52.1 Adding ScalaTest as an external testing dependency

```
// file build.sbt

libraryDependencies +=
  "org.scalatest" %% "scalatest" % "3.2.9" % "test"
```
Declaring the dependency restricted to test only

The extra configuration % "test" indicates to use the dependency only in test code. This prevents using the library in your application's source code.

When executing the command sbt test in the root folder of your project, sbt will download your external dependencies, compile both the source and test code, and search for tests to run:

```
$ sbt test
// …
[info] Run completed in 56 milliseconds.
[info] Total number of tests run: 0
[info] Suites: completed 0, aborted 0
[info] Tests: succeeded 0, failed 0, canceled 0, ignored 0, pending 0
[info] No tests were executed.
```

You haven't written any tests yet, so it executes none.

 ## 52.2 Your first test

Suppose that you wrote a function that computes the frequency of the characters in a text. For example, for the text "test," it should count the character "t" twice and the others once. The function is called count and lives in a class called org.example.frequency.Frequency.

Listing 52.2 The count function

```
// file src/main/scala/org/example/frequency/Frequency.scala

package org.example.frequency
```
It is a source file because it is inside the directory src/main.

```
class Frequency {

  def count(text: String): Set[(Char, Int)] =
    text.groupBy(char => char).map { case (char, occurrences) =>
      char -> occurrences.length
    }.toSet

}
```

Let's write a test for it. First, let's create a test file under src/test using the same package name and define which scenarios you want to verify.

Listing 52.3 The skeleton for FrequencyTest

```
// file src/test/scala/org/example/frequency/FrequencyTest.scala
```
It is a test file because it is inside the directory src/test.

```
package org.example.frequency
```

```
import org.scalatest.flatspec.AnyFlatSpec
```
It enables the test-specific DSL.

```
class FrequencyTest extends AnyFlatSpec {
```

```
"Frequency" should "count no frequency for the empty string" in fail()
it should "count the frequency of the characters in a text" in fail()
}
```
The code elements are part of the test DSL.

The command sbt test detects the two tests as failed because they throw a NoImplementationError exception:

```
$ sbt test
// ...
[info] FrequencyTest:
[info] Frequency
[info] - should count no frequency for the empty string *** FAILED ***
[info]   org.scalatest.exceptions.TestFailedException was thrown.
          (FrequencyTest.scala:7)
[info] - should count the frequency of the characters in a text ***
          FAILED ***
[info]   org.scalatest.exceptions.TestFailedException was thrown.
          (FrequencyTest.scala:9)
[info] Run completed in 535 milliseconds.
[info] Total number of tests run: 2
[info] Suites: completed 1, aborted 0
```

```
[info] Tests: succeeded 0, failed 2, canceled 0, ignored 0, pending 0
[info] *** 2 TESTS FAILED ***
[error] Failed tests:
[error] org.example.frequency.FrequencyTest
[error] (Test / test) sbt.TestsFailedException: Tests unsuccessful
[error] Total time: 2 s, completed 5 Feb 2021, 11:18:38
```

You can now implement the tests and check if they pass.

Listing 52.4 The class FrequencyTest

```
// file src/test/scala/org/example/frequency/FrequencyTest.scala

package org.example.frequency

import org.scalatest.flatspec.AnyFlatSpec
import org.scalatest.matchers.should.Matchers

class FrequencyTest extends AnyFlatSpec with Matchers {

  val frequency = new Frequency

  "Frequency" should "count no frequency for the empty string" in {
    val result = frequency.count("")
    result.shouldEqual(Set.empty)
  }

  it should "count the frequency of the characters in a text" in {
    val result = frequency.count("test")
    val expected = Set('t' -> 2, 'e' -> 1, 's' -> 1)
    result.shouldEqual(expected)
  }
}
```

It enables the test-specific DSL.

It enables a DSL to express assertions using the verb "should."

The instance of type Frequency to test

The method shouldEqual is added to the scope by the trait Matchers.

You can now use the command sbt test to check that the tests are now passing:

```
$ sbt test
// …
[info] FrequencyTest:
[info] Frequency
[info] - should count no frequency for the empty string
[info] - should count the frequency of the characters in a text
[info] Run completed in 401 milliseconds.
[info] Total number of tests run: 2
```

```
[info] Suites: completed 1, aborted 0
[info] Tests: succeeded 2, failed 0, canceled 0, ignored 0, pending 0
[info] All tests passed.
[success] Total time: 6 s, completed 5 Feb 2021, 11:37:53
```

The ScalaTest library allows you to write tests for your Scala code. First, you need to define a class that extends one of its specification classes (e.g., org.scalatest.flatspec .AnyFlatSpec). Then you need to select one of its matchers (e.g., org.scalatest.matchers .should.Matchers) to define the style of your assertions. ScalaTest is a rich and flexible library. Its website (www.scalatest.org) offers a comprehensive list and guide on the several supported testing styles.

> **Quick Check 52.1**   You received two bug reports on your implementation of count.
> 1   The function is incorrectly counting characters that are not letters nor digits (e.g., white space, punctuation, etc.); you should ignore them.
> 2   It should consider each character as case insensitive. For example, it should add the occurrences of the character "A" to those of the character "a."
>
> For example, the text "Test test!" should return the following count (and nothing else): the character "t" four times, the characters "e" and "s" twice. Write new test scenarios to replicate the bugs and fix them.

 ## 52.3 Asynchronous testing

Suppose your program needs to compute the frequency of the characters in a file. Your implementation reuses the function count you defined previously.

Listing 52.5 **The function countFromFile**

```
package org.example.frequency

import scala.concurrent.{ExecutionContext, Future}
import scala.io.Source

class Frequency {

  def countFromFile(filename: String)
     (using ec: ExecutionContext): Future[Set[(Char, Int)]] =
     readFromFile(filename).map(count)
```

```
private def readFromFile(filename: String)
    (using ec: ExecutionContext): Future[String] =
  Future {
    val source = Source.fromFile(filename)
    try {
      source.getLines().mkString
    } finally source.close()
  }

  def count(text: String): Set[(Char, Int)] =
    text.groupBy(char => char).map { case (char, occurrences) =>
      char -> occurrences.length
    }.toSet

}
```

Executing the function asynchronously because it reads from a file, which is a slow operation

Closing the file resource to avoid memory leaks

You now want to write a test for this new asynchronous function. First, you need to create a test resource for your test. Create a new file containing the word "test" called myFile.txt in the directory src/test/resources. You can now use the specification class AsyncFlatSpec to define assertions on both synchronous and asynchronous values.

Listing 52.6 Adding an asynchronous test

```
package org.example.frequency

import org.scalatest.flatspec.AsyncFlatSpec
import org.scalatest.matchers.should

class FrequencyTest extends AsyncFlatSpec with should.Matchers {

  val frequency = new Frequency

  // …

  it should "asynchronously count characters from a file" in {
    val filename = getClass.getResource("/myFile.txt").getPath
    val result = frequency.countFromFile(filename)
    val expected = Set('t' -> 2, 'e' -> 1, 's' -> 1)
    result.map(_.shouldEqual(expected))
  }
}
```

Allows you to assert on synchronous and asynchronous values

Retrieving the path of your test resource

Defining an assertion for your asynchronous value

The specification class AnyFlatSpec offers the same testing style as AnyFlatSpec with dedicated support for values of type Future. The assertion is valid only if the Future completes successfully and its value respects the given assumption.

Quick Check 52.2 The function countFromFile currently returns an asynchronous failure if the given file does not exist. Modify its implementation to return an empty set instead. Write a test for this use case. HINT: The recover function of a Future instance allows you to define recovery values to use when throwing specific exceptions. It was the following signature:

```
def recover[T](pf: PartialFunction[Throwable, T])
              (using executor: ExecutionContext): Future[T]
```

Testing with IO: Use unsafeRunSync
If your application uses cats.effect.IO to represent asynchronous computation, you do not need dedicated support when writing tests for it. Thanks to its clear separation between the definition and the execution of some computation, you can use the function unsafeRunSync for its evaluation, which allows you to evaluate your side effects synchronously, making your tests easier to write.

 **Summary**

In this lesson, my objective was to introduce you to the basics of writing tests in Scala.

- You saw how to write a test using the specification class AnyFlatSpec from the library ScalaTest and how to run it in sbt.
- You discovered how to test asynchronous code thanks to its specification class AsyncFlatSpec.

Let's see if you got this!

TRY THIS You wrote a test that reads from a file in listing 52.6. This approach can be inconvenient because reading from an actual file is a slow operation, and you may not want to create a file for each of your test cases. Write new test cases that assert the behavior of countFromFile without relying on actual files but rather simulating (or stubbing) their content. HINT: Modify the access modifier of readFromFile from private to protected and define a new subclass of Frequency that overrides it to rely on a dictionary to link a filename to its content instead.

Answers to quick checks

Quick Check 52.1 First, you should replicate the bug by adding new test assertions and scenarios. For example, you could do something similar to the following:

```scala
class FrequencyTest extends AnyFlatSpec with should.Matchers {

  // …

  it should "count the frequency of the characters in a text" in
      {
    val resultA = frequency.count("test")
    val expectedA = Set('t' -> 2, 'e' -> 1, 's' -> 1)
    resultA.shouldEqual(expectedA)

    val resultB = frequency.count("Test test")
    val expectedB = Set('t' -> 4, 'e' -> 2, 's' -> 2)
    resultB.shouldEqual(expectedB)
  }

  it should "consider characters as case insensitive" in {
    val result = frequency.count("AaA")
    result.shouldEqual(Set('a' -> 3))
  }

  it should "consider only letters and digits" in {
    val result = frequency.count(" ,..?! ")
    result.shouldEqual(Set.empty)
  }
}
```

You should check that the new test assertions replicate the bugs:

```
$ sbt test
// …
[info] FrequencyTest:
[info] Frequency
[info] - should count no frequency for the empty string[info] -
         should count the frequency of the characters in a text
         *** FAILED ***
[info]   HashSet((T,1), ( ,1), (e,2), (t,3), (s,2)) did not equal
         Set((t,4), (e,2), (s,2)) (FrequencyTest.scala:20)
```

```
(continued)
[info]    Analysis:
[info]    HashSet(missingInLeft: [(t,4)], missingInRight: [(T,1), (
           ,1), (t,3)])
[info] - should consider characters as case insensitive *** FAILED
           ***
[info]    Set((A,2), (a,1)) did not equal Set((a,3))
           (FrequencyTest.scala:25)
[info]    Analysis:
[info]    Set(missingInLeft: [(a,3)], missingInRight: [(A,2), (a,1)])
[info] - should consider only letters and digits *** FAILED ***
[info]    HashSet((?,1), ( ,2), (!,1), (.,1), (,,1)) did not equal
           Set() (FrequencyTest.scala:30)
[info]    Analysis:
[info]    HashSet(missingInRight: [(?,1), ( ,2), (!,1), (.,1),
           (,,1)])
[info] Run completed in 433 milliseconds.
[info] Total number of tests run: 4
[info] Suites: completed 1, aborted 0
[info] Tests: succeeded 1, failed 3, canceled 0, ignored 0, pending
           0
[info] *** 3 TESTS FAILED ***
```

Finally, you change your implementation and verify that all tests are passing:

```
class Frequency {

  def count(text: String): Set[(Char, Int)] =
    text.toLowerCase.filter(_.isLetterOrDigit)
        .groupBy(char => char).map { case (char, occurrences) =>
      char -> occurrences.length
    }.toSet

}


$ sbt test
// …
[info] FrequencyTest:
[info] Frequency
[info] - should count no frequency for the empty string
[info] - should count the frequency of the characters in a text
[info] - should consider characters as case insensitive
```

```
[info] - should consider only letters and digits
[info] Run completed in 399 milliseconds.
[info] Total number of tests run: 4
[info] Suites: completed 1, aborted 0
[info] Tests: succeeded 4, failed 0, canceled 0, ignored 0,
         pending 0
[info] All tests passed.
[success] Total time: 5 s, completed 5 Feb 2021, 12:34:43
```

Quick Check 52.2 First, you add a new test case for your function countFromFile and verify that it fails:

```
it should "return the empty set if the file does not exist" in {
    val result = frequency.countFromFile("I-do-not-exist.txt")
    result.map(_.shouldEqual(Set.empty))
}
```

You can now change your implementation of countFromFile and make the tests pass:

```
def countFromFile(filename: String)
  (using ec: ExecutionContext): Future[Set[(Char, Int)]] =
  readFromFile(filename).map(count).recover {
    case _: FileNotFoundException => Set.empty
  }
```

THE QUIZ APPLICATION: PART 2

In this capstone, you will

- Lazily evaluate side effects using the type IO
- Define an HTTP API to send and receive requests using http4s
- Serialize and deserialize HTTP responses in JSON format using circe
- Write tests to assert that your business logic is correct

In this capstone, you'll complete the quiz application you started in unit 7 by defining its service and API layers. In particular, you'll implement a server that offers its users an HTTP API to perform the following operations:

- Inform about the status of your application.
- Display a list of categories a user can choose.
- Generate a quiz by randomly choosing 10 questions for a given category.
- Calculate the quiz score based on the received answers.

In your application, you'll focus on processing existing data rather than creating new data. Your database will contain preloaded data. However, you can easily add endpoints to allow users to add new categories, questions, and answers following the same patterns if you wish to do so.

You will structure your application in layers to have a clear separation of concerns (see figure 53.1):

- The DAO layer defines how to communicate with the database. It exposes records, which are a close representation of the structure of the database's tables.
- The service layer defines the business logic of your application. A service class accesses a specific DAO instance, and it returns entities, not records. Your application can expose entities through its API, so they should have JSON encoders and decoders defined for them.
- The API layer defines the structure of each endpoint. An API class does not contain any business logic since this is the responsibility of the service layer.

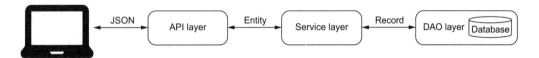

Figure 53.1 Each layer of your application has specific concerns. The DAO layer defines how to communicate with the database, and it produces records, which are a close representation of the database's tables. The service layer creates entities that the API layer can expose in JSON format. The API layer defines each endpoint's structure.

> **This lesson uses Scala 2**
> The code examples in this lesson use Scala 2 because, at the time of this publication, the library Quill doesn't support Scala 3 yet. An experimental Quill version for Scala 3 is currently under development, and it will be released once feature-complete and stable.

 ## 53.1 Download the base project

The first task you need to perform is downloading the base project you are going to use. Navigate to an empty directory and execute the following git commands to see the remote branch:

```
$ git init
$ git remote add get-prog-with-scala https://github.com/DanielaSfregola/
        get-programming-with-scala.git
$ git fetch get-prog-with-scala
$ git checkout -b my_lesson53 get-prog-with-scala/baseline_unit8_
        lesson53
```

The code contains the code you implemented in the previous unit's capstone with a few minor additions. First, your database will now have preloaded categories, questions, and answers (look at its src/main/resource/init.sql and TestDatabase object to learn how to do this). Its data has been extracted from Open Trivia DB (opentdb.com), a free and user-contributed collection of trivia questions. Finally, its build.sbt file has a few new dependencies: it now lists cats-effect, circe, http4s, and ScalaTest among its external libraries.

Listing 53.1 The build.sbt file

```
// file build.sbt

// …

val CirceVersion  = "0.14.1"
val Http4sVersion = "0.22.0"

libraryDependencies ++= Seq(
  // …
    "org.typelevel" %% "cats-effect" % "2.5.1",
    "io.circe" %% "circe-core" % CirceVersion,
    "io.circe" %% "circe-generic" % CirceVersion,
    "io.circe" %% "circe-parser" % CirceVersion,
    "org.http4s" %% "http4s-blaze-server" % Http4sVersion,
    "org.http4s" %% "http4s-dsl" % Http4sVersion,
    "org.http4s" %% "http4s-circe" % Http4sVersion,
    "org.scalatest" %% "scalatest" % "3.2.9" % "test"
  )
```

You can now run the sbt compile from your project's root directory to download all its external dependencies and compile its code.

53.2 Generic endpoints

The first set of endpoints you are going to implement is not specific to your application domain. Offering a few endpoints to ensure your system is responsive and healthy is good practice. The healthCheck endpoint is useful for monitoring systems, while ping allows its users to ensure they can successfully communicate with it by performing a concise and lightweight request.

Listing 53.2 shows you how to create a GenericService class inside the package org .example.quiz.service with the logic to produce an informative message about the connectivity to its internal dependencies.

Listing 53.2 The GenericService class

```scala
// file src/main/scala/org/example/quiz/service/GenericService.scala
package org.example.quiz.service

import cats.effect.{ContextShift, IO}
import org.example.quiz.dao.GenericDao

class GenericService(dao: GenericDao)(implicit cs: ContextShift[IO]) {

  def healthCheck: IO[String] =
    checkDbConnectivity().map { success =>
      s"Database Connectivity: ${if (success) "OK" else "FAILURE"}"
    }

  private def checkDbConnectivity(): IO[Boolean] =
    IO.fromFuture(IO(dao.testConnection()))
      .handleErrorWith (_ => IO(false))
}
```

The function IO.fromFuture needs an implicit ContextShift parameter.

Converting a Future instance into IO

During its evaluation, if it throws an exception, it returns IO(false) instead.

The function IO.fromFuture allows you to convert an instance of Future into one of type IO. It has the following signature:

```scala
def fromFuture[A](iof: IO[Future[A]])
    (implicit cs: ContextShift[IO]): IO[A]
```

Rather than refactoring the DAO layer to use IO instead of Future, you can invoke the IO.fromFuture function to perform the conversion in the service layer. You can now define the generic routes to reply to ping messages and inform about the status of your application's internal dependencies.

Listing 53.3 The GenericApi class

```scala
// file src/main/scala/org/example/quiz/api/GenericApi.scala
package org.example.quiz.api

import cats.effect.IO
import org.example.quiz.service.GenericService
import org.http4s.HttpRoutes
import org.http4s.dsl.Http4sDsl

class GenericApi(genericService: GenericService) extends Http4sDsl[IO] {
```

```scala
val routes = HttpRoutes.of[IO] {
  case GET -> Root / "ping" => Ok("pong")
  case GET -> Root / "healthCheck" => Ok(genericService.healthCheck)
}

}
```

You'll integrate these endpoints into your server and expose them as part of your HTTP API.

53.3 Displaying the available categories

The next endpoint allows users to see all the available quiz categories. First, you need to decide what information you are willing to expose in your HTTP API by implementing the CategoryEntity class.

Listing 53.4 The CategoryEntity class

```scala
// file src/main/scala/org/example/quiz/entities/CategoryEntity.scala
package org.example.quiz.entities

import org.example.quiz.dao.records.Category
import io.circe.generic.semiauto._
import io.circe._

case class CategoryEntity(id: Long, name: String)

object CategoryEntity {

  implicit val encoder: Encoder[CategoryEntity] =
    deriveEncoder[CategoryEntity]
  implicit val decoder: Decoder[CategoryEntity] =
    deriveDecoder[CategoryEntity]

  def fromRecord(record: Category): CategoryEntity =
    apply(id = record.id, name = record.name)
}
```

> Defining JSON encoder and decoder for CategoryEntity

> Converting a record (i.e., data read from the database) into an entity (i.e., data that the API exposes)

Its service needs to read all the categories from the database and convert them into entities so that the API can expose them in JSON format. It also needs to retrieve a category by its ID. You'll use this when processing a quiz generation request.

Listing 53.5 The CategoryService class

```scala
// file src/main/scala/org/example/quiz/service/CategoryService.scala
package org.example.quiz.service

import cats.effect.{ContextShift, IO}
import org.example.quiz.dao.CategoryDao
import org.example.quiz.dao.records.Category
import org.example.quiz.entities.CategoryEntity

class CategoryService(dao: CategoryDao)(implicit cs: ContextShift[IO]) {

  def get(id: Long): IO[Option[CategoryEntity]] =
    IO.fromFuture(IO(dao.findById(id))).map { maybeRecord =>
      maybeRecord.map(CategoryEntity.fromRecord)
    }

  def all(): IO[List[CategoryEntity]] =
    IO.fromFuture(IO(dao.all())).map { records =>
      records.toList.map(CategoryEntity.fromRecord)
    }
}
```

The function IO.fromFuture needs an implicit ContextShift parameter.

Converting a Future instance into IO

You can now define the route to display the categories.

Listing 53.6 The CategoryApi class

```scala
package org.example.quiz.api

import cats.effect.IO
import org.example.quiz.entities.CategoryEntity
import org.example.quiz.service.CategoryService
import org.http4s.HttpRoutes
import org.http4s.circe._
import org.http4s.dsl.Http4sDsl

class CategoryApi(categoryService: CategoryService)
    extends Http4sDsl[IO] {

  private implicit val categoriesEncoder =
    jsonEncoderOf[IO, List[CategoryEntity]]

  val routes = HttpRoutes.of[IO] {
    case GET -> Root => Ok(categoryService.all())
  }
}
```

Importing http4s functionalities to generate a JSON entity encoder

It defines a JSON encoder for an HTTP entity containing a list of categories. It implicitly requires an instance of Encoder[CategoryEntity].

When defining your server, you'll map the category routes to the prefix "categories" so that a user can receive all the categories by performing a GET request to the endpoint/ categories.

 ## 53.4 Creating a quiz

Let's implement the endpoint that will generate a quiz with 10 random questions for a given category. Implement a class QuizEntity in the package org.example.quiz.entities to define how to display the quiz questions. You want to make sure you don't reveal the correct answers at this stage.

Listing 53.7 The QuizEntity class

```scala
// file src/main/scala/org/example/quiz/entities/QuizEntity.scala
package org.example.quiz.entities

import io.circe._
import io.circe.generic.semiauto._
import org.example.quiz.dao.records.{Answer, Question}

case class QuizEntity(questions: List[QuestionEntity])

object QuizEntity {
  implicit val encoder: Encoder[QuizEntity] =
    deriveEncoder[QuizEntity]
  implicit val decoder: Decoder[QuizEntity] =
    deriveDecoder[QuizEntity]
}

case class QuestionEntity(id: Long,
                          text: String,
                          possibleAnswers: Set[PossibleAnswerEntity])

object QuestionEntity {

  implicit val encoder: Encoder[QuestionEntity] =
    deriveEncoder[QuestionEntity]
  implicit val decoder: Decoder[QuestionEntity] =
    deriveDecoder[QuestionEntity]

  def fromRecord(question: Question,
                 answers: Seq[Answer]): QuestionEntity = {
```

Defining JSON encoder and decoder for the entity

Converting a record (i.e., data read from the database) into an entity (i.e., data that the API exposes)

```
        val possibleAnswers =
              answers.map(PossibleAnswerEntity.fromRecord).toSet
        apply(question.id, question.text, possibleAnswers)
      }
```

Defining JSON encoder and decoder for the entity

```
    }

    case class PossibleAnswerEntity(id: Long, text: String)

    object PossibleAnswerEntity {

      implicit val encoder: Encoder[PossibleAnswerEntity] =
        deriveEncoder[PossibleAnswerEntity]
      implicit val decoder: Decoder[PossibleAnswerEntity] =
        deriveDecoder[PossibleAnswerEntity]

      def fromRecord(answer: Answer): PossibleAnswerEntity =
        apply(answer.id, answer.text)
    }
```

Converting a record (i.e., data read from the database) into an entity (i.e., data that the API exposes)

You can now implement the QuizService class that defines how to generate a quiz from a given category ID.

> **Listing 53.8 The QuizService: Generating a quiz**

```
// file src/main/scala/org/example/quiz/service/QuizService.scala
package org.example.quiz.service

import cats.effect.{ContextShift, IO}
import org.example.quiz.dao.QuestionAnswerDao
import org.example.quiz.entities._

class QuizService(dao: QuestionAnswerDao,
                  categoryService: CategoryService)
                 (implicit cs: ContextShift[IO]) {

  private val numberOfQuestions = 10

  def generate(categoryId: Long): IO[Option[QuizEntity]] =
    categoryService.get(categoryId).flatMap {
      case Some(category) =>
        pickQuestions(category, numberOfQuestions).map(qs =>
          Some(QuizEntity(qs)))
```

The function IO.fromFuture needs an implicit ContextShift parameter.

```
    case None => IO(None)
  }

 private def pickQuestions(category: CategoryEntity,
                           n: Int): IO[List[QuestionEntity]] = {
   val randomQAs = IO.fromFuture(IO(
                   dao.pickByCategoryId(category.id, n = n)))
   randomQAs.map { qas =>
     qas.map { case (q, as) =>
         QuestionEntity.fromRecord(q, as)
     }.toList
   }
 }
}
```

Converting a Future
instance into IO

Finally, let's define an endpoint that responds to a GET request passing a query parameter category_id with either a QuizEntity instance or a 404 Not Found error code.

Listing 53.9 The QuizApi: Generating a quiz

```
// file src/main/scala/org/example/quiz/api/QuizApi.scala
package org.example.quiz.api

import cats.effect.IO
import org.example.quiz.entities._
import org.example.quiz.service.QuizService
import org.http4s.HttpRoutes
import org.http4s.dsl._
import org.http4s.circe._

class QuizApi(quizService: QuizService) extends Http4sDsl[IO] {

  private implicit val quizEncoder = jsonEncoderOf[IO, QuizEntity]

  private object CategoryParam
    extends QueryParamDecoderMatcher[Long]("category_id")

  val routes = HttpRoutes.of[IO] {
    case GET -> Root :? CategoryParam(categoryId) =>
      quizService.generate(categoryId).flatMap {
        case Some(quiz) => Ok(quiz)
        case None => NotFound(s"Category $categoryId does not exist")
      }
  }
}
```

It defines a JSON encoder for an HTTP entity containing a quiz entity. It implicitly requires an instance of Encoder[QuizEntity].

Importing http4s functionalities to generate a JSON entity encoder.

It matches a query parameter with name category_id and a value of type Long.

In the server, you'll map the quiz routes to a "quiz" prefix. For example, a user can request a quiz for the category with ID 10 by sending a GET request to the /quiz?category_id=10 endpoint.

 ## 53.5 Answering a quiz

The last endpoint you'll implement allows users to send their quiz answers and receive their quiz score with both the percentage of given correct answers and a summary of which are correct and which are not.

The class GivenAnswerEntity defines the format users must follow for each of their answers, while the class ScoreEntity specifies what information to display when replying with their score.

Listing 53.10 The GivenAnswerEntity and ScoreEntity classes

```scala
// src/main/scala/org/example/quiz/entities/GivenAnswerEntity.scala
package org.example.quiz.entities

import io.circe._
import io.circe.generic.semiauto._

case class GivenAnswerEntity(questionId: Long, answerId: Long)

object GivenAnswerEntity {

  implicit val encoder: Encoder[GivenAnswerEntity] =
    deriveEncoder[GivenAnswerEntity]
  implicit val decoder: Decoder[GivenAnswerEntity] =
    deriveDecoder[GivenAnswerEntity]
}
```

Defining JSON encoder and decoder for the entity

```scala
// file src/main/scala/org/example/quiz/entities/ScoreEntity.scala
package org.example.quiz.entities

import io.circe._
import io.circe.generic.semiauto._

case class ScoreEntity(score: Double,
                       correct: List[GivenAnswerEntity],
                       wrong: List[GivenAnswerEntity])
```

```scala
object ScoreEntity {

  implicit val encoder: Encoder[ScoreEntity] =
    deriveEncoder[ScoreEntity]
  implicit val decoder: Decoder[ScoreEntity] =
    deriveDecoder[ScoreEntity]

}
```

Defining JSON encoder and decoder for the entity

You can now add the logic to create a ScoreEntity instance from an instance of type List[GivenAnswerEntity] in the QuizService class.

Listing 53.11 The QuizService class: Computing the score

```scala
// file src/main/scala/org/example/quiz/services/QuizService.scala
package org.example.quiz.service

import cats.effect.{ContextShift, IO}
import org.example.quiz.dao.QuestionAnswerDao
import org.example.quiz.entities._

class QuizService(dao: QuestionAnswerDao,
                  categoryService: CategoryService)
                 (implicit cs: ContextShift[IO]) {

  // ...

  def score(givenAnswers: List[GivenAnswerEntity]): IO[ScoreEntity] = {
    val questionIds = givenAnswers.map(_.questionId)
    IO.fromFuture(
      IO(dao.getCorrectQuestionAnswers(questionIds))
    ).map { correctAnswers =>
      val goodAnswers = givenAnswers.filter { answer =>
        correctAnswers.exists { case (q, a) =>
          q == answer.questionId && a == answer.answerId
        }
      }
      val badAnswers = givenAnswers.diff(goodAnswers)
      val score = 1.0 * goodAnswers.size / givenAnswers.size
      ScoreEntity(score, correct = goodAnswers, wrong = badAnswers)
    }
  }
}
```

Converting a Future instance into IO

Finally, let's define an endpoint for it in the `QuizApi` class for the users to post their responses.

Listing 53.12 The QuizApi class: Computing the score

```scala
// file src/main/scala/org/example/quiz/api/QuizApi.scala
package org.example.quiz.api

import cats.effect.IO
import org.example.quiz.entities._
import org.example.quiz.service.QuizService
import org.http4s.HttpRoutes
import org.http4s.dsl._          ⟵  Importing http4s
import org.http4s.circe._        ⟵  functionalities to generate
                                     a JSON entity encoder

class QuizApi(quizService: QuizService) extends Http4sDsl[IO] {

  // …
                                                 It creates a JSON decoder
                                                 for an HTTP entity contain-
                                                 ing a list of given answers.
  private implicit val givenAnswersDecoder =     It implicitly requires an
    jsonOf[IO, List[GivenAnswerEntity]]    ⟵     instance of Decoder[Given-
  private implicit val quizScoreEncoder =        AnswerEntity].
    jsonEncoderOf[IO, ScoreEntity]   ⟵
                                          It defines a JSON encoder
                                          for an HTTP entity containing
                                          a score entity. It implicitly
  val routes = HttpRoutes.of[IO] {        requires an instance of
    //..                                  Encoder[ScoreEntity].
    case request @ POST -> Root =>
      val response = for {
        answers <- request.as[List[GivenAnswerEntity]]
        score <- quizService.score(answers)
      } yield score
      Ok(response)
  }
}
```

You will map the quiz routes to the prefix `quiz`. Users can send a `POST` request to the endpoint/quiz with their responses in JSON format as its body and receive their score in response.

53.6 The HTTP server

The core implementation is now over. Let's see how to connect all the components and define an HTTP server for your quiz application.

First, let's define classes representing each layer of your application.

Listing 53.13 Defining each layer

```scala
// file src/main/scala/org/example/quiz/dao/Daos.scala
package org.example.quiz.dao

import io.getquill.{PostgresJAsyncContext, SnakeCase}

import scala.concurrent.ExecutionContext

class Dao(ctx: PostgresJAsyncContext[SnakeCase.type])
        (implicit ec: ExecutionContext) {

  val category = new CategoryDao(ctx)
  val generic = new GenericDao(ctx)
  val questionAnswer = new QuestionAnswerDao(ctx)

}
```

The DAO layer can only access the database.

```scala
// file src/main/scala/org/example/quiz/services/Services.scala
package org.example.quiz.service

import cats.effect.{ContextShift, IO}
import org.example.quiz.dao.Dao

class Services(dao: Dao)(implicit cs: ContextShift[IO]) {

  val generic = new GenericService(dao.generic)
  val category = new CategoryService(dao.category)
  val quiz = new QuizService(dao.questionAnswer, category)

}
```

The service can only access the DAO layer.

```scala
// file src/main/scala/org/example/quiz/api/Api.scala
package org.example.quiz.api
```

```
import org.example.quiz.service.Services
```
The API layer can
only access the
service layer.
```
class Api(services: Services) {

  val category = new CategoryApi(services.category)
  val generic = new GenericApi(services.generic)
  val quiz = new QuizApi(services.quiz)

}
```

The final step of your implementation is to define an HTTP server. You need to bind it to
a port and host and mount the routes you want to expose in your HTTP API.

Listing 53.14 The QuizApp executable object

```
// file src/main/scala/org/example/quiz/QuizApp.scala
package org.example.quiz

import cats.effect.{ExitCode, IO, IOApp}
import org.example.quiz.api.Api
import org.example.quiz.dao.Dao
import org.example.quiz.service.Services
import org.http4s.server.Router

import org.http4s.implicits._
import org.http4s.blaze.server.BlazeServerBuilder
import scala.concurrent.ExecutionContext
```
An executable app using
IO that provides an
implicit context shift
instance
```
object QuizApp extends IOApp {

  private val dao = new Dao(TestDatabase.ctx)(ExecutionContext.global)
  private val services = new Services(dao)
  private val api = new Api(services)

  private val httpApp = Router(
    "/" -> api.generic.routes,
    "categories" -> api.category.routes,
    "quiz" -> api.quiz.routes
  ).orNotFound
```
Return a 404 error if the
server does not find a
matching endpoint for
the received request.
```

  override def run(args: List[String]): IO[ExitCode] =
    stream(args).compile.drain.as(ExitCode.Success)
```

```
    private def stream(args: List[String]) =
      BlazeServerBuilder[IO](ExecutionContext.global)
      .bindHttp(8000, "0.0.0.0")
      .withHttpApp(httpApp)
      .serve
}
```

The implementation of your quiz application is now complete.

 ## 53.7 Writing tests

This section will show you a possible strategy to use when writing tests for your application. You can follow one or many testing strategies. You can write tests that start your application using a test database, send HTTP requests to it, and assert its HTTP responses. You can also write tests specific to its business logic independent from the other components of your application, such as its API and DAO layers.

Let's write a test for the class CategoryService. The tests for the other services follow the same structure. A CategoryService has one parameter of type CategoryDao. You need to define a class that simulates its behavior by reading some predefined test data, called *fixtures*, rather than querying a database.

Listing 53.15 Simulating CategoryDao

```
// file src/test/scala/org/example/quiz/stubs/dao/Fixtures.scala

package org.example.quiz.stubs.dao

import org.example.quiz.dao.records._

object Fixtures {

  val catA = Category(id = 1, name = "General")
  val catB = Category(id = 2, name = "History")

  val categories: List[Category] = List(catA, catB)

}


// src/test/scala/org/example/quiz/stubs/dao/FakeCategoryDao.scala
```

```
package org.example.quiz.stubs.dao

import org.example.quiz.dao.CategoryDao
import org.example.quiz.dao.records.Category

import scala.concurrent.{ExecutionContext, Future}

class FakeCategoryDao(implicit ec: ExecutionContext)
    extends CategoryDao(ctx = null /* unused */) {

  private var fakeCategories = Fixtures.categories

  private def safelyModify(f: List[Category] => List[Category]): Unit =
    synchronized { fakeCategories = f(fakeCategories) }

  override def save(category: Category): Future[Long] = {
    safelyModify(_ :+ category)
    Future(category.id)
  }

  override def all(): Future[List[Category]] = Future(fakeCategories)

  override def findById(id: Long): Future[Option[Category]] =
    Future(fakeCategories.find(_.id == id))

  override def deleteById(id: Long): Future[Boolean] = {
    val isPresent = fakeCategories.exists(_.id == id)
    safelyModify(_.filterNot(_.id == id))
    Future(isPresent)
  }

}
```

Leaves the database context not initialized because it's unused

Ensures only one thread at a time can modify the list of categories

Overriding the behavior of the function to rely on the list of categories rather than querying a database

You can now use your FakeCategoryDao implementation to test the business logic defined in CategoryService.

Listing 53.16 Writing a test for CategoryService

```
// src/test/scala/org/example/quiz/service/CategoryServiceTest.scala
package org.example.quiz.service
```

```scala
import cats.effect.{ContextShift, IO}
import org.example.quiz.entities.CategoryEntity
import org.example.quiz.stubs.dao.{FakeCategoryDao, Fixtures}
import org.scalatest.flatspec.AnyFlatSpec
import org.scalatest.matchers.should.Matchers

import scala.concurrent.ExecutionContext

class CategoryServiceTest extends AnyFlatSpec with Matchers {

  private def mkService() = {
    implicit val ec: ExecutionContext = ExecutionContext.global
    implicit val cs: ContextShift[IO] = IO.contextShift(ec)

    new CategoryService(new FakeCategoryDao)
  }

  "CategoryService" should "return all the categories" in {
    val service = mkService()
    val entities = service.all().unsafeRunSync()
    val expectedEntities =
      Fixtures.categories.map(CategoryEntity.fromRecord)
    entities.shouldEqual(expectedEntities)
  }

  it should "return a category if the id exists" in {
    val service = mkService()
    val entity = CategoryEntity.fromRecord(Fixtures.catA)
    val optRes = service.get(entity.id).unsafeRunSync()
    optRes.shouldEqual(Some(entity))
  }

  it should "return no category if the id is invalid" in {
    val service = mkService()
    val optRes = service.get(-1).unsafeRunSync()
    optRes.shouldEqual(None)
  }

}
```

You can use this pattern to write tests for all the remaining services. Once your tests pass using the command sbt test, you are ready to run your application.

53.8 Let's give it a try!

It's time to see your quiz application in action. Navigate the root directory of your project and execute the command sbt run to start your server. Once ready, you will see the following message in your console:

```
Service bound to address /0:0:0:0:0:0:0:0:8000

  _   _   _   _ _     _ _
 | |_| |_| |_  _ __| | | ___
 | ' \ _|  _| '_ \_  _(_-<
 |_||_\__|\__| .__/ |_|/__/
             |_|
http4s v0.22.0 on blaze v0.15.1 started at http://[::]:8000/
```

First, let's ensure you can connect to the service by performing a GET request to http://localhost:8000/ping:

```
$ curl -i http://localhost:8000/ping
HTTP/1.1 200 OK
Content-Type: text/plain; charset=UTF-8
Date: Sun, 11 Apr 2021 11:34:56 GMT
Content-Length: 4

pong
```

You can also check that your application is healthy and that it can talk to the database by sending a GET request to http://localhost:8000/healthCheck:

```
$ curl -i http://localhost:8000/healthCheck
HTTP/1.1 200 OK
Content-Type: text/plain; charset=UTF-8
Date: Sun, 11 Apr 2021 11:36:12 GMT
Content-Length: 25

Database Connectivity: OK
```

Sending a request to an endpoint that does not exist should return a 404 – Not found error:

```
$ curl -i http://localhost:8000/invalid-endpoint
HTTP/1.1 404 Not Found
Content-Type: text/plain; charset=UTF-8
Date: Sun, 11 Apr 2021 11:40:32 GMT
Content-Length: 9

Not found
```

You can see the list of available categories at http://localhost:8000/categories:

```
$ curl -i http://localhost:8000/categories
HTTP/1.1 200 OK
Content-Type: application/json
Date: Sun, 11 Apr 2021 11:43:30 GMT
Content-Length: 898

[{"id":9,"name":"General Knowledge"},
{"id":10,"name":"Entertainment: Books"},
{"id":11,"name":"Entertainment: Film"},
{"id":12,"name":"Entertainment: Music"},
{"id":13,"name":"Entertainment: Musicals & Theatres"},
// …truncating output…
{"id":32,"name":"Entertainment: Cartoon & Animations"}]
```

First, let's request a quiz for a category that does not exist and ensure that it fails with a meaningful message:

```
$ curl -i http://localhost:8000/quiz?category_id=42
HTTP/1.1 404 Not Found
Content-Type: text/plain; charset=UTF-8
Date: Sun, 11 Apr 2021 11:47:46 GMT
Content-Length: 26

Category 42 does not exist
```

Let's try again, this time by requesting a category, for example "General Knowledge" with ID 9:

```
$ curl -i http://localhost:8000/quiz?category_id=9
HTTP/1.1 200 OK
Content-Type: application/json
Date: Sun, 11 Apr 2021 11:50:37 GMT
Content-Length: 2299

{"questions":[{"id":17,"text":"What is the right way to spell the
capital of Hungary?","possibleAnswers":[{"id":62,"text":
"Bhudapest"},{"id":63,"text":"Budapast"},{"id":64,"text":
"Budapest"},{"id":65,"text":"Boodapest"}]},
//…truncating output…
{"id":9,"text":"Complete the following analogy: Audi is to Volkswagen
as Infiniti is to ?","possibleAnswers":[{"id":30,"text":
```

```
"Subaru"},{"id":31,"text":"Nissan"},{"id":32,"text":"Honda"},
{"id":33,"text":"Hyundai"}]}]}
```

The application will calculate your score when sending your answers as a POST request
to `http://localhost:8000/quiz`:

```
$ curl -i -X POST -d '[{"questionId": 22, "answerId": 80 }, {
        "questionId": 17, "answerId": 62 }]'
        http://localhost:8000/quiz
// sending only two answers rather than ten for briefty

HTTP/1.1 200 OK
Content-Type: application/json
Date: Sun, 11 Apr 2021 12:00:25 GMT
Content-Length: 99

{"score":0.5,"correct":[{"questionId":22,"answerId":80}],
"wrong":[{"questionId":17,"answerId":62}]}
```

You sent two answers. Only one of them was correct, so you receive a score of 50%.

Summary

In this capstone, you implemented an HTTP server that exposes an HTTP API to generate and answer quizzes.

- You implemented endpoints to monitor the status of your application.
- You defined its business logic in its service layer and wrote tests for it.
- You designed its endpoints in its API layer.
- You implemented a server that exposes an HTTP API, and you consumed its data
  to monitor its status and play a quiz.

INDEX

Symbols

:: class 231
:+ method 232–233
:help command 12
:load <path> 12
:quit command 12
:replay command 12
:reset command 12
@tailrec annotation 464
& method 305
-- method 305, 314
+ method 295, 313
+: method 232–233
++ method 305, 314
-> method 312

A

PartialFunction 132
about command 21
abstract classes 58–61
abstract function 46
abstract keyword 49
access modifiers 79–85
   choosing access levels 83
   private access 81–82, 84
   protected access 82–83, 85
   public access 80, 84
ad hoc polymorphism 388
andThen function 133
anonymous functions 46, 123–129
   concise notation for 126–127, 129
   functions vs. 124–126, 129
App trait 98
application.properties 429
apply method 92–94, 159, 161, 204, 220, 229, 252, 324, 350
   companion objects 161–162

equivalent expressions 94, 96
apply(0) function 253
ArithmeticException 174
arrow constructor 207
as method 431
asJson function 455
AsyncFlatSpec class 499–500
asynchronous testing 498–500, 503
Await.ready function 419
Await.result method 420

B

BigDecimal type 255
BigInt type 272
bindHttp function 144
Blaze 140
BlazeServerBuilder[IO] 144
Boolean type 48, 160, 255
build.properties 25
build.sbt 23
by-name parameters 464–466, 470
Byte type 255, 272
bytecode 5

C

CamelCase 428–429
case classes 7, 157–165
   apply function 161–162
   case objects 164–165
   companion object 161–162
   copy function 159
   equals function 159–160
   getters 158
   hashCode function 159–160
   pattern matching and 163–165
   toString function 159–160
   unapply function 161–162